Vol. 5

Created by
Shoko Conami

HAMBURG // LONDON // LOS ANGELES // TOKYO

Shinobi Life 5
Created by Shoko Conami

Translation - Lori Riser
English Adaptation - Ysabet Reinhardt MacFarlane
Copy Editor - Carol Fan
Retouch and Lettering - Star Print Brokers
Production Artist - Rui Kyo
Graphic Designer - Chelsea Windlinger

Editor - Lillian Diaz-Przybyl
Print Production Manager - Lucas Rivera
Managing Editor - Vy Nguyen
Senior Designer - Louis Csontos
Art Director - Al-Insan Lashley
Director of Sales and Manufacturing - Allyson De Simone
Associate Publisher - Marco F. Pavia
President and C.O.O. - John Parker
C.E.O. and Chief Creative Officer - Stu Levy

A **TOKYOPOP** Manga

TOKYOPOP Inc.
5900 Wilshire Blvd. Suite 2000
Los Angeles, CA 90036

E-mail: info@TOKYOPOP.com
Come visit us online at www.TOKYOPOP.com

ISBN: 978-1-4278-1646-7

First TOKYOPOP printing: June 2010
10 9 8 7 6 5 4 3 2 1
Printed in the USA

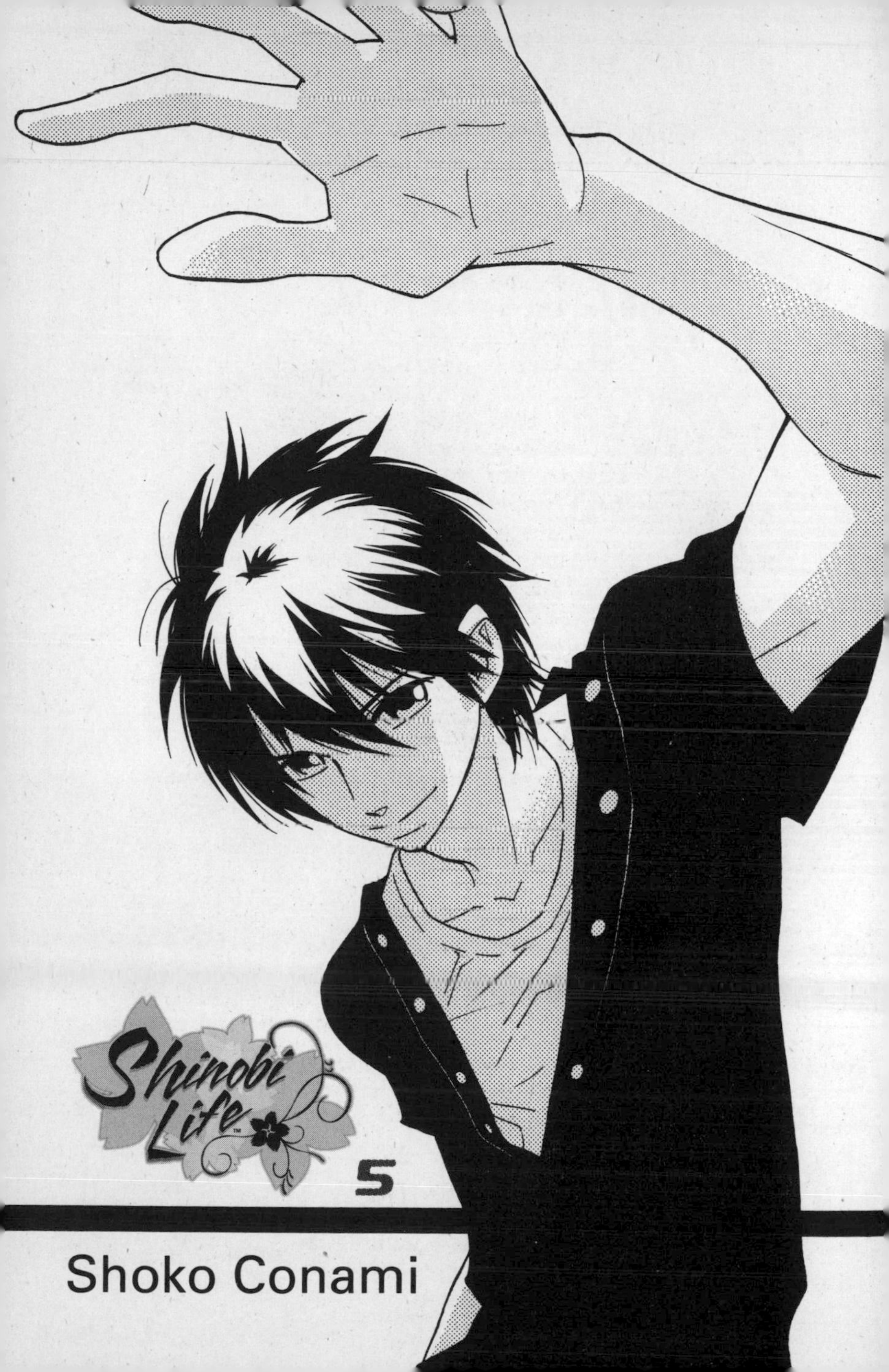

Shinobi Life™ 5

Shoko Conami

Character Introduction

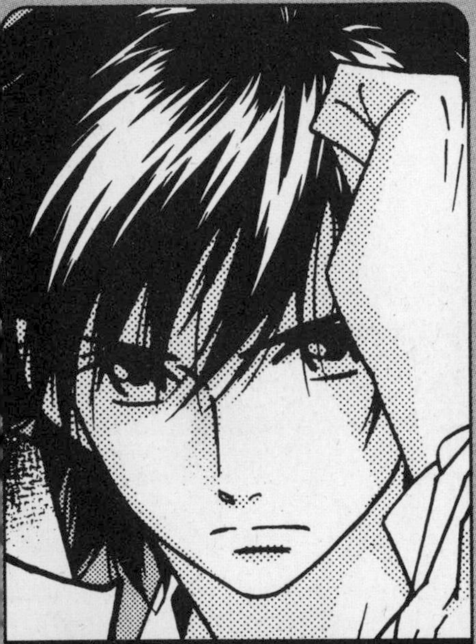

KAGETORA

A NINJA FROM THE PAST. HE'S DECIDED TO LIVE IN THE PRESENT WITH BENI.

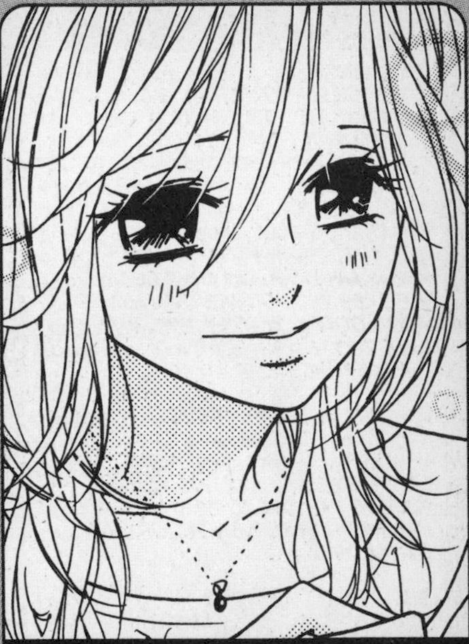

BENI FUJIWARA

A HIGH SCHOOL GIRL WHO'S FALLING IN LOVE WITH KAGETORA (?!).

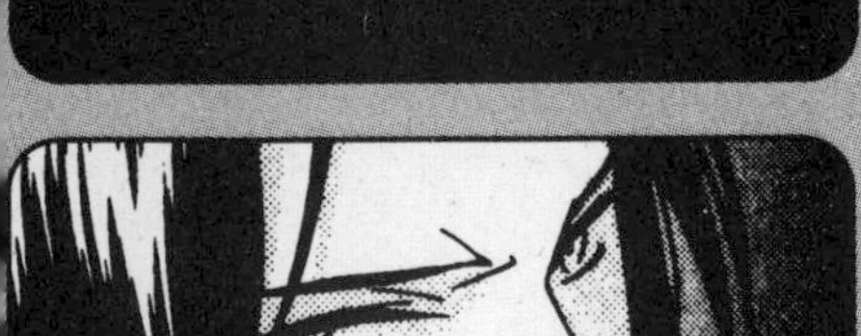

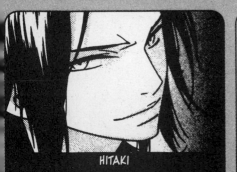

HITAKI

KAGETORA'S NINJA COMRADE. HE'S OUT TO DESTROY KAGETORA'S LIFE.

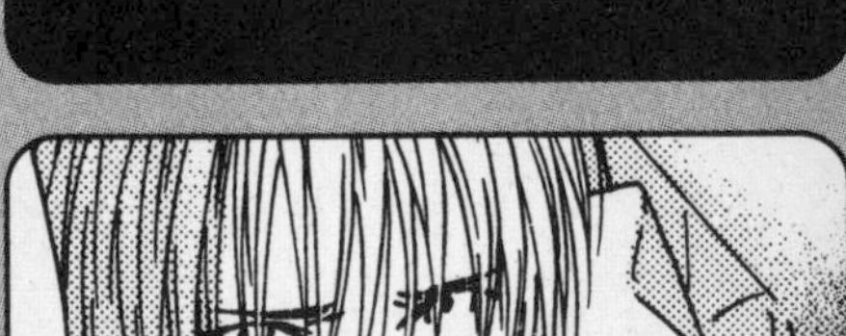

RIHITO IWATSURU

BENI'S CLASSMATE AND FIANCÉ.

Summary &

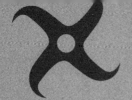

BENI FUJIWARA, A HIGH SCHOOL GIRL WHO LONGS FOR DEATH AS REVENGE AGAINST HER ARROGANT FATHER, IS UNEXPECTEDLY RESCUED ONE DAY WHEN SHE FALLS OFF A BUILDING. HER SAVIOR? A NINJA NAMED KAGETORA, WHO FALLS FROM THE SKY AT THE RIGHT MOMENT. KAGETORA CALLS BENI "BENI HIME," AND DEVOTES HIMSELF TO PROTECTING HER AT ANY COST...AT FIRST BECAUSE HE MISTAKES HER FOR HER OWN ANCESTOR, WHO LOOKED EXACTLY LIKE HER. YES, KAGETORA IS A NINJA WHO HAS TRAVELED THROUGH TIME FROM THE PAST!

AS TIME PASSES, BENI GRADUALLY BECOMES FOND OF KAGETORA AFTER HE REPEATEDLY SAVES HER FROM DANGER AND PLEDGES HIS ETERNAL LOYALTY. SHE TRIES TO PRETEND TO BE BENI HIME FOR HIM, AND THEY SLOWLY BECOME CLOSER AND CLOSER.

BUT WHEN THE PAIR UNEXPECTEDLY TRAVELS BACK TO KAGETORA'S TIME, HE RUNS INTO THE REAL BENI HIME AND REALIZES THAT THE TWO WOMEN ARE NOT THE SAME PERSON. AFTER BENI HIME TELLS KAGETORA THAT SHE WANTS TO LIVE AS A NORMAL VILLAGER, HE LOSES HIS PURPOSE IN LIFE. WHEN A FELLOW NINJA, HITAKI, BRANDS HIM A TRAITOR AND TRIES TO KILL HIM, KAGETORA DECIDES TO RETURN TO THE PRESENT WITH BENI AND LIVE WITH HER.

THINGS SEEM TO BE GOING SMOOTHLY FOR BENI AND KAGETORA'S FLEDGLING ROMANCE, BUT THAT COMES TO AN ABRUPT END WHEN BENI'S FATHER REVEALS THAT BENI ALREADY HAS A FIANCÉ--RIHITO IWATSURU! BENI AND KAGETORA FLEE HER FATHER'S HOUSE TO ESCAPE HIS CONTROL AND RIHITO'S AGGRESSION, AND FOR A BRIEF TIME THEY'RE ABLE TO ACT ON THEIR FEELINGS FOR EACH OTHER. AND THEN BENI SUGGESTS THAT THEY RUN WHERE HER FATHER CAN NEVER FIND THEM: THE PAST.

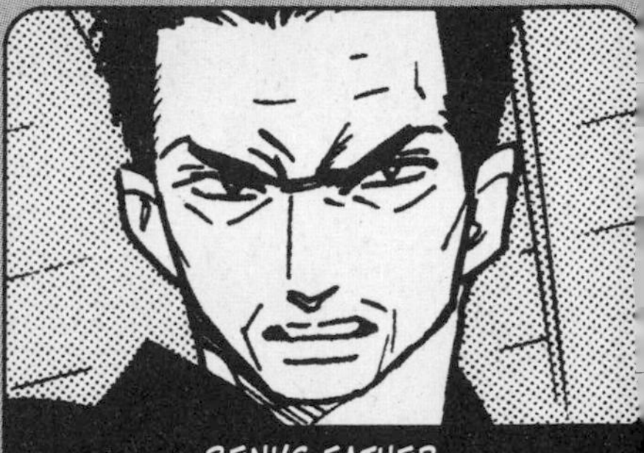

BENI'S FATHER

A COLD MAN, UNINTERESTED IN HIS DAUGHTER.

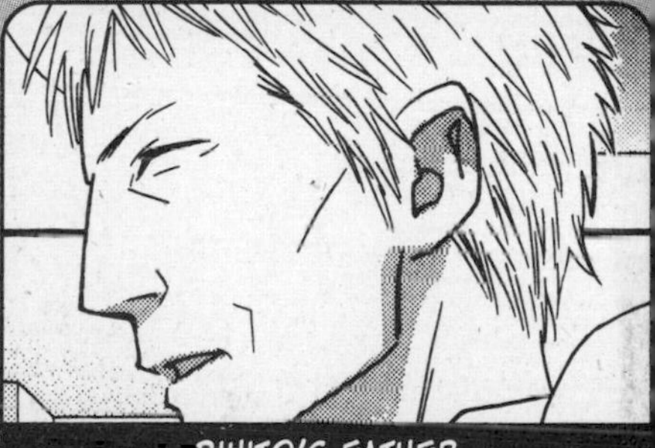

RIHITO'S FATHER

A MAN WHO CRAVES THE FUJIWARA FAMILY'S ABILITY TO PREDICT THE FUTURE.

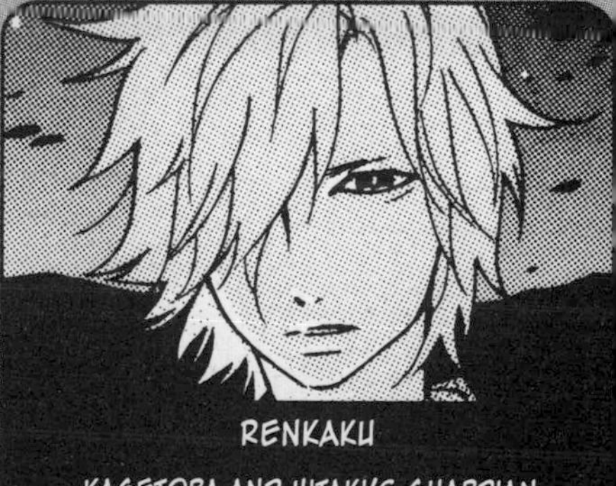

RENKAKU

KAGETORA AND HITAKI'S GUARDIAN IN THE PAST.

CONTENTS

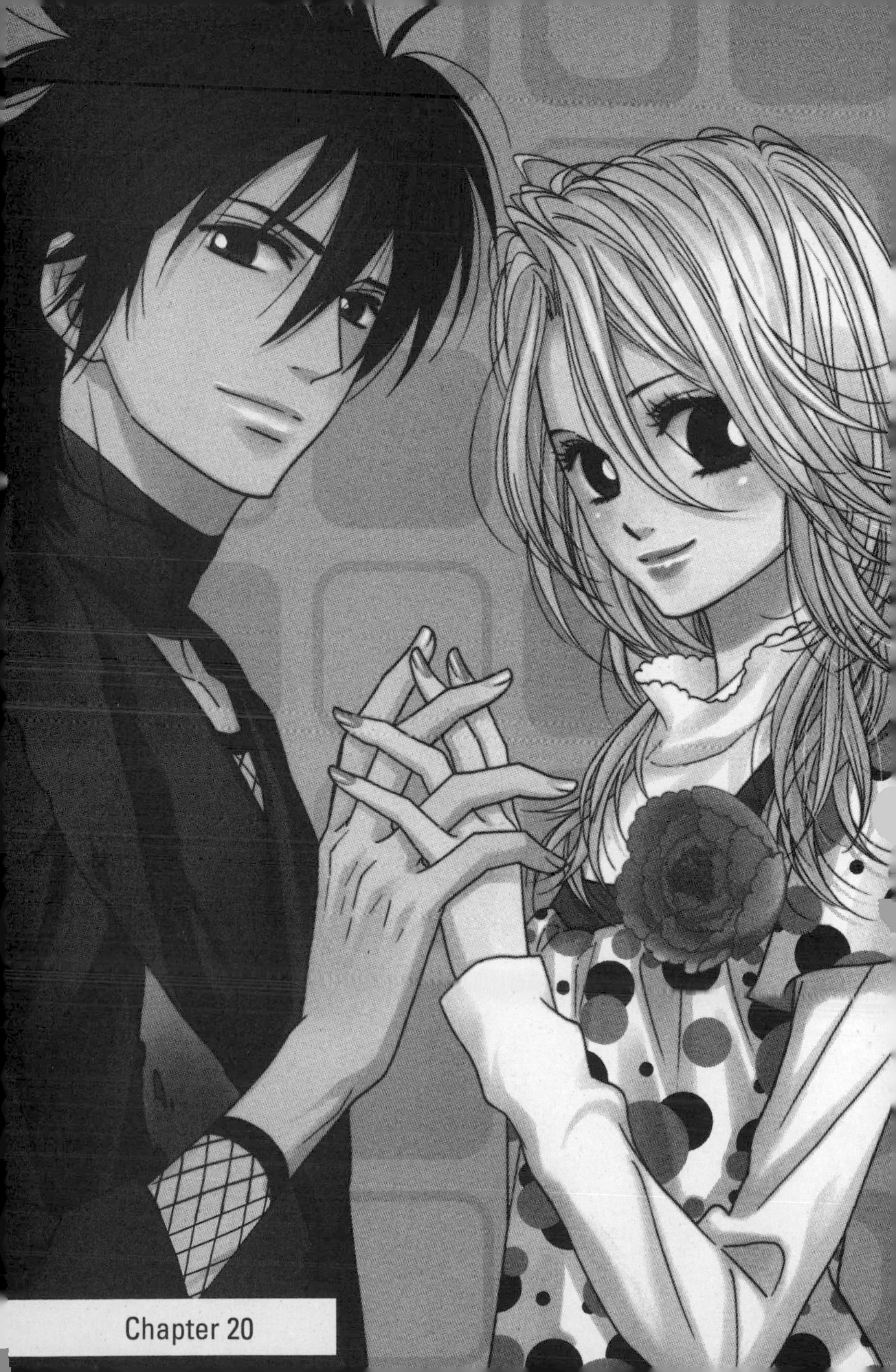

Chapter 20

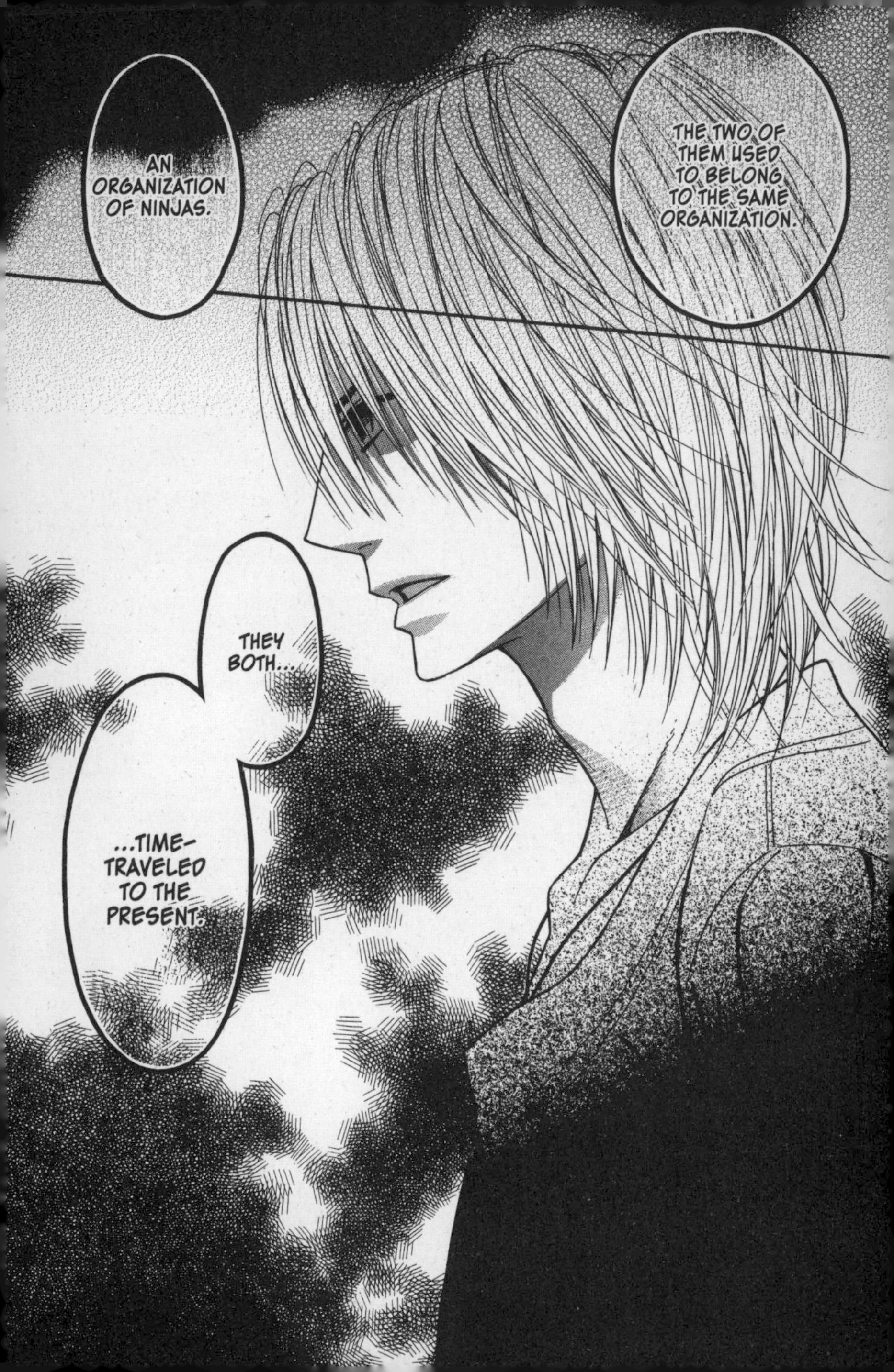
THE TWO OF THEM USED TO BELONG TO THE SAME ORGANIZATION.
AN ORGANIZATION OF NINJAS.
THEY BOTH...
...TIME-TRAVELED TO THE PRESENT.

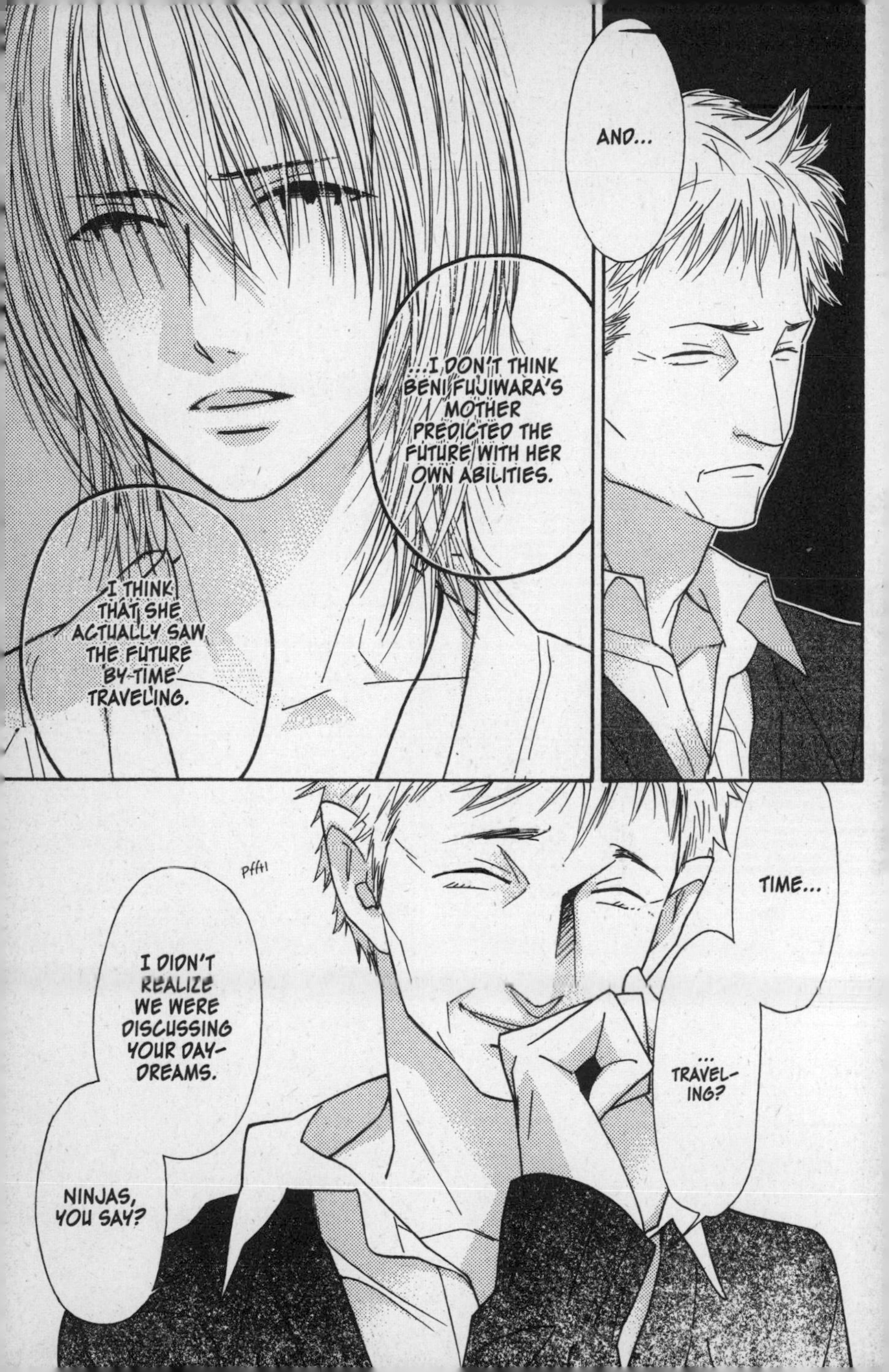
AND...
...I DON'T THINK BENI FUJIWARA'S MOTHER PREDICTED THE FUTURE WITH HER OWN ABILITIES.
I THINK THAT SHE ACTUALLY SAW THE FUTURE BY TIME TRAVELING.
TIME...
...TRAVEL-ING?
Pfft!
I DIDN'T REALIZE WE WERE DISCUSSING YOUR DAY-DREAMS.
NINJAS, YOU SAY?

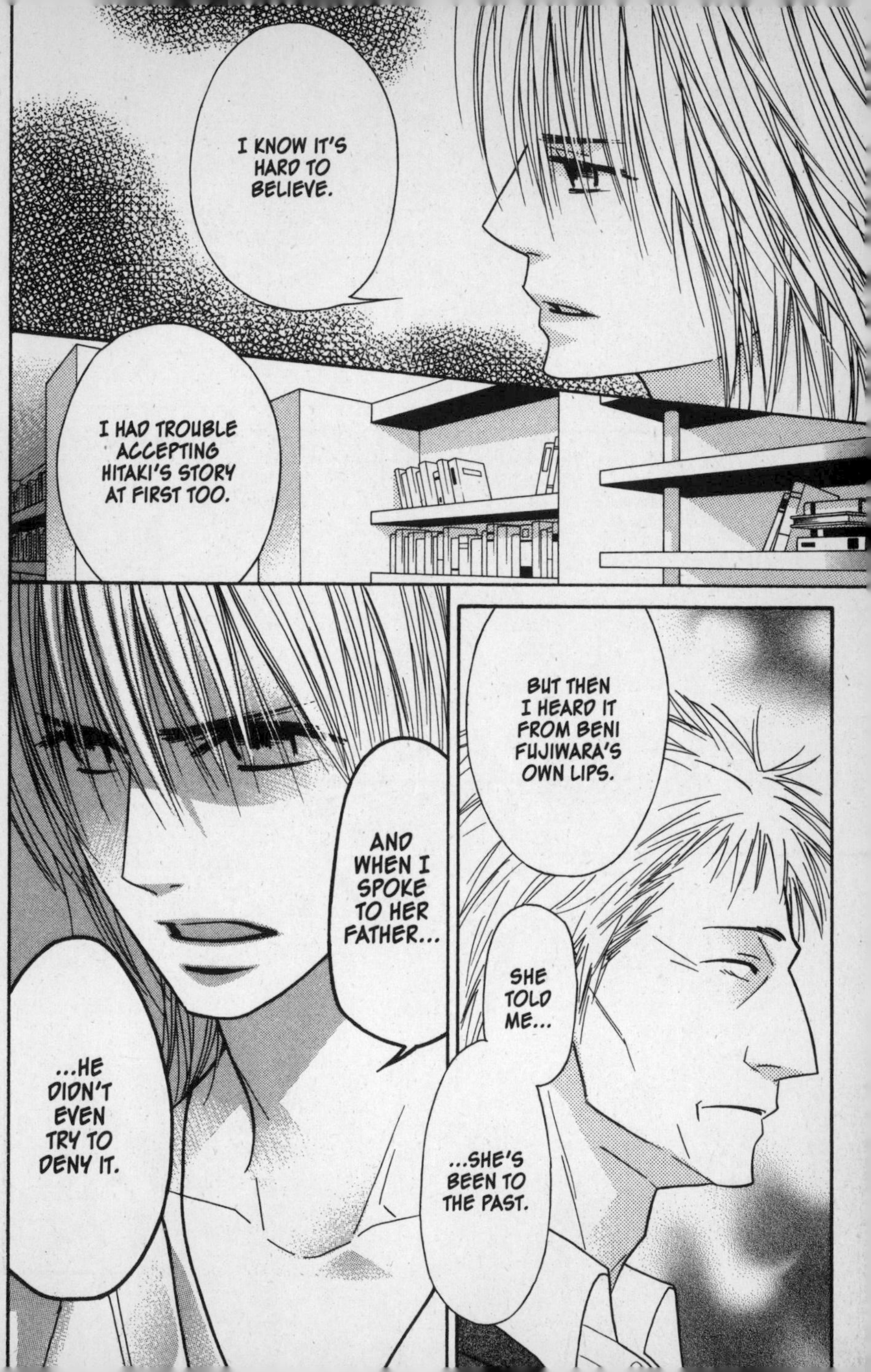
I KNOW IT'S HARD TO BELIEVE.
I HAD TROUBLE ACCEPTING HITAKI'S STORY AT FIRST TOO.
BUT THEN I HEARD IT FROM BENI FUJIWARA'S OWN LIPS.
SHE TOLD ME...
...SHE'S BEEN TO THE PAST.
AND WHEN I SPOKE TO HER FATHER...
...HE DIDN'T EVEN TRY TO DENY IT.

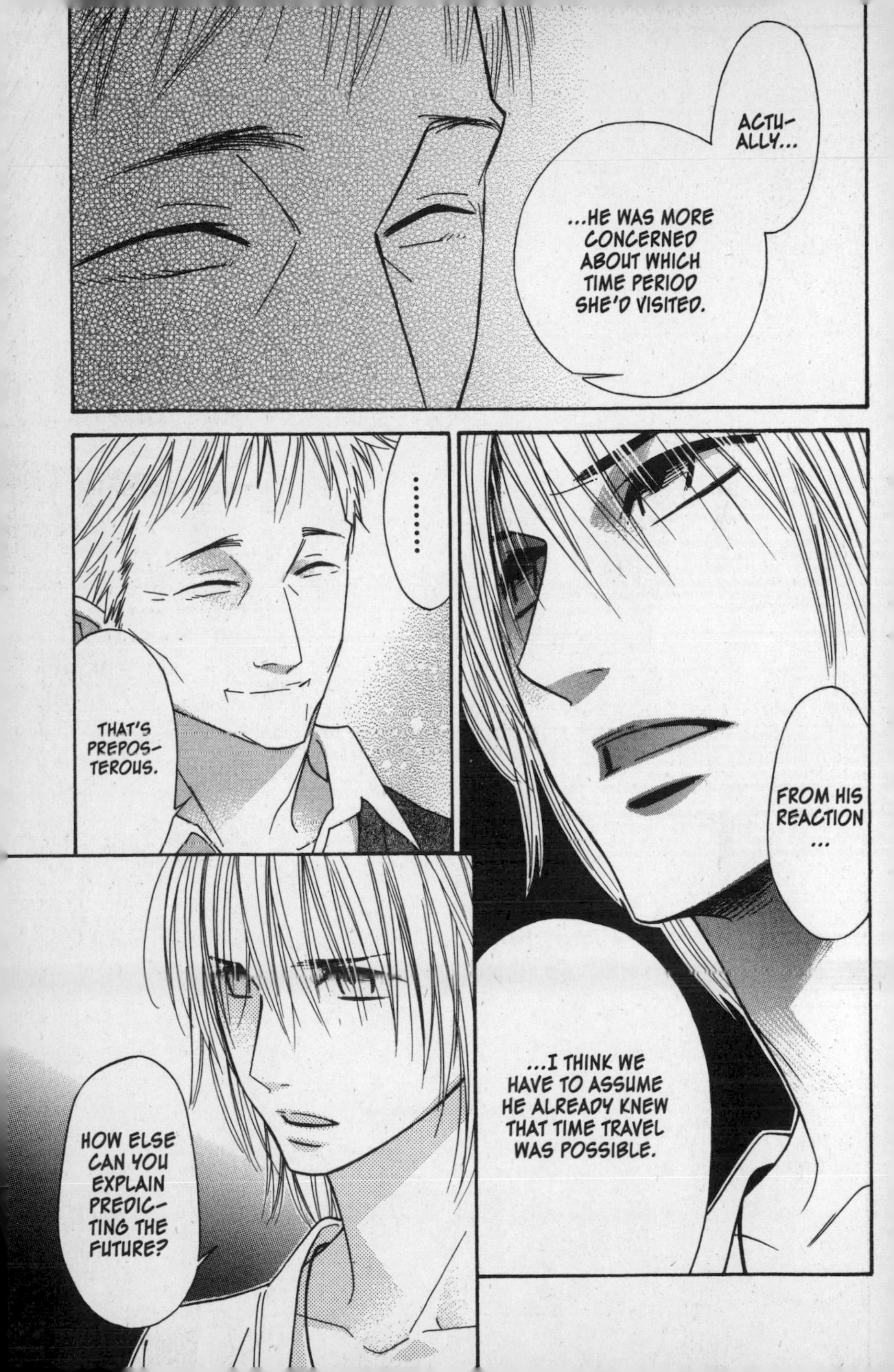
ACTU-
ALLY...
...HE WAS MORE CONCERNED ABOUT WHICH TIME PERIOD SHE'D VISITED.
FROM HIS REACTION...
...I THINK WE HAVE TO ASSUME HE ALREADY KNEW THAT TIME TRAVEL WAS POSSIBLE.
......
THAT'S PREPOSTEROUS.
HOW ELSE CAN YOU EXPLAIN PREDICTING THE FUTURE?

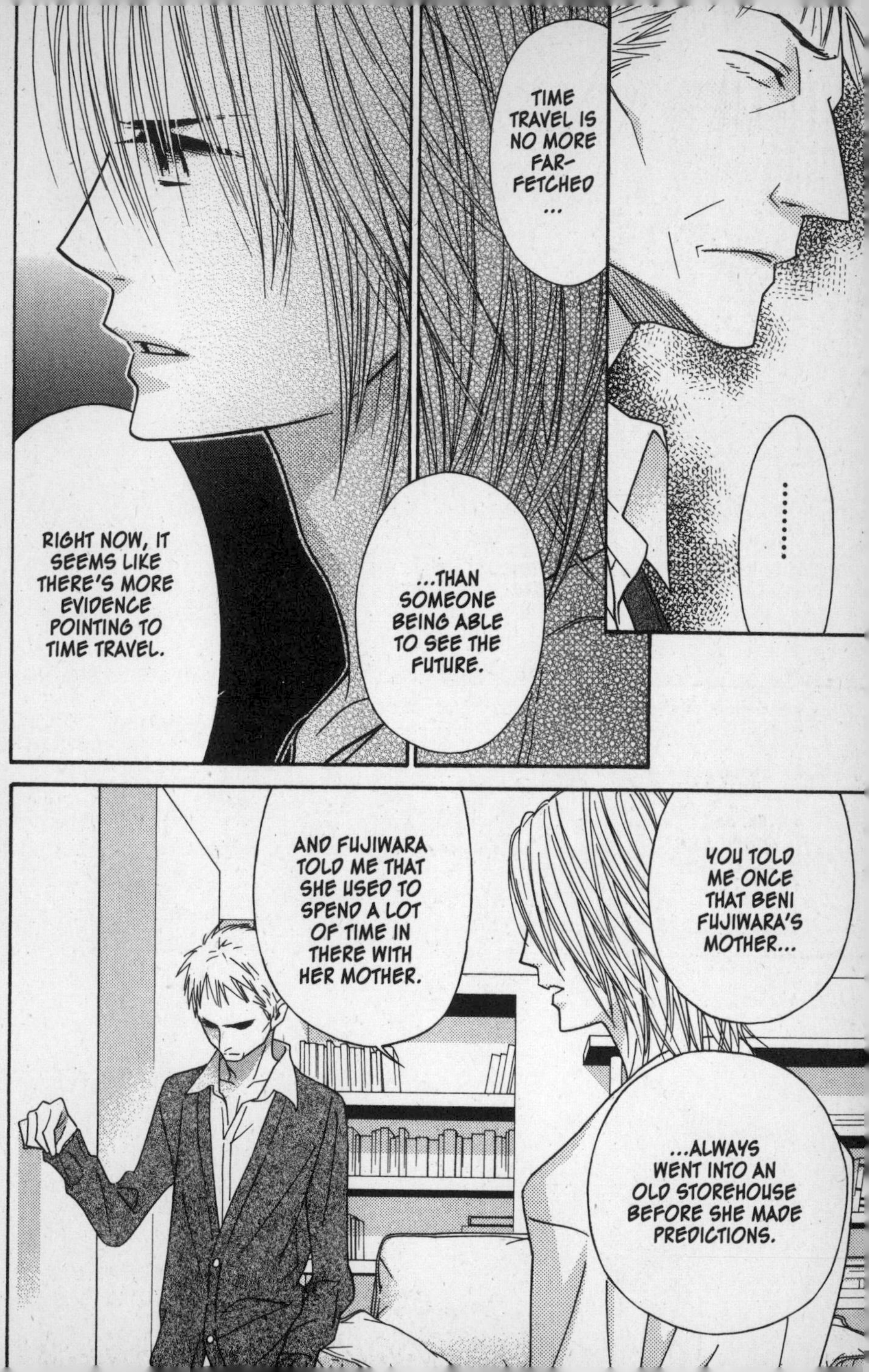
TIME TRAVEL IS NO MORE FAR-FETCHED ...
...THAN SOMEONE BEING ABLE TO SEE THE FUTURE.
......
RIGHT NOW, IT SEEMS LIKE THERE'S MORE EVIDENCE POINTING TO TIME TRAVEL.
YOU TOLD ME ONCE THAT BENI FUJIWARA'S MOTHER...
...ALWAYS WENT INTO AN OLD STOREHOUSE BEFORE SHE MADE PREDICTIONS.
AND FUJIWARA TOLD ME THAT SHE USED TO SPEND A LOT OF TIME IN THERE WITH HER MOTHER.

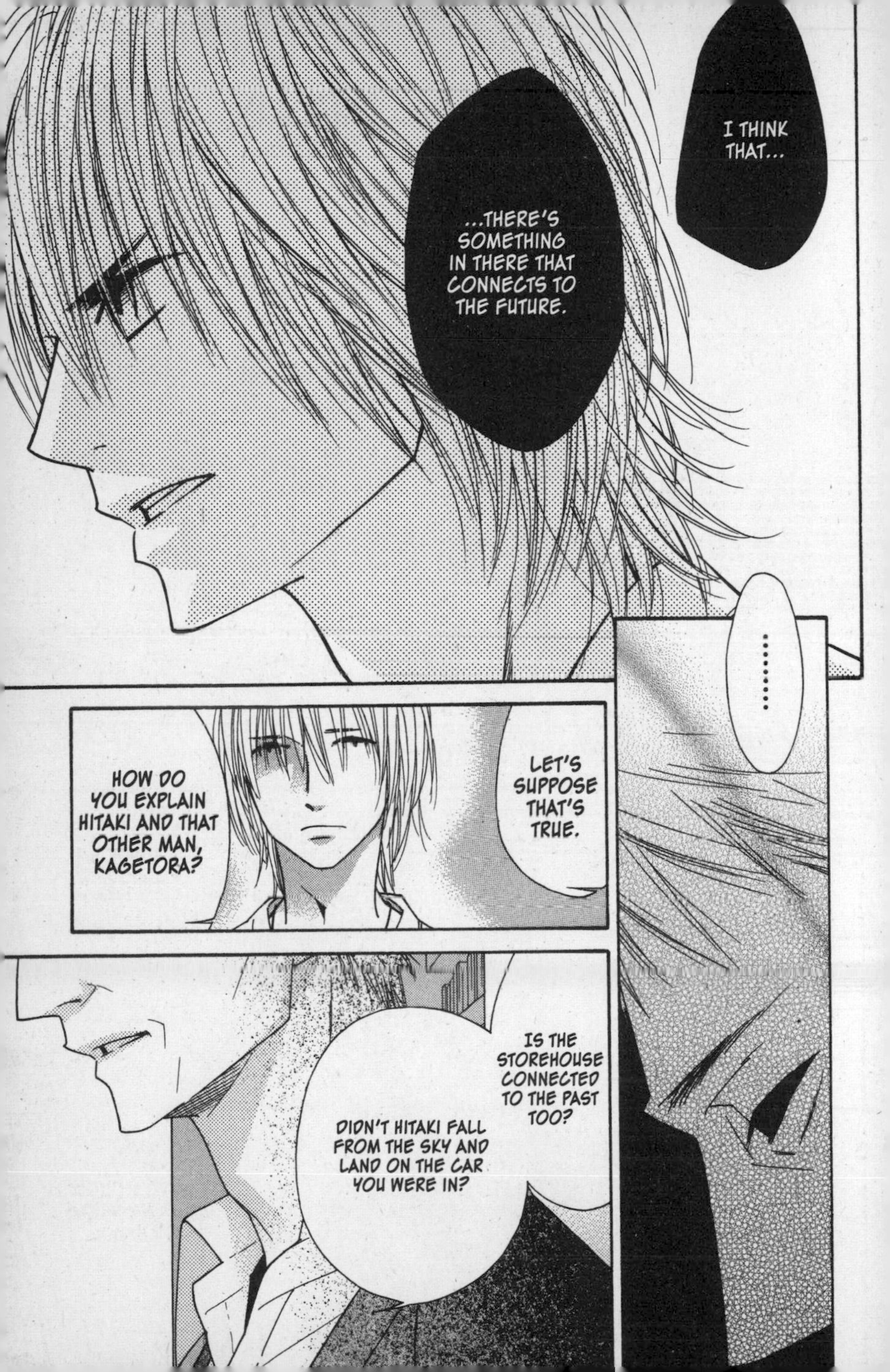
I THINK THAT...
...THERE'S SOMETHING IN THERE THAT CONNECTS TO THE FUTURE.
......
LET'S SUPPOSE THAT'S TRUE.
HOW DO YOU EXPLAIN HITAKI AND THAT OTHER MAN, KAGETORA?
IS THE STOREHOUSE CONNECTED TO THE PAST TOO?
DIDN'T HITAKI FALL FROM THE SKY AND LAND ON THE CAR YOU WERE IN?

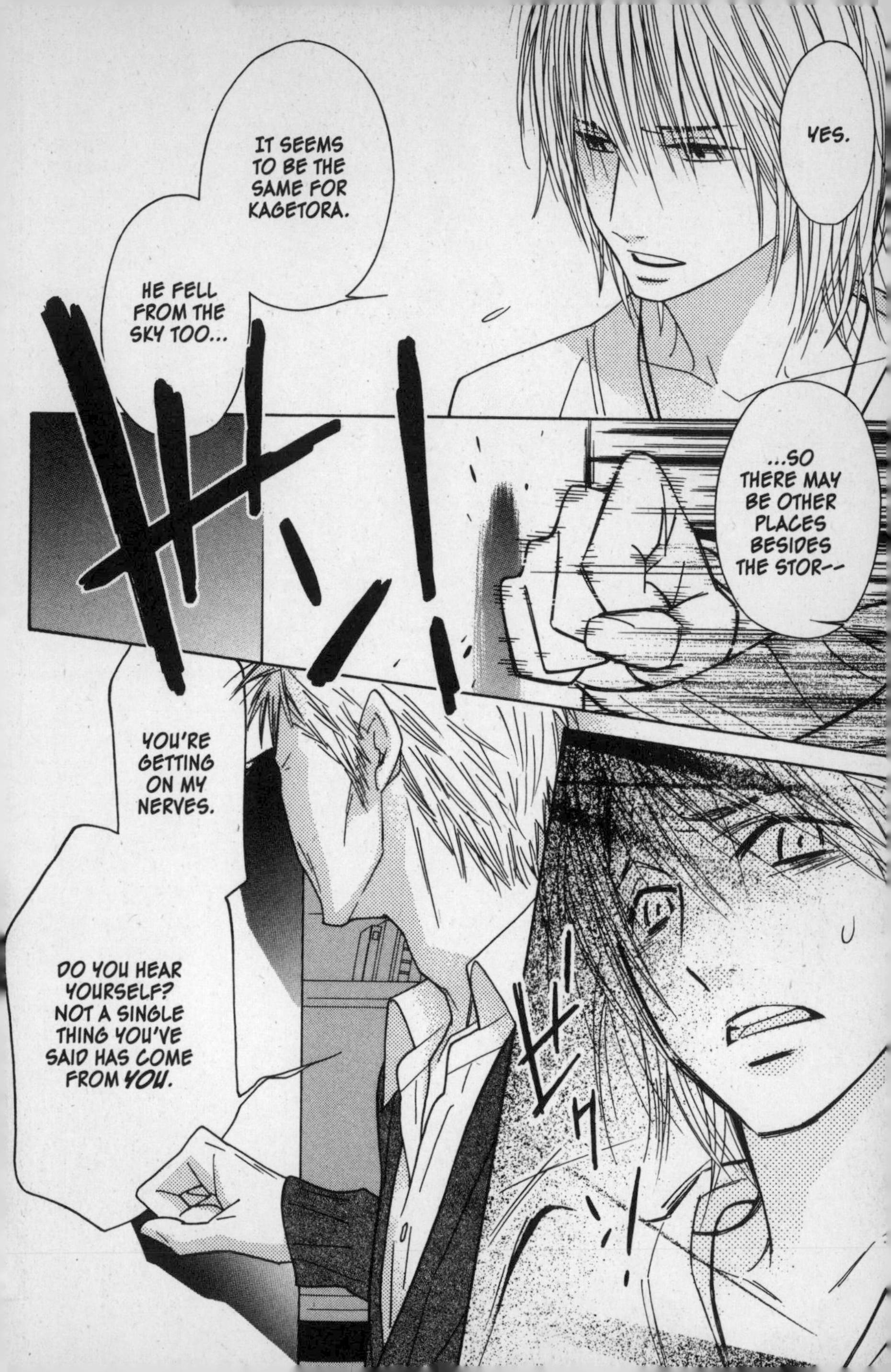
YES.
IT SEEMS TO BE THE SAME FOR KAGETORA.
HE FELL FROM THE SKY TOO...
...SO THERE MAY BE OTHER PLACES BESIDES THE STOR--
YOU'RE GETTING ON MY NERVES.
DO YOU HEAR YOURSELF? NOT A SINGLE THING YOU'VE SAID HAS COME FROM YOU.

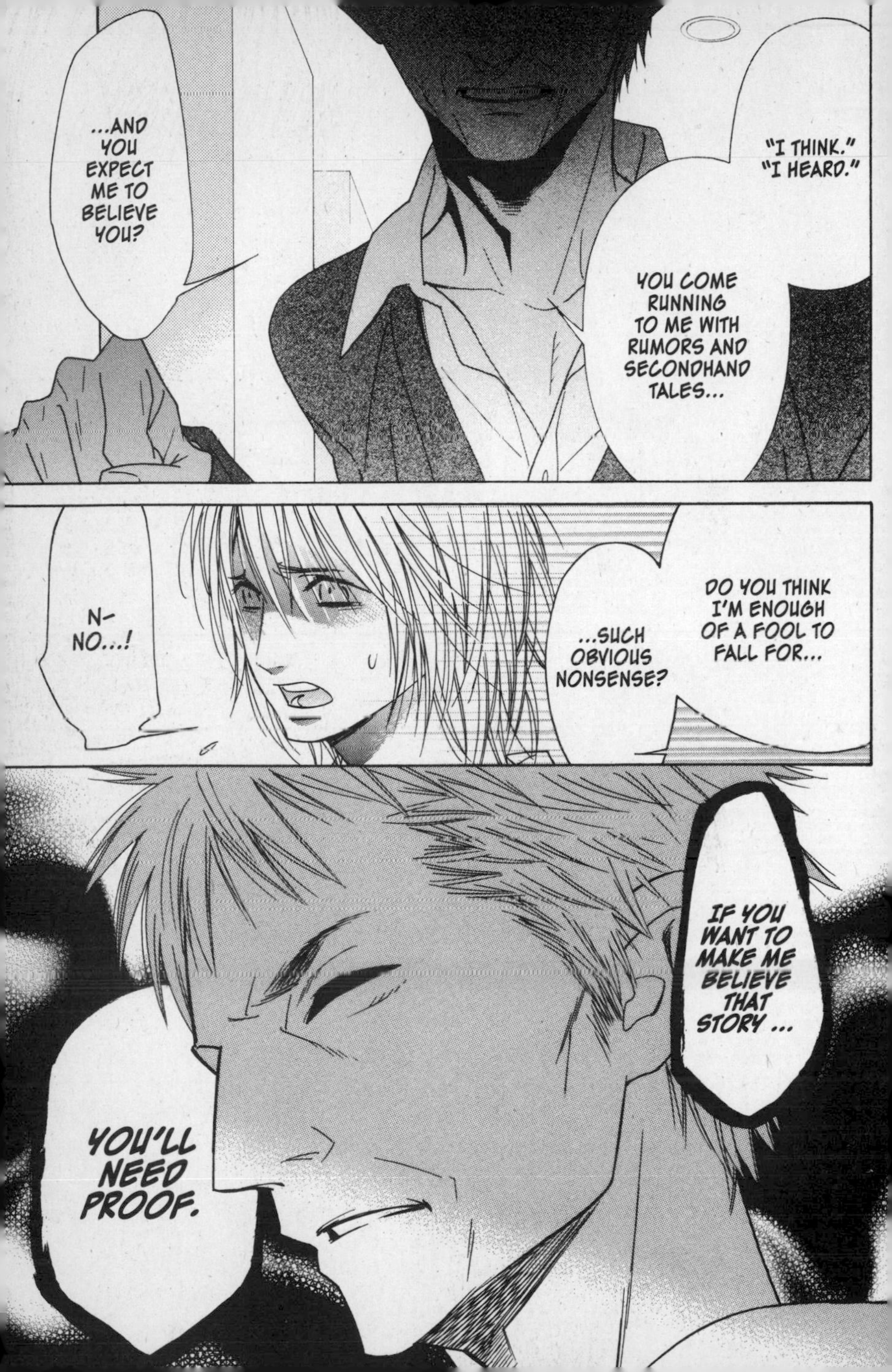
"I THINK." "I HEARD."
YOU COME RUNNING TO ME WITH RUMORS AND SECONDHAND TALES...
...AND YOU EXPECT ME TO BELIEVE YOU?
DO YOU THINK I'M ENOUGH OF A FOOL TO FALL FOR...
...SUCH OBVIOUS NONSENSE?
N-NO...!
IF YOU WANT TO MAKE ME BELIEVE THAT STORY ...
YOU'LL NEED PROOF.

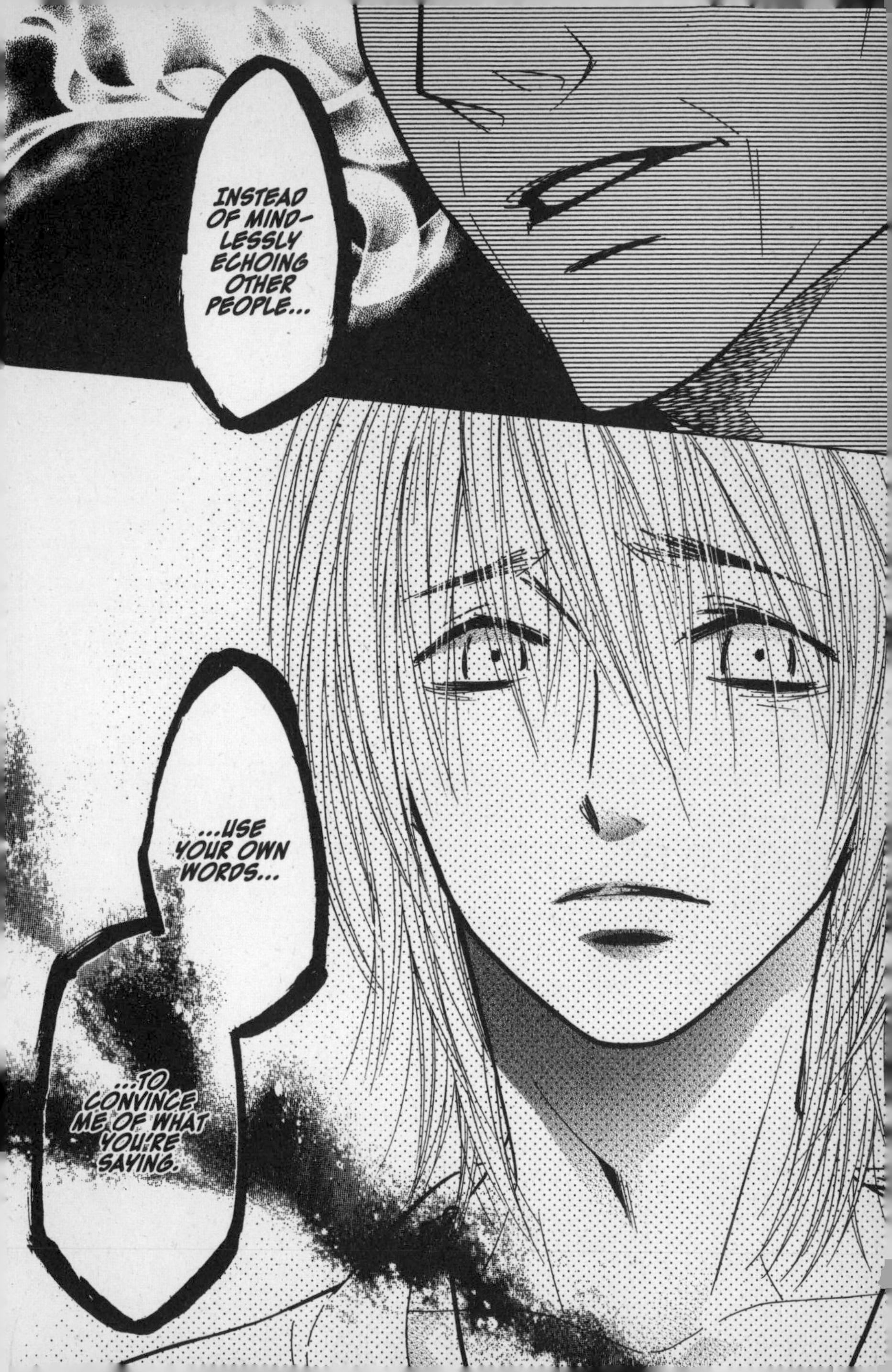
INSTEAD OF MIND-LESSLY ECHOING OTHER PEOPLE...
...USE YOUR OWN WORDS...
...TO CONVINCE ME OF WHAT YOU'RE SAYING.

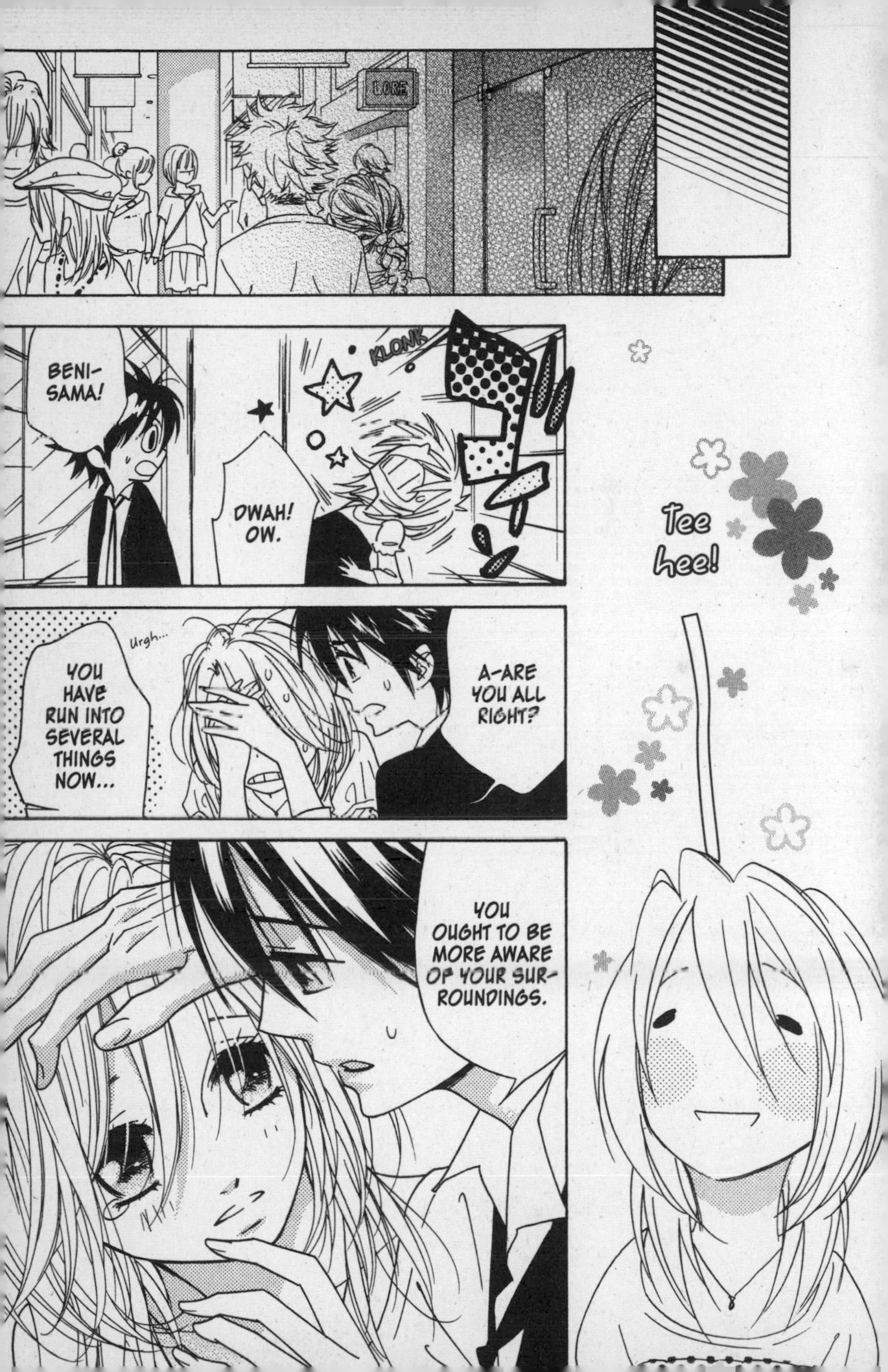
LORE
Tee hee!
KLONK
DWAH! OW.
BENI-SAMA!
A-ARE YOU ALL RIGHT?
Urgh...
YOU HAVE RUN INTO SEVERAL THINGS NOW...
YOU OUGHT TO BE MORE AWARE OF YOUR SUR-ROUNDINGS.

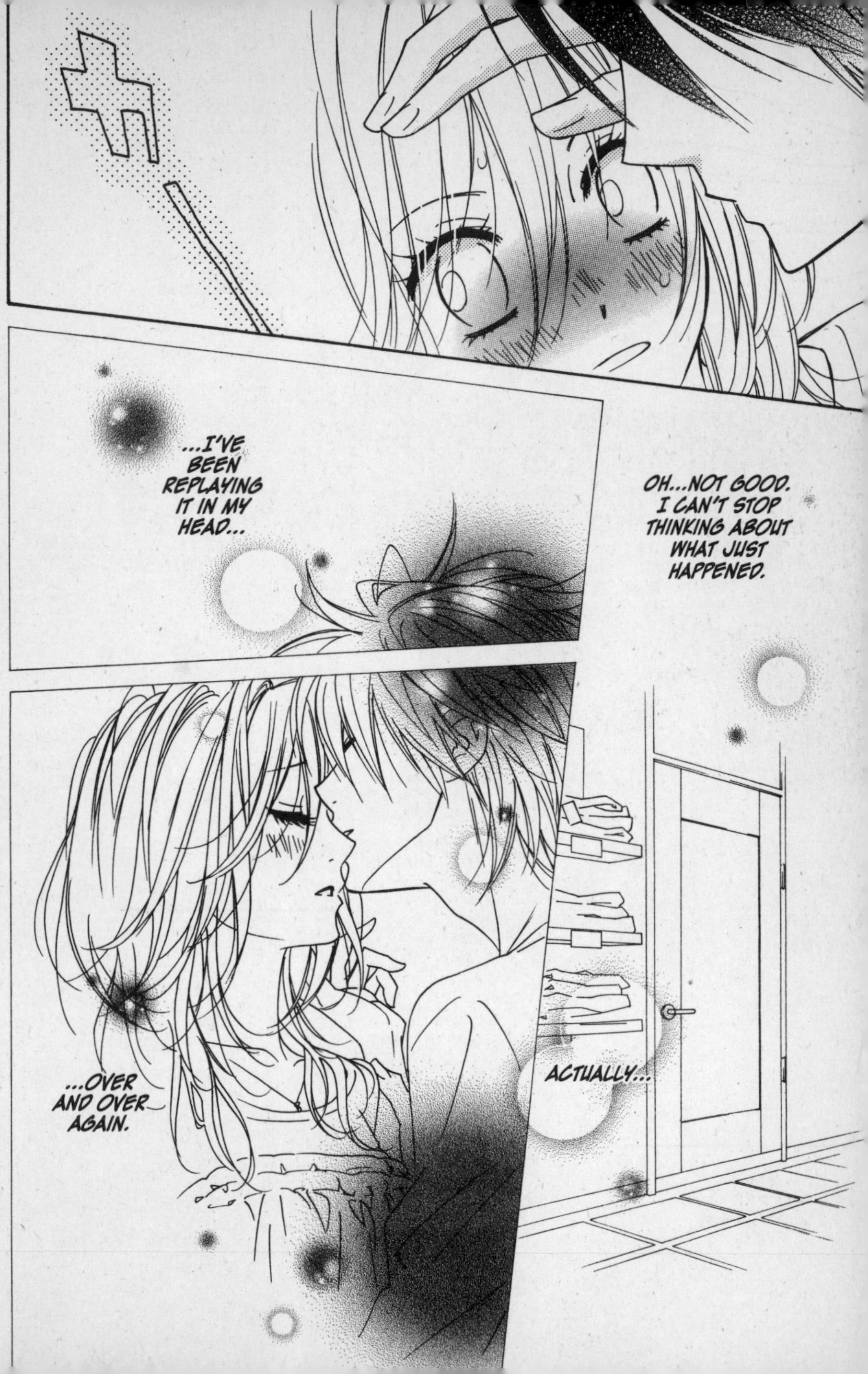
OH...NOT GOOD. I CAN'T STOP THINKING ABOUT WHAT JUST HAPPENED.
...I'VE BEEN REPLAYING IT IN MY HEAD...
ACTUALLY...
...OVER AND OVER AGAIN.

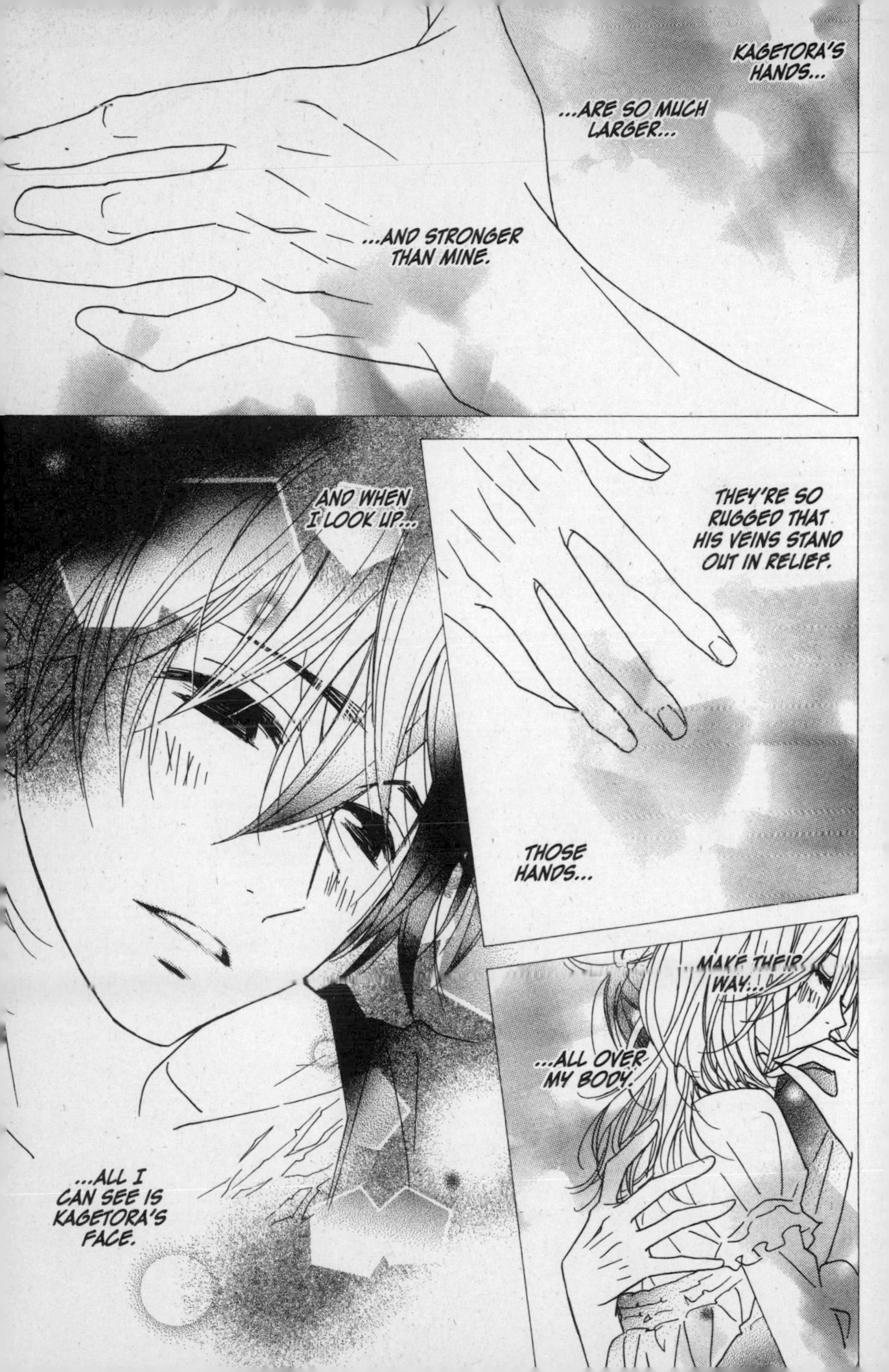
KAGETORA'S HANDS...
...ARE SO MUCH LARGER...
...AND STRONGER THAN MINE.
THEY'RE SO RUGGED THAT HIS VEINS STAND OUT IN RELIEF.
AND WHEN I LOOK UP...
THOSE HANDS...
...MAKE THEIR WAY...
...ALL OVER MY BODY.
...ALL I CAN SEE IS KAGETORA'S FACE.

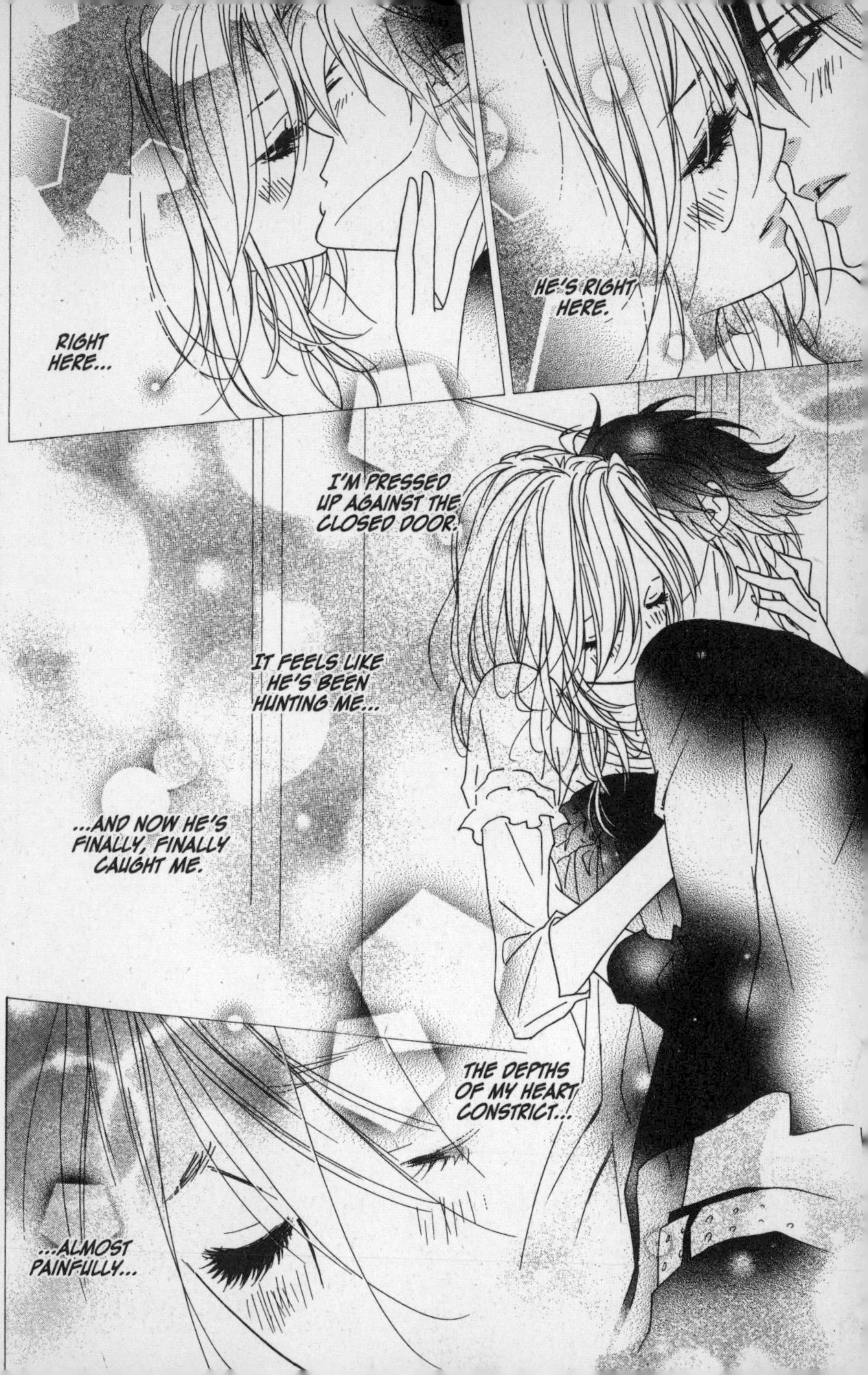
HE'S RIGHT HERE.
RIGHT HERE...
I'M PRESSED UP AGAINST THE CLOSED DOOR.
IT FEELS LIKE HE'S BEEN HUNTING ME...
...AND NOW HE'S FINALLY, FINALLY CAUGHT ME.
THE DEPTHS OF MY HEART CONSTRICT...
...ALMOST PAINFULLY...

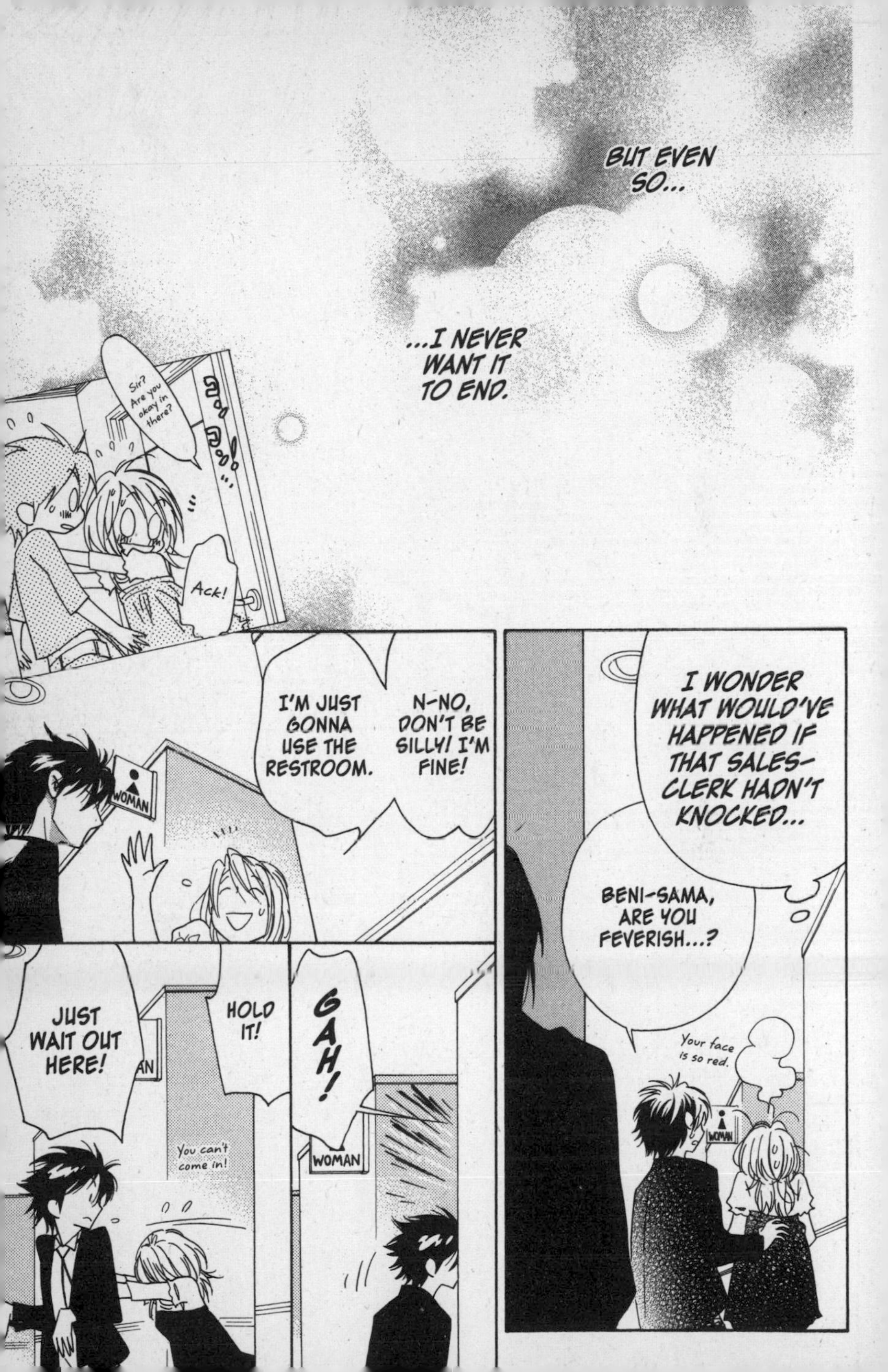
BUT EVEN SO...
...I NEVER WANT IT TO END.
Sir? Are you okay in there?
Ack!
N-NO, DON'T BE SILLY! I'M FINE!
I'M JUST GONNA USE THE RESTROOM.
WOMAN
I WONDER WHAT WOULD'VE HAPPENED IF THAT SALES-CLERK HADN'T KNOCKED...
BENI-SAMA, ARE YOU FEVERISH...?
Your face is so red.
GAH!
HOLD IT!
JUST WAIT OUT HERE!
You can't come in!
WOMAN

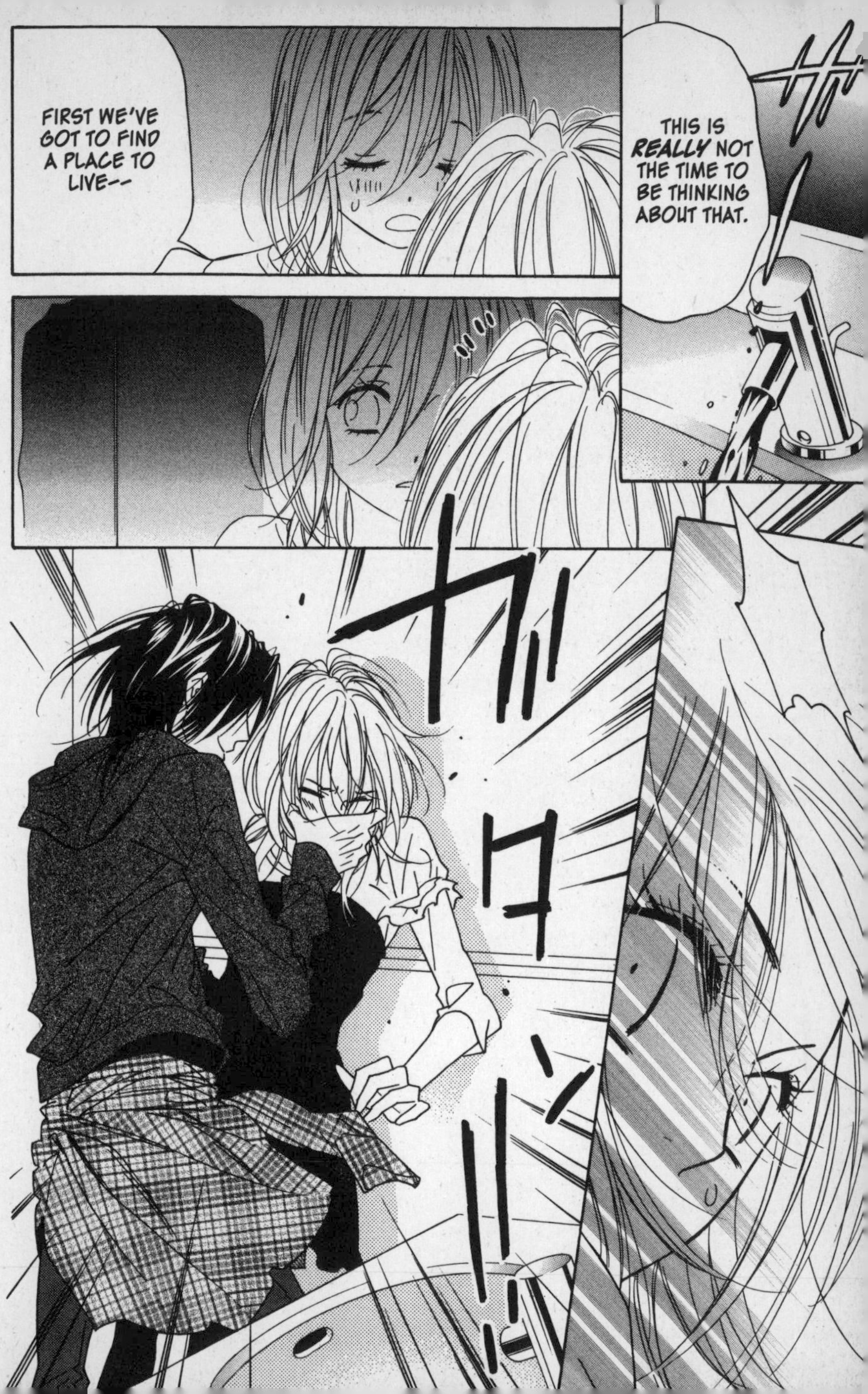
THIS IS REALLY NOT THE TIME TO BE THINKING ABOUT THAT.
FIRST WE'VE GOT TO FIND A PLACE TO LIVE--

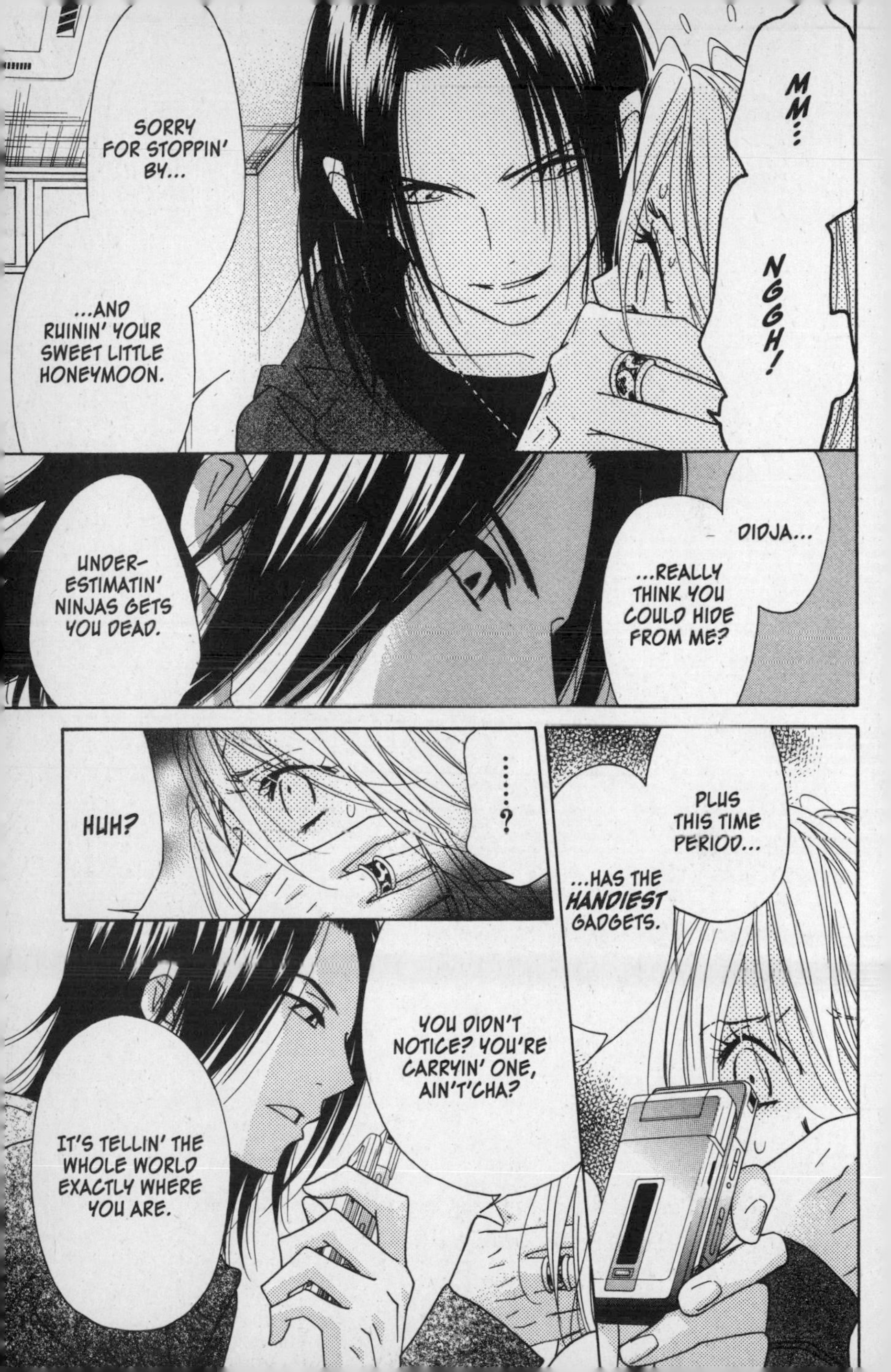
MM...
NGGH!
SORRY FOR STOPPIN' BY...
...AND RUININ' YOUR SWEET LITTLE HONEYMOON.
DIDJA...
...REALLY THINK YOU COULD HIDE FROM ME?
UNDER-ESTIMATIN' NINJAS GETS YOU DEAD.
PLUS THIS TIME PERIOD...
...HAS THE **HANDIEST** GADGETS.
.....?
HUH?
YOU DIDN'T NOTICE? YOU'RE CARRYIN' ONE, AIN'T'CHA?
IT'S TELLIN' THE WHOLE WORLD EXACTLY WHERE YOU ARE.

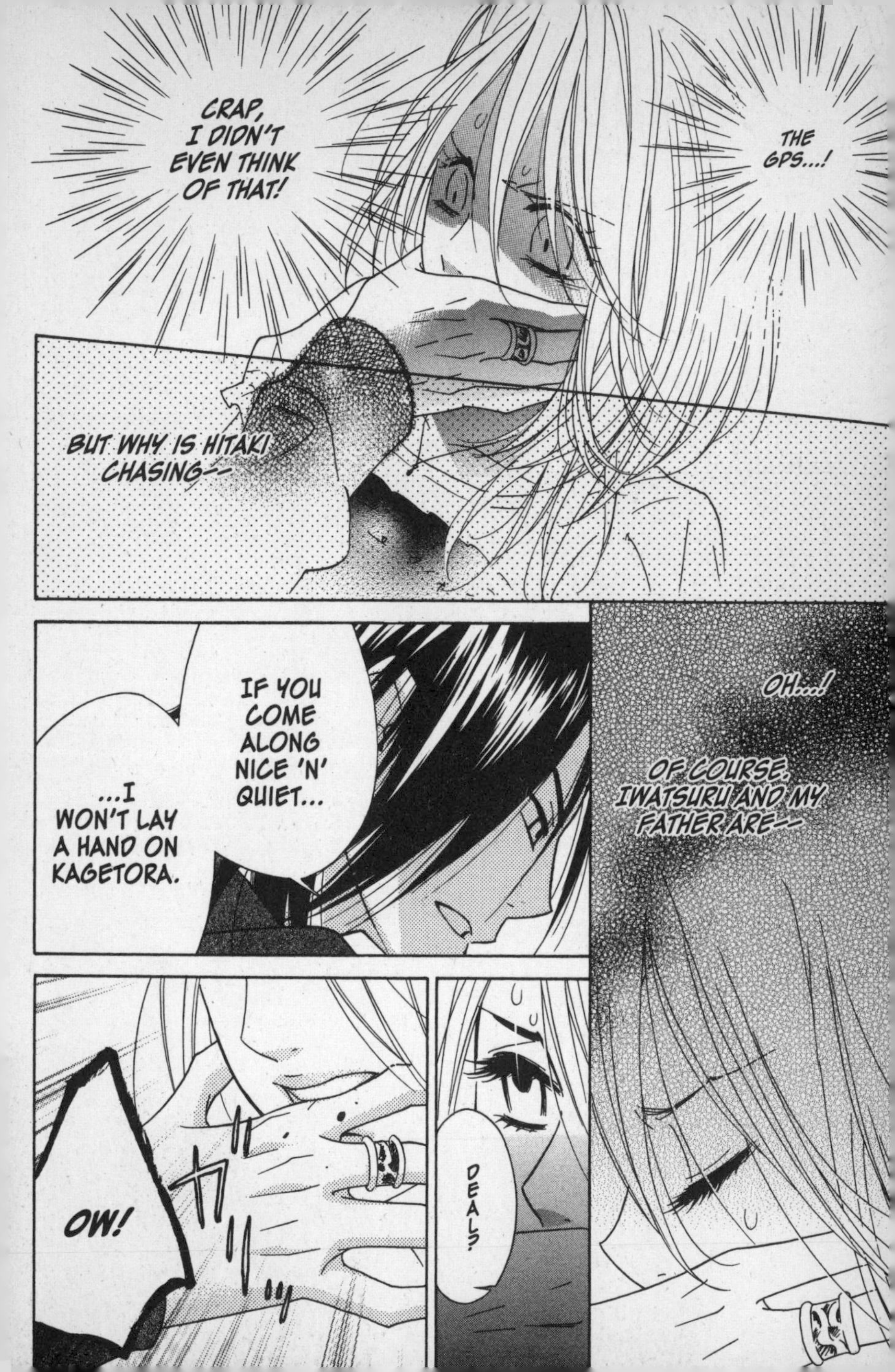
THE GPS...!
CRAP, I DIDN'T EVEN THINK OF THAT!
BUT WHY IS HITAKI CHASING--
OH...!
OF COURSE. IWATSURU AND MY FATHER ARE--
IF YOU COME ALONG NICE 'N' QUIET...
...I WON'T LAY A HAND ON KAGETORA.
DEAL?
OW!

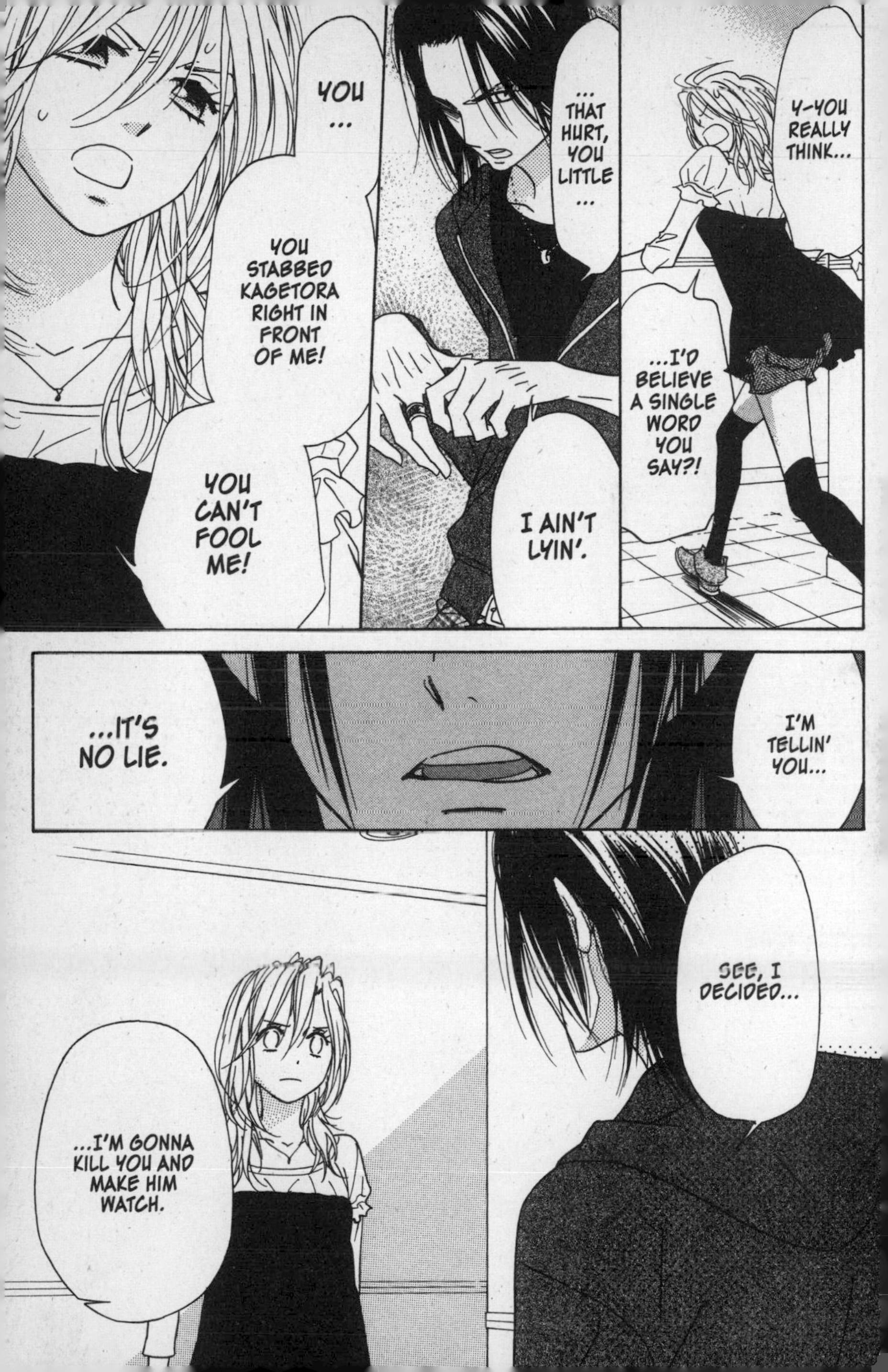
Y-YOU REALLY THINK...
...I'D BELIEVE A SINGLE WORD YOU SAY?!
...THAT HURT, YOU LITTLE...
I AIN'T LYIN'.
YOU...
YOU STABBED KAGETORA RIGHT IN FRONT OF ME!
YOU CAN'T FOOL ME!
I'M TELLIN' YOU...
...IT'S NO LIE.
SEE, I DECIDED...
...I'M GONNA KILL YOU AND MAKE HIM WATCH.

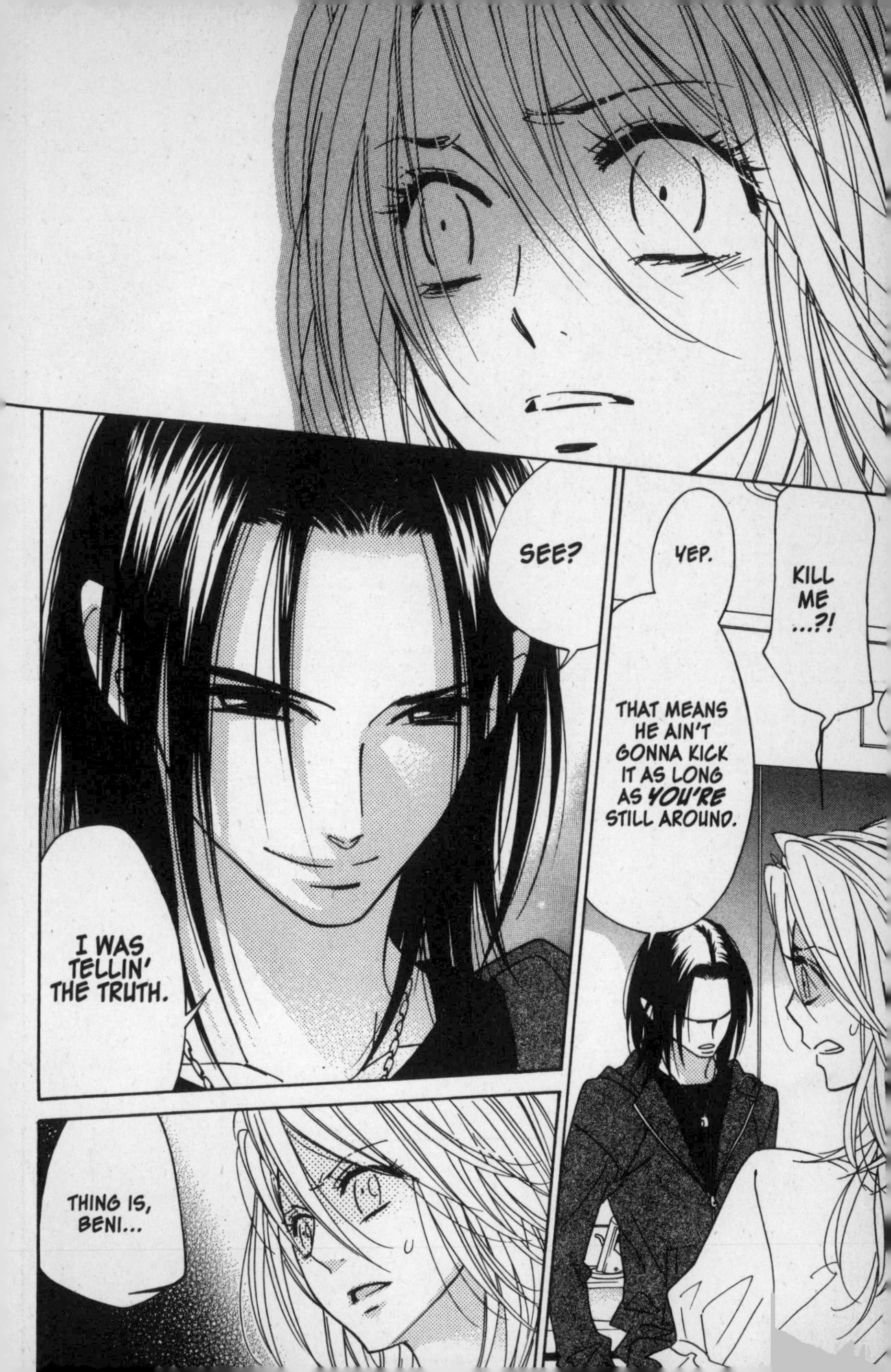
KILL ME ...?!
YEP.
THAT MEANS HE AIN'T GONNA KICK IT AS LONG AS YOU'RE STILL AROUND.
SEE?
I WAS TELLIN' THE TRUTH.
THING IS, BENI...

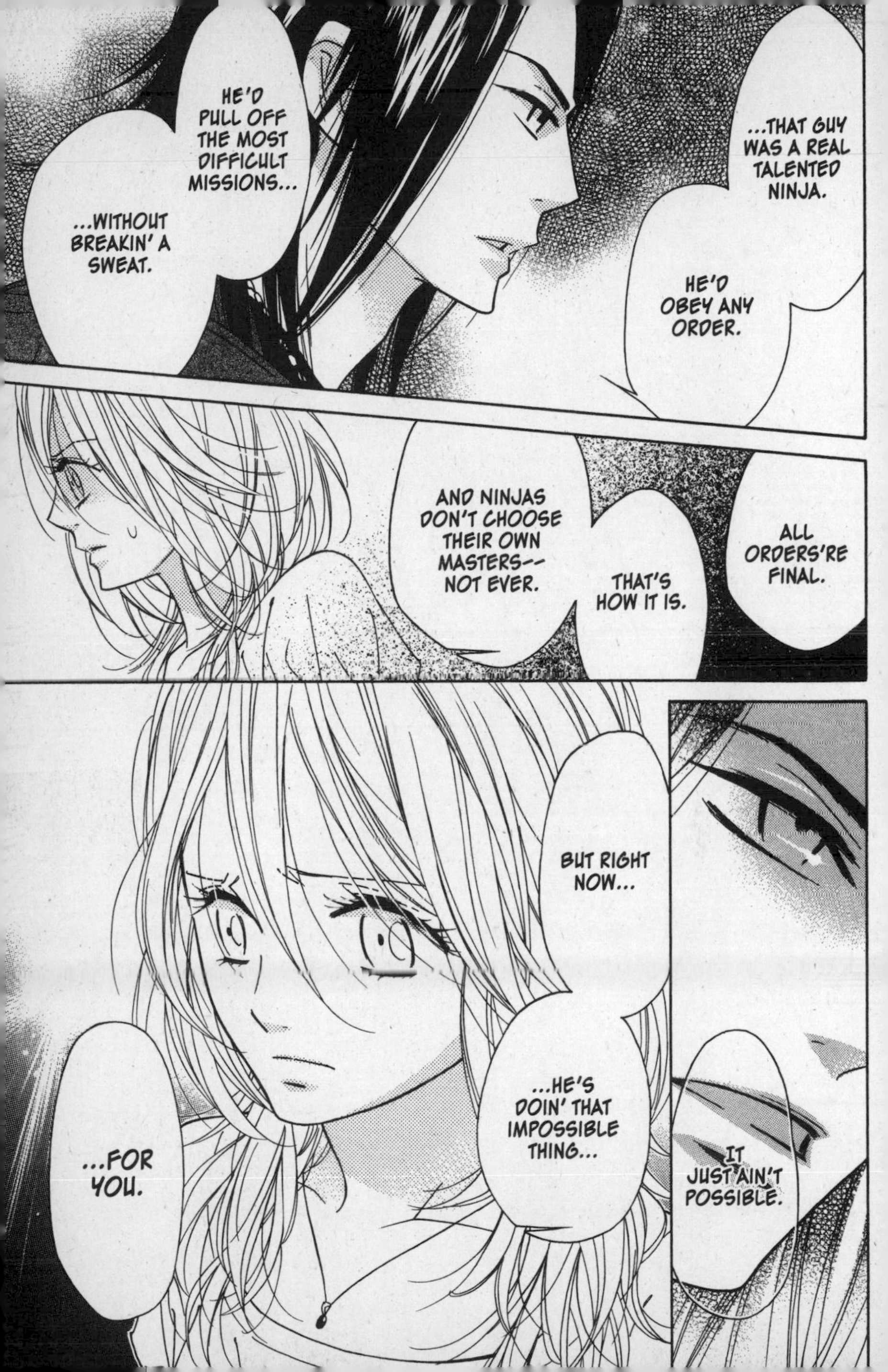
...THAT GUY WAS A REAL TALENTED NINJA.
HE'D OBEY ANY ORDER.
HE'D PULL OFF THE MOST DIFFICULT MISSIONS...
...WITHOUT BREAKIN' A SWEAT.
ALL ORDERS'RE FINAL.
THAT'S HOW IT IS.
AND NINJAS DON'T CHOOSE THEIR OWN MASTERS--NOT EVER.
IT JUST AIN'T POSSIBLE.
BUT RIGHT NOW...
...HE'S DOIN' THAT IMPOSSIBLE THING...
...FOR YOU.

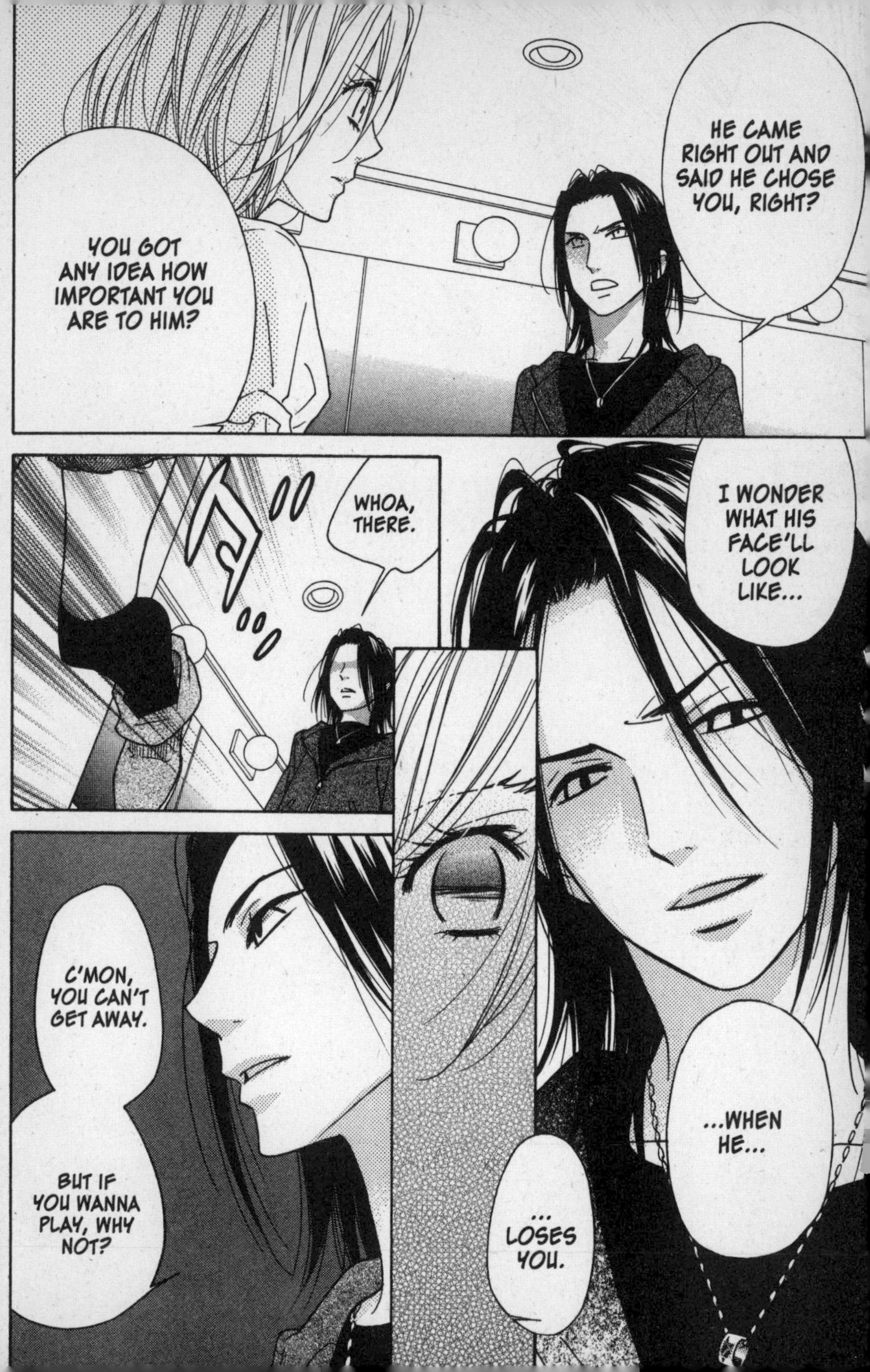
HE CAME RIGHT OUT AND SAID HE CHOSE YOU, RIGHT?
YOU GOT ANY IDEA HOW IMPORTANT YOU ARE TO HIM?
WHOA, THERE.
C'MON, YOU CAN'T GET AWAY.
BUT IF YOU WANNA PLAY, WHY NOT?
I WONDER WHAT HIS FACE'LL LOOK LIKE...
...WHEN HE...
...LOSES YOU.

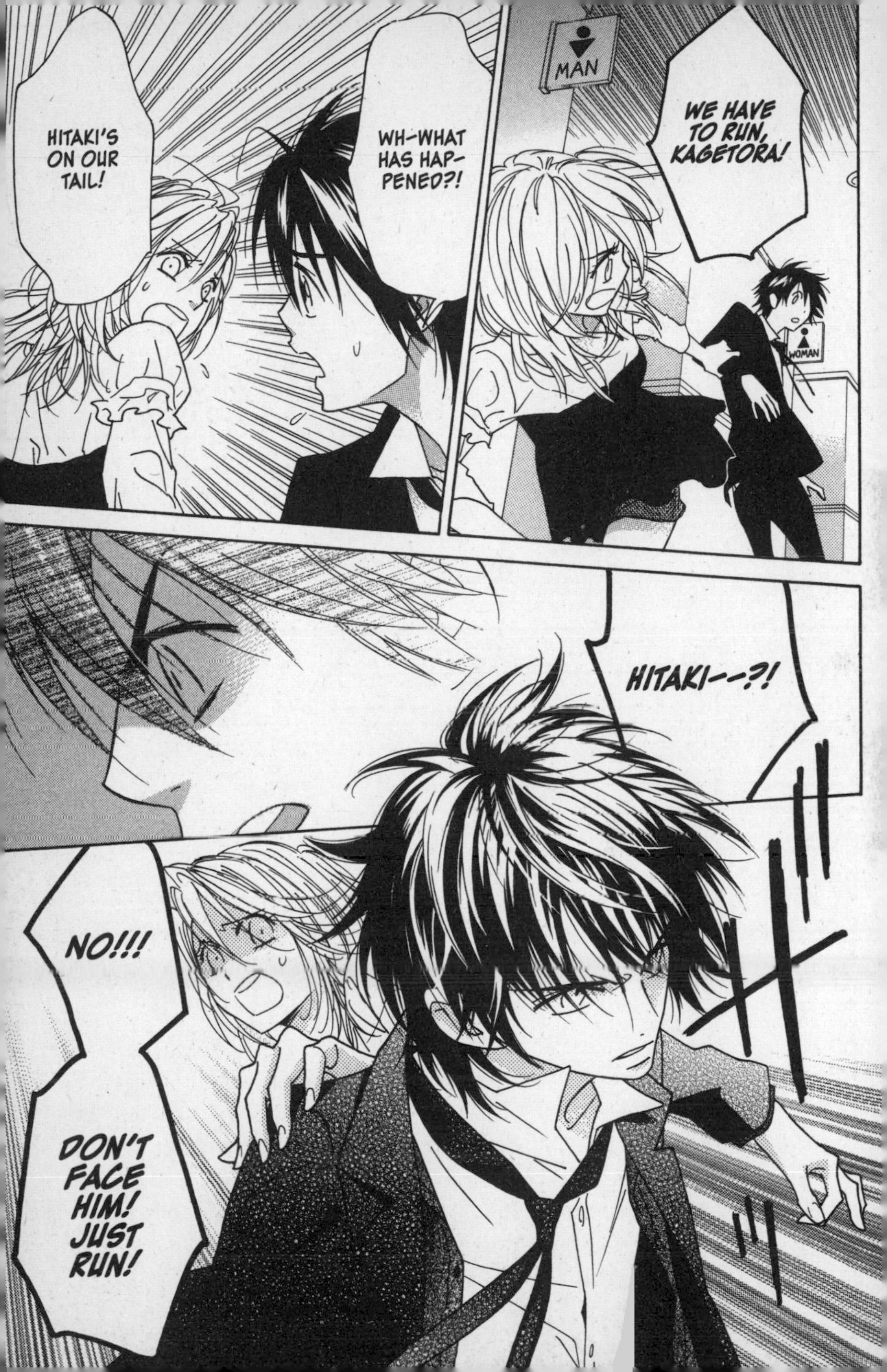
MAN
WOMAN
WE HAVE TO RUN, KAGETORA!
WH-WHAT HAS HAP-PENED?!
HITAKI'S ON OUR TAIL!
HITAKI--?!
NO!!!
DON'T FACE HIM! JUST RUN!

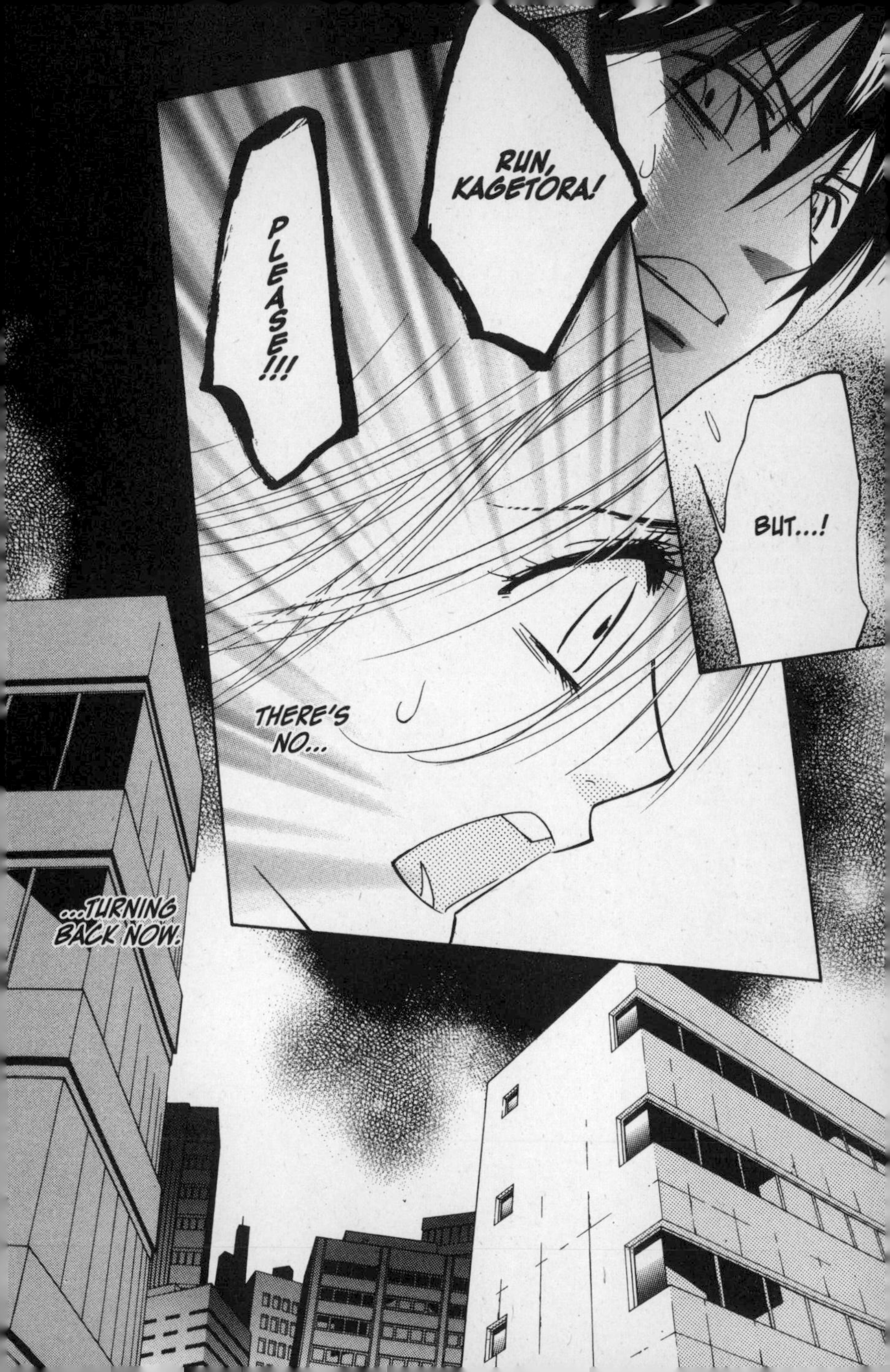
RUN, KAGETORA!
PLEASE!!!
BUT...!
THERE'S NO...
...TURNING BACK NOW.

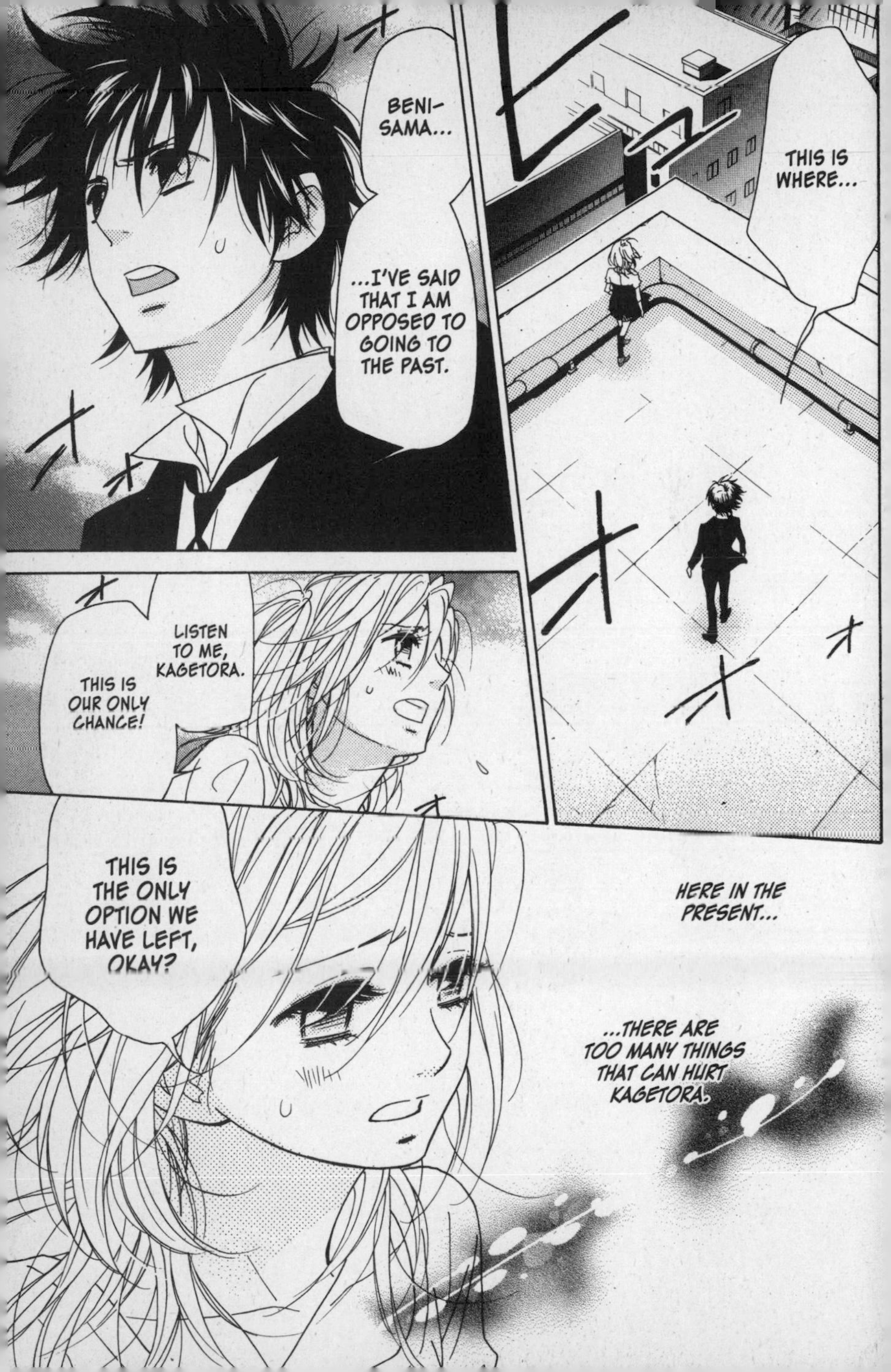
THIS IS WHERE...
BENI-SAMA...
...I'VE SAID THAT I AM OPPOSED TO GOING TO THE PAST.
LISTEN TO ME, KAGETORA.
THIS IS OUR ONLY CHANCE!
HERE IN THE PRESENT...
...THERE ARE TOO MANY THINGS THAT CAN HURT KAGETORA.
THIS IS THE ONLY OPTION WE HAVE LEFT, OKAY?

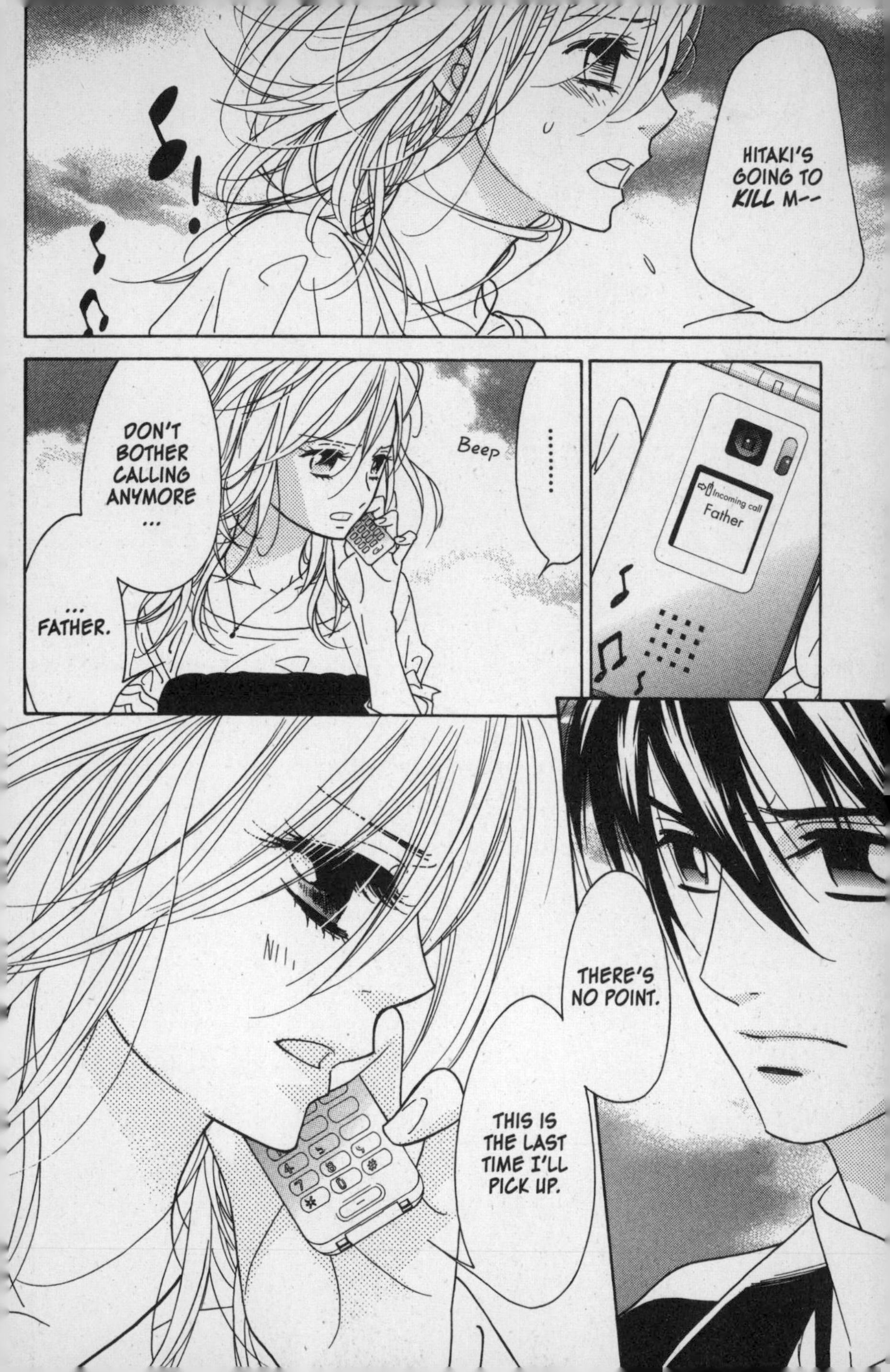
HITAKI'S GOING TO KILL M--
Incoming call
Father
......
Beep
DON'T BOTHER CALLING ANYMORE ...
... FATHER.
THERE'S NO POINT.
THIS IS THE LAST TIME I'LL PICK UP.

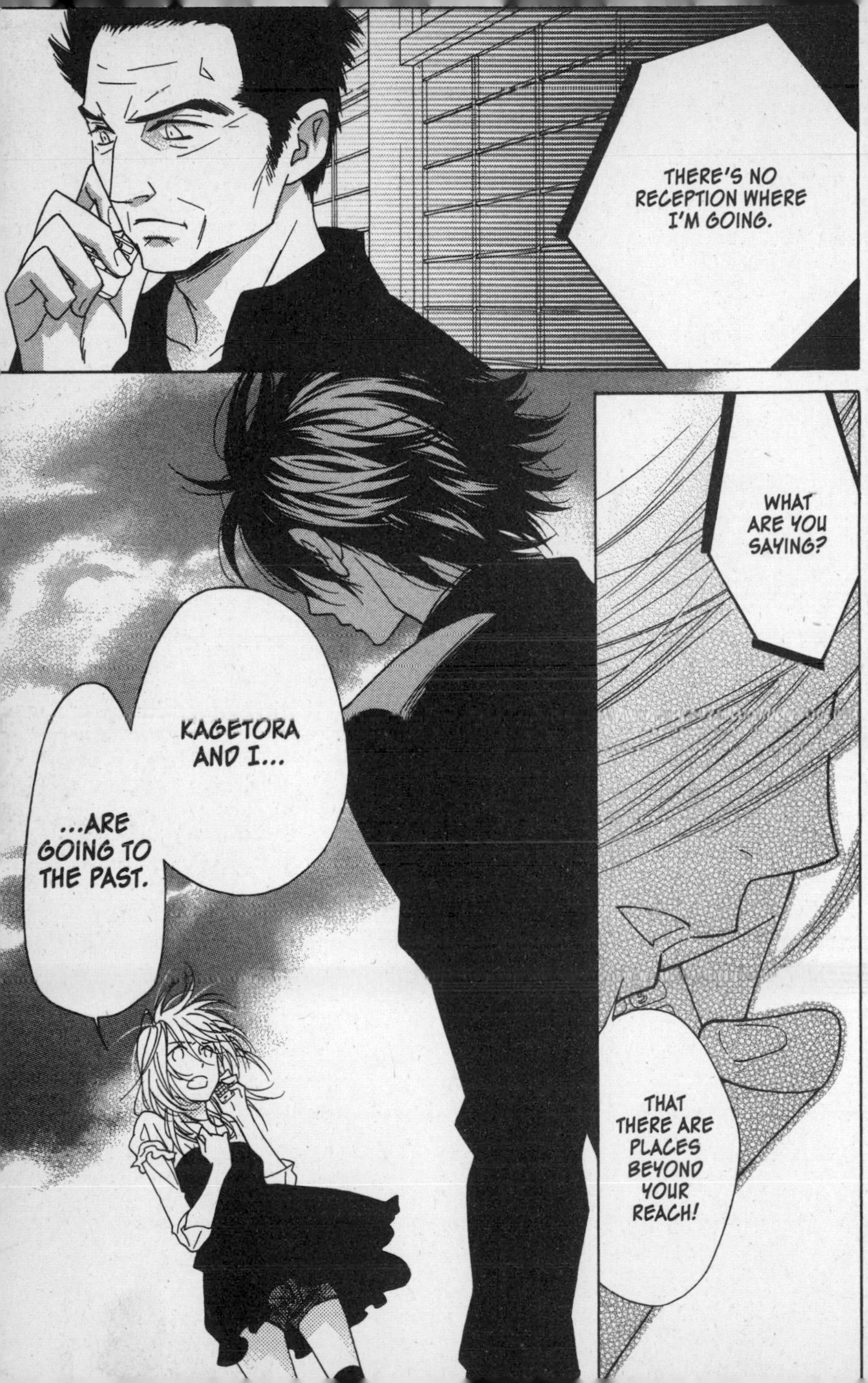
THERE'S NO RECEPTION WHERE I'M GOING.
WHAT ARE YOU SAYING?
THAT THERE ARE PLACES BEYOND YOUR REACH!
KAGETORA AND I...
...ARE GOING TO THE PAST.

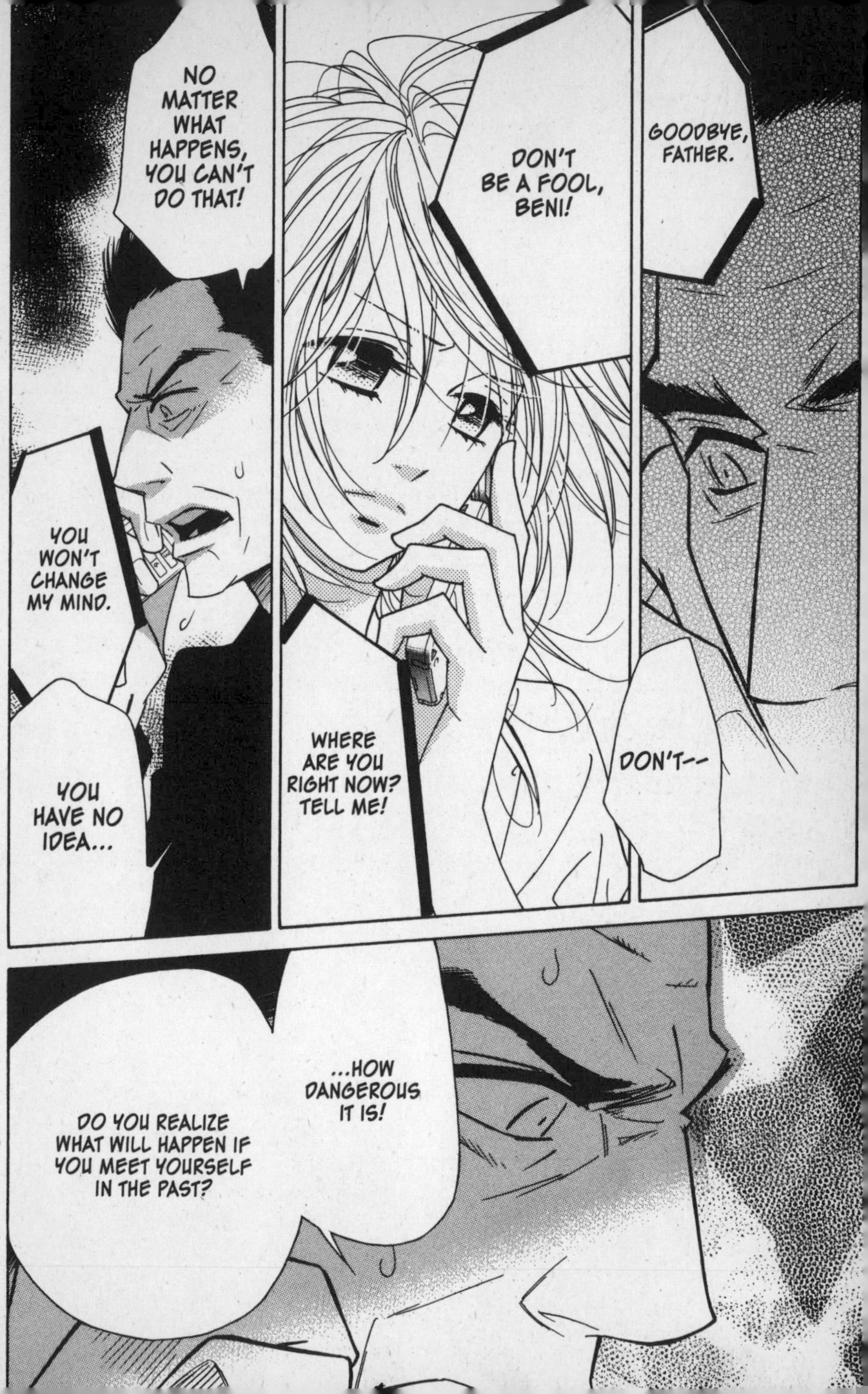
GOODBYE, FATHER.
DON'T--
DON'T BE A FOOL, BENI!
WHERE ARE YOU RIGHT NOW? TELL ME!
NO MATTER WHAT HAPPENS, YOU CAN'T DO THAT!
YOU WON'T CHANGE MY MIND.
YOU HAVE NO IDEA...
...HOW DANGEROUS IT IS!
DO YOU REALIZE WHAT WILL HAPPEN IF YOU MEET YOURSELF IN THE PAST?

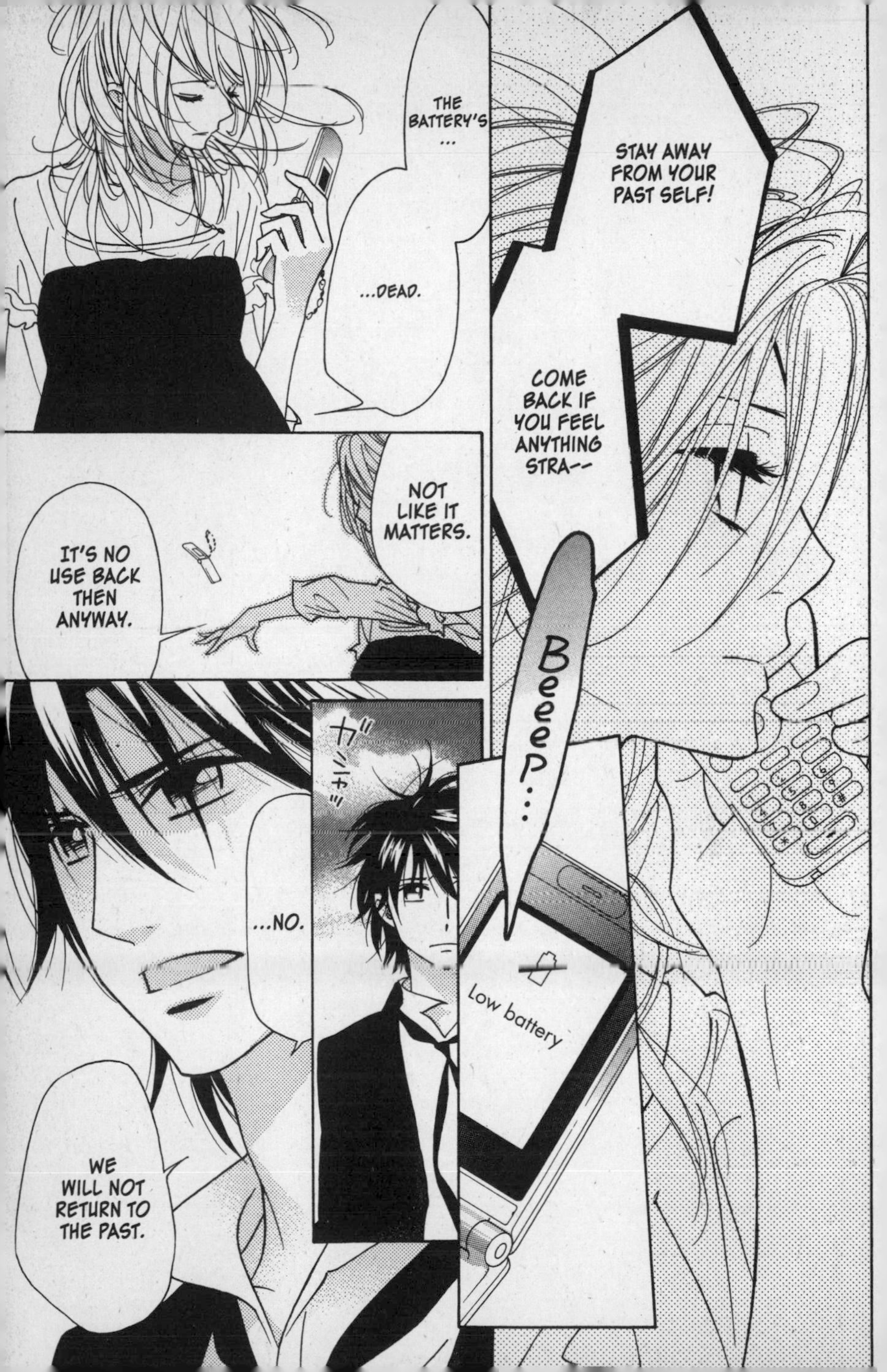
STAY AWAY FROM YOUR PAST SELF!
COME BACK IF YOU FEEL ANYTHING STRA--
Beeep...
Low battery
THE BATTERY'S ...
...DEAD.
NOT LIKE IT MATTERS.
IT'S NO USE BACK THEN ANYWAY.
ガシャッ
...NO.
WE WILL NOT RETURN TO THE PAST.

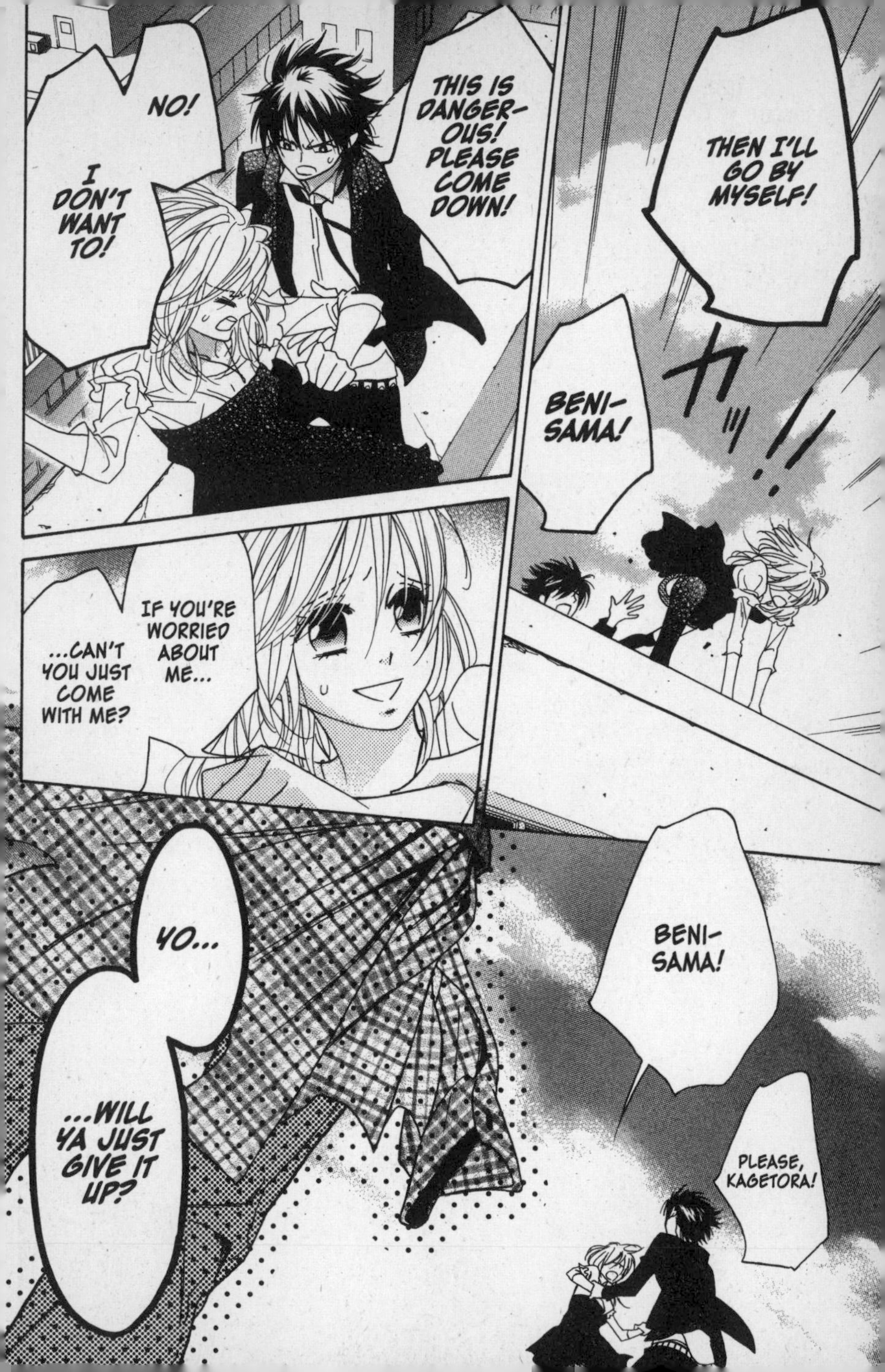
THEN I'LL GO BY MYSELF!
THIS IS DANGEROUS! PLEASE COME DOWN!
NO!
I DON'T WANT TO!
BENI-SAMA!
IF YOU'RE WORRIED ABOUT ME...
...CAN'T YOU JUST COME WITH ME?
BENI-SAMA!
PLEASE, KAGETORA!
YO...
...WILL YA JUST GIVE IT UP?

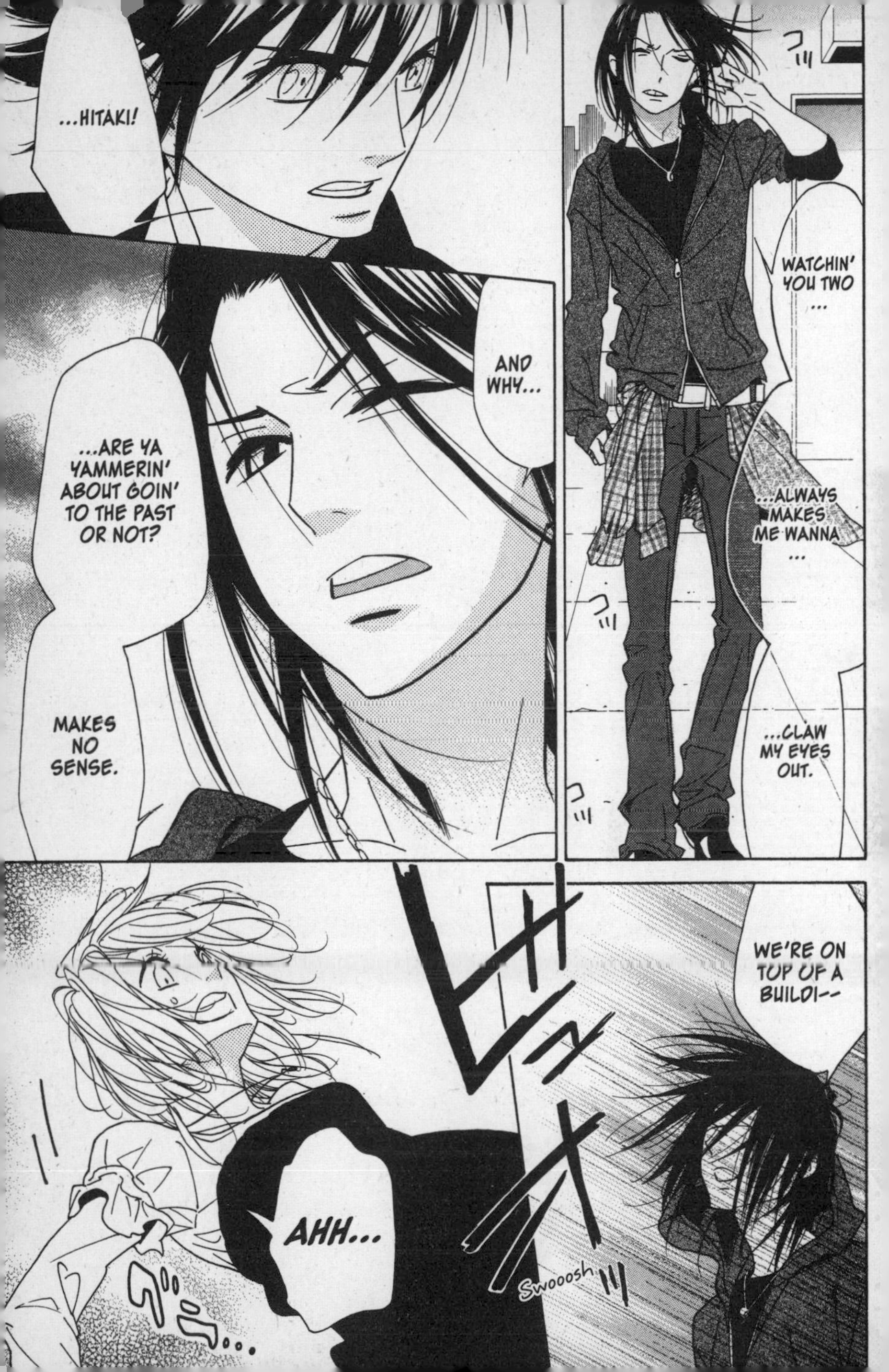

WATCHIN' YOU TWO ...
...ALWAYS MAKES ME WANNA ...
...CLAW MY EYES OUT.
...HITAKI!
AND WHY...
...ARE YA YAMMERIN' ABOUT GOIN' TO THE PAST OR NOT?
MAKES NO SENSE.
WE'RE ON TOP OF A BUILDI--
Swooosh
AHH...

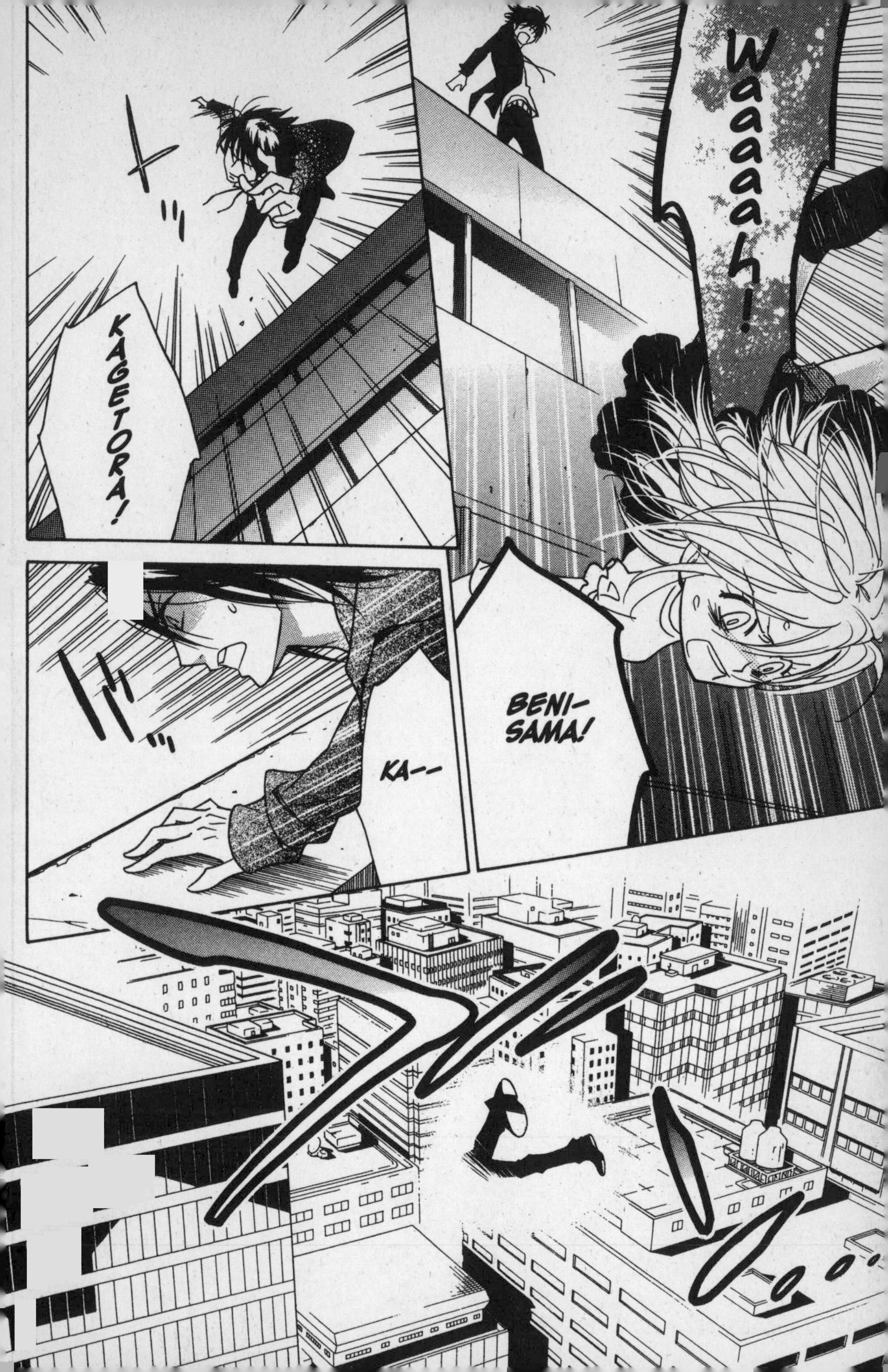
Waaaaah!
KAGETORA!
BENI-SAMA!
KA--

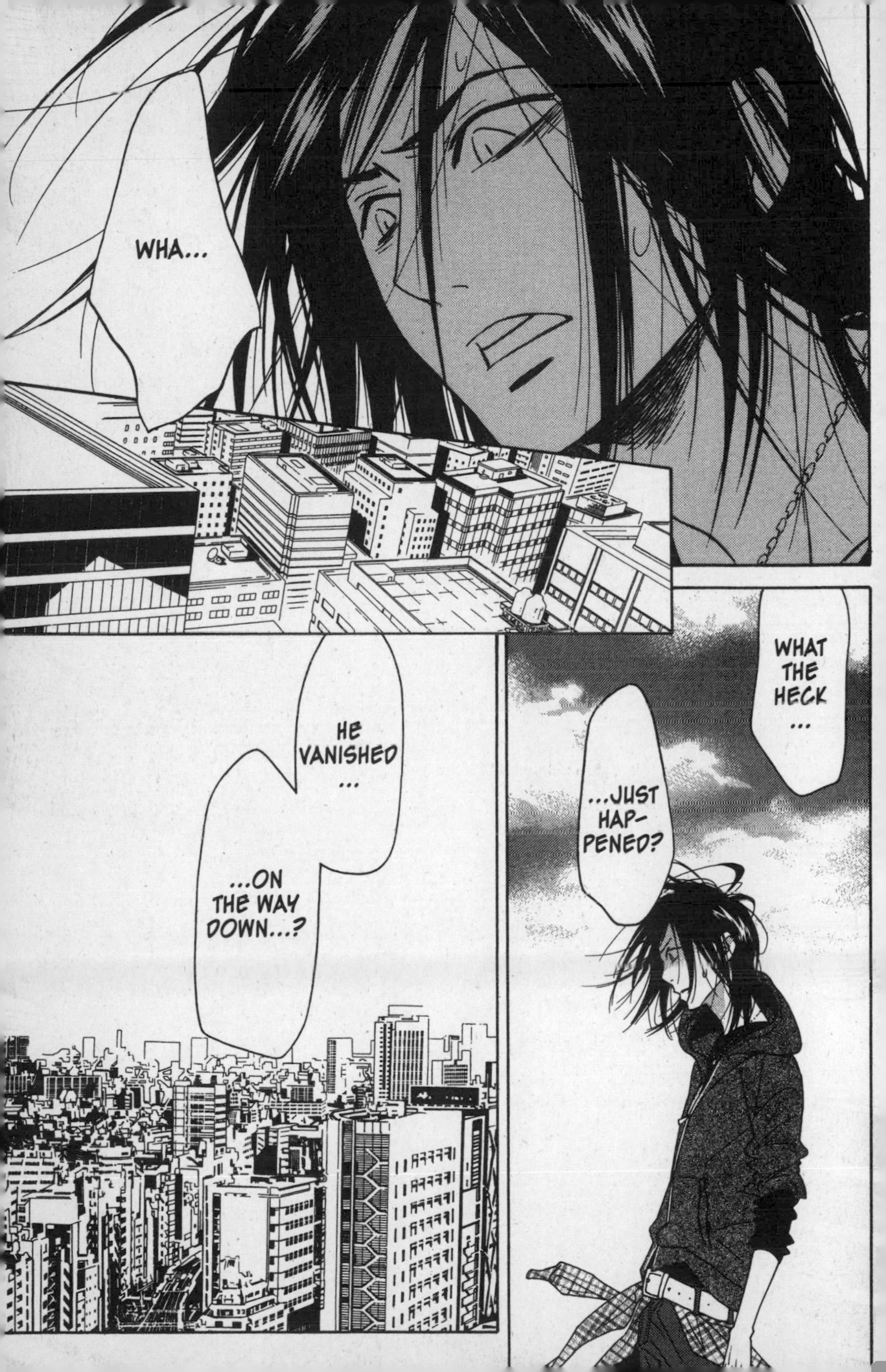
WHA...
WHAT THE HECK ...
...JUST HAP-PENED?
HE VANISHED ...
...ON THE WAY DOWN...?

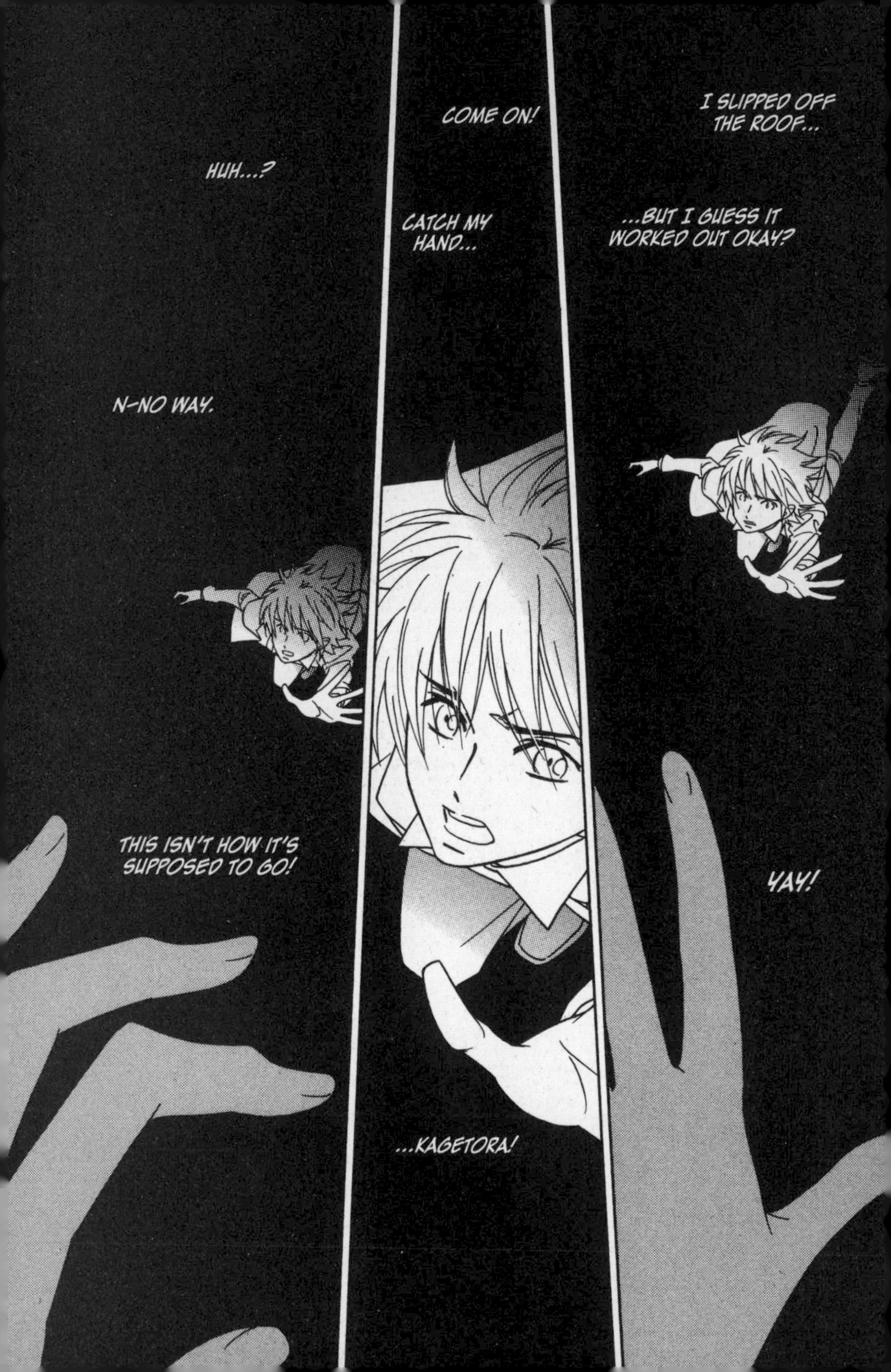
I SLIPPED OFF THE ROOF...
...BUT I GUESS IT WORKED OUT OKAY?
YAY!
COME ON!
CATCH MY HAND...
...KAGETORA!
HUH...?
N-NO WAY.
THIS ISN'T HOW IT'S SUPPOSED TO GO!

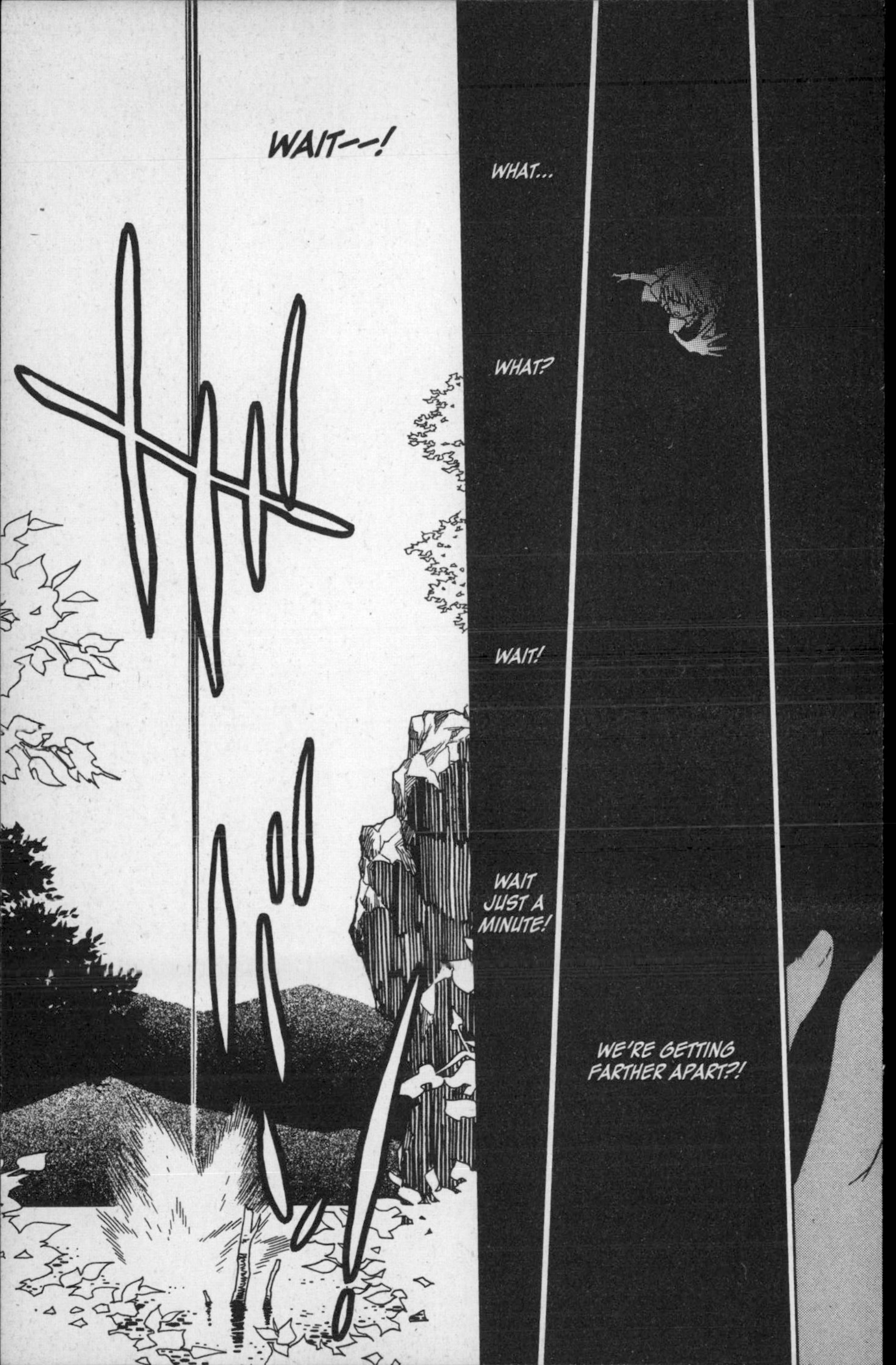
WAIT--!
WHAT...
WHAT?
WAIT!
WAIT JUST A MINUTE!
WE'RE GETTING FARTHER APART?!

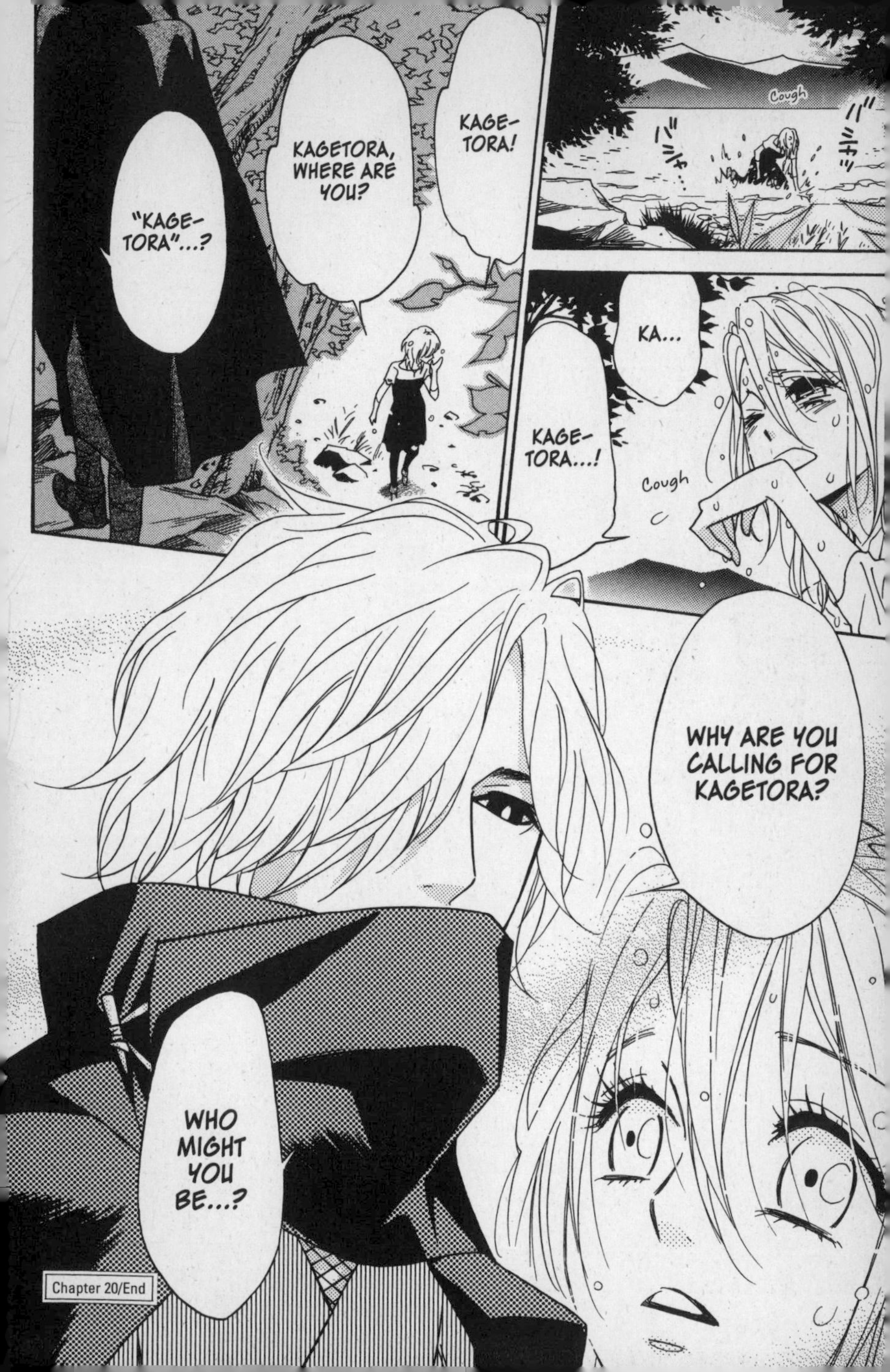
Cough
KA...
KAGE-TORA...!
Cough
KAGE-TORA!
KAGETORA, WHERE ARE YOU?
"KAGE-TORA"...?
WHY ARE YOU CALLING FOR KAGETORA?
WHO MIGHT YOU BE...?
Chapter 20/End

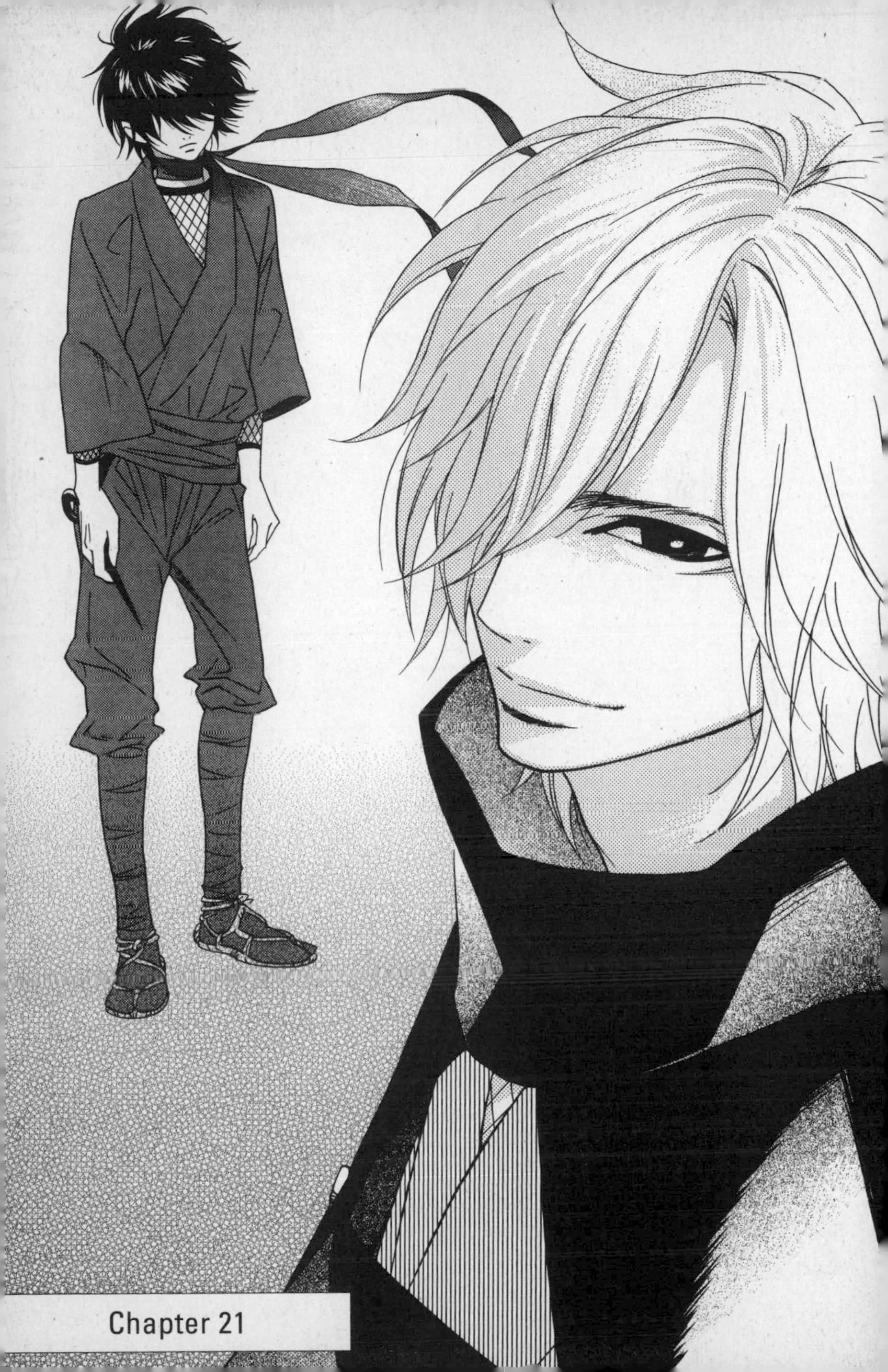

Chapter 21

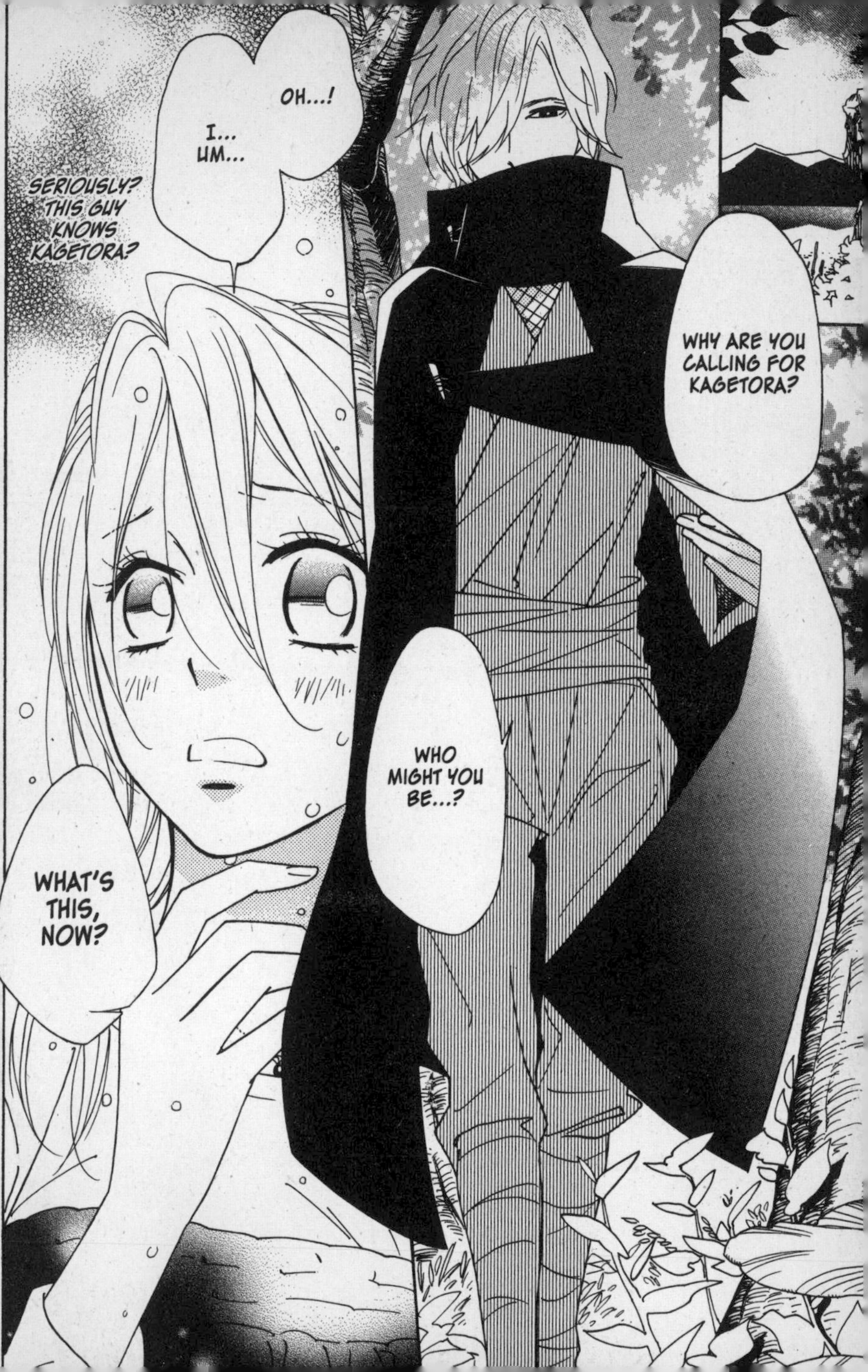
WHY ARE YOU CALLING FOR KAGETORA?
OH...!
I... UM...
SERIOUSLY? THIS GUY KNOWS KAGETORA?
WHO MIGHT YOU BE...?
WHAT'S THIS, NOW?

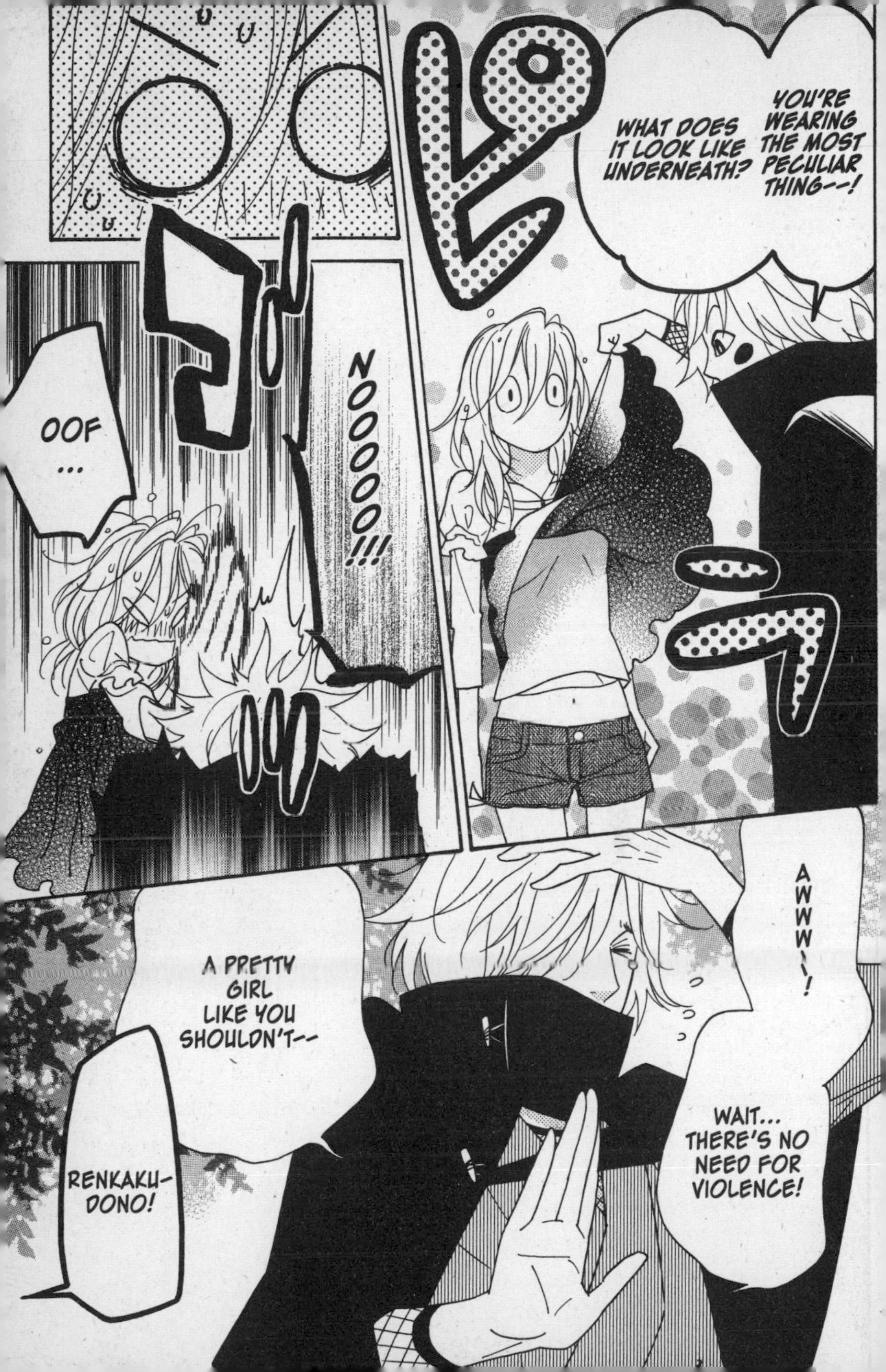
YOU'RE WEARING THE MOST PECULIAR THING--!
WHAT DOES IT LOOK LIKE UNDERNEATH?
NOOOOOOO!!!
OOF ...
AWWW~!
A PRETTY GIRL LIKE YOU SHOULDN'T--
WAIT... THERE'S NO NEED FOR VIOLENCE!
RENKAKU-DONO!

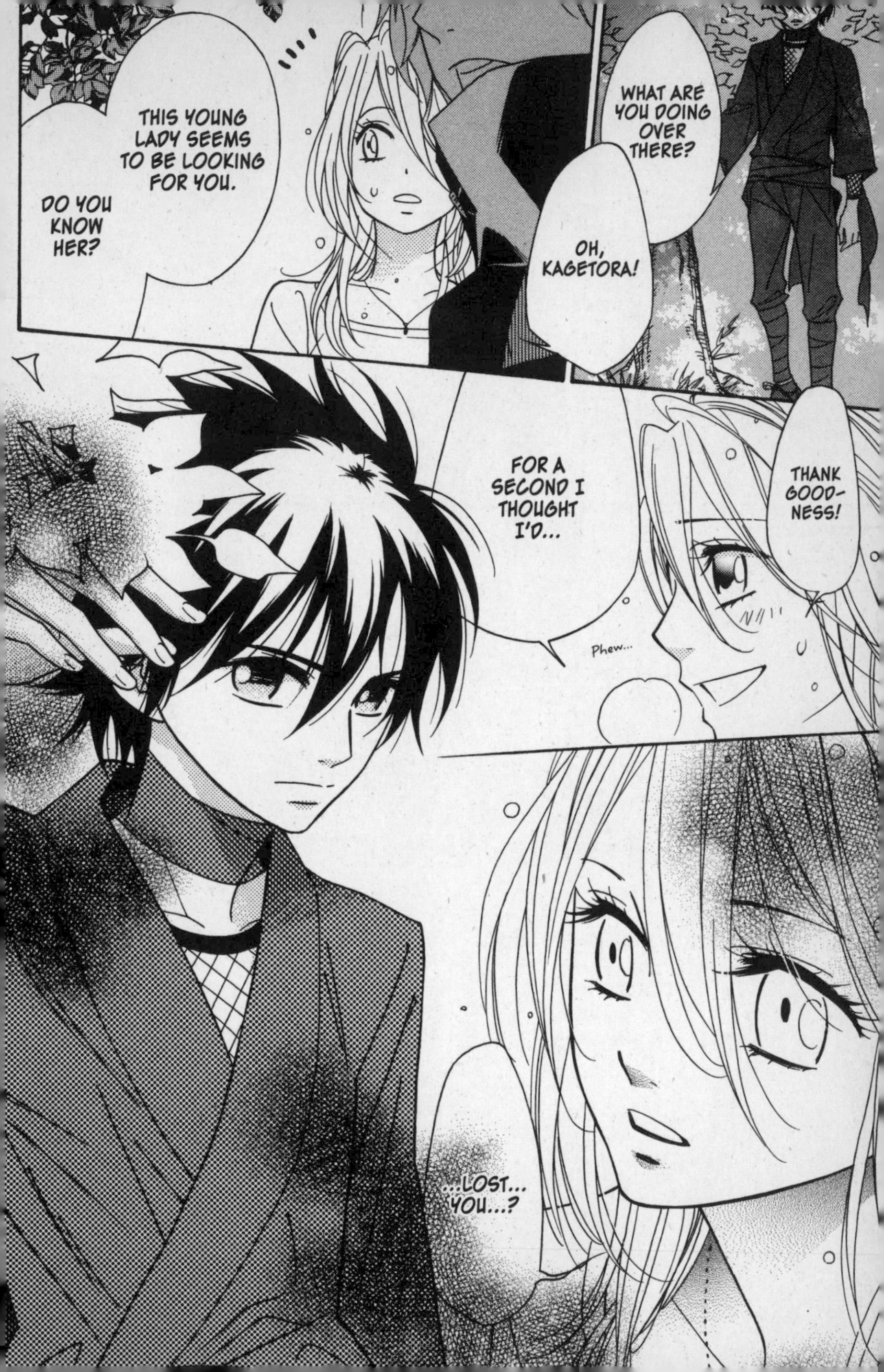
WHAT ARE YOU DOING OVER THERE?
OH, KAGETORA!
THIS YOUNG LADY SEEMS TO BE LOOKING FOR YOU.
DO YOU KNOW HER?
THANK GOODNESS!
FOR A SECOND I THOUGHT I'D...
Phew...
...LOST... YOU...?

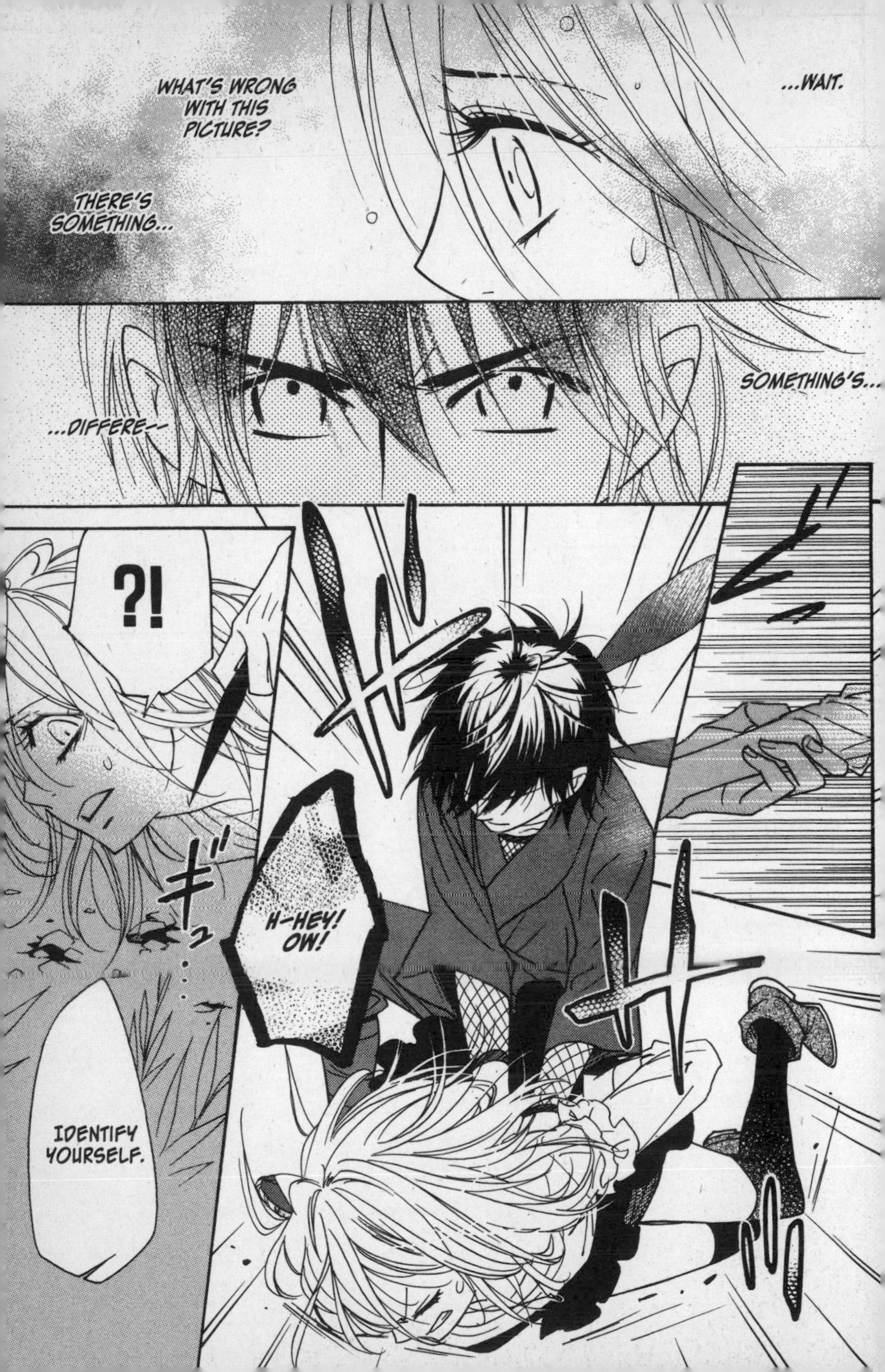
...WAIT.
WHAT'S WRONG WITH THIS PICTURE?
THERE'S SOMETHING...
SOMETHING'S...
...DIFFERE--
?!
H-HEY! OW!
IDENTIFY YOURSELF.

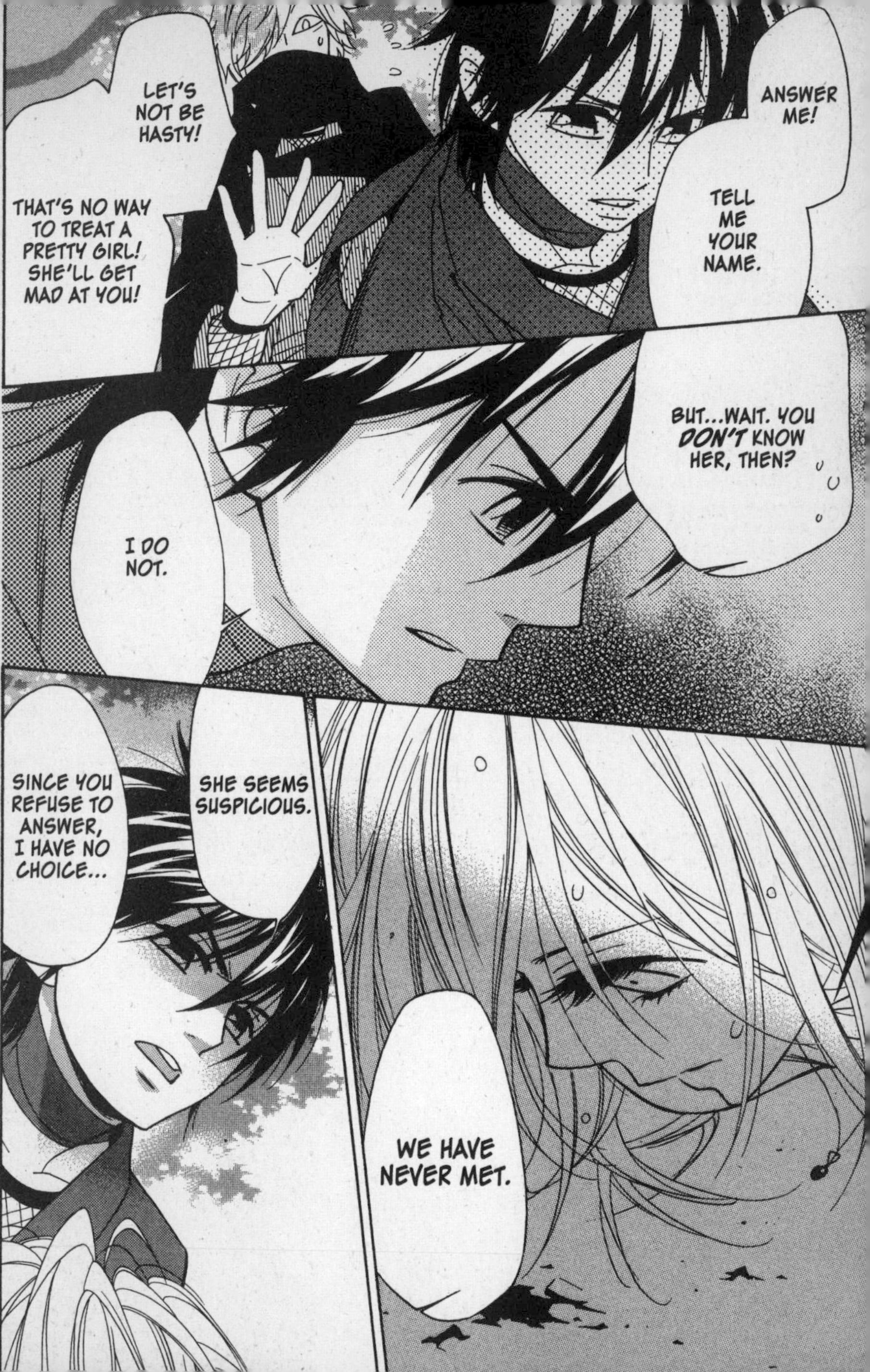
ANSWER ME!
TELL ME YOUR NAME.
LET'S NOT BE HASTY!
THAT'S NO WAY TO TREAT A PRETTY GIRL! SHE'LL GET MAD AT YOU!
BUT...WAIT. YOU *DON'T* KNOW HER, THEN?
I DO NOT.
WE HAVE NEVER MET.
SHE SEEMS SUSPICIOUS.
SINCE YOU REFUSE TO ANSWER, I HAVE NO CHOICE...

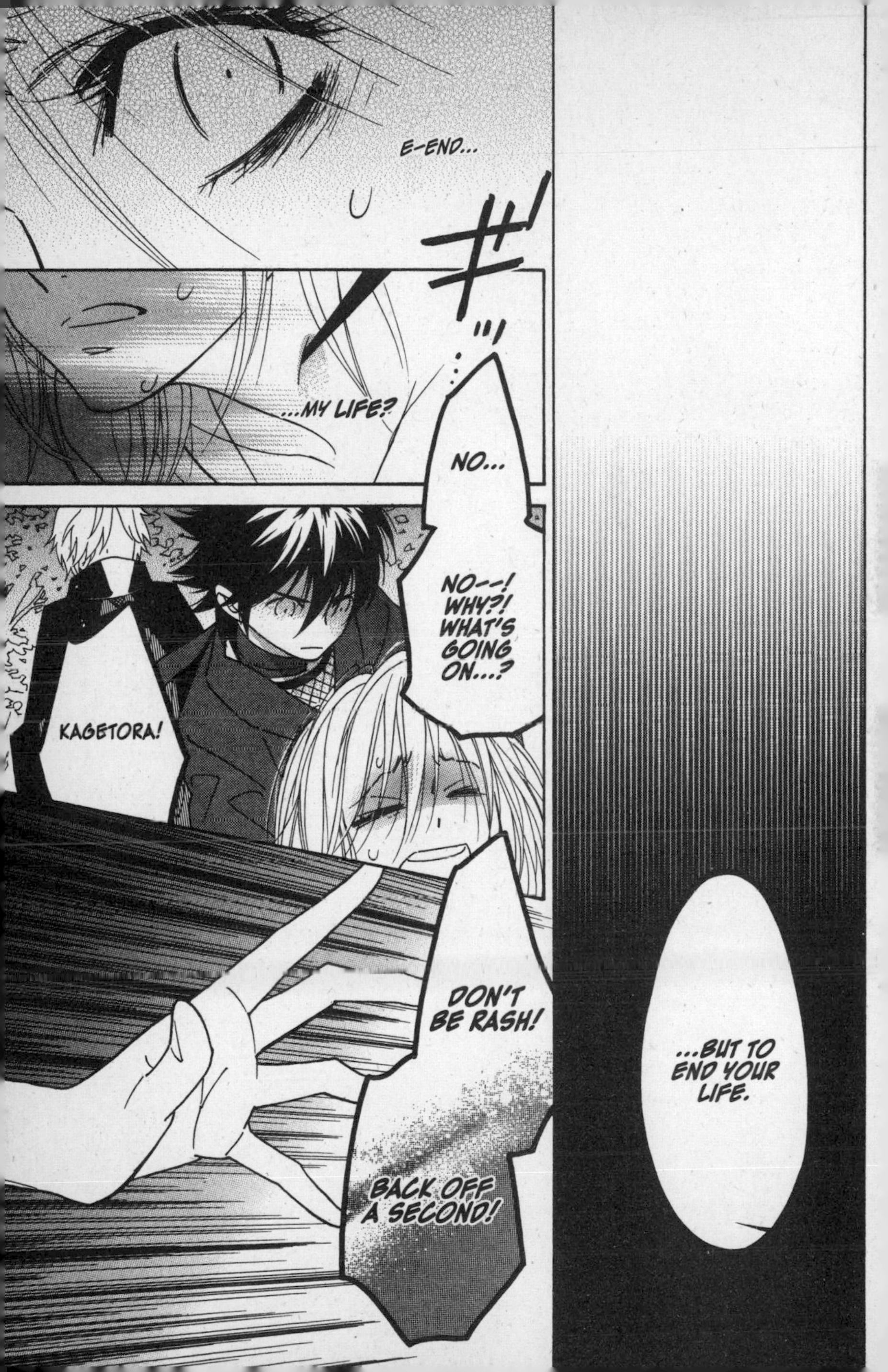
E-END...
...MY LIFE?
NO...
NO--! WHY?! WHAT'S GOING ON...?
KAGETORA!
DON'T BE RASH!
BACK OFF A SECOND!
...BUT TO END YOUR LIFE.

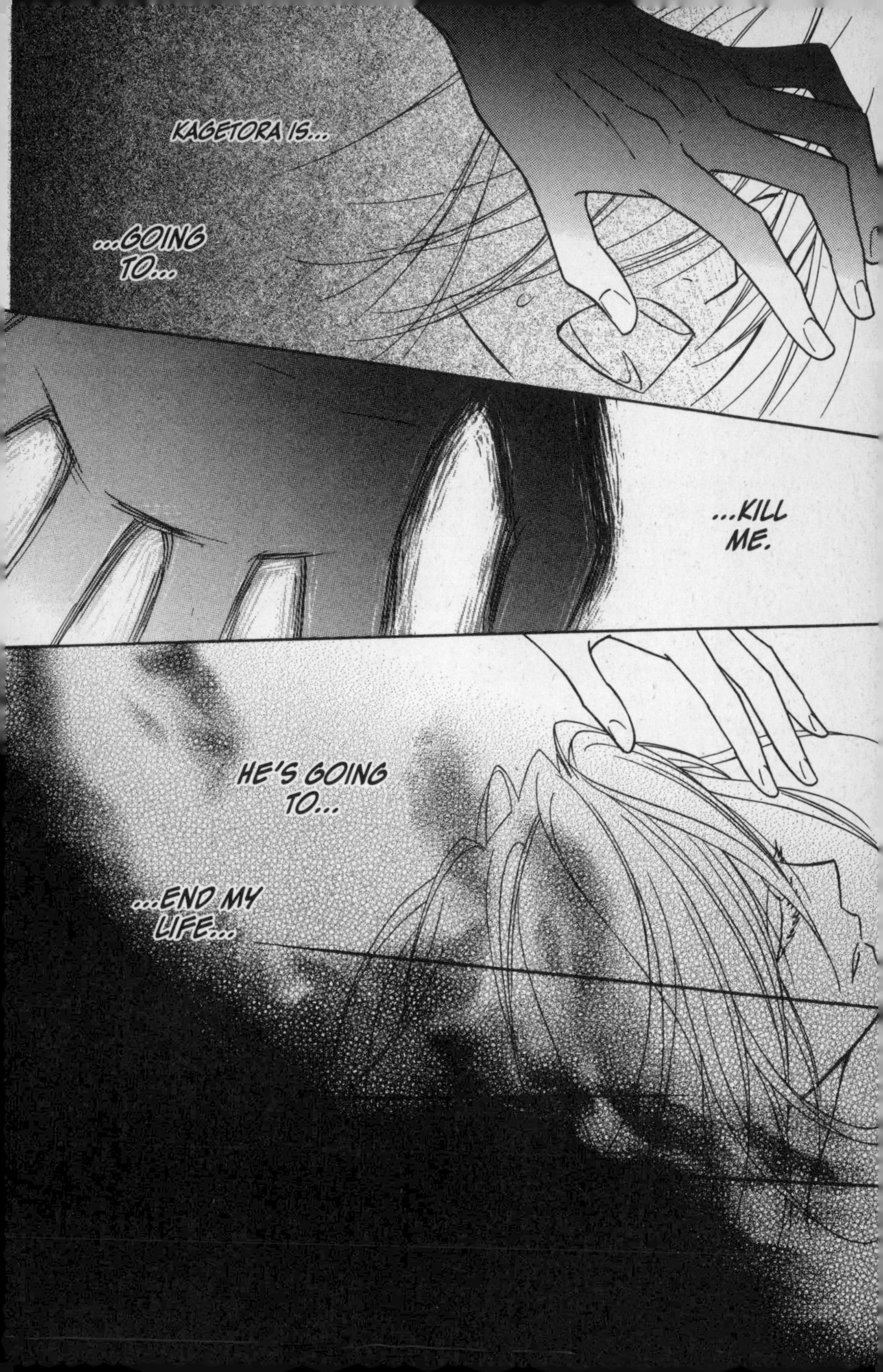
KAGETORA IS...
...GOING TO...
...KILL ME.
HE'S GOING TO...
...END MY LIFE...

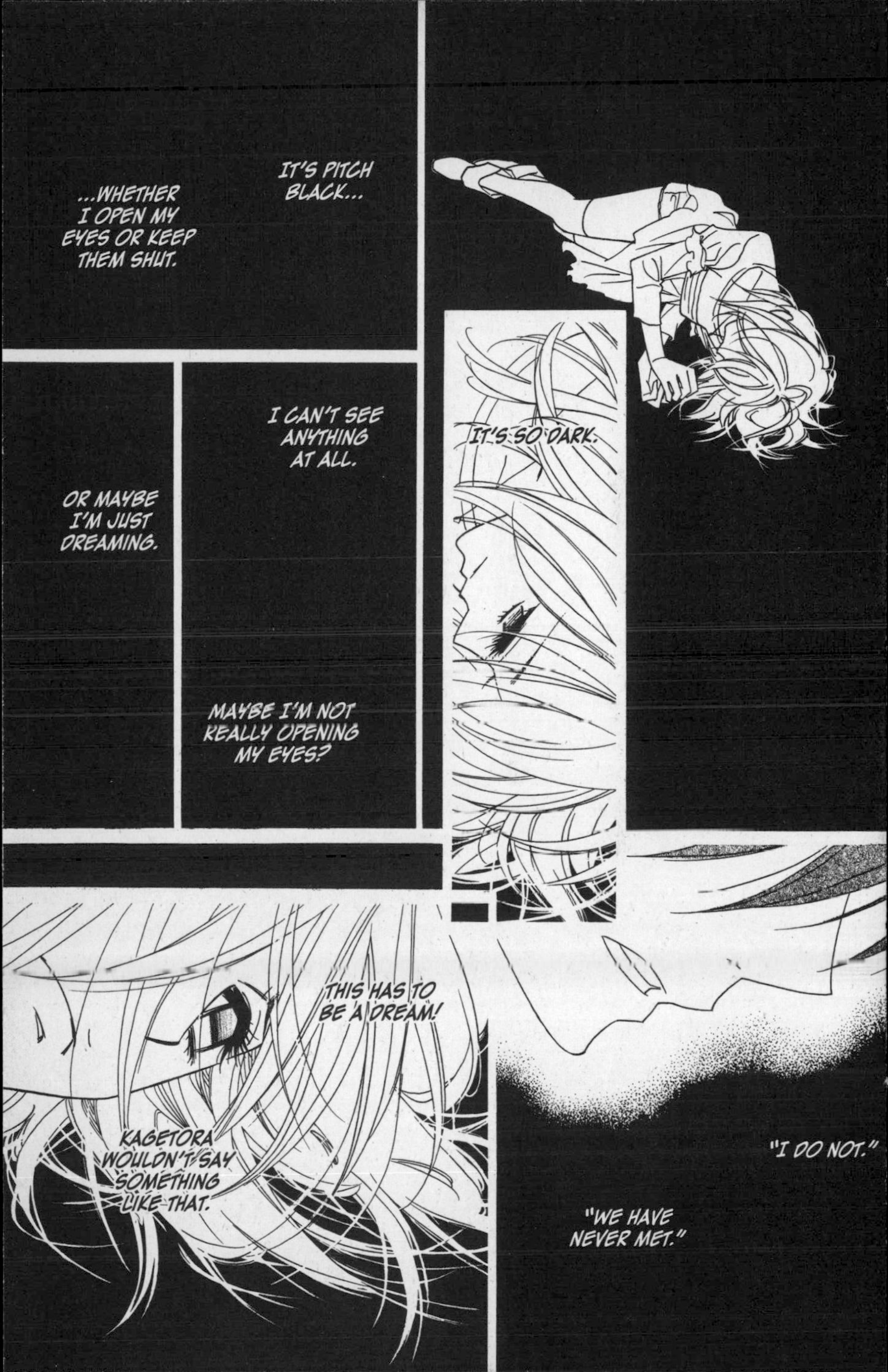
IT'S PITCH BLACK...
...WHETHER I OPEN MY EYES OR KEEP THEM SHUT.
IT'S SO DARK.
I CAN'T SEE ANYTHING AT ALL.
OR MAYBE I'M JUST DREAMING.
MAYBE I'M NOT REALLY OPENING MY EYES?
"I DO NOT."
"WE HAVE NEVER MET."
THIS HAS TO BE A DREAM!
KAGETORA WOULDN'T SAY SOMETHING LIKE THAT.

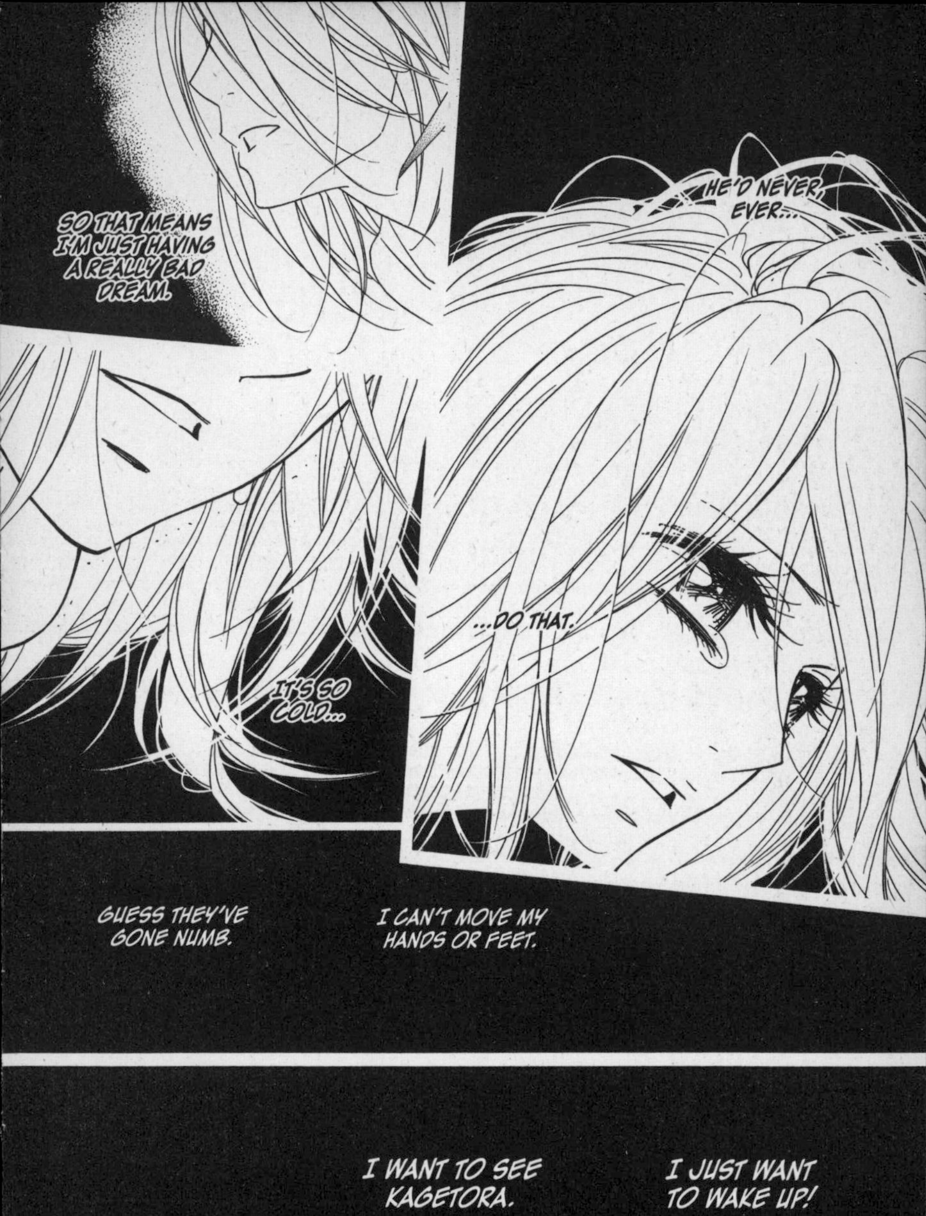
HE'D NEVER, EVER...
...DO THAT.
SO THAT MEANS I'M JUST HAVING A REALLY BAD DREAM.
IT'S SO COLD...
I CAN'T MOVE MY HANDS OR FEET.
GUESS THEY'VE GONE NUMB.
I JUST WANT TO WAKE UP!
I WANT TO SEE KAGETORA.

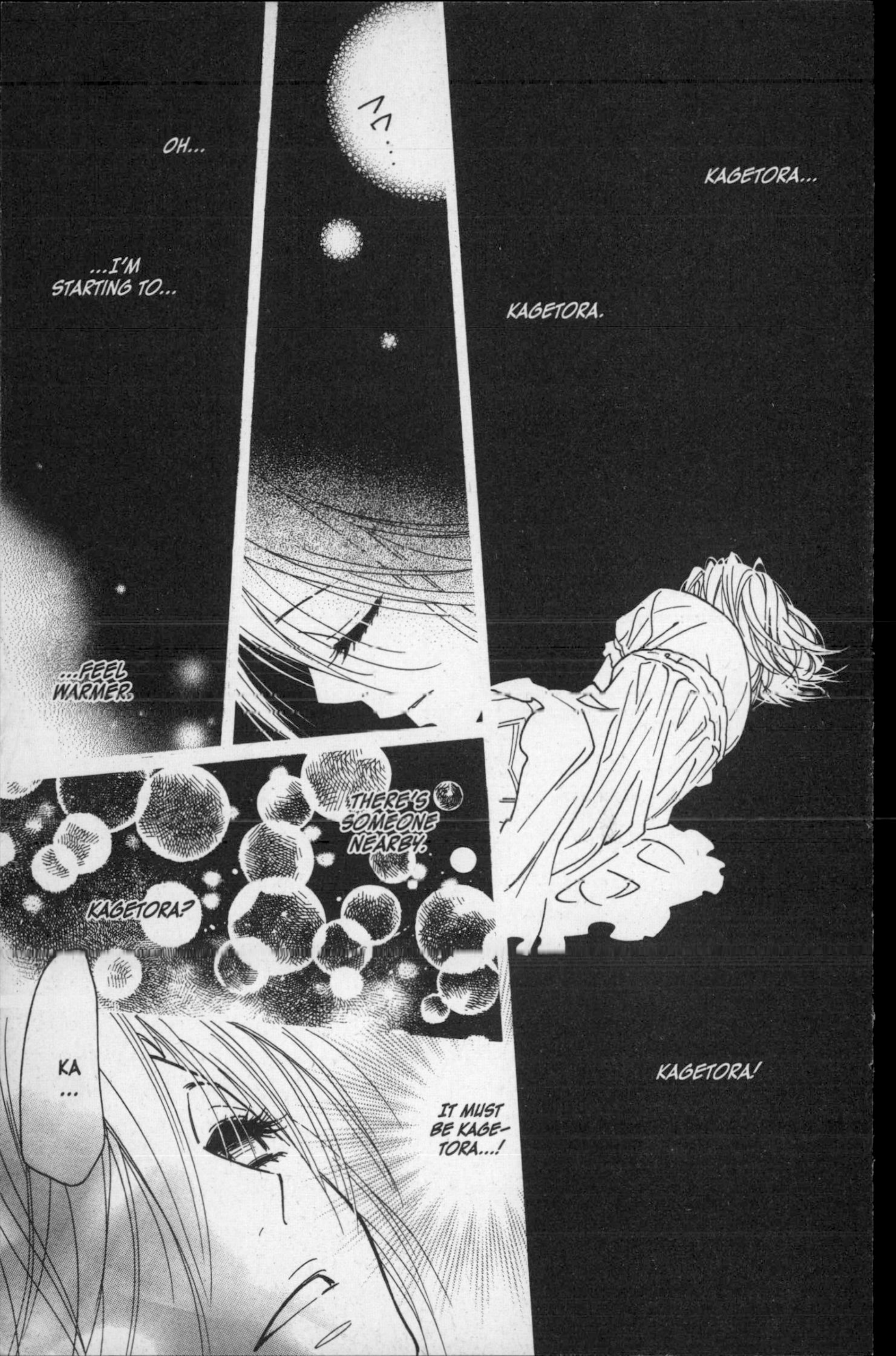
KAGETORA...
OH...
KAGETORA.
...I'M STARTING TO...
...FEEL WARMER.
THERE'S SOMEONE NEARBY.
KAGETORA?
KAGETORA!
IT MUST BE KAGE-TORA...!
KA ...

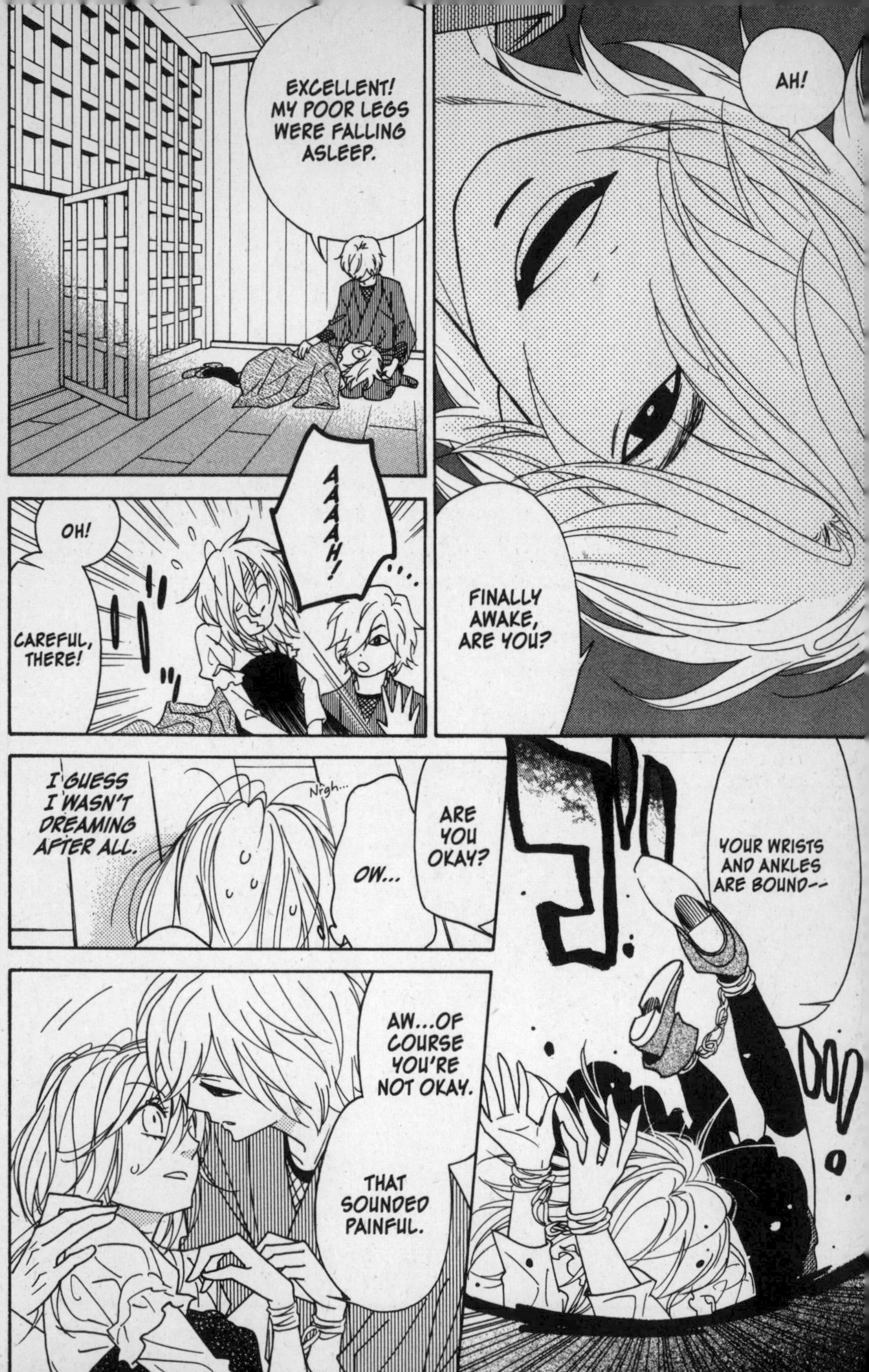
AH!
FINALLY AWAKE, ARE YOU?
EXCELLENT! MY POOR LEGS WERE FALLING ASLEEP.
AAAAH!
OH!
CAREFUL, THERE!
YOUR WRISTS AND ANKLES ARE BOUND--
ARE YOU OKAY?
OW...
Nrgh...
I GUESS I WASN'T DREAMING AFTER ALL.
AW...OF COURSE YOU'RE NOT OKAY.
THAT SOUNDED PAINFUL.

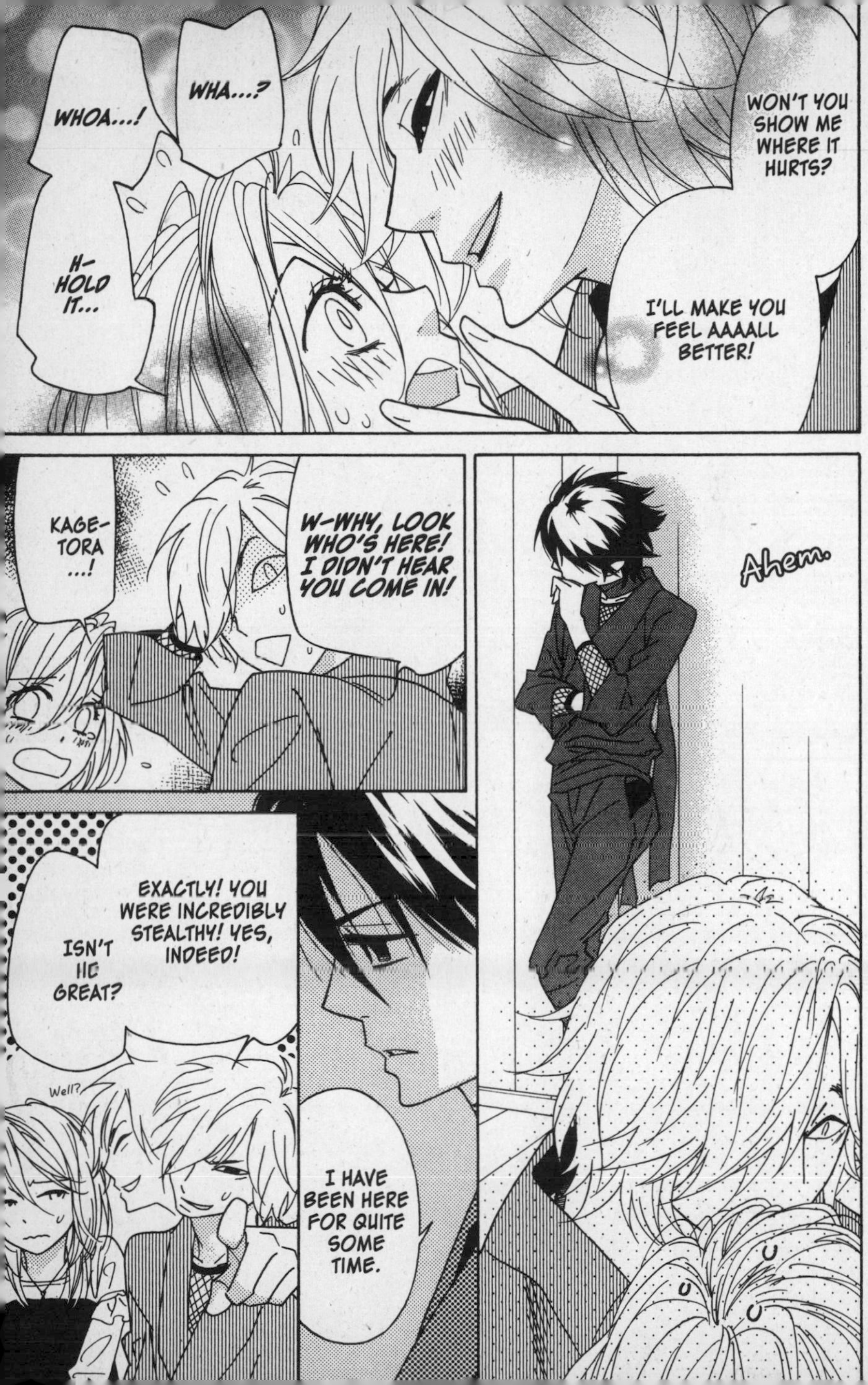
WON'T YOU SHOW ME WHERE IT HURTS?
I'LL MAKE YOU FEEL AAAALL BETTER!
WHA...?
WHOA...!
H-HOLD IT...
Ahem.
W-WHY, LOOK WHO'S HERE! I DIDN'T HEAR YOU COME IN!
KAGE-TORA...!
I HAVE BEEN HERE FOR QUITE SOME TIME.
EXACTLY! YOU WERE INCREDIBLY STEALTHY! YES, INDEED!
ISN'T HE GREAT?
Well?

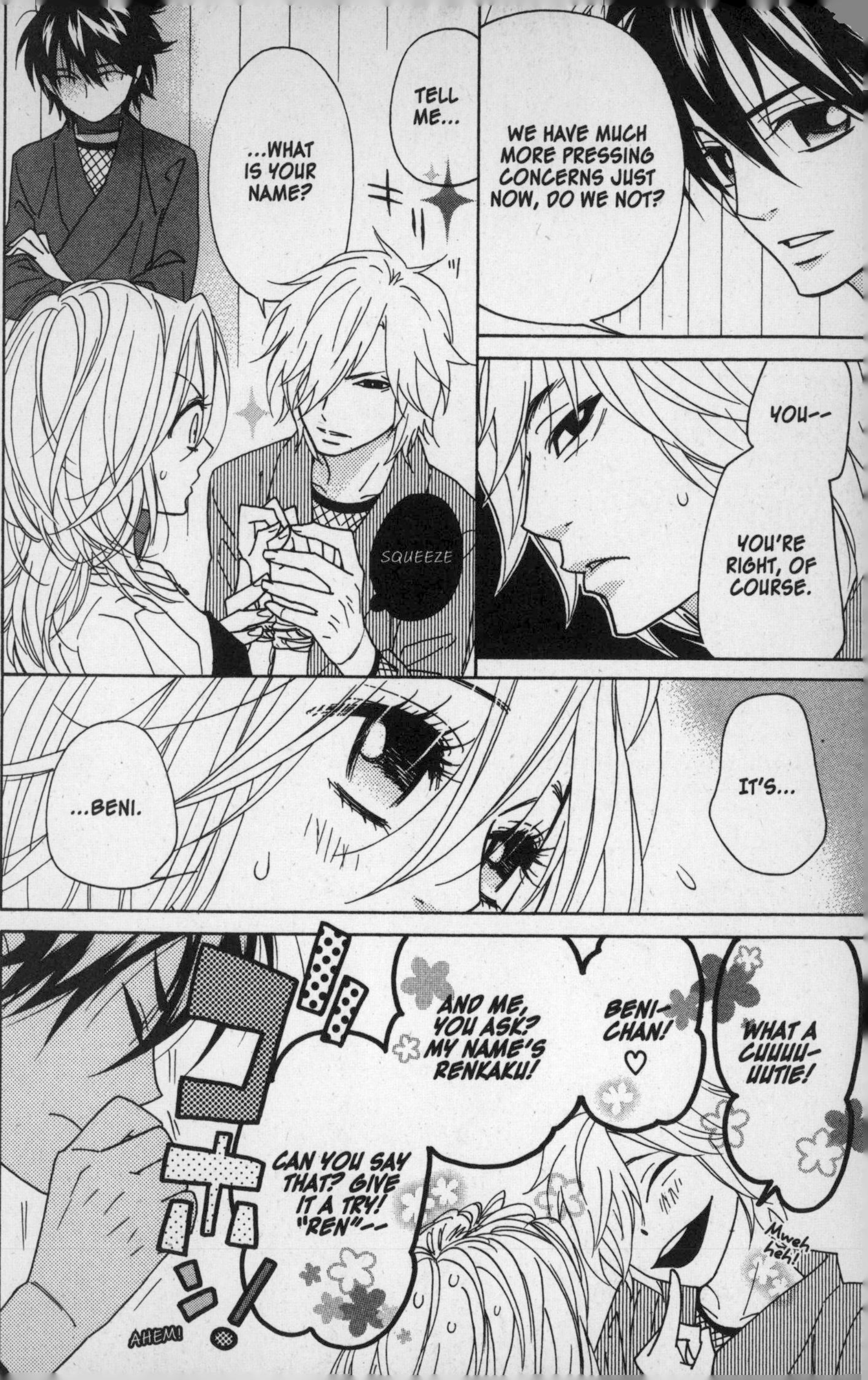
TELL ME...
...WHAT IS YOUR NAME?
SQUEEZE
WE HAVE MUCH MORE PRESSING CONCERNS JUST NOW, DO WE NOT?
YOU--
YOU'RE RIGHT, OF COURSE.
IT'S...
...BENI.
WHAT A CUUUU-UUTIE!
BENI-CHAN! ♡
AND ME, YOU ASK? MY NAME'S RENKAKU!
CAN YOU SAY THAT? GIVE IT A TRY! "REN"--
Mweh heh!
AHEM!

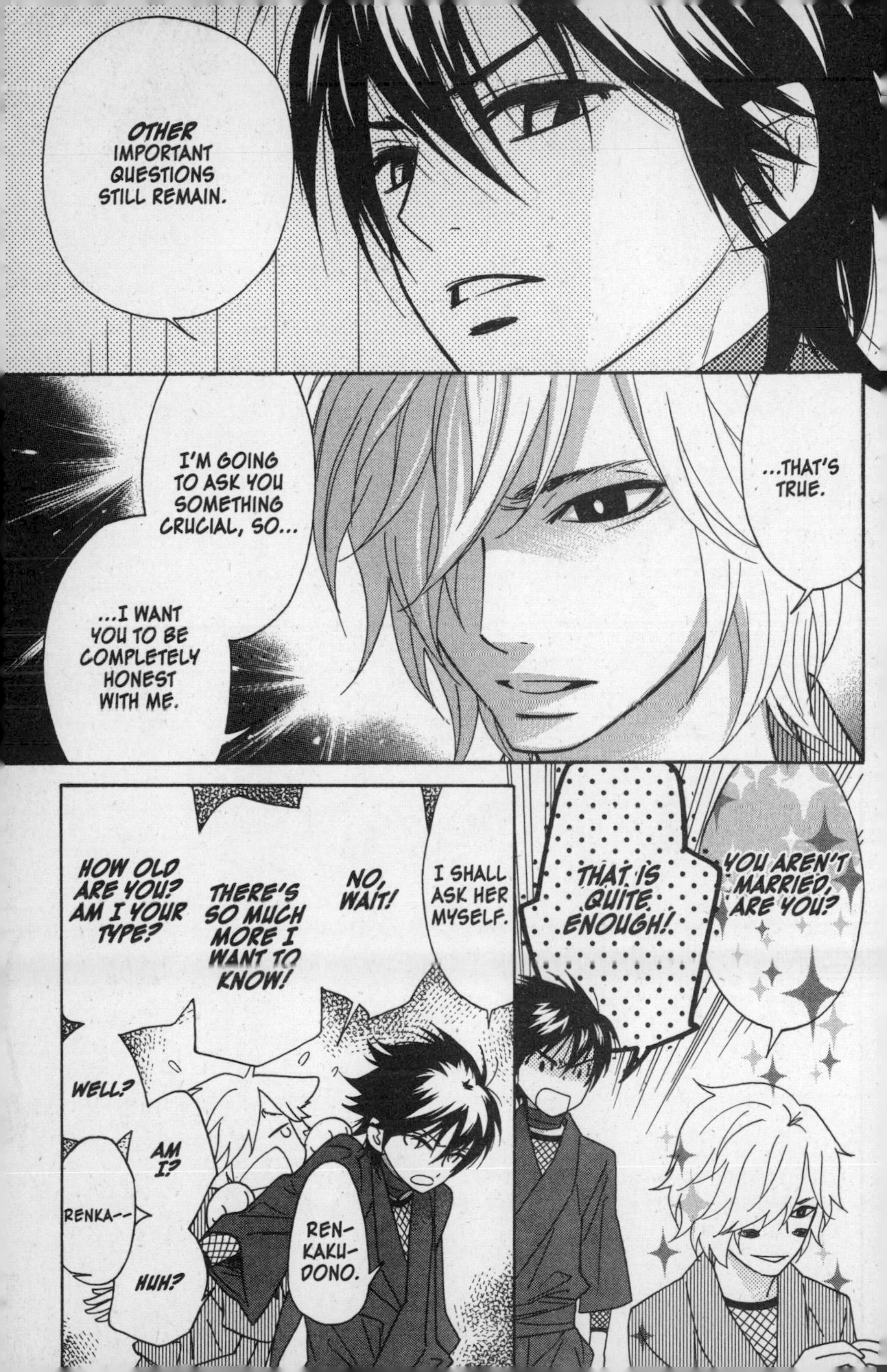
OTHER IMPORTANT QUESTIONS STILL REMAIN.
...THAT'S TRUE.
I'M GOING TO ASK YOU SOMETHING CRUCIAL, SO...
...I WANT YOU TO BE COMPLETELY HONEST WITH ME.
YOU AREN'T MARRIED, ARE YOU?
THAT IS QUITE ENOUGH!
I SHALL ASK HER MYSELF.
NO, WAIT!
THERE'S SO MUCH MORE I WANT TO KNOW!
HOW OLD ARE YOU? AM I YOUR TYPE?
WELL?
AM I?
RENKA--
HUH?
REN-KAKU-DONO.

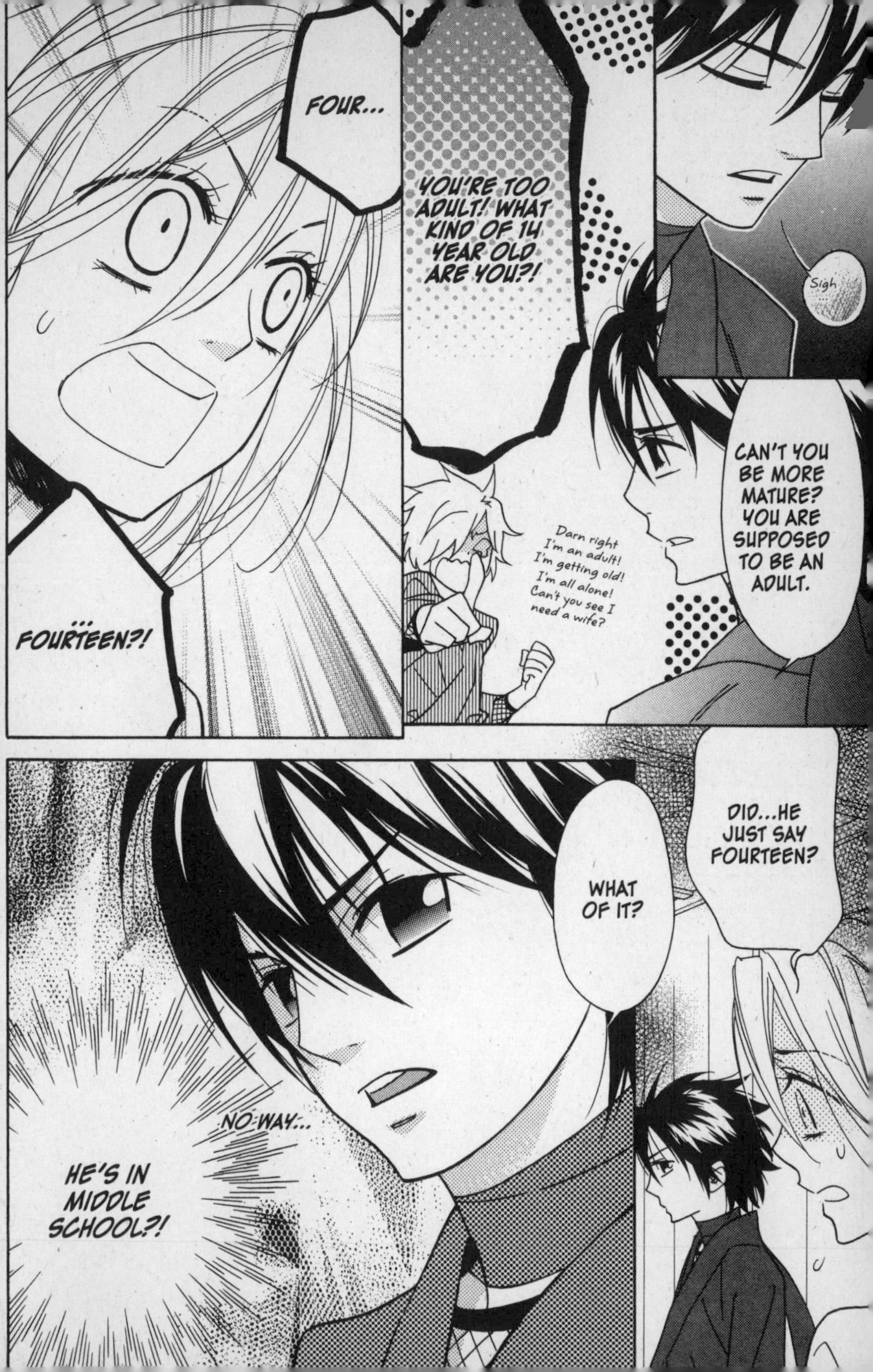
Sigh
CAN'T YOU BE MORE MATURE? YOU ARE SUPPOSED TO BE AN ADULT.
Darn right I'm an adult! I'm getting old! I'm all alone! Can't you see I need a wife?
YOU'RE TOO ADULT! WHAT KIND OF 14 YEAR OLD ARE YOU?!
FOUR...
...FOURTEEN?!
DID...HE JUST SAY FOURTEEN?
WHAT OF IT?
NO WAY...
HE'S IN MIDDLE SCHOOL?!

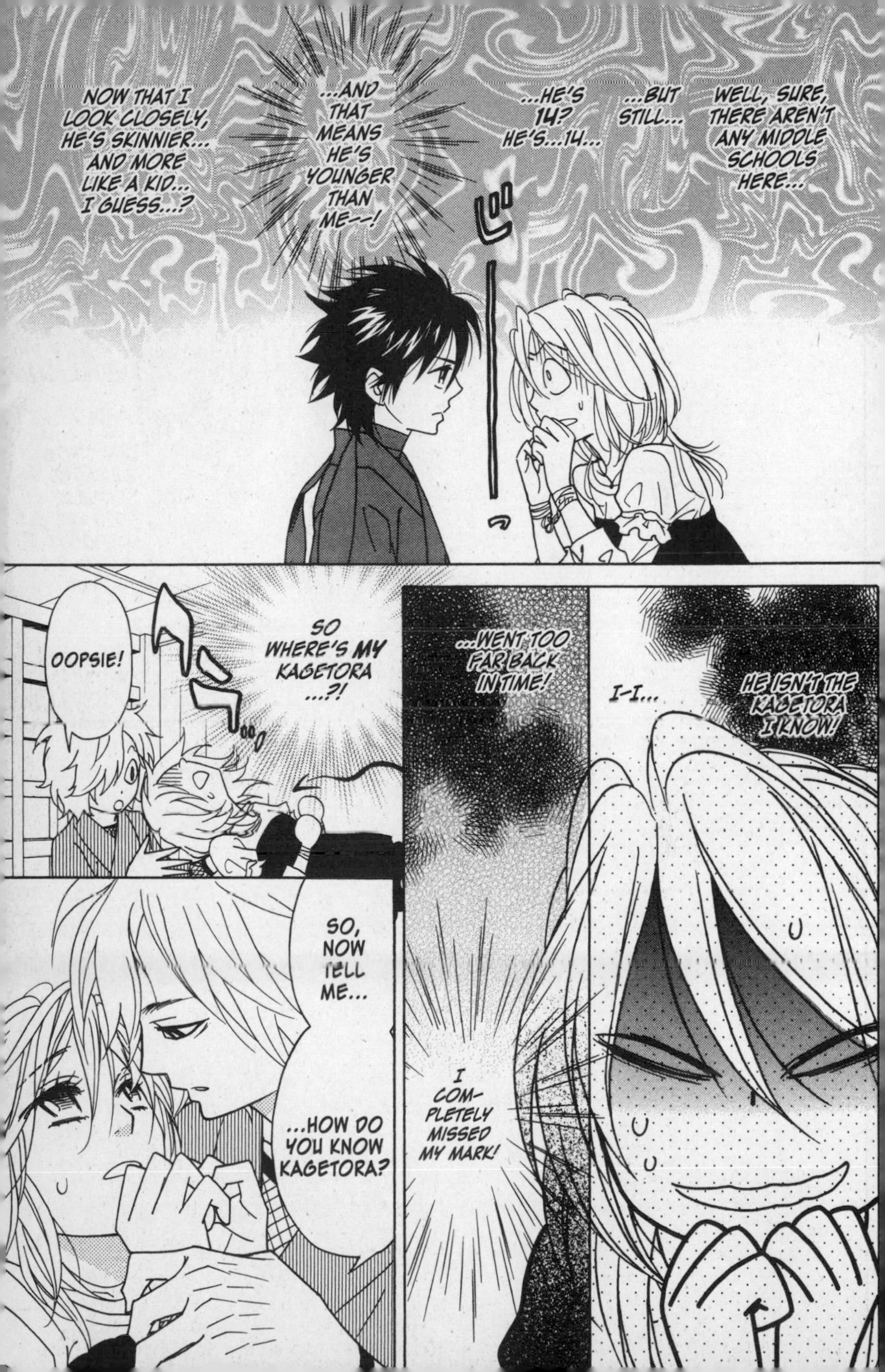
WELL, SURE, THERE AREN'T ANY MIDDLE SCHOOLS HERE...
...BUT STILL...
...HE'S 14? HE'S...14...
...AND THAT MEANS HE'S YOUNGER THAN ME--!
NOW THAT I LOOK CLOSELY, HE'S SKINNIER... AND MORE LIKE A KID... I GUESS...?
I-I...
HE ISN'T THE KAGETORA I KNOW!
...WENT TOO FAR BACK IN TIME!
SO WHERE'S MY KAGETORA ...?!
OOPSIE!
I COMPLETELY MISSED MY MARK!
SO, NOW TELL ME...
...HOW DO YOU KNOW KAGETORA?

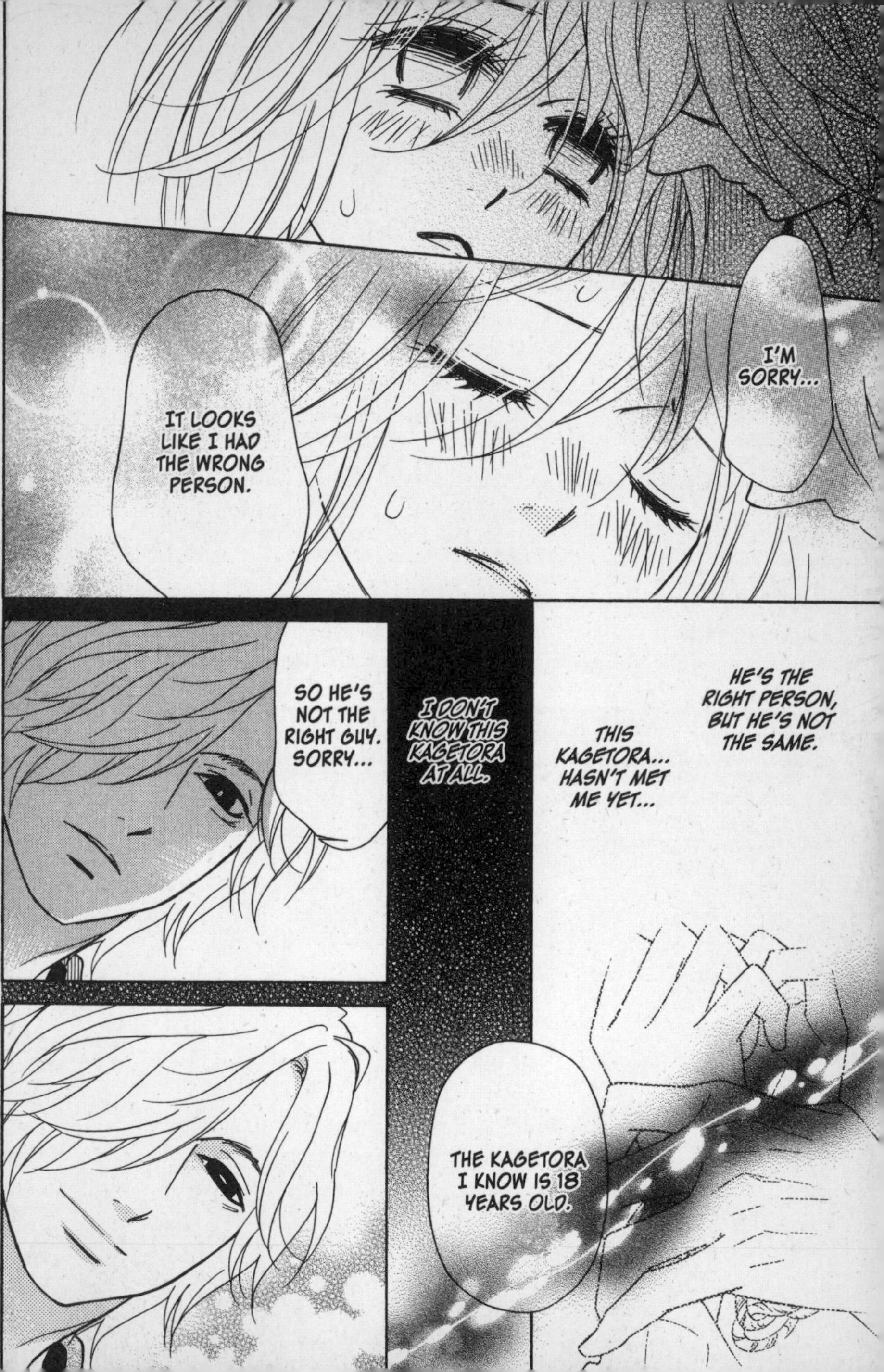
I'M SORRY...
IT LOOKS LIKE I HAD THE WRONG PERSON.
HE'S THE RIGHT PERSON, BUT HE'S NOT THE SAME.
THIS KAGETORA... HASN'T MET ME YET...
I DON'T KNOW THIS KAGETORA AT ALL.
SO HE'S NOT THE RIGHT GUY. SORRY...
THE KAGETORA I KNOW IS 18 YEARS OLD.

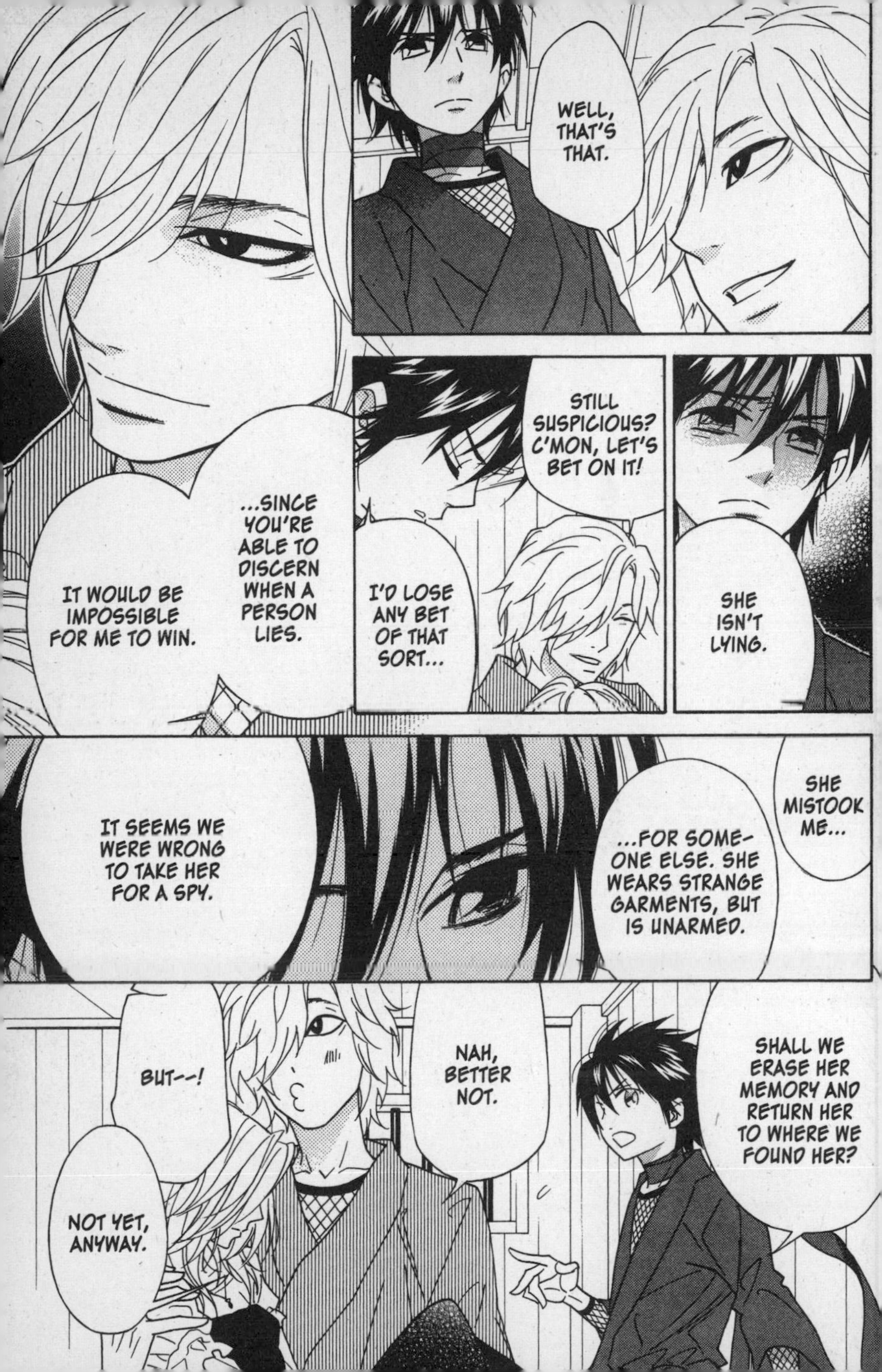
WELL, THAT'S THAT.
SHE ISN'T LYING.
STILL SUSPICIOUS? C'MON, LET'S BET ON IT!
I'D LOSE ANY BET OF THAT SORT...
...SINCE YOU'RE ABLE TO DISCERN WHEN A PERSON LIES.
IT WOULD BE IMPOSSIBLE FOR ME TO WIN.
SHE MISTOOK ME...
...FOR SOME-ONE ELSE. SHE WEARS STRANGE GARMENTS, BUT IS UNARMED.
IT SEEMS WE WERE WRONG TO TAKE HER FOR A SPY.
SHALL WE ERASE HER MEMORY AND RETURN HER TO WHERE WE FOUND HER?
NAH, BETTER NOT.
BUT--!
NOT YET, ANYWAY.

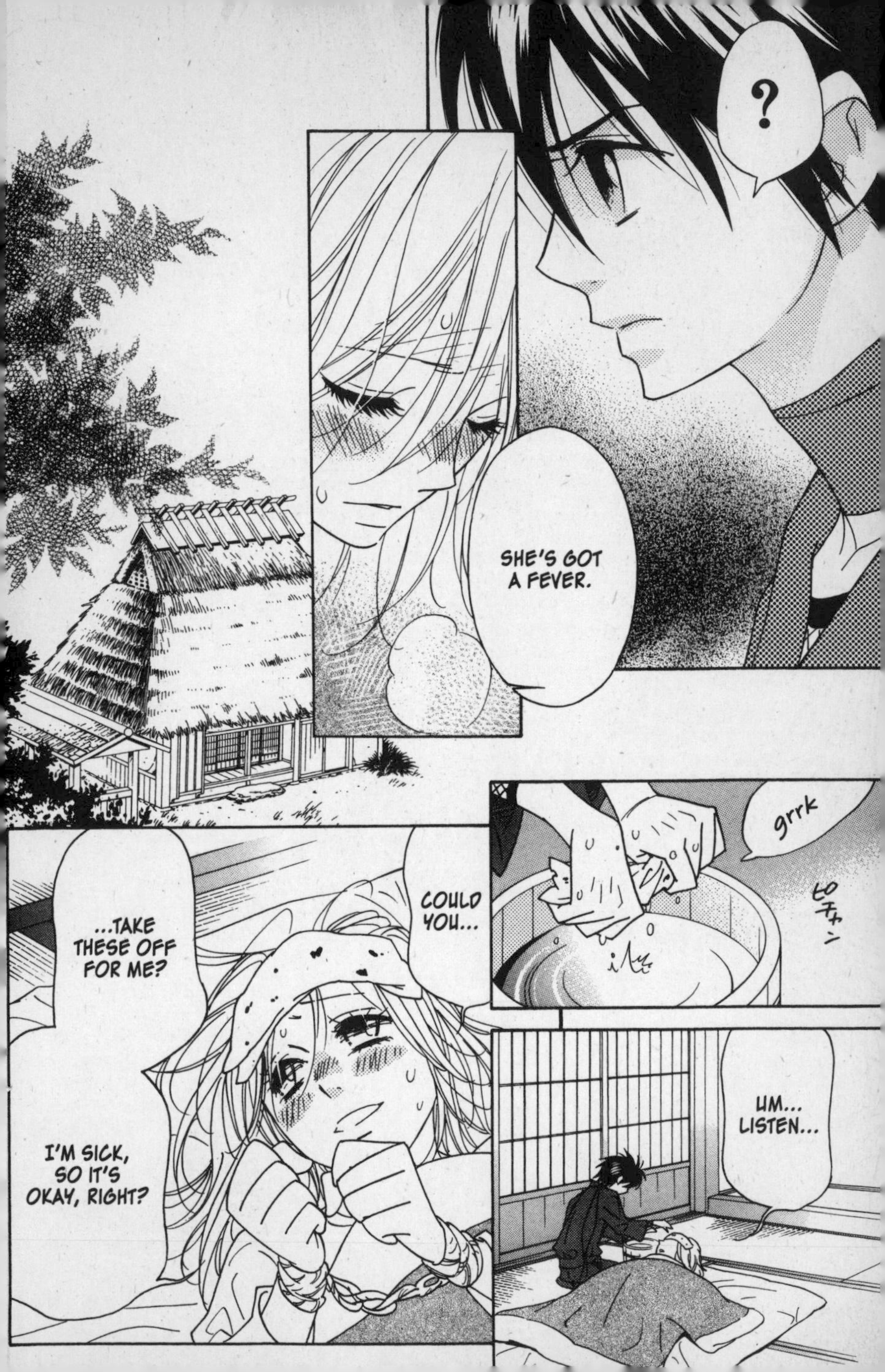
?
SHE'S GOT A FEVER.
grrk
ピチャン
UM... LISTEN...
COULD YOU...
...TAKE THESE OFF FOR ME?
I'M SICK, SO IT'S OKAY, RIGHT?

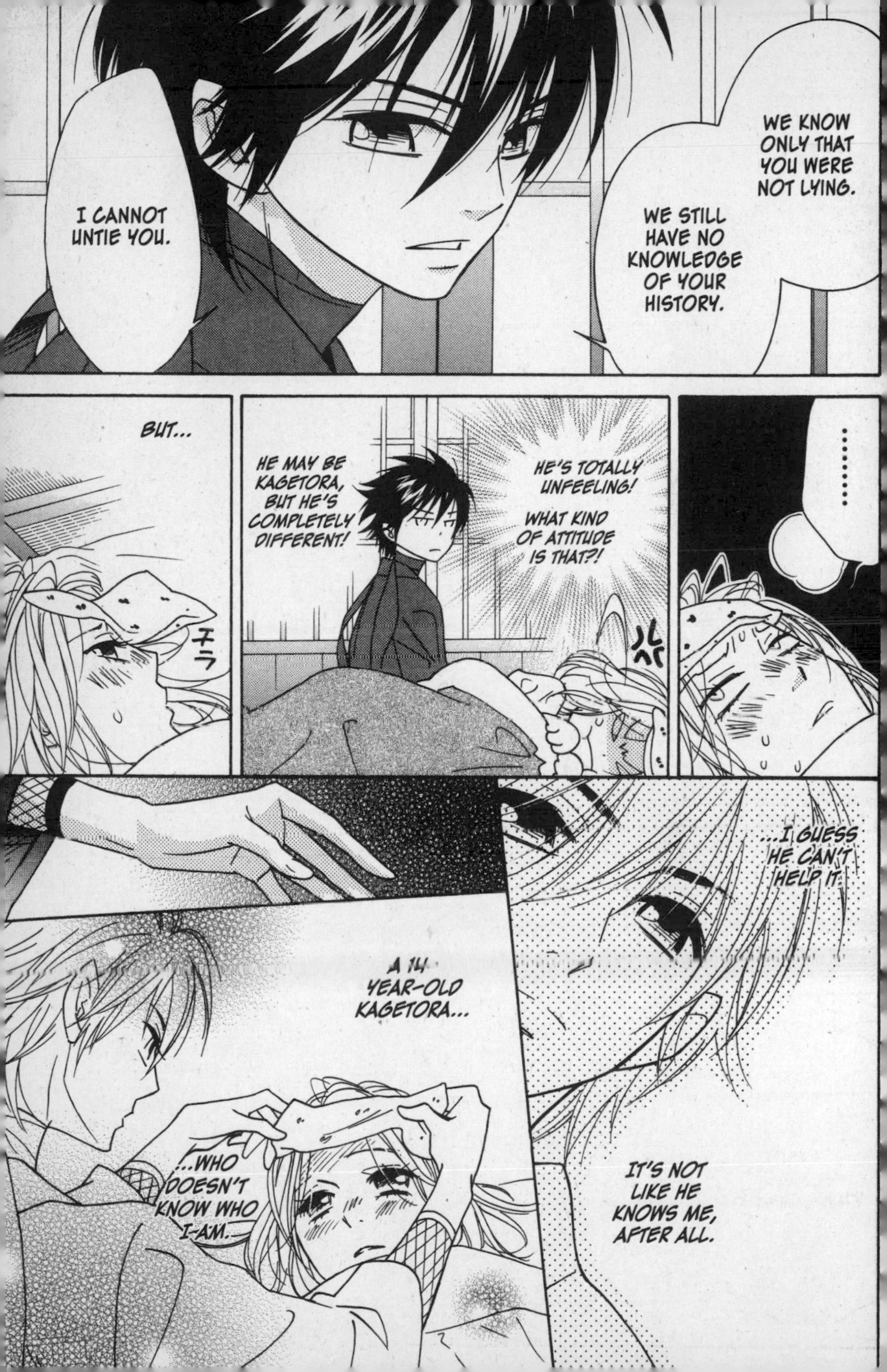

WE KNOW ONLY THAT YOU WERE NOT LYING.
WE STILL HAVE NO KNOWLEDGE OF YOUR HISTORY.
I CANNOT UNTIE YOU.
......
HE'S TOTALLY UNFEELING!
WHAT KIND OF ATTITUDE IS THAT?!
HE MAY BE KAGETORA, BUT HE'S COMPLETELY DIFFERENT!
BUT...
チラ
...I GUESS HE CAN'T HELP IT.
IT'S NOT LIKE HE KNOWS ME, AFTER ALL.
A 14 YEAR-OLD KAGETORA...
...WHO DOESN'T KNOW WHO I AM.

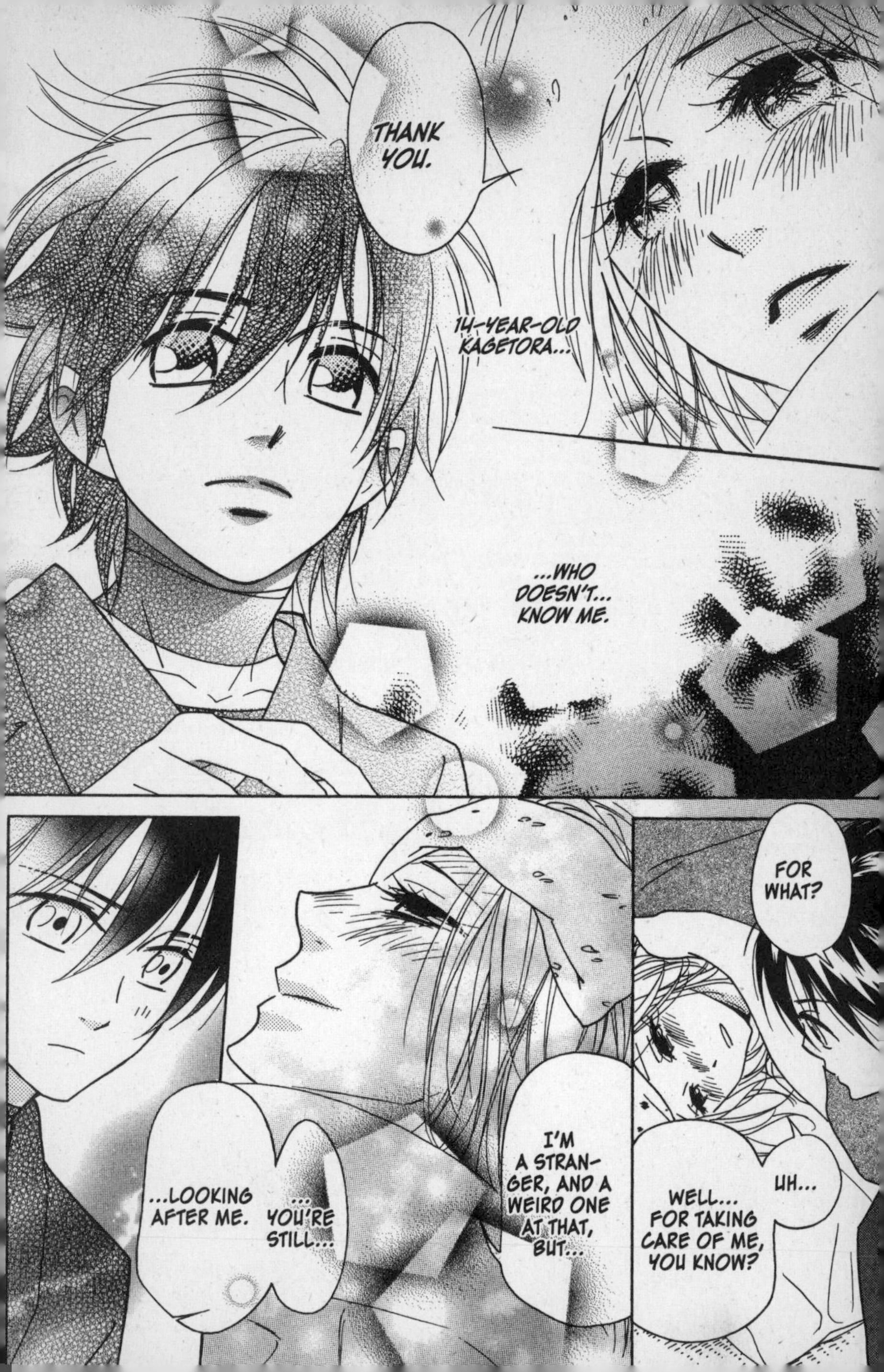
THANK YOU.
14-YEAR-OLD KAGETORA...
...WHO DOESN'T... KNOW ME.
FOR WHAT?
UH...
WELL... FOR TAKING CARE OF ME, YOU KNOW?
I'M A STRANGER, AND A WEIRD ONE AT THAT, BUT...
...YOU'RE STILL...
...LOOKING AFTER ME.

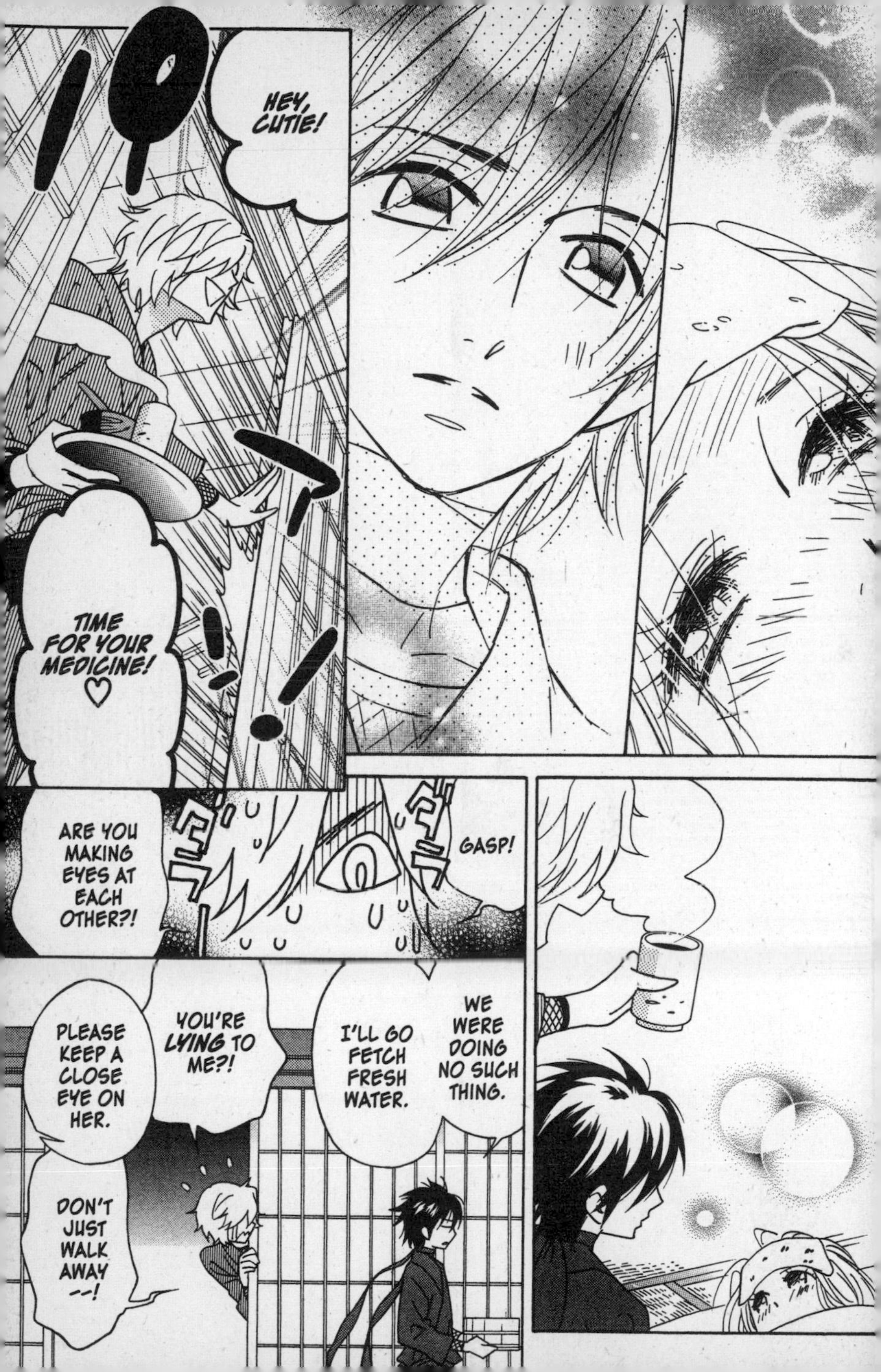
HEY, CUTIE!
TIME FOR YOUR MEDICINE! ♡
GASP!
ARE YOU MAKING EYES AT EACH OTHER?!
WE WERE DOING NO SUCH THING.
I'LL GO FETCH FRESH WATER.
YOU'RE *LYING* TO ME?!
PLEASE KEEP A CLOSE EYE ON HER.
DON'T JUST WALK AWAY --!

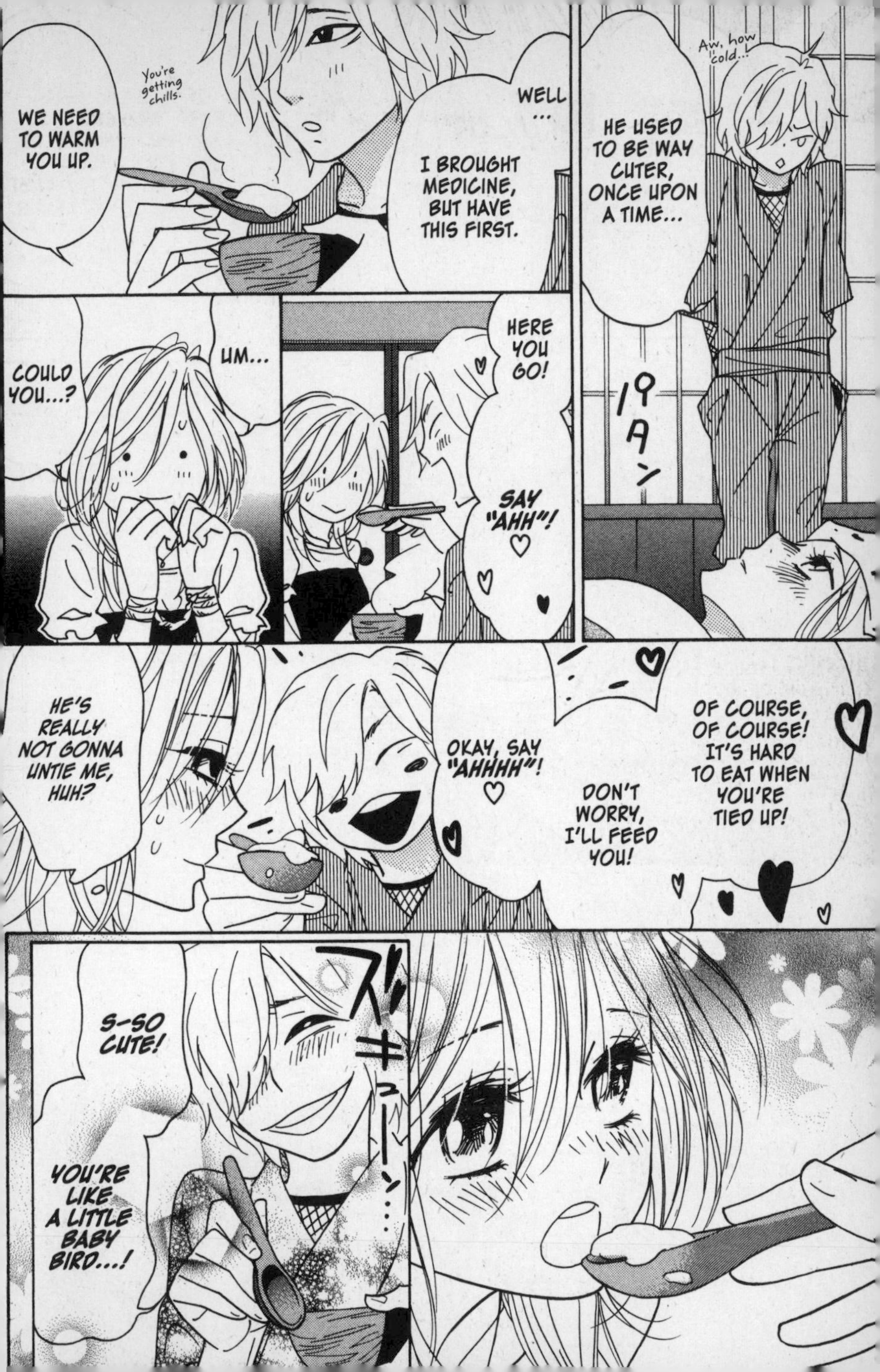
Aw, how cold...!
HE USED TO BE WAY CUTER, ONCE UPON A TIME...
パタン
WELL...
I BROUGHT MEDICINE, BUT HAVE THIS FIRST.
You're getting chills.
WE NEED TO WARM YOU UP.
HERE YOU GO!
SAY "AHH"!
UM...
COULD YOU...?
OF COURSE, OF COURSE! IT'S HARD TO EAT WHEN YOU'RE TIED UP!
DON'T WORRY, I'LL FEED YOU!
OKAY, SAY "AHHHH"!
HE'S REALLY NOT GONNA UNTIE ME, HUH?
ズキューン...
S-SO CUTE!
YOU'RE LIKE A LITTLE BABY BIRD...!

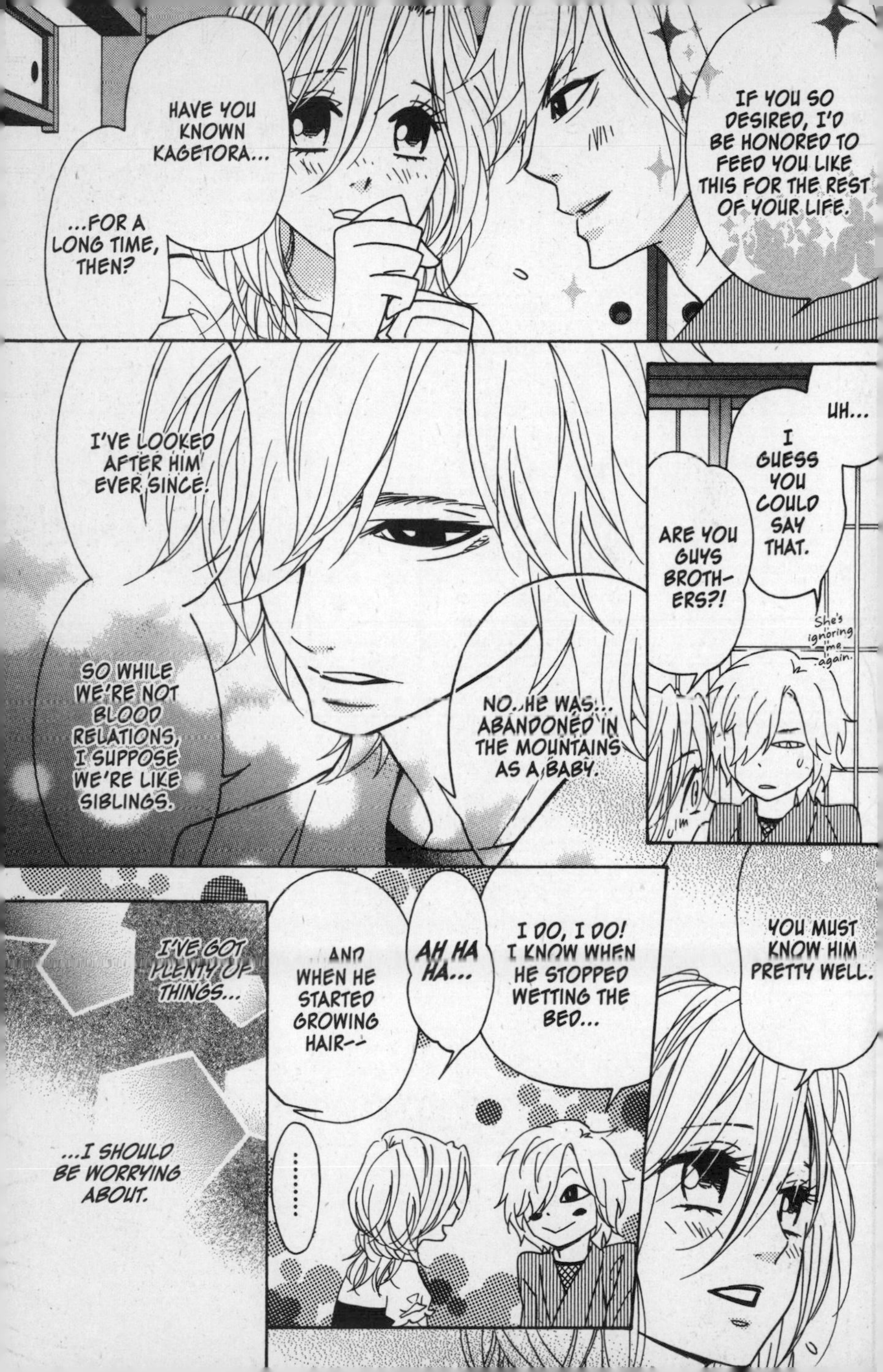
IF YOU SO DESIRED, I'D BE HONORED TO FEED YOU LIKE THIS FOR THE REST OF YOUR LIFE.
HAVE YOU KNOWN KAGETORA...
...FOR A LONG TIME, THEN?
UH...
I GUESS YOU COULD SAY THAT.
ARE YOU GUYS BROTHERS?!
She's ignoring me again.
NO. HE WAS... ABANDONED IN THE MOUNTAINS AS A BABY.
I'VE LOOKED AFTER HIM EVER SINCE.
SO WHILE WE'RE NOT BLOOD RELATIONS, I SUPPOSE WE'RE LIKE SIBLINGS.
YOU MUST KNOW HIM PRETTY WELL.
I DO, I DO! I KNOW WHEN HE STOPPED WETTING THE BED...
AH HA HA...
AND WHEN HE STARTED GROWING HAIR--
......
I'VE GOT PLENTY OF THINGS...
...I SHOULD BE WORRYING ABOUT.

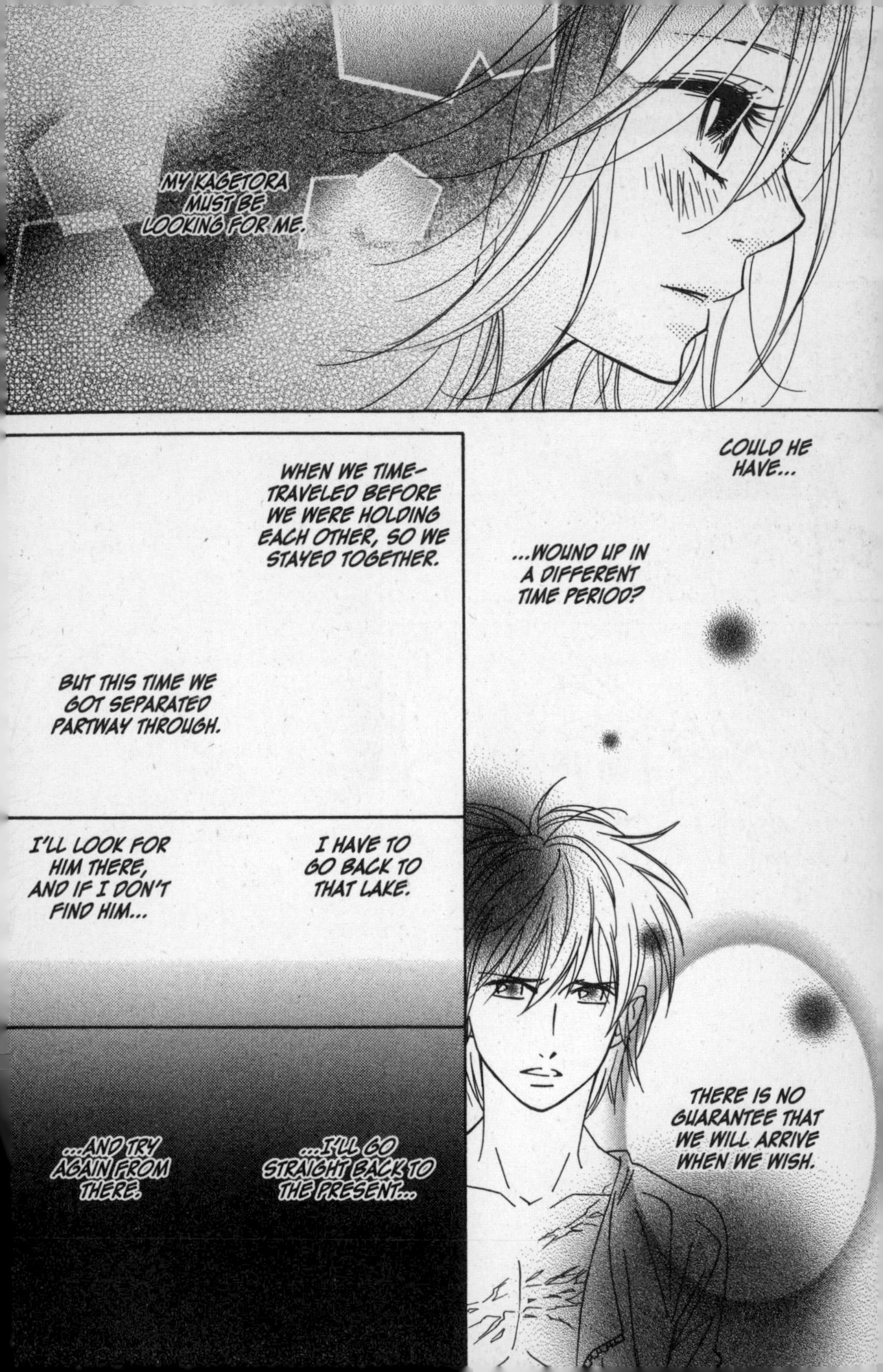
MY KAGETORA MUST BE LOOKING FOR ME.
COULD HE HAVE...
...WOUND UP IN A DIFFERENT TIME PERIOD?
WHEN WE TIME-TRAVELED BEFORE WE WERE HOLDING EACH OTHER, SO WE STAYED TOGETHER.
BUT THIS TIME WE GOT SEPARATED PARTWAY THROUGH.
THERE IS NO GUARANTEE THAT WE WILL ARRIVE WHEN WE WISH.
I HAVE TO GO BACK TO THAT LAKE.
I'LL LOOK FOR HIM THERE, AND IF I DON'T FIND HIM...
...I'LL GO STRAIGHT BACK TO THE PRESENT...
...AND TRY AGAIN FROM THERE.

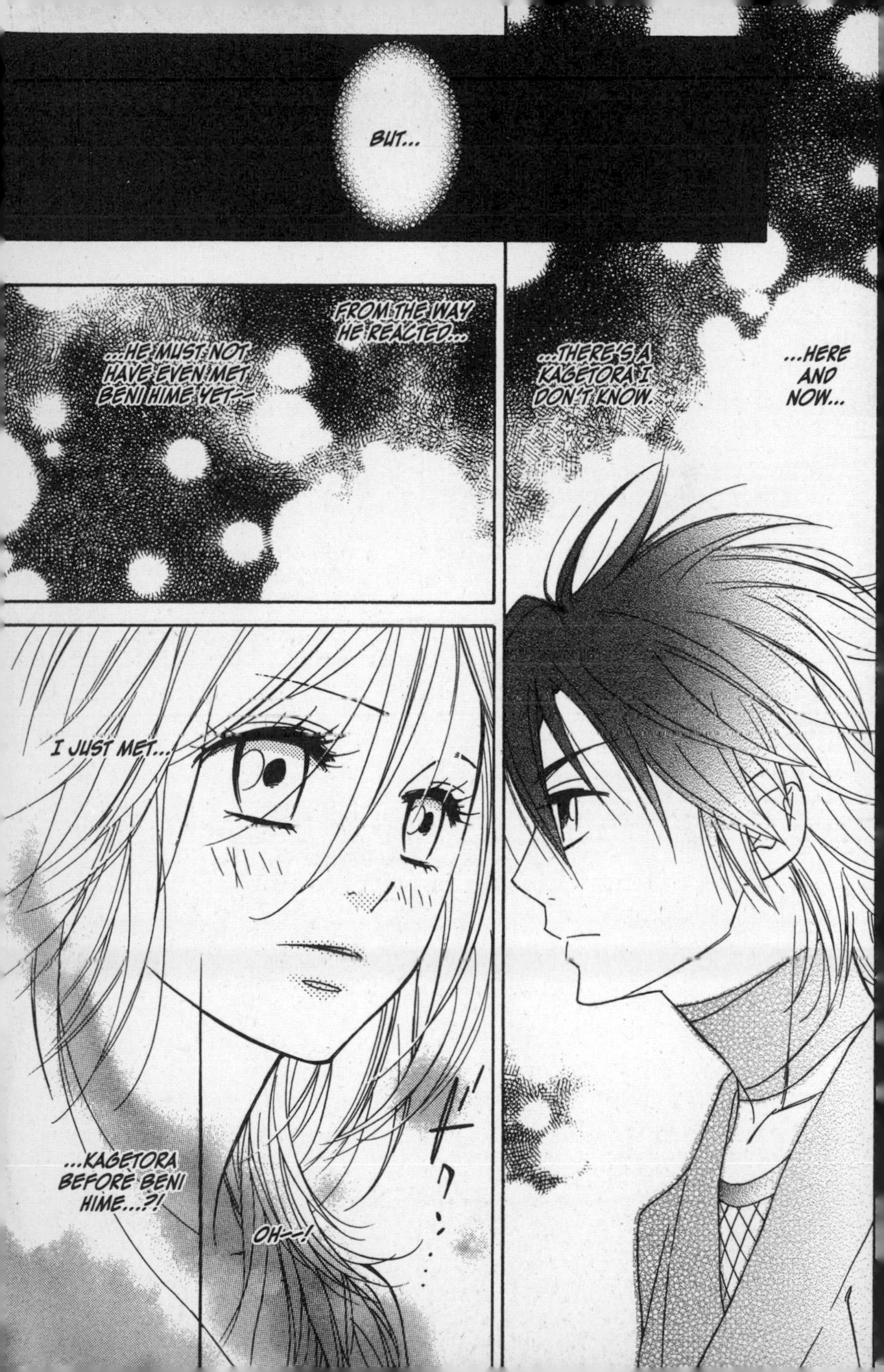
BUT...
...HERE AND NOW...
...THERE'S A KAGETORA I DON'T KNOW.
FROM THE WAY HE REACTED...
...HE MUST NOT HAVE EVEN MET BENI HIME YET--
I JUST MET...
...KAGETORA BEFORE BENI HIME...?!
OH--!

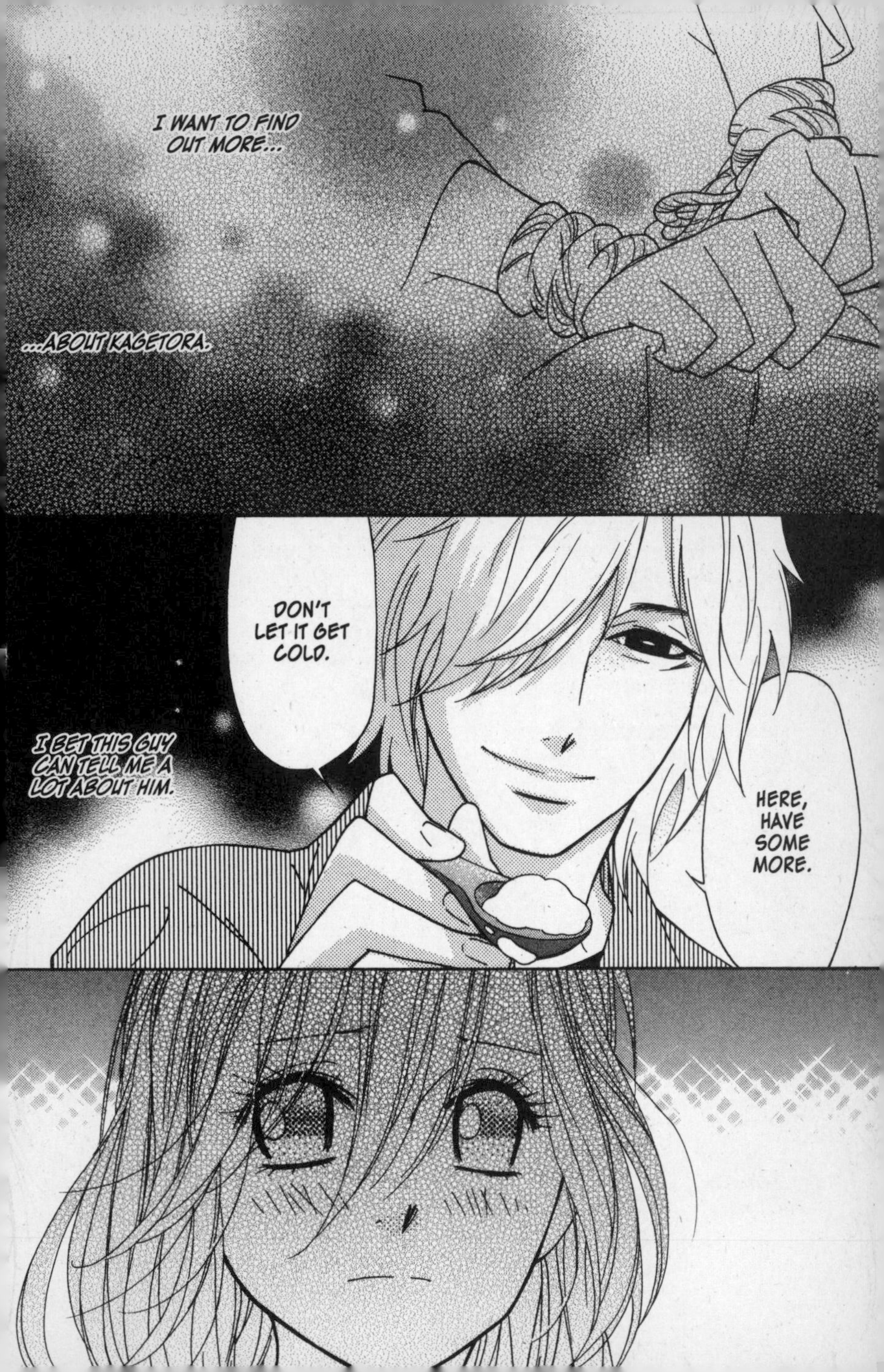
I WANT TO FIND OUT MORE...
...ABOUT KAGETORA.
HERE, HAVE SOME MORE.
DON'T LET IT GET COLD.
I BET THIS GUY CAN TELL ME A LOT ABOUT HIM.

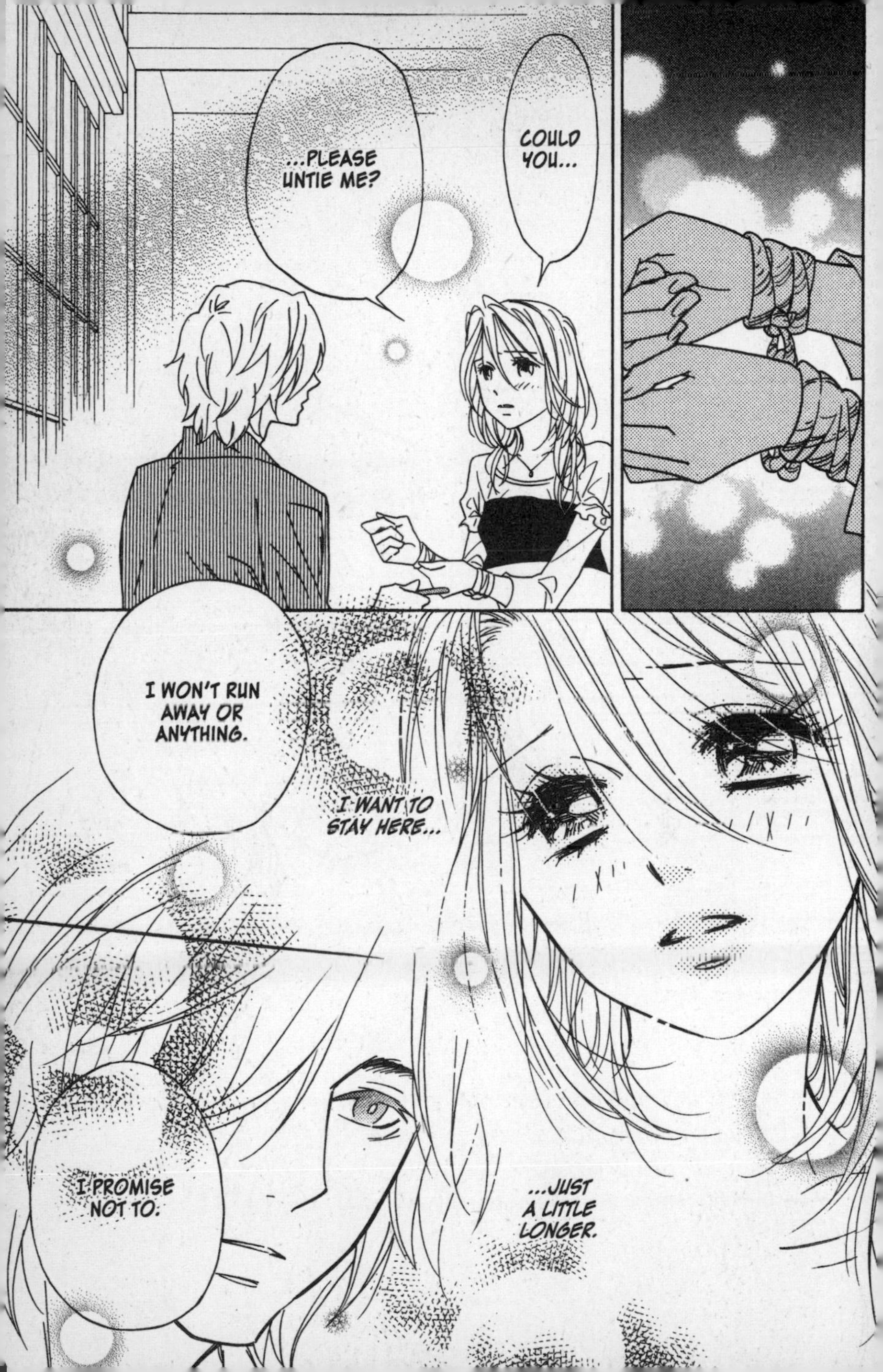
COULD YOU...
...PLEASE UNTIE ME?
I WON'T RUN AWAY OR ANYTHING.
I WANT TO STAY HERE...
...JUST A LITTLE LONGER.
I PROMISE NOT TO.

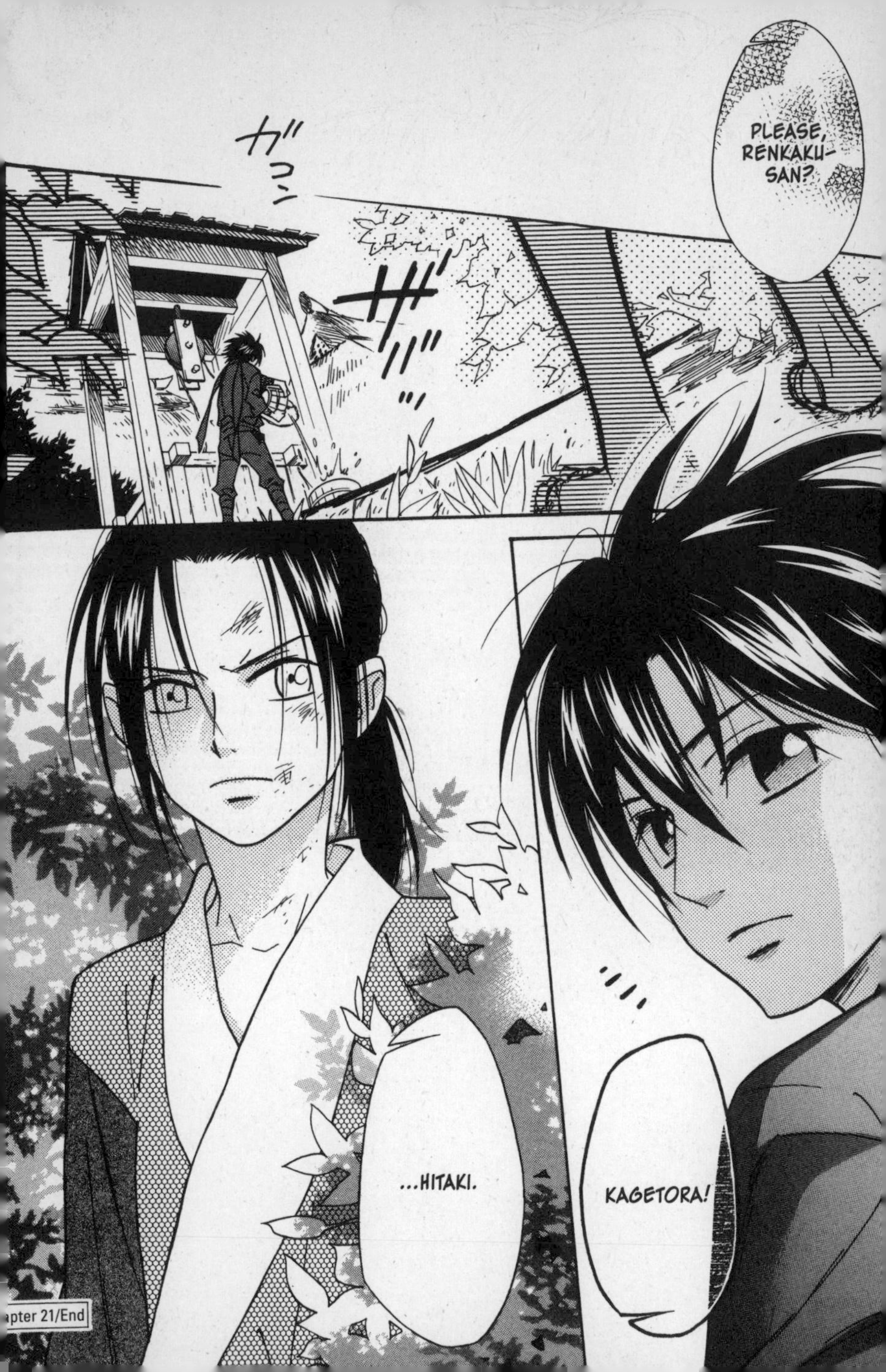
PLEASE, RENKAKU-SAN?
ガコン
ザザッ
KAGETORA!
...HITAKI.
apter 21/End

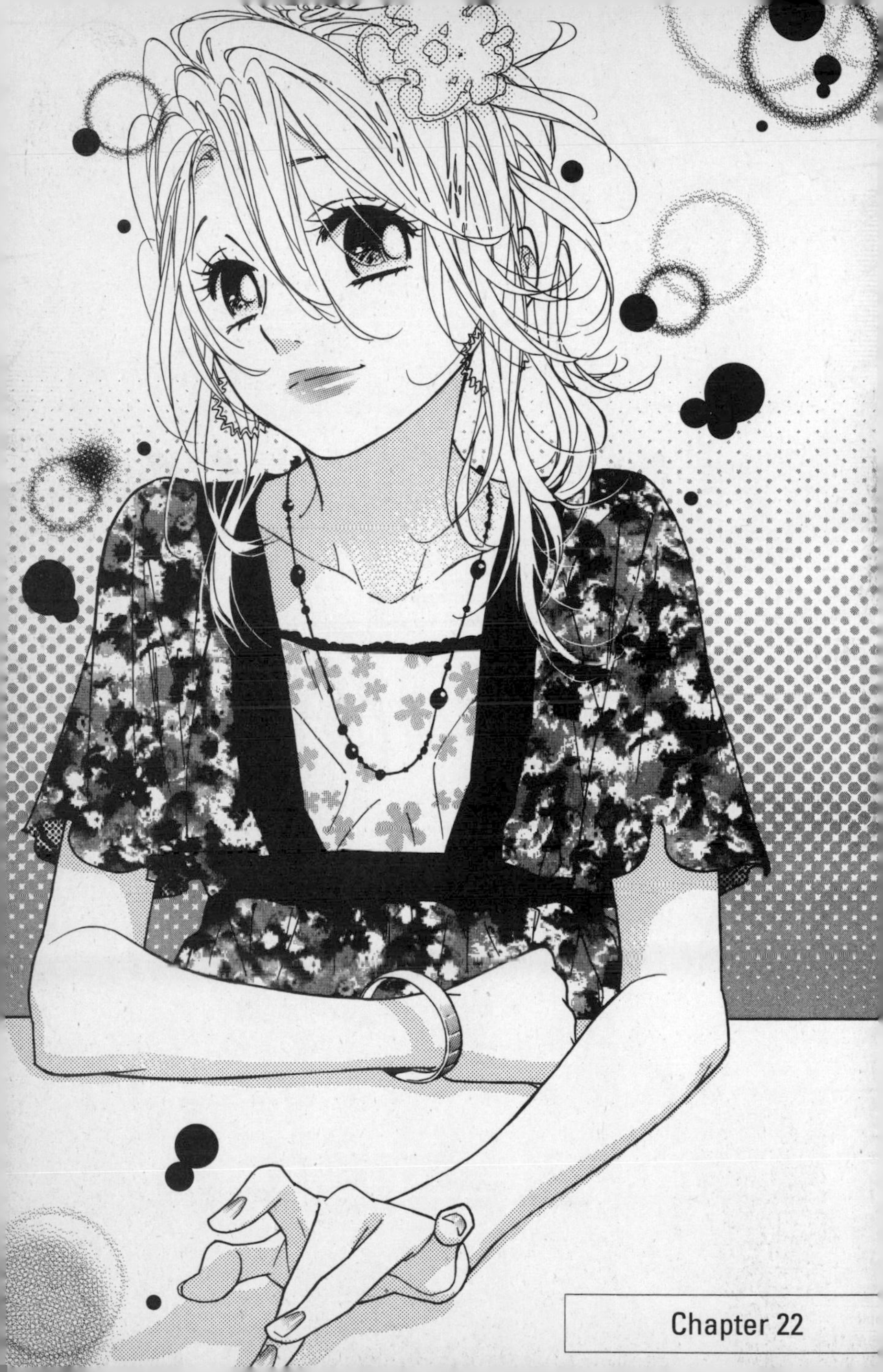

Chapter 22

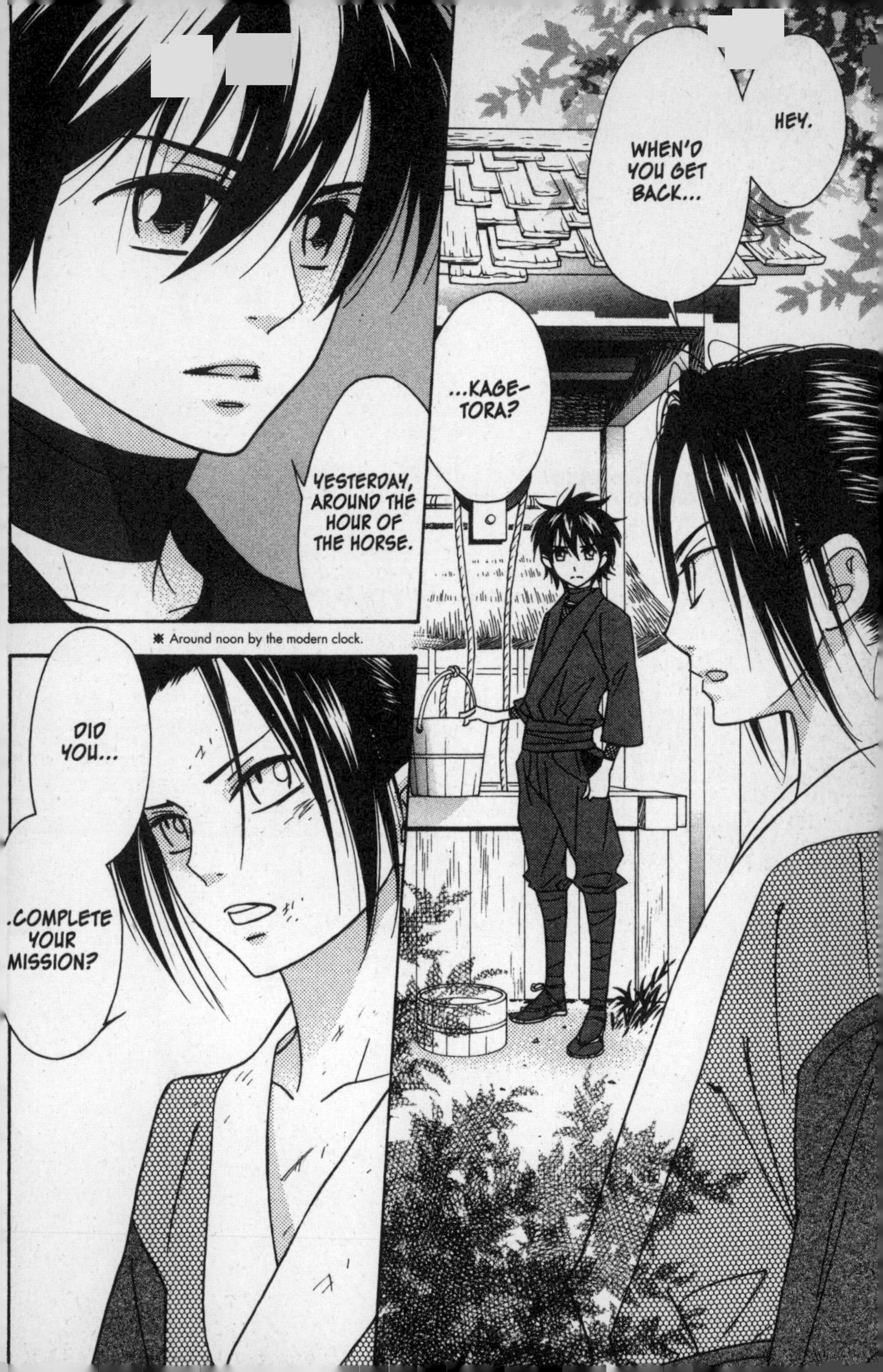
HEY.
WHEN'D YOU GET BACK...
...KAGE-TORA?
YESTERDAY, AROUND THE HOUR OF THE HORSE.
DID YOU...
.COMPLETE YOUR MISSION?

※ Around noon by the modern clock.

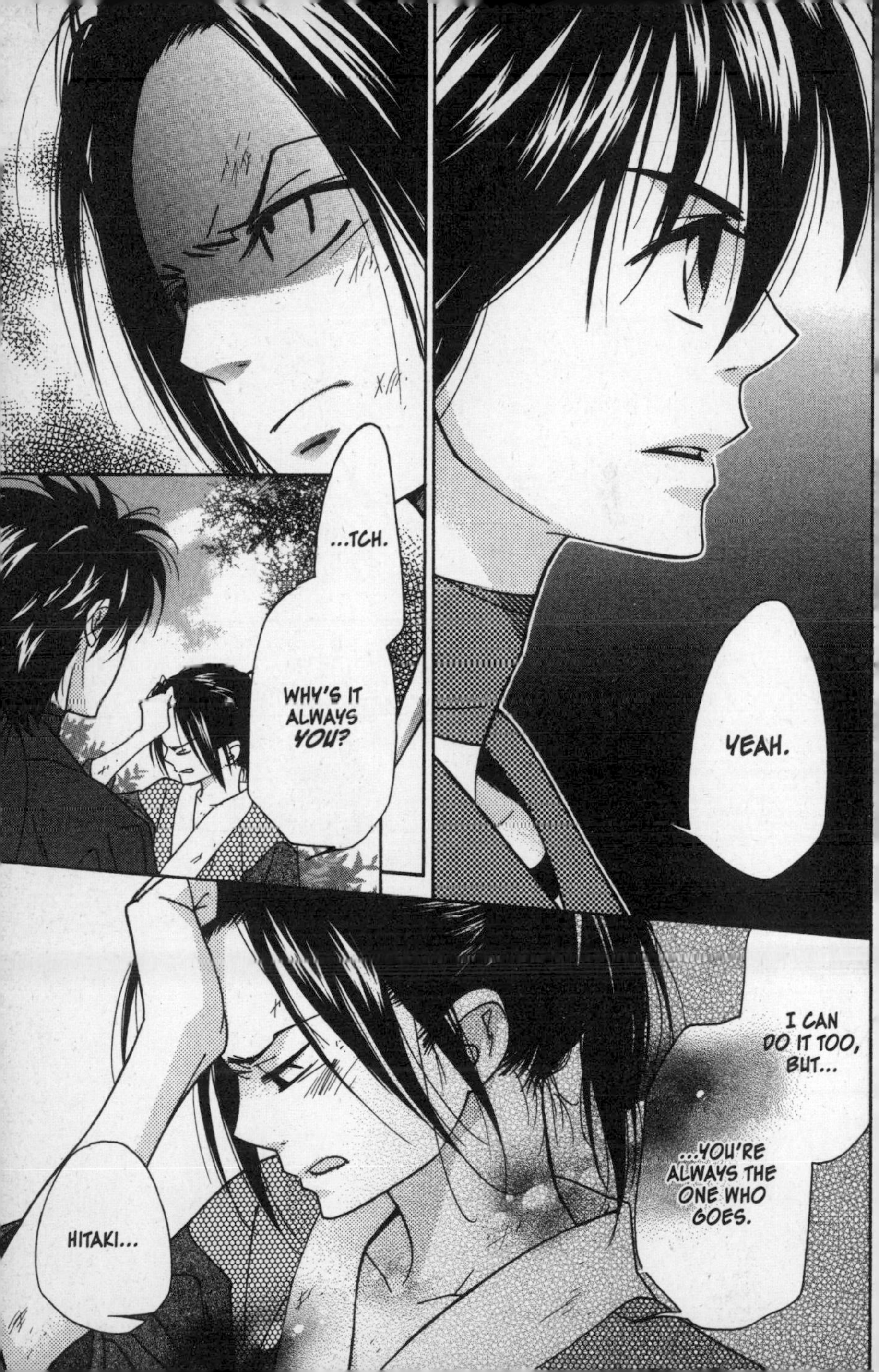
YEAH.
...TCH.
WHY'S IT ALWAYS YOU?
I CAN DO IT TOO, BUT...
...YOU'RE ALWAYS THE ONE WHO GOES.
HITAKI...

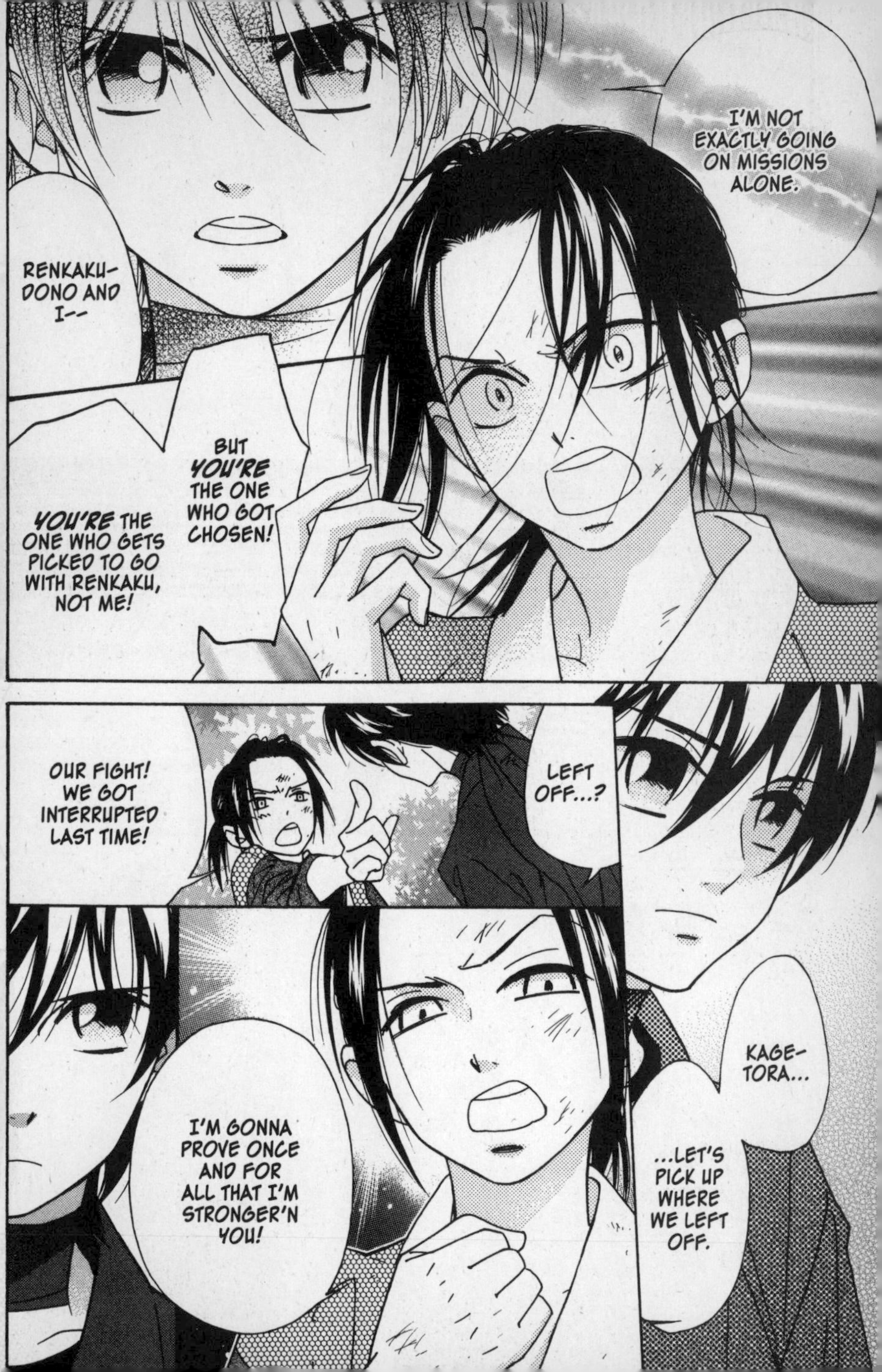
I'M NOT EXACTLY GOING ON MISSIONS ALONE.
RENKAKU-DONO AND I--
BUT *YOU'RE* THE ONE WHO GOT CHOSEN!
YOU'RE THE ONE WHO GETS PICKED TO GO WITH RENKAKU, NOT ME!
KAGE-TORA...
...LET'S PICK UP WHERE WE LEFT OFF.
LEFT OFF...?
OUR FIGHT! WE GOT INTERRUPTED LAST TIME!
I'M GONNA PROVE ONCE AND FOR ALL THAT I'M STRONGER'N YOU!

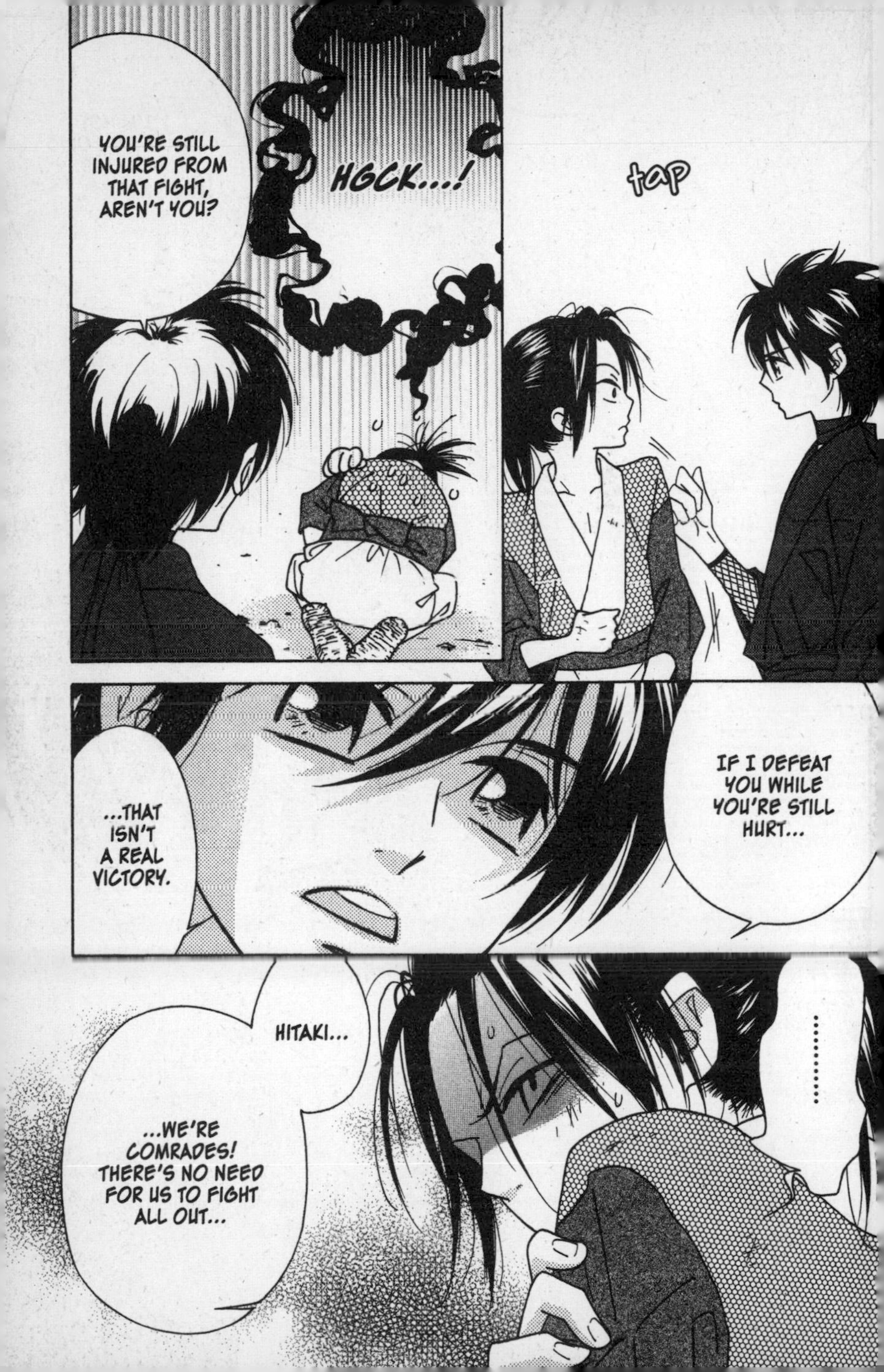
tap
HGCK...!
YOU'RE STILL INJURED FROM THAT FIGHT, AREN'T YOU?
IF I DEFEAT YOU WHILE YOU'RE STILL HURT...
...THAT ISN'T A REAL VICTORY.
......
HITAKI...
...WE'RE COMRADES! THERE'S NO NEED FOR US TO FIGHT ALL OUT...

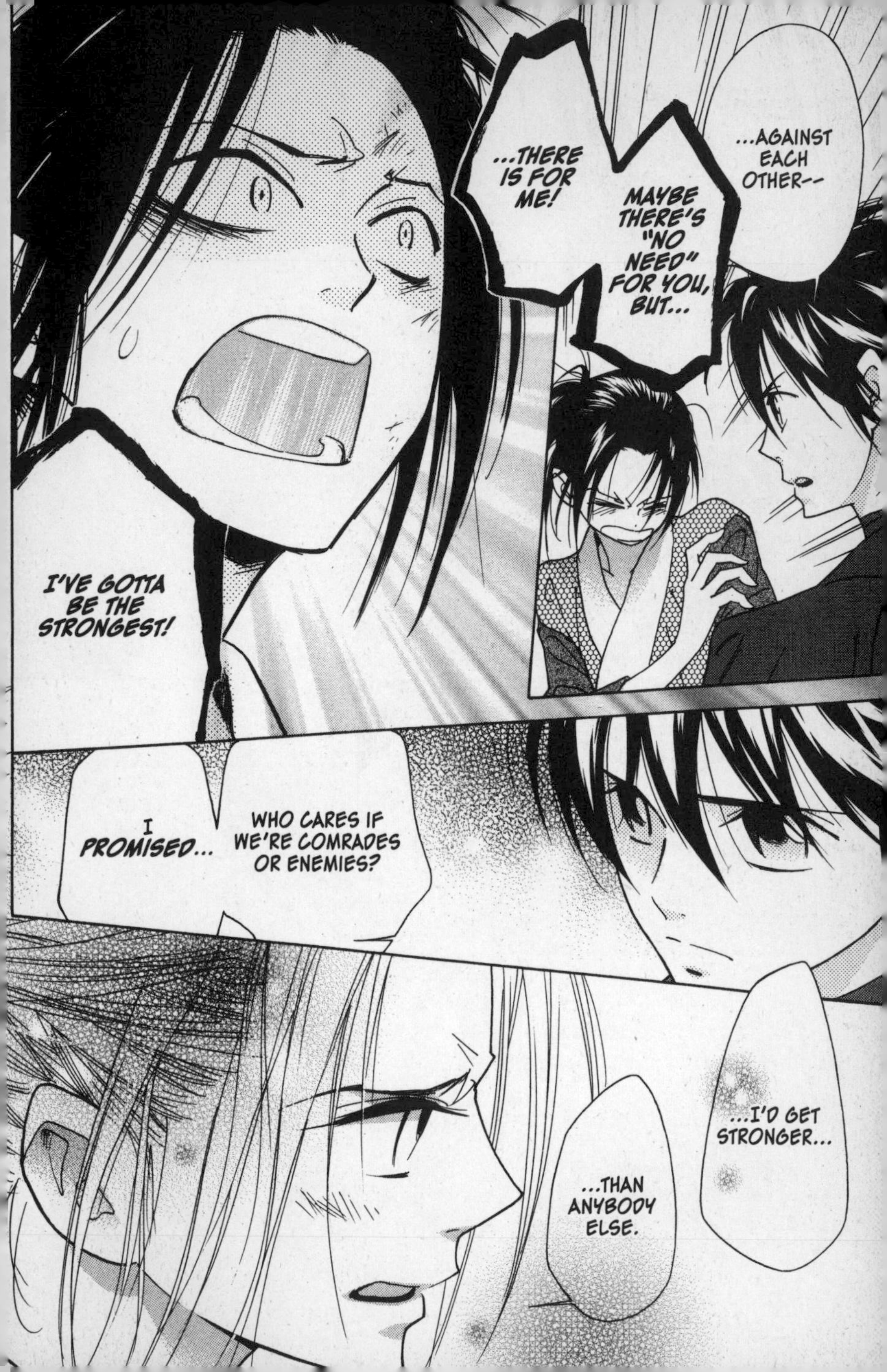
...AGAINST EACH OTHER--
MAYBE THERE'S "NO NEED" FOR YOU, BUT...
...THERE IS FOR ME!
I'VE GOTTA BE THE STRONGEST!
WHO CARES IF WE'RE COMRADES OR ENEMIES?
I PROMISED...
...I'D GET STRONGER...
...THAN ANYBODY ELSE.

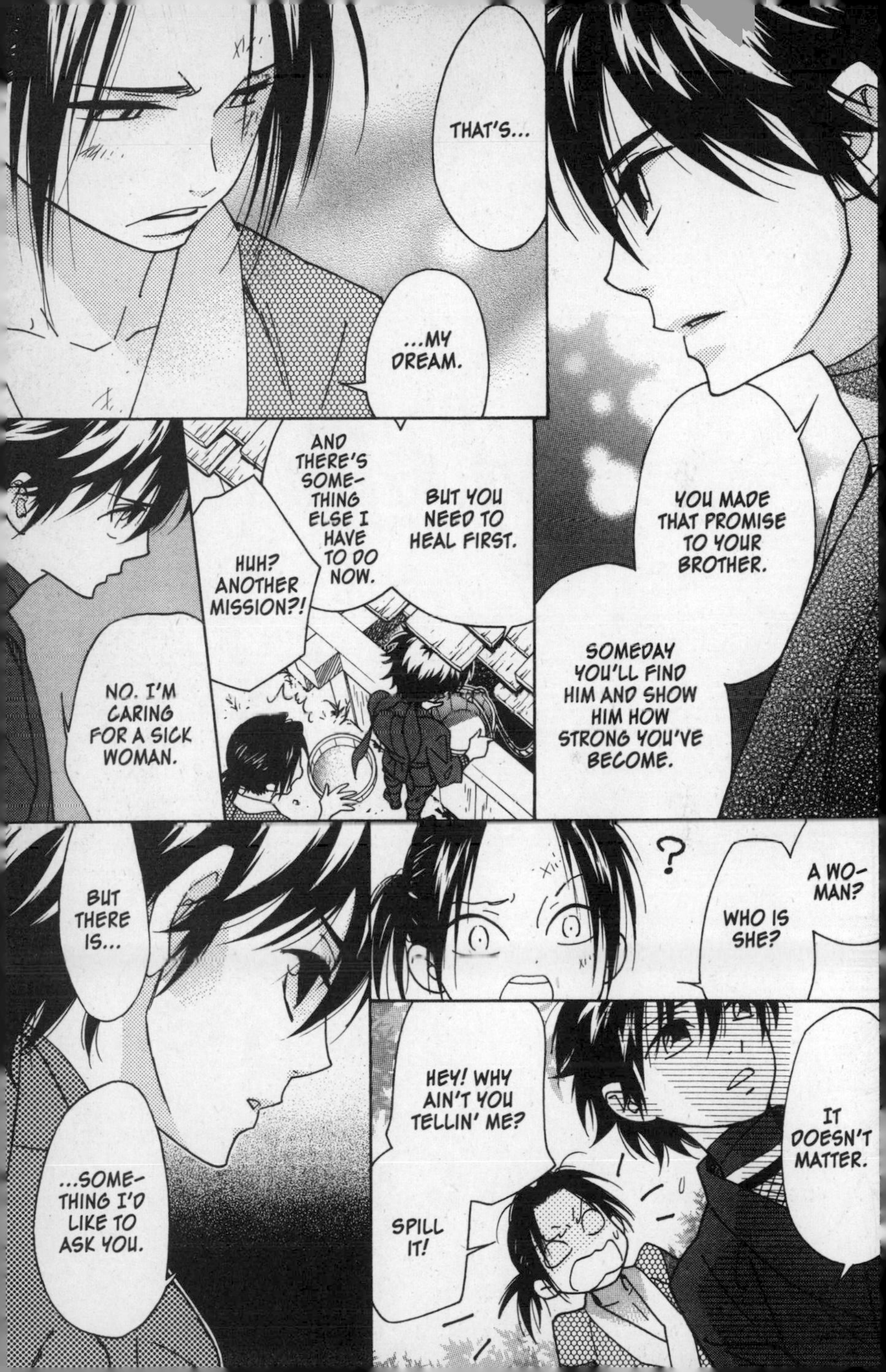
YOU MADE THAT PROMISE TO YOUR BROTHER.
SOMEDAY YOU'LL FIND HIM AND SHOW HIM HOW STRONG YOU'VE BECOME.
THAT'S...
...MY DREAM.
AND THERE'S SOME-THING ELSE I HAVE TO DO NOW.
BUT YOU NEED TO HEAL FIRST.
HUH? ANOTHER MISSION?!
NO. I'M CARING FOR A SICK WOMAN.
?
A WO-MAN?
WHO IS SHE?
IT DOESN'T MATTER.
HEY! WHY AIN'T YOU TELLIN' ME?
SPILL IT!
BUT THERE IS...
...SOME-THING I'D LIKE TO ASK YOU.

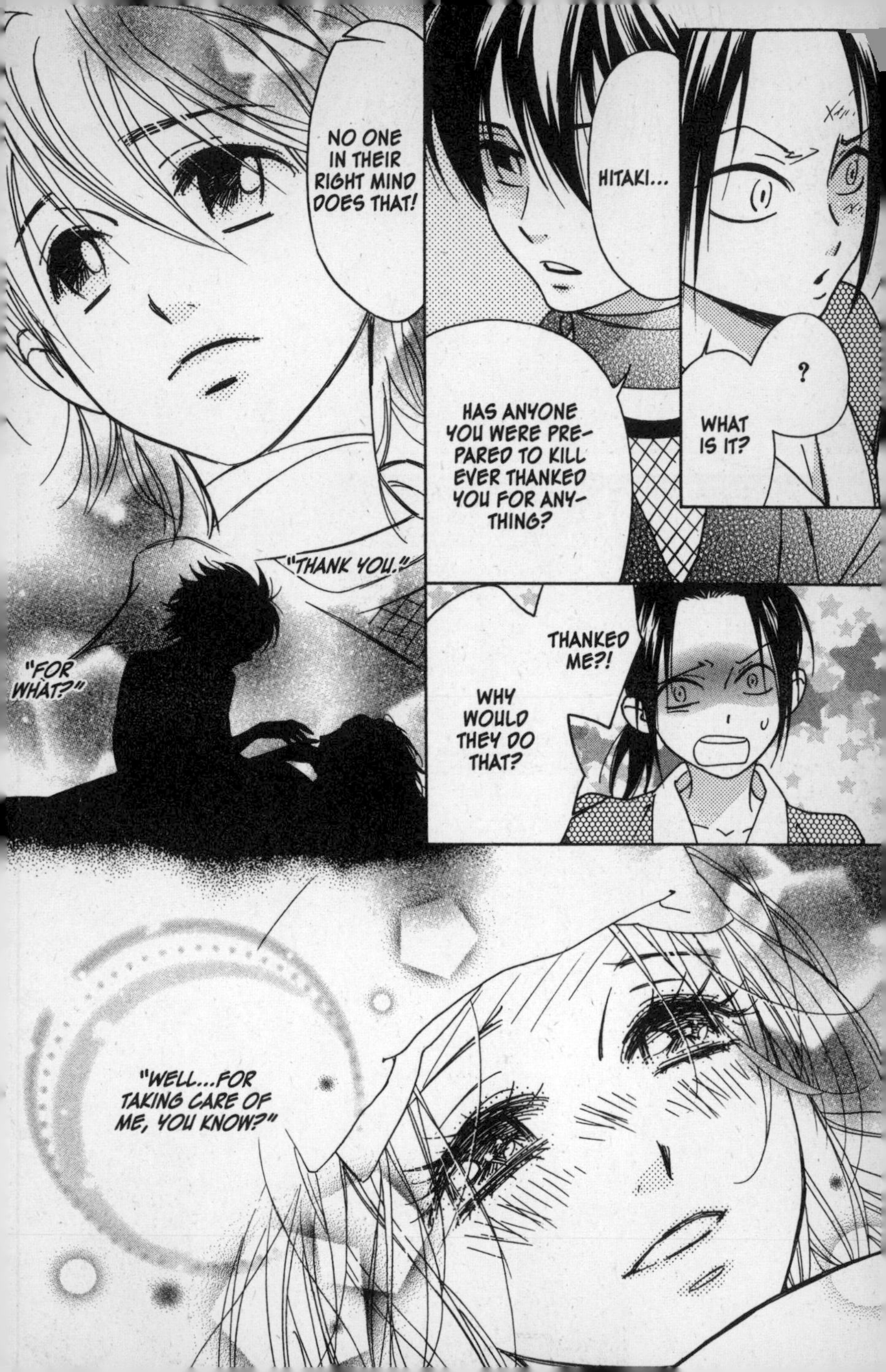
HITAKI...
?
WHAT IS IT?
HAS ANYONE YOU WERE PRE-PARED TO KILL EVER THANKED YOU FOR ANY-THING?
NO ONE IN THEIR RIGHT MIND DOES THAT!
THANKED ME?!
WHY WOULD THEY DO THAT?
"THANK YOU."
"FOR WHAT?"
"WELL...FOR TAKING CARE OF ME, YOU KNOW?"

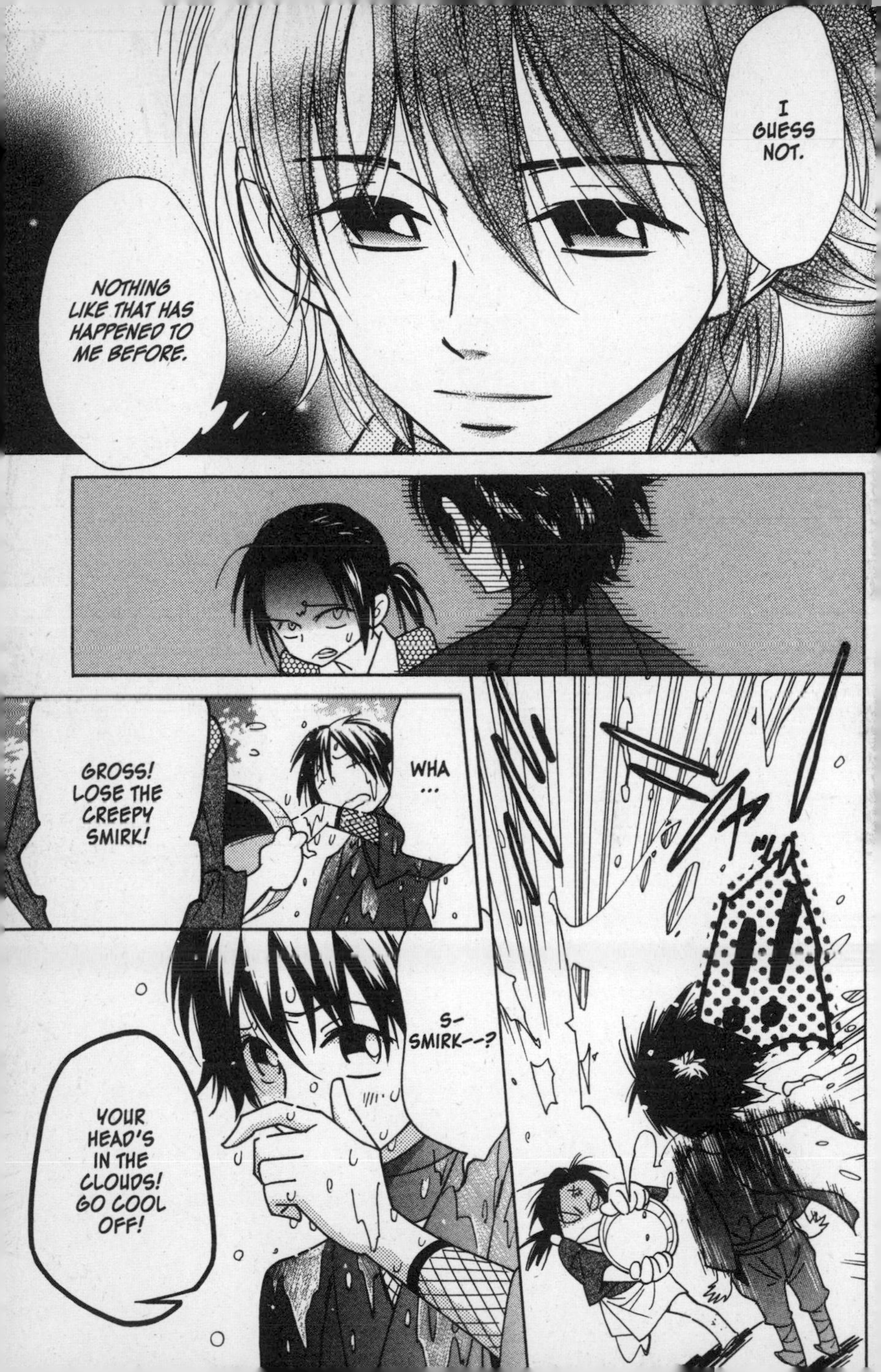
I GUESS NOT.
NOTHING LIKE THAT HAS HAPPENED TO ME BEFORE.
WHA ...
GROSS! LOSE THE CREEPY SMIRK!
S-SMIRK--?
YOUR HEAD'S IN THE CLOUDS! GO COOL OFF!

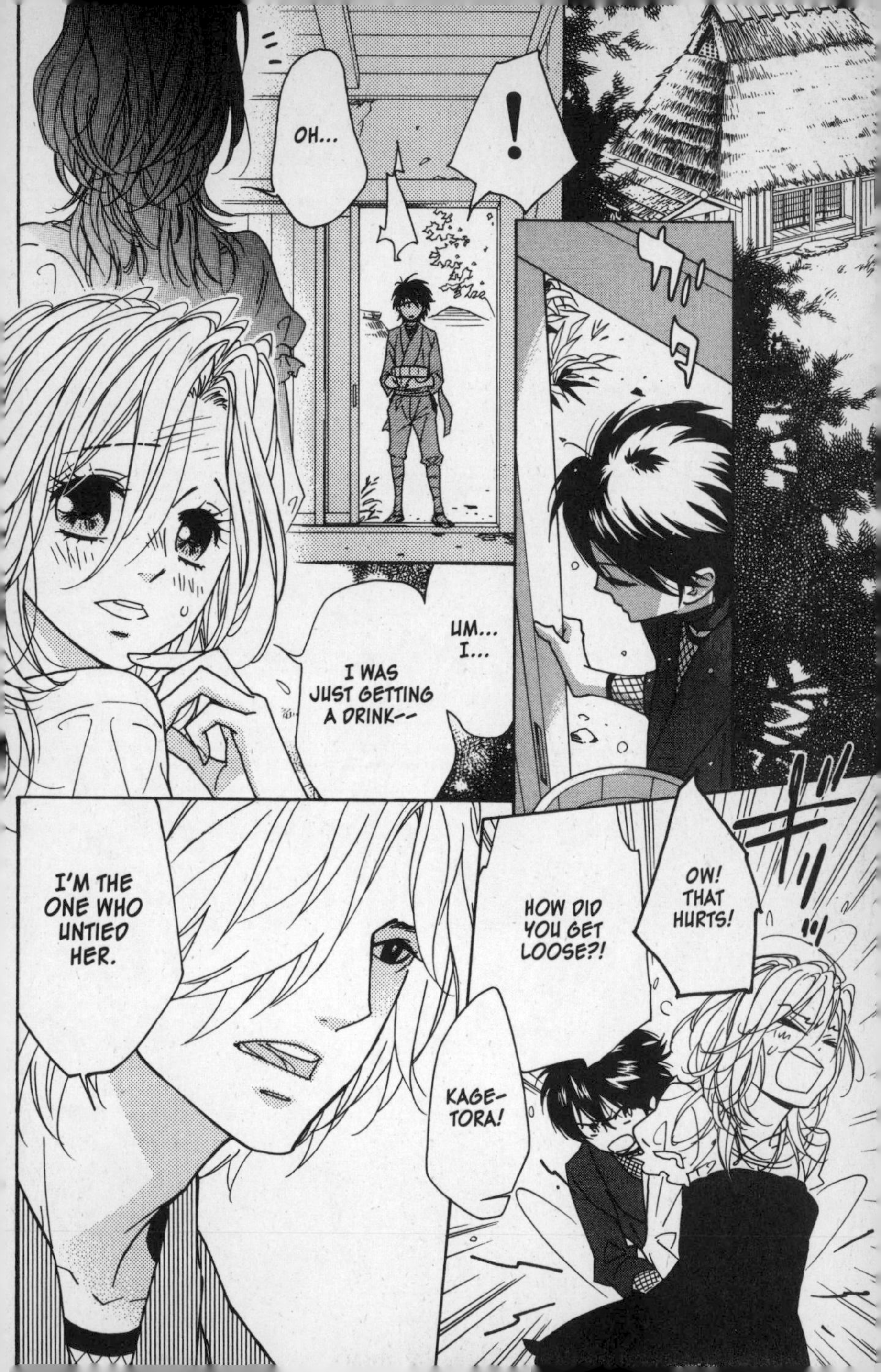
ガタ
!
OH...
UM... I...
I WAS JUST GETTING A DRINK--
ギリ
OW! THAT HURTS!
HOW DID YOU GET LOOSE?!
KAGE-TORA!
I'M THE ONE WHO UNTIED HER.

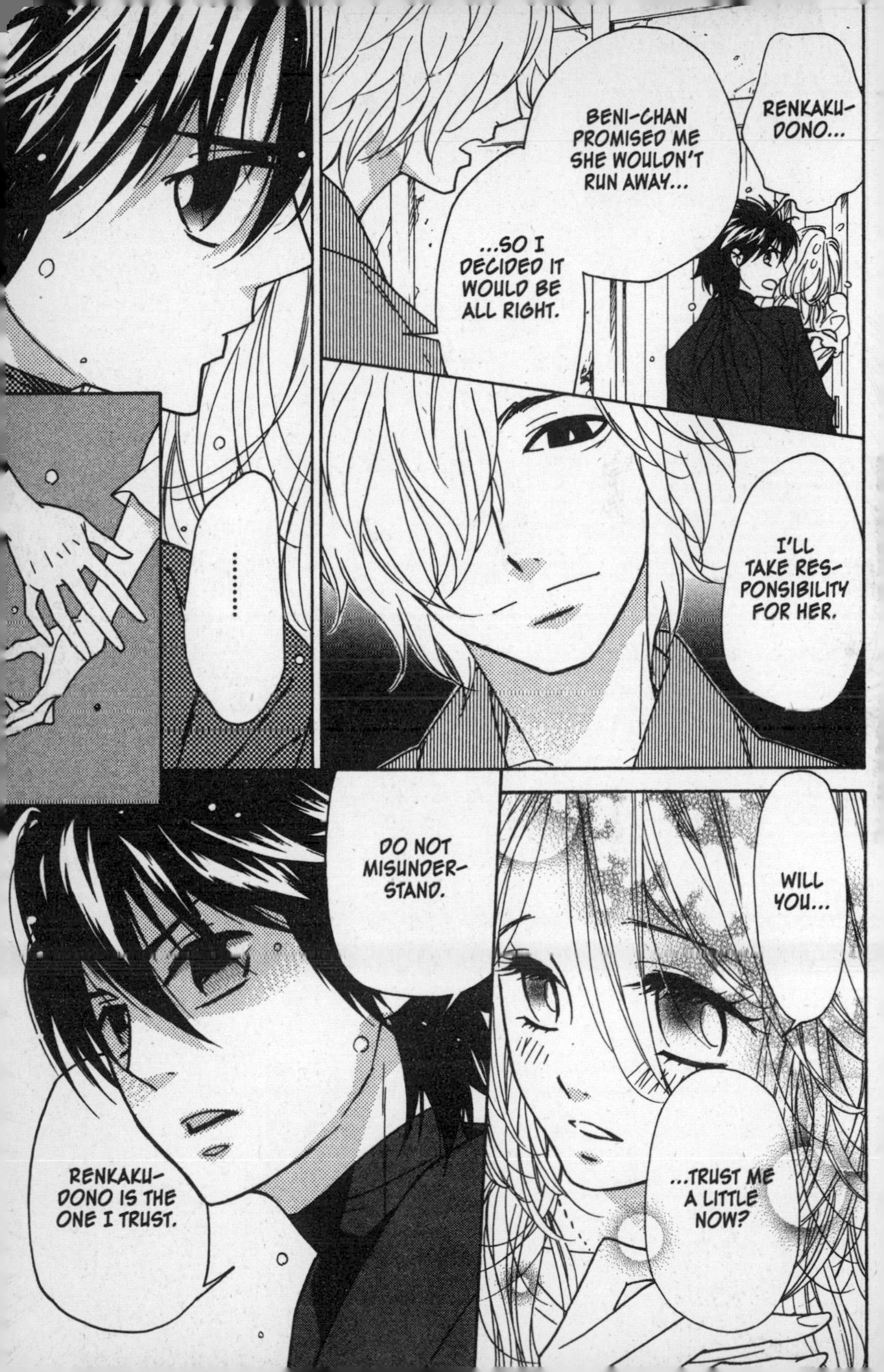
RENKAKU-DONO...
BENI-CHAN PROMISED ME SHE WOULDN'T RUN AWAY...
...SO I DECIDED IT WOULD BE ALL RIGHT.
I'LL TAKE RES-PONSIBILITY FOR HER.
....
WILL YOU...
...TRUST ME A LITTLE NOW?
DO NOT MISUNDER-STAND.
RENKAKU-DONO IS THE ONE I TRUST.

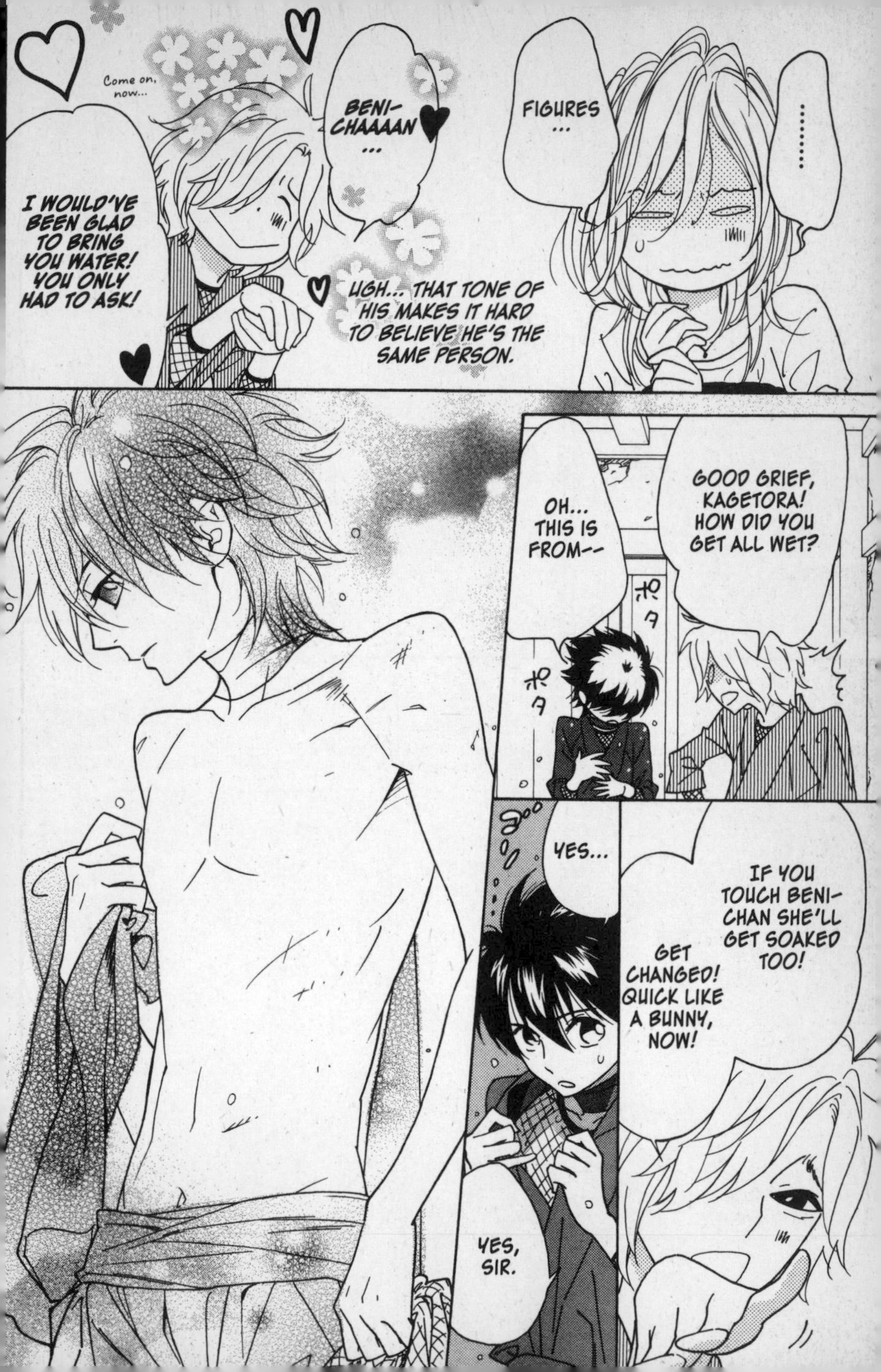

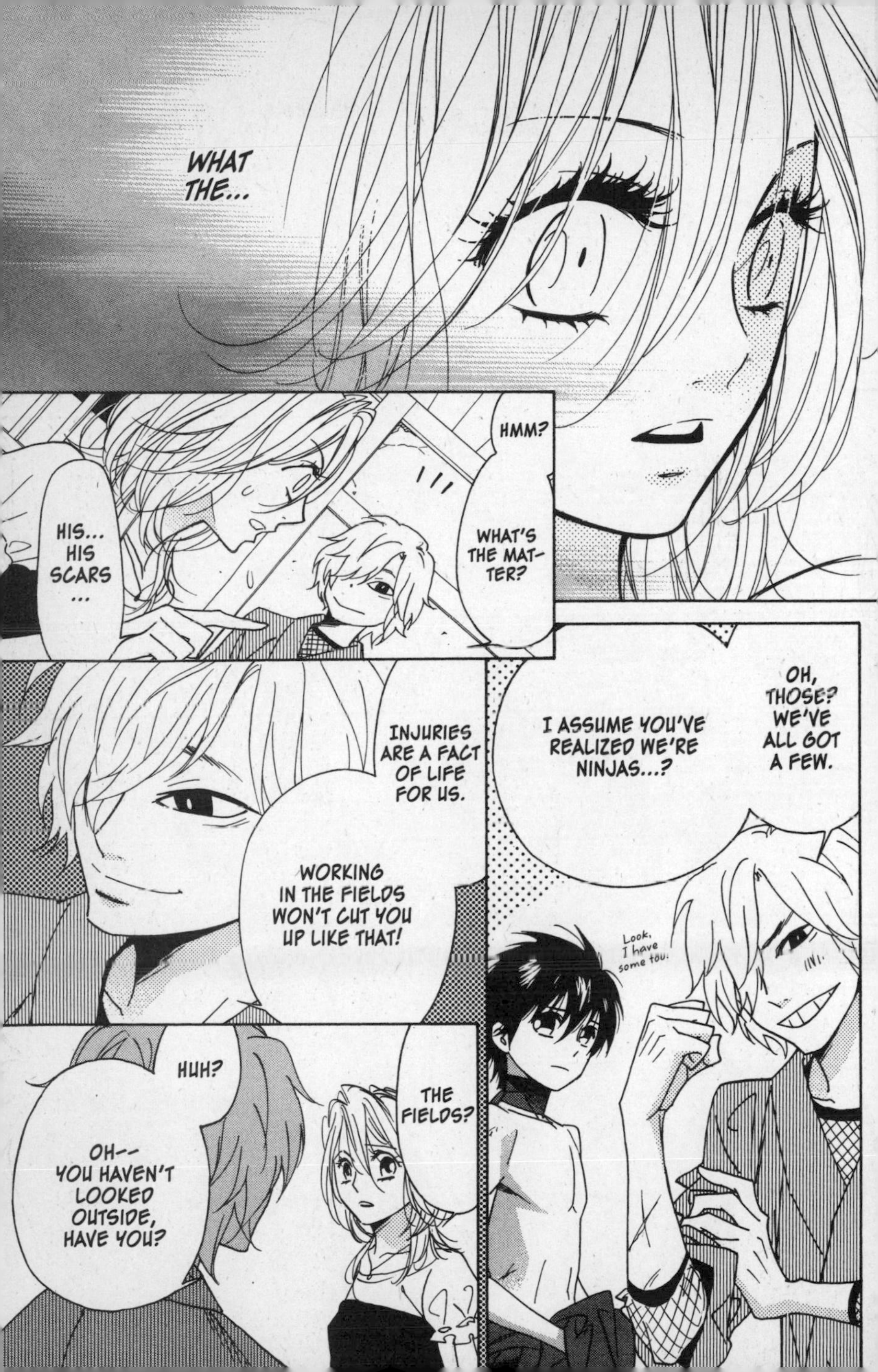
WHAT THE...
HMM?
WHAT'S THE MAT-TER?
HIS... HIS SCARS ...
OH, THOSE? WE'VE ALL GOT A FEW.
I ASSUME YOU'VE REALIZED WE'RE NINJAS...?
Look, I have some too.
INJURIES ARE A FACT OF LIFE FOR US.
WORKING IN THE FIELDS WON'T CUT YOU UP LIKE THAT!
THE FIELDS?
HUH?
OH-- YOU HAVEN'T LOOKED OUTSIDE, HAVE YOU?

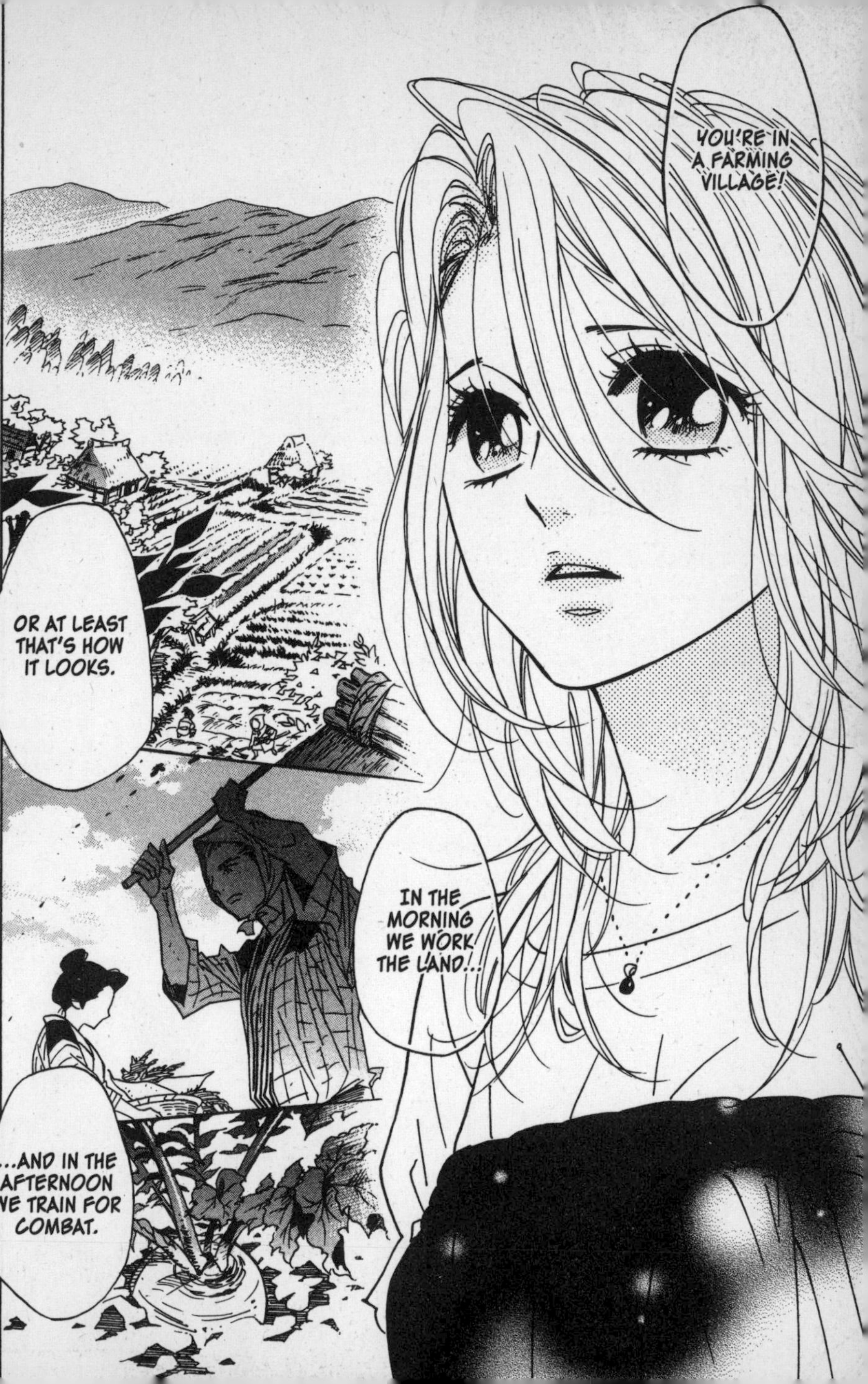
YOU'RE IN A FARMING VILLAGE!
OR AT LEAST THAT'S HOW IT LOOKS.
IN THE MORNING WE WORK THE LAND...
...AND IN THE AFTERNOON WE TRAIN FOR COMBAT.

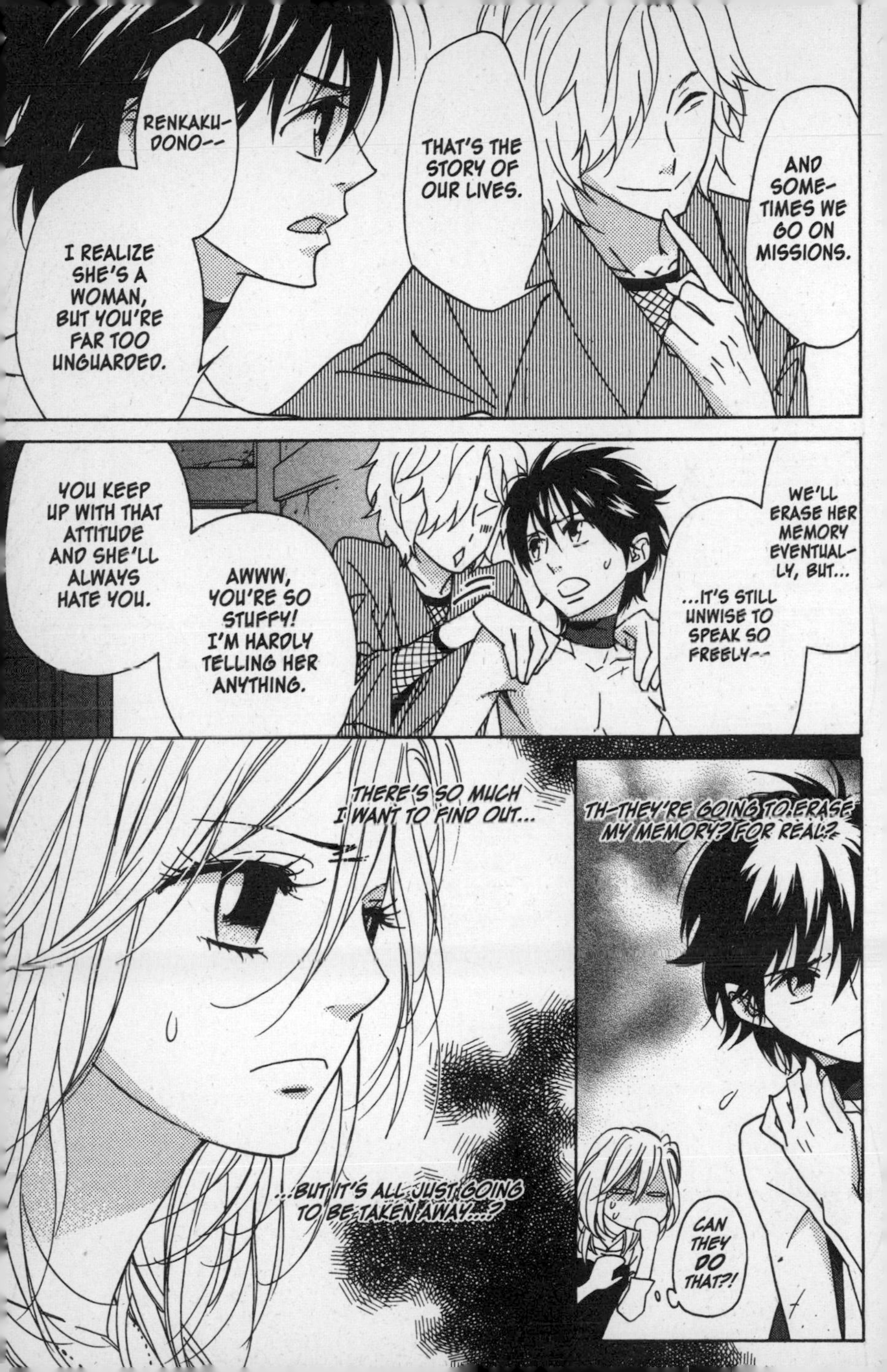
AND SOMETIMES WE GO ON MISSIONS.
THAT'S THE STORY OF OUR LIVES.
RENKAKU-DONO--
I REALIZE SHE'S A WOMAN, BUT YOU'RE FAR TOO UNGUARDED.
WE'LL ERASE HER MEMORY EVENTUALLY, BUT...
...IT'S STILL UNWISE TO SPEAK SO FREELY--
AWWW, YOU'RE SO STUFFY! I'M HARDLY TELLING HER ANYTHING.
YOU KEEP UP WITH THAT ATTITUDE AND SHE'LL ALWAYS HATE YOU.
TH-THEY'RE GOING TO ERASE MY MEMORY? FOR REAL?!
CAN THEY DO THAT?!
THERE'S SO MUCH I WANT TO FIND OUT...
...BUT IT'S ALL JUST GOING TO BE TAKEN AWAY...?

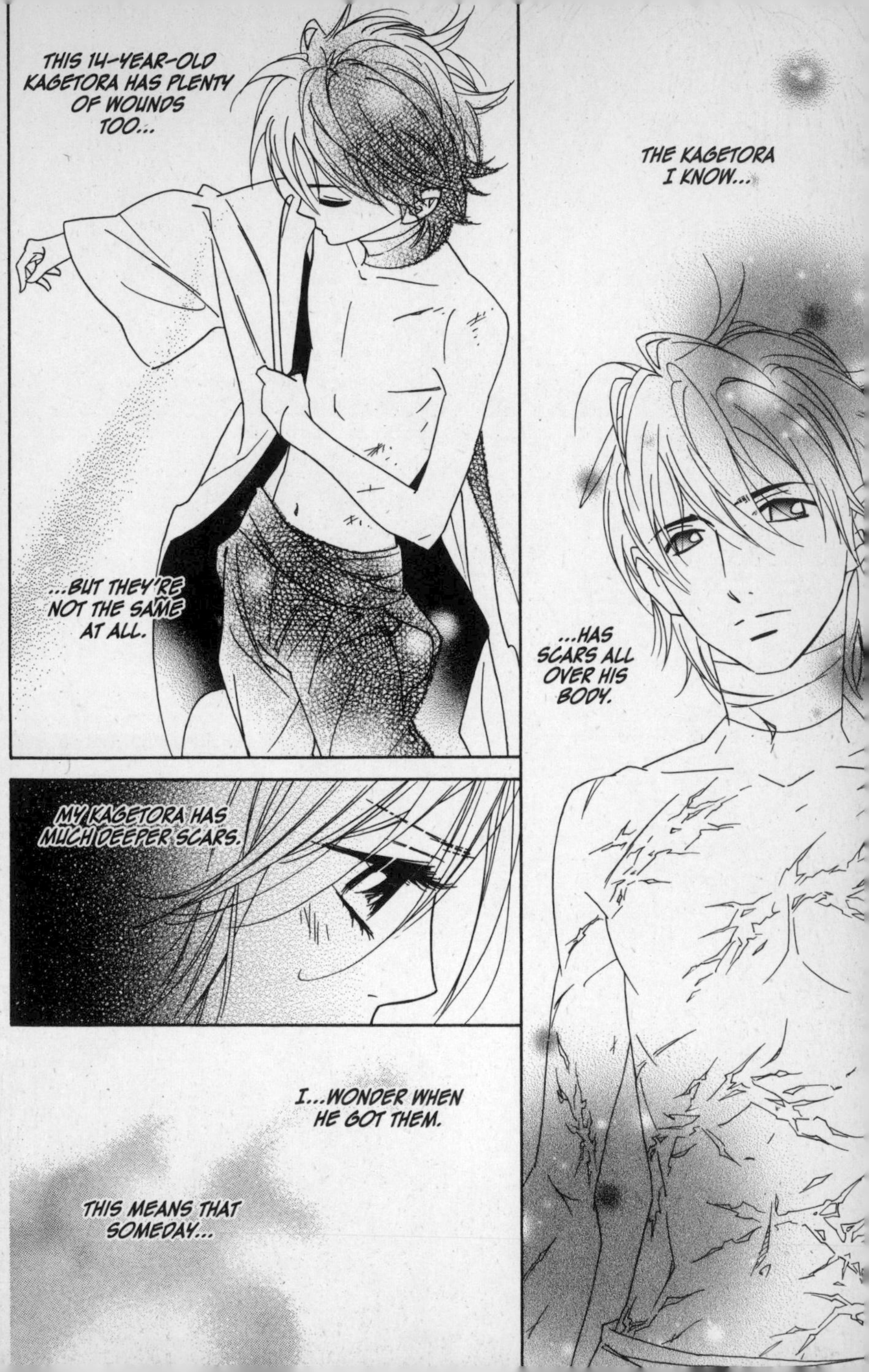
THE KAGETORA I KNOW...
...HAS SCARS ALL OVER HIS BODY.
THIS 14-YEAR-OLD KAGETORA HAS PLENTY OF WOUNDS TOO...
...BUT THEY'RE NOT THE SAME AT ALL.
MY KAGETORA HAS MUCH DEEPER SCARS.
I...WONDER WHEN HE GOT THEM.
THIS MEANS THAT SOMEDAY...

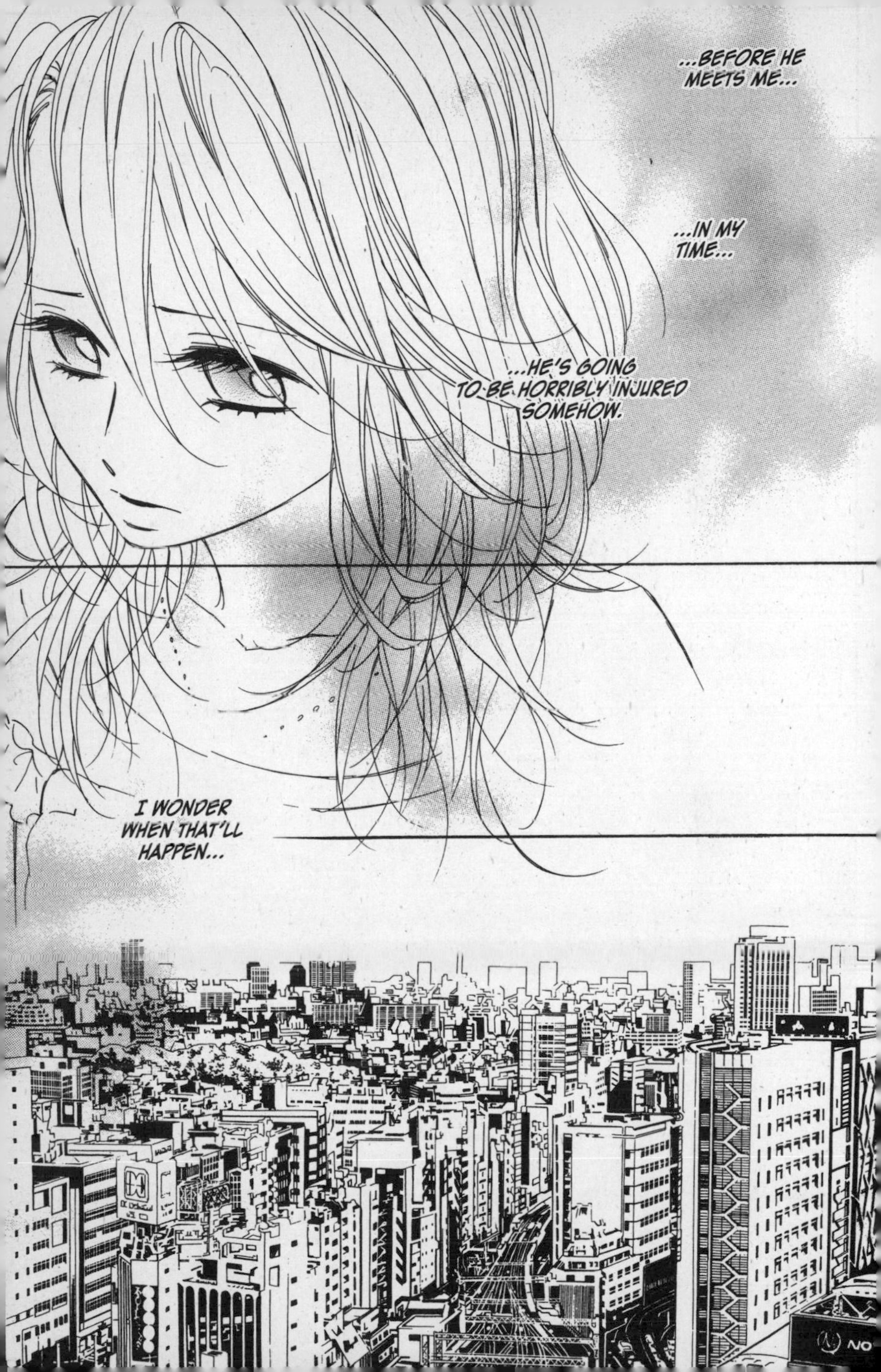
...BEFORE HE MEETS ME...
...IN MY TIME...
...HE'S GOING TO BE HORRIBLY INJURED SOMEHOW.
I WONDER WHEN THAT'LL HAPPEN...

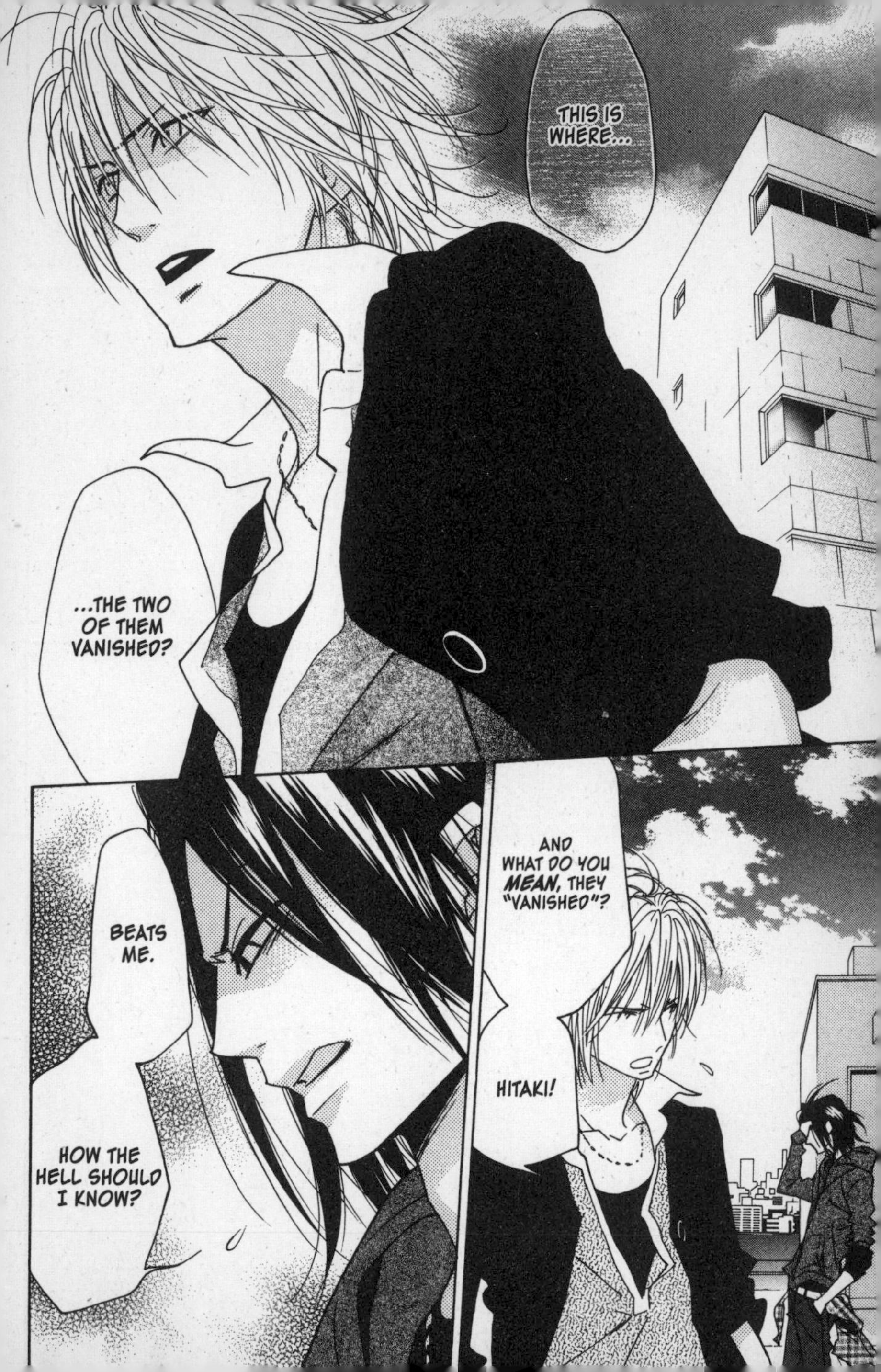
THIS IS WHERE...
...THE TWO OF THEM VANISHED?
AND WHAT DO YOU MEAN, THEY "VANISHED"?
HITAKI!
BEATS ME.
HOW THE HELL SHOULD I KNOW?

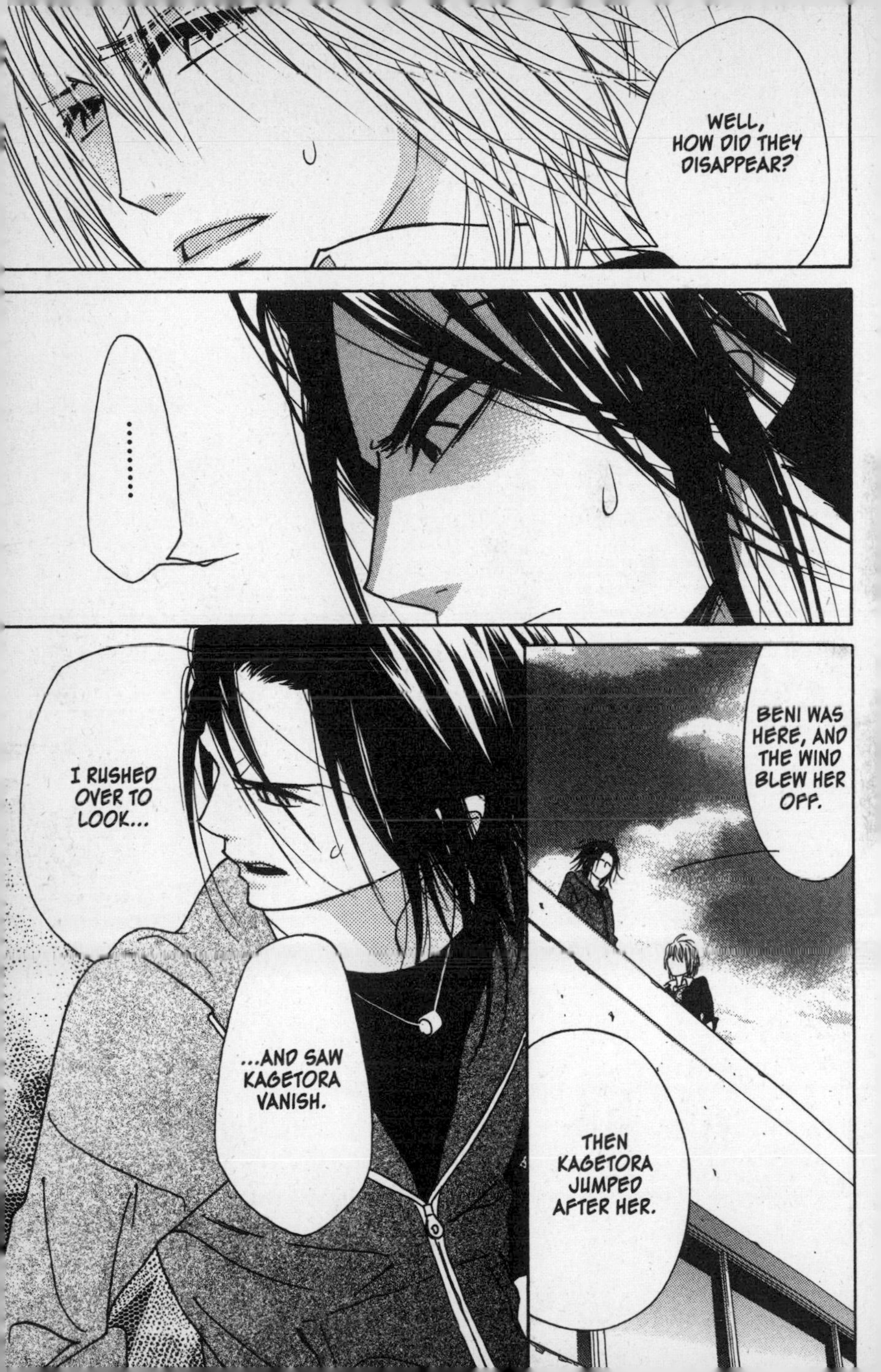
WELL, HOW DID THEY DISAPPEAR?
....
BENI WAS HERE, AND THE WIND BLEW HER OFF.
THEN KAGETORA JUMPED AFTER HER.
I RUSHED OVER TO LOOK...
...AND SAW KAGETORA VANISH.

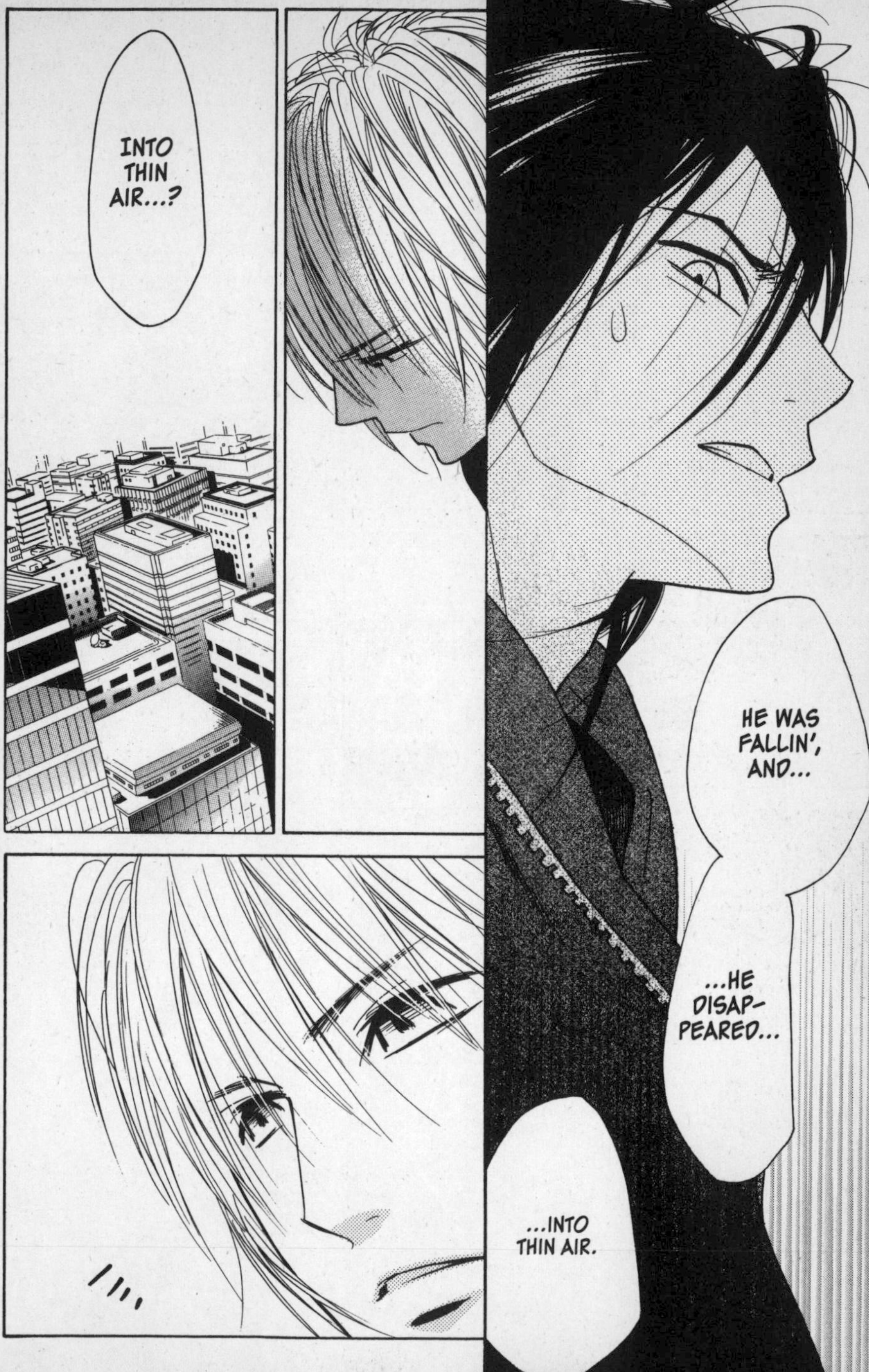
HE WAS FALLIN', AND...
...HE DISAP-PEARED...
...INTO THIN AIR.
INTO THIN AIR...?

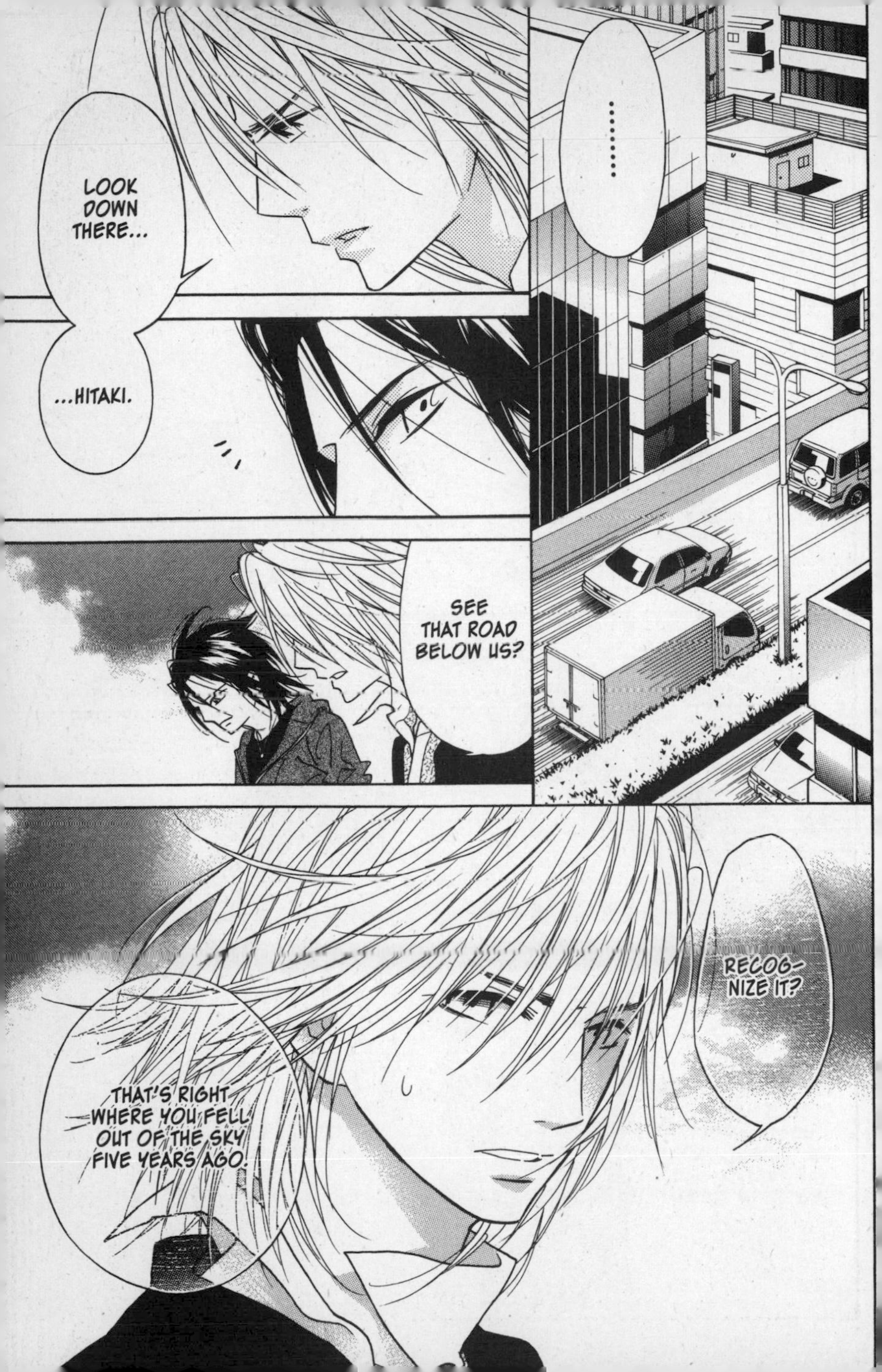
......
LOOK DOWN THERE...
...HITAKI.
SEE THAT ROAD BELOW US?
RECOG-NIZE IT?
THAT'S RIGHT WHERE YOU FELL OUT OF THE SKY FIVE YEARS AGO.

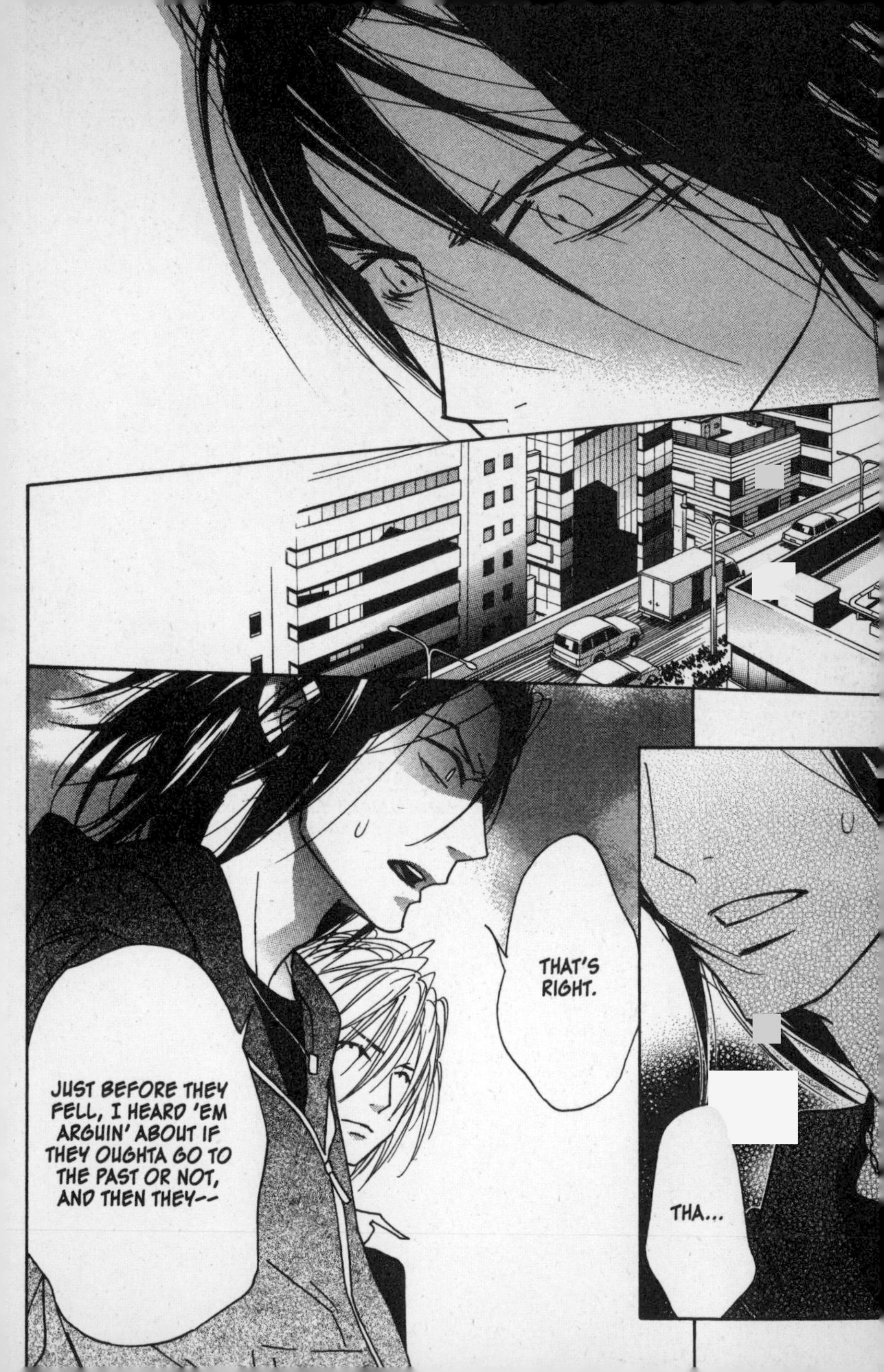
JUST BEFORE THEY FELL, I HEARD 'EM ARGUIN' ABOUT IF THEY OUGHTA GO TO THE PAST OR NOT, AND THEN THEY--
THAT'S RIGHT.
THA...

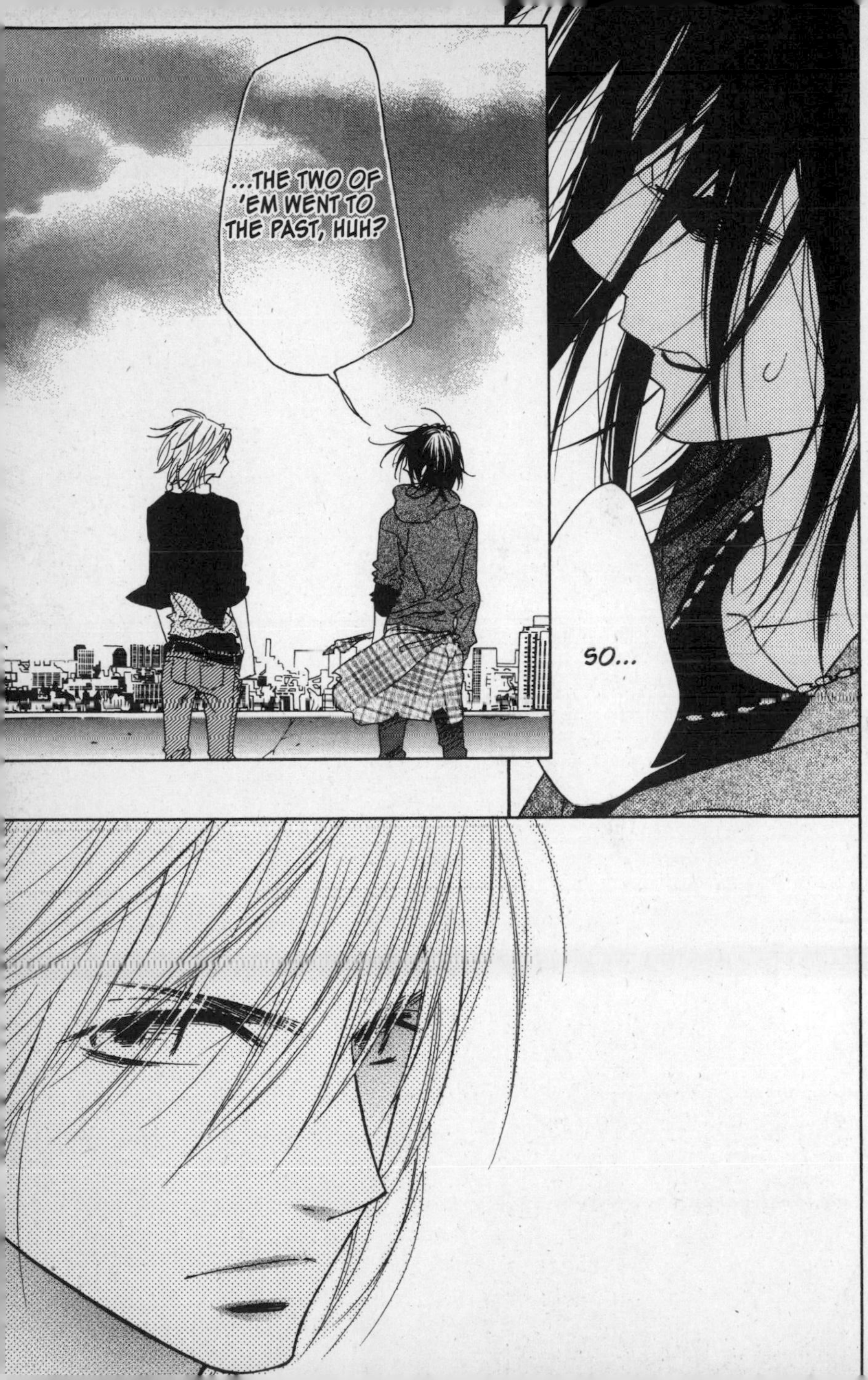
SO...
...THE TWO OF 'EM WENT TO THE PAST, HUH?

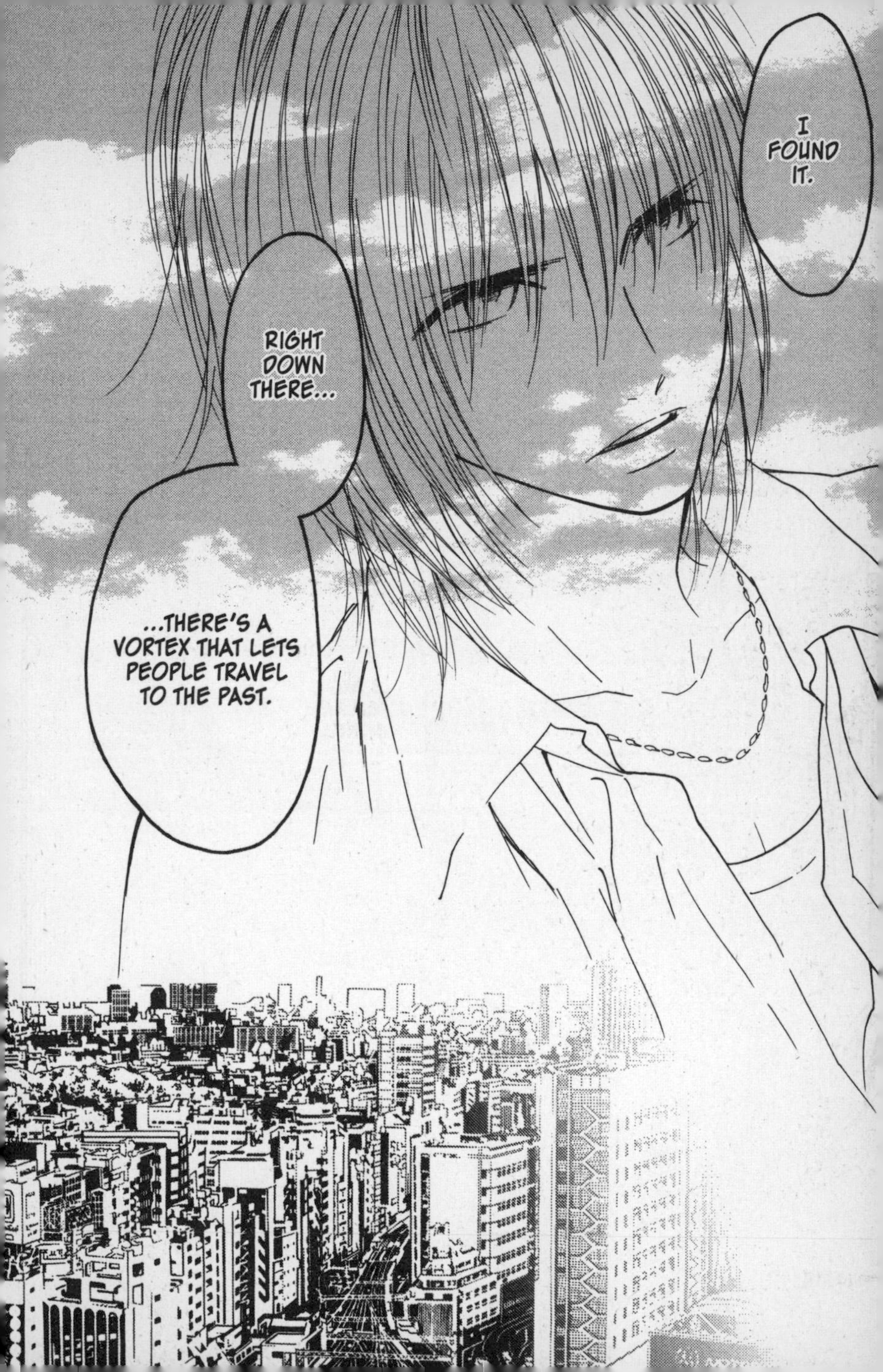
I FOUND IT.
RIGHT DOWN THERE...
...THERE'S A VORTEX THAT LETS PEOPLE TRAVEL TO THE PAST.

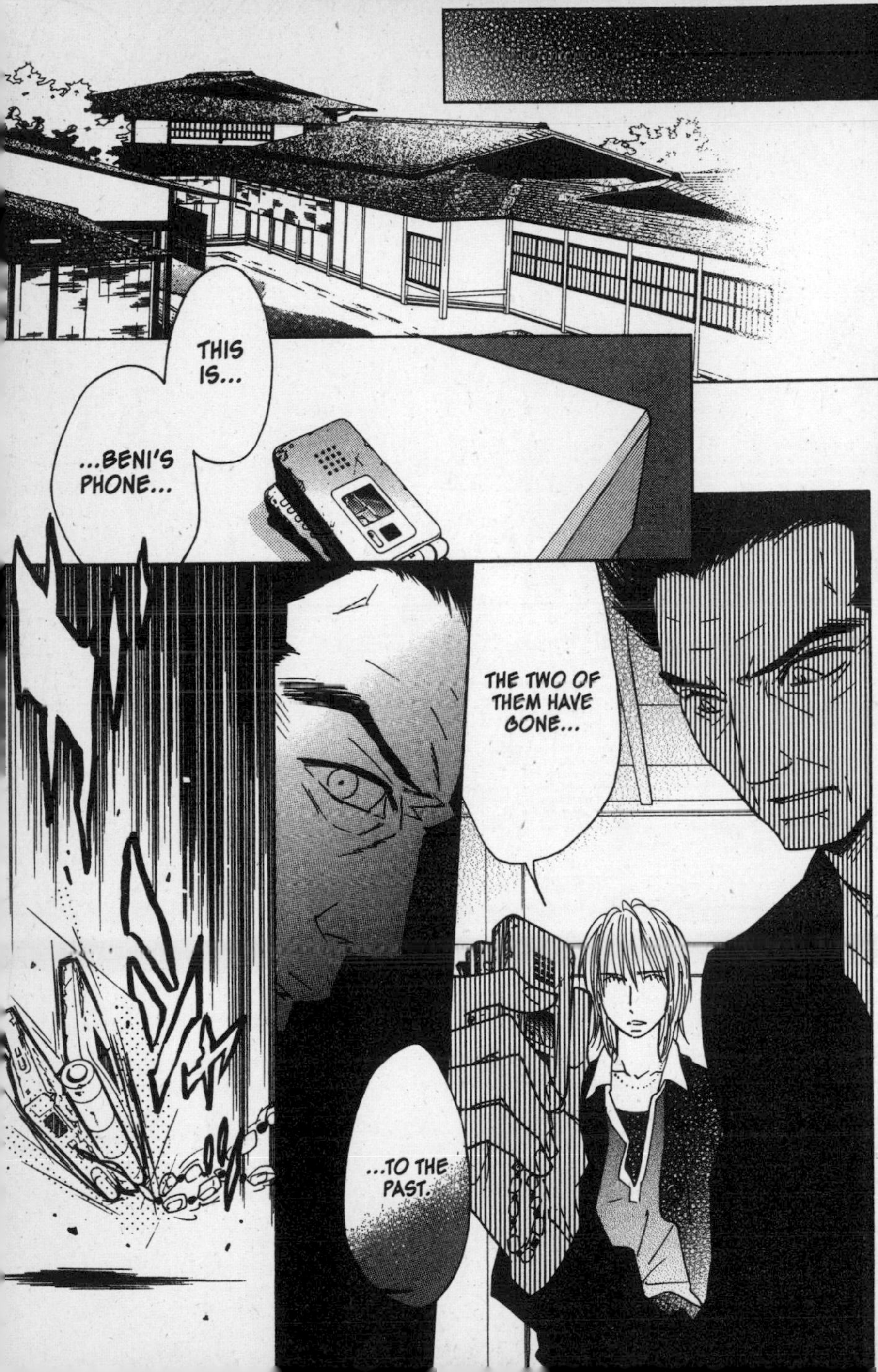
THIS IS...
...BENI'S PHONE...
THE TWO OF THEM HAVE GONE...
...TO THE PAST.

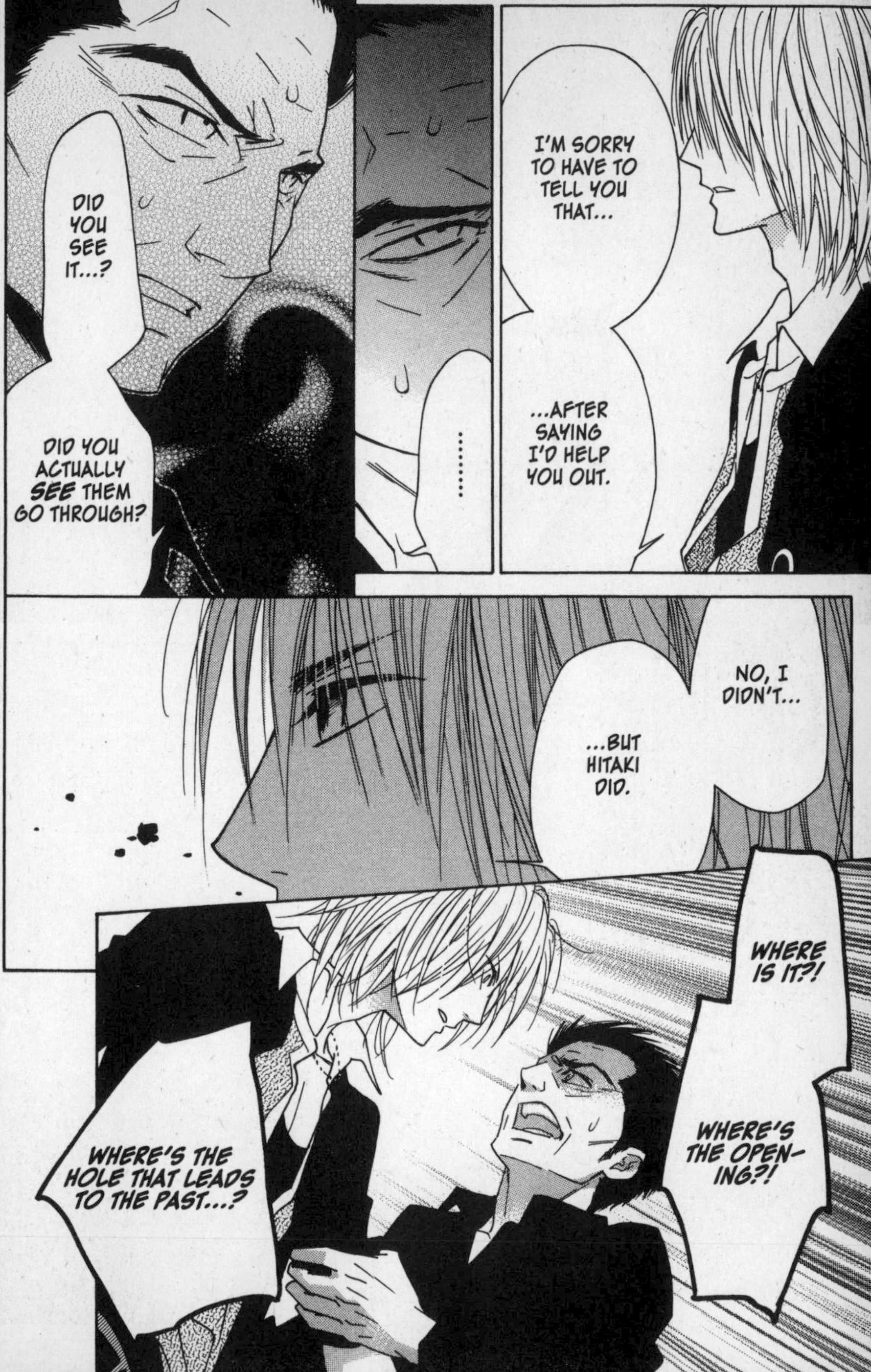
I'M SORRY TO HAVE TO TELL YOU THAT...
...AFTER SAYING I'D HELP YOU OUT.
......
DID YOU SEE IT...?
DID YOU ACTUALLY SEE THEM GO THROUGH?
NO, I DIDN'T...
...BUT HITAKI DID.
WHERE IS IT?!
WHERE'S THE OPENING?!
WHERE'S THE HOLE THAT LEADS TO THE PAST...?

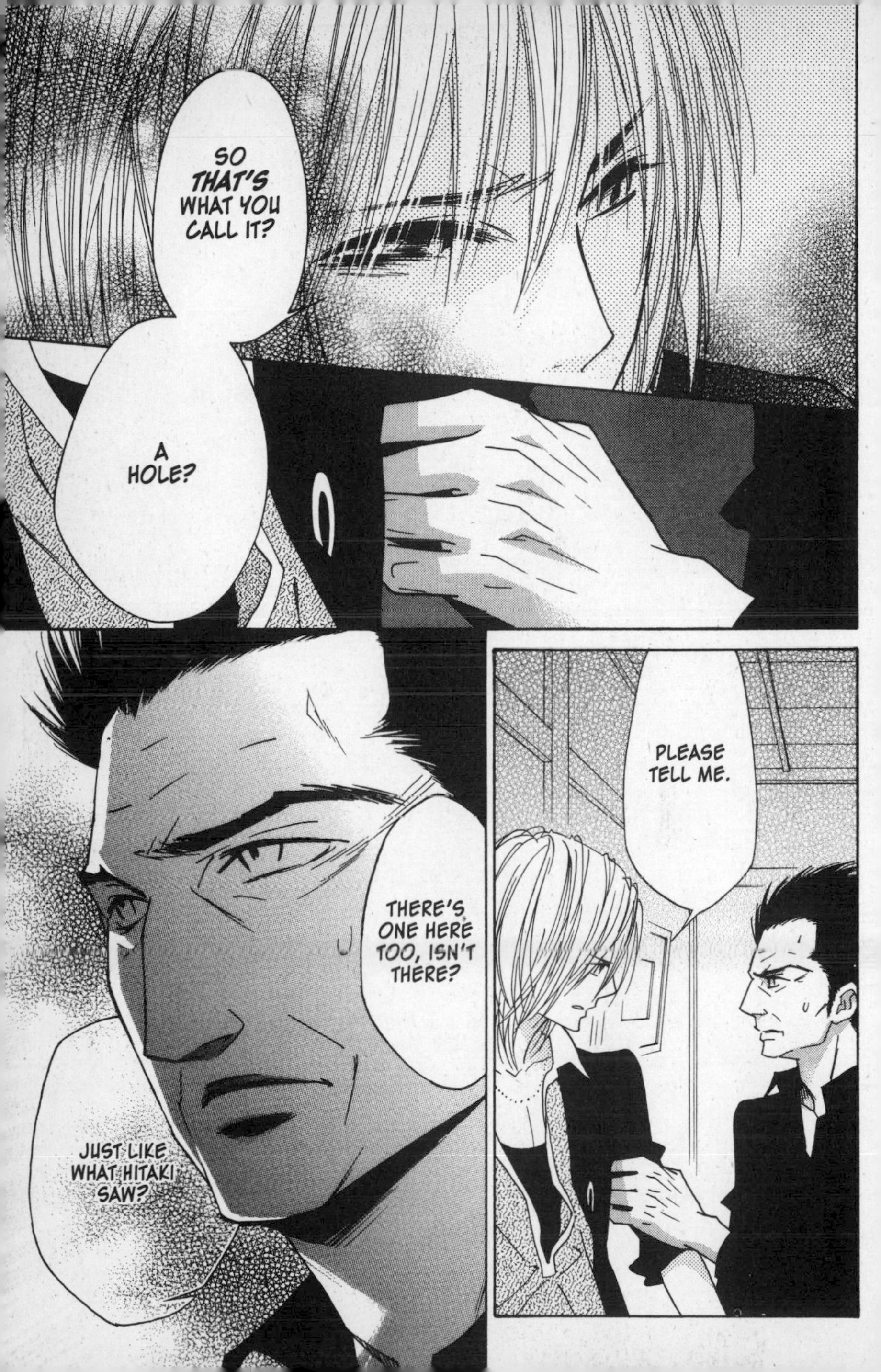
SO THAT'S WHAT YOU CALL IT?
A HOLE?
PLEASE TELL ME.
THERE'S ONE HERE TOO, ISN'T THERE?
JUST LIKE WHAT HITAKI SAW?

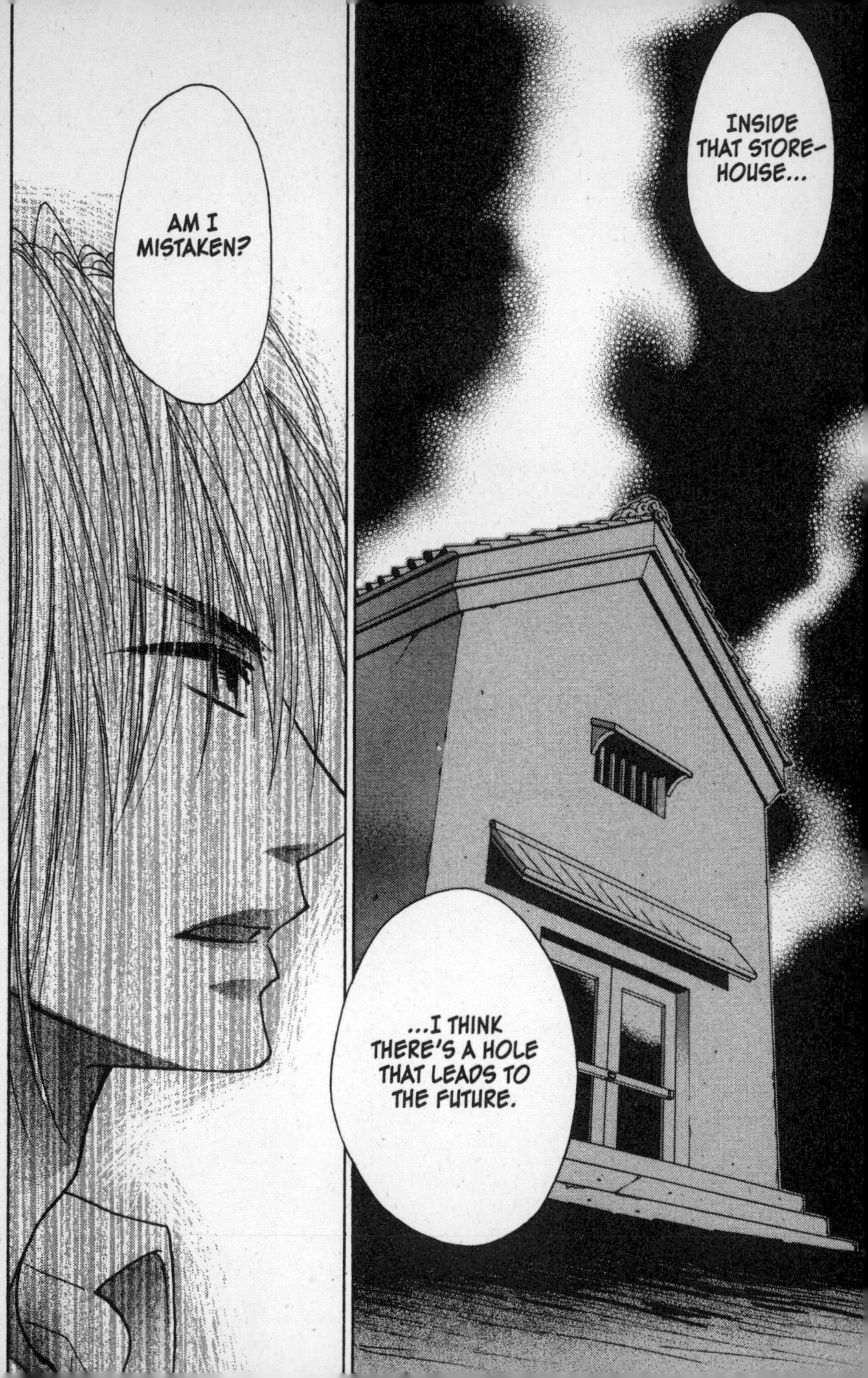
INSIDE THAT STORE-HOUSE...
...I THINK THERE'S A HOLE THAT LEADS TO THE FUTURE.
AM I MISTAKEN?

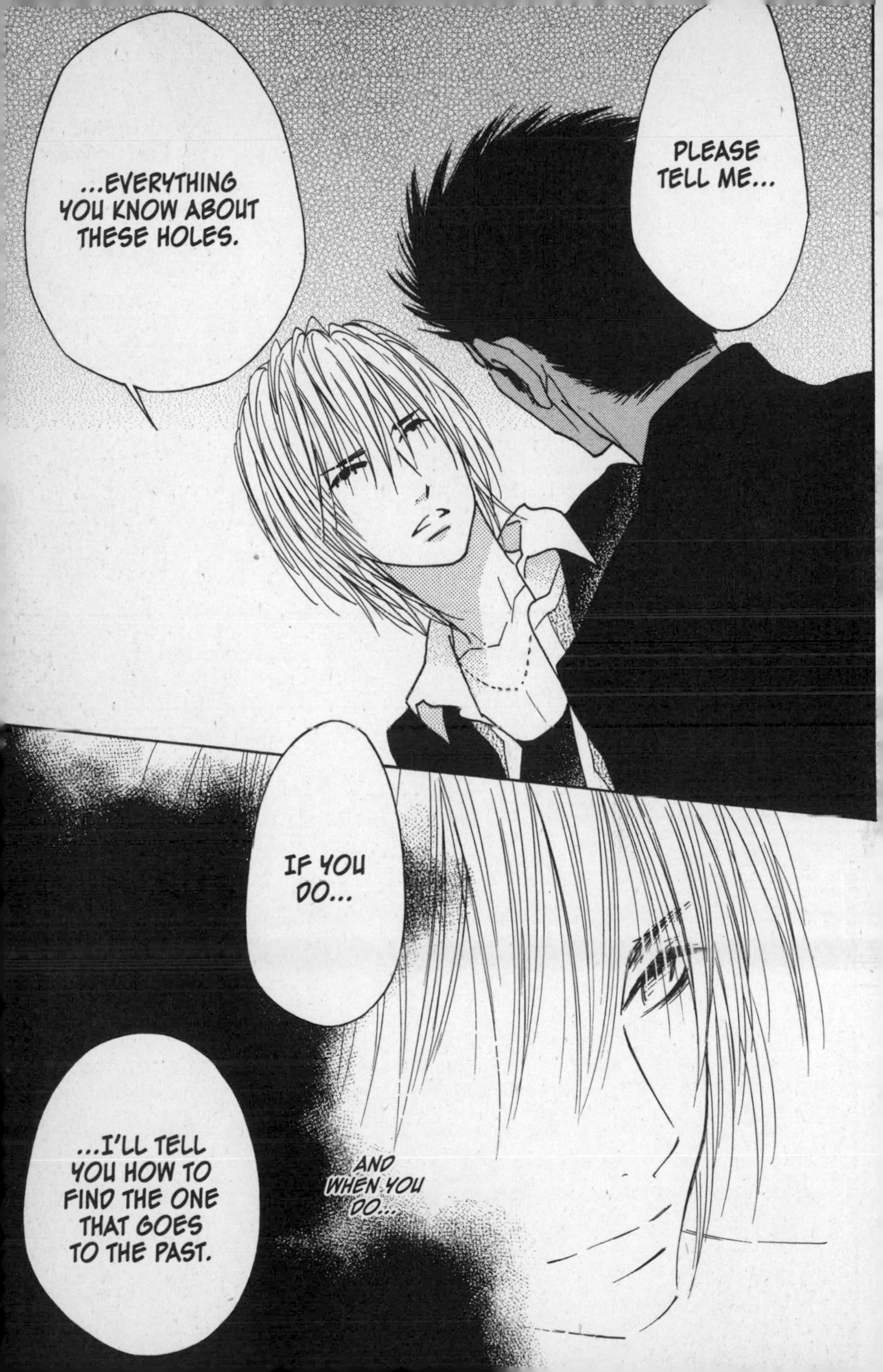
PLEASE TELL ME...
...EVERYTHING YOU KNOW ABOUT THESE HOLES.
IF YOU DO...
AND WHEN YOU DO...
...I'LL TELL YOU HOW TO FIND THE ONE THAT GOES TO THE PAST.

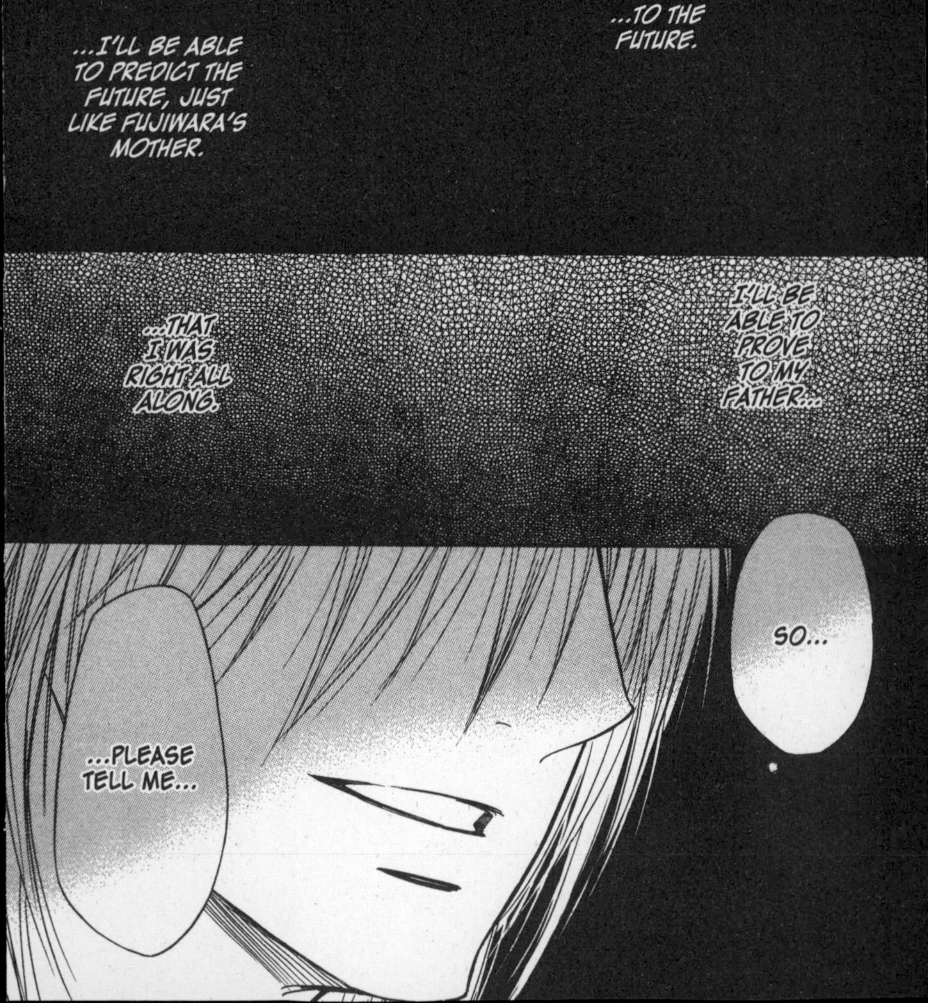
...TO THE FUTURE.
...I'LL BE ABLE TO PREDICT THE FUTURE, JUST LIKE FUJIWARA'S MOTHER.
I'LL BE ABLE TO PROVE TO MY FATHER...
...THAT I WAS RIGHT ALL ALONG.
SO...
...PLEASE TELL ME...

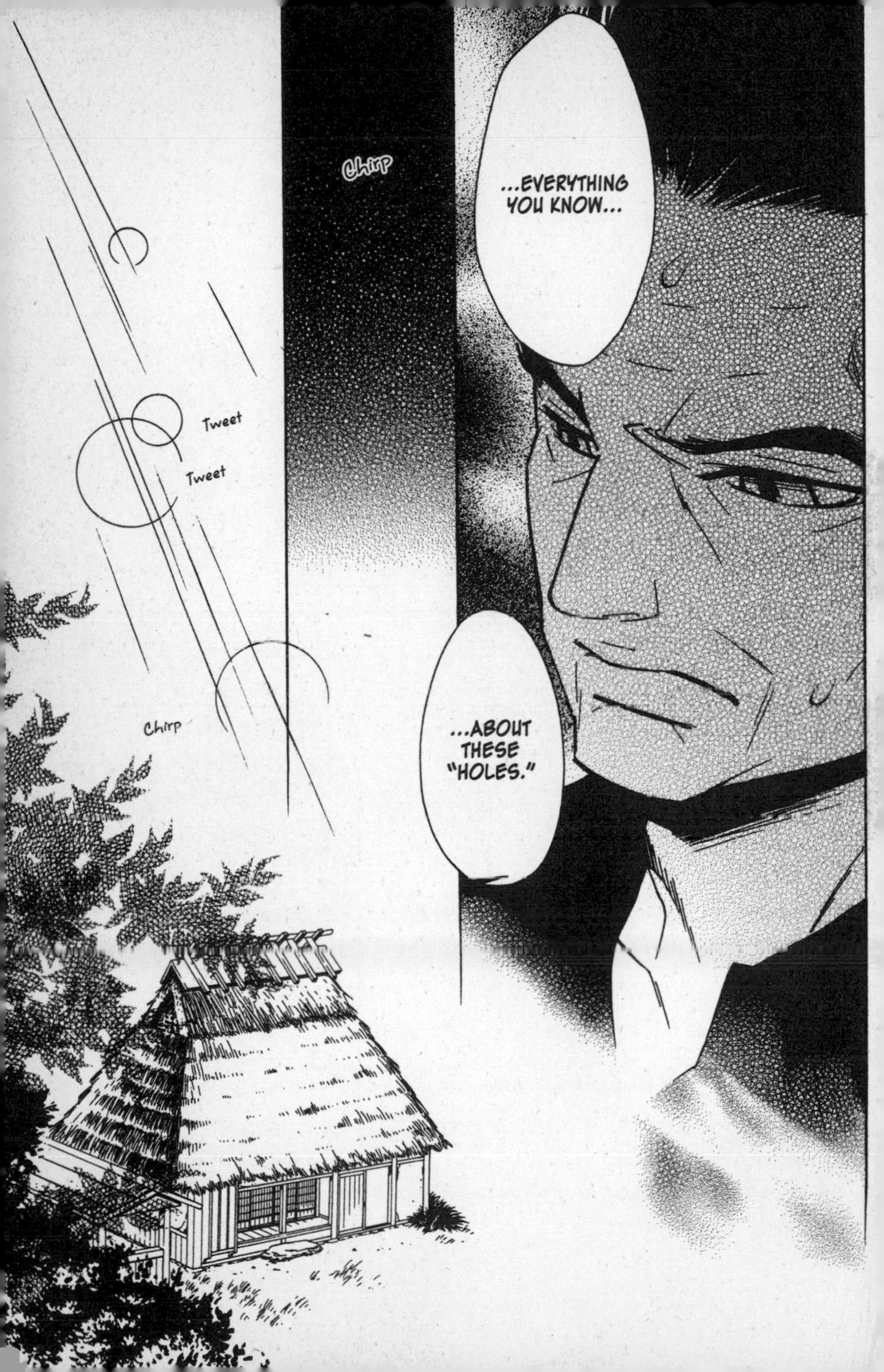
...EVERYTHING YOU KNOW...
...ABOUT THESE "HOLES."
Chirp
Tweet
Tweet
Chirp

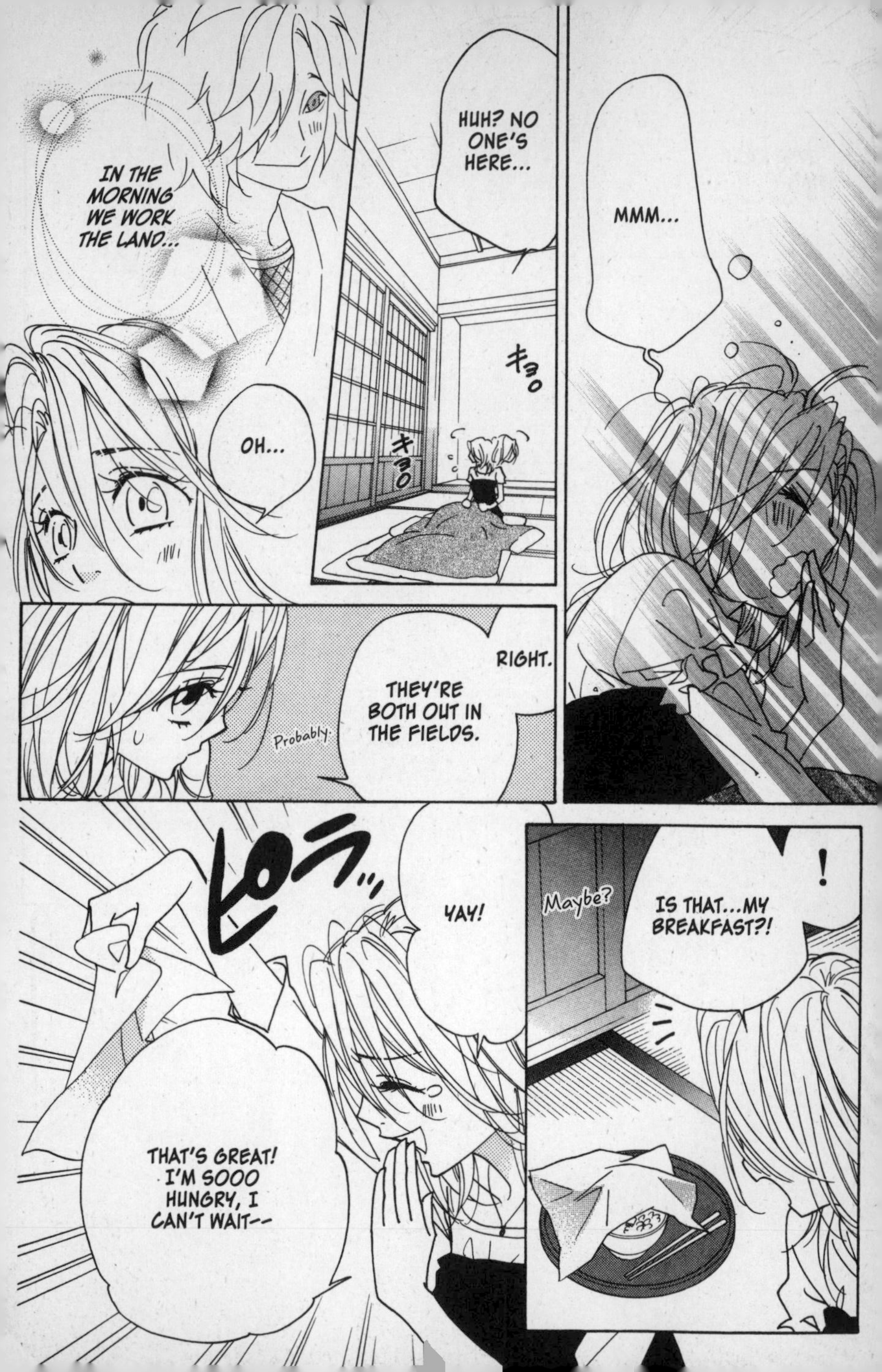
MMM...
HUH? NO ONE'S HERE...
キョロ
キョロ
IN THE MORNING WE WORK THE LAND...
OH...
RIGHT.
THEY'RE BOTH OUT IN THE FIELDS.
Probably.
!
IS THAT...MY BREAKFAST?!
Maybe?
YAY!
THAT'S GREAT! I'M SOOO HUNGRY, I CAN'T WAIT--

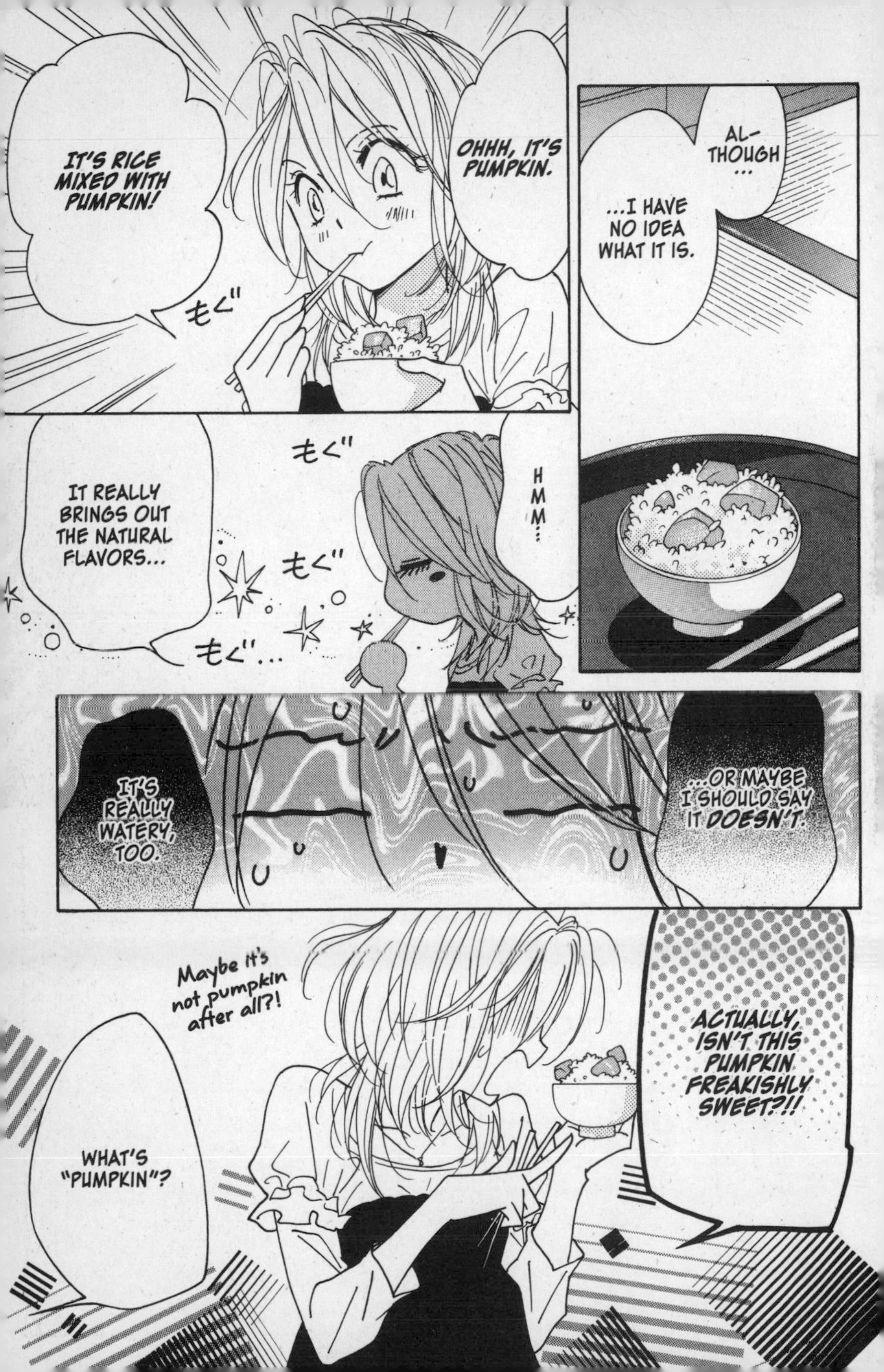
OHHH, IT'S PUMPKIN.
IT'S RICE MIXED WITH PUMPKIN!
もぐ"
AL-THOUGH ...
...I HAVE NO IDEA WHAT IT IS.
HMM...
もぐ"
もぐ"
もぐ"...
IT REALLY BRINGS OUT THE NATURAL FLAVORS...
...OR MAYBE I SHOULD SAY IT DOESN'T.
IT'S REALLY WATERY, TOO.
ACTUALLY, ISN'T THIS PUMPKIN FREAKISHLY SWEET?!!
Maybe it's not pumpkin after all?!
WHAT'S "PUMPKIN"?

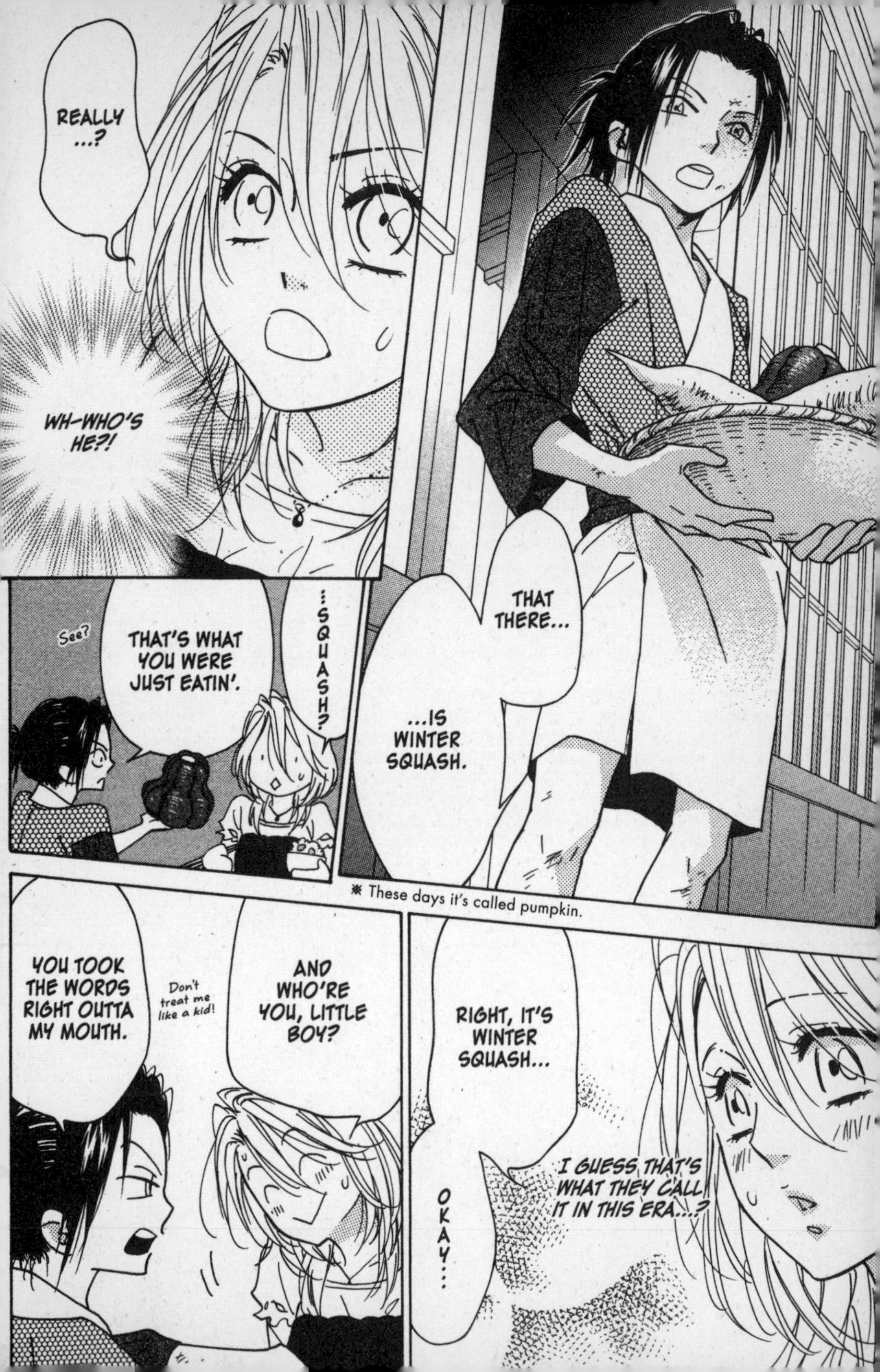
THAT THERE...
...IS WINTER SQUASH.
REALLY ...?
WH-WHO'S HE?!
...SQUASH?
THAT'S WHAT YOU WERE JUST EATIN'.
See?
RIGHT, IT'S WINTER SQUASH...
OKAY...
I GUESS THAT'S WHAT THEY CALL IT IN THIS ERA...?
AND WHO'RE YOU, LITTLE BOY?
Don't treat me like a kid!
YOU TOOK THE WORDS RIGHT OUTTA MY MOUTH.

※ These days it's called pumpkin.

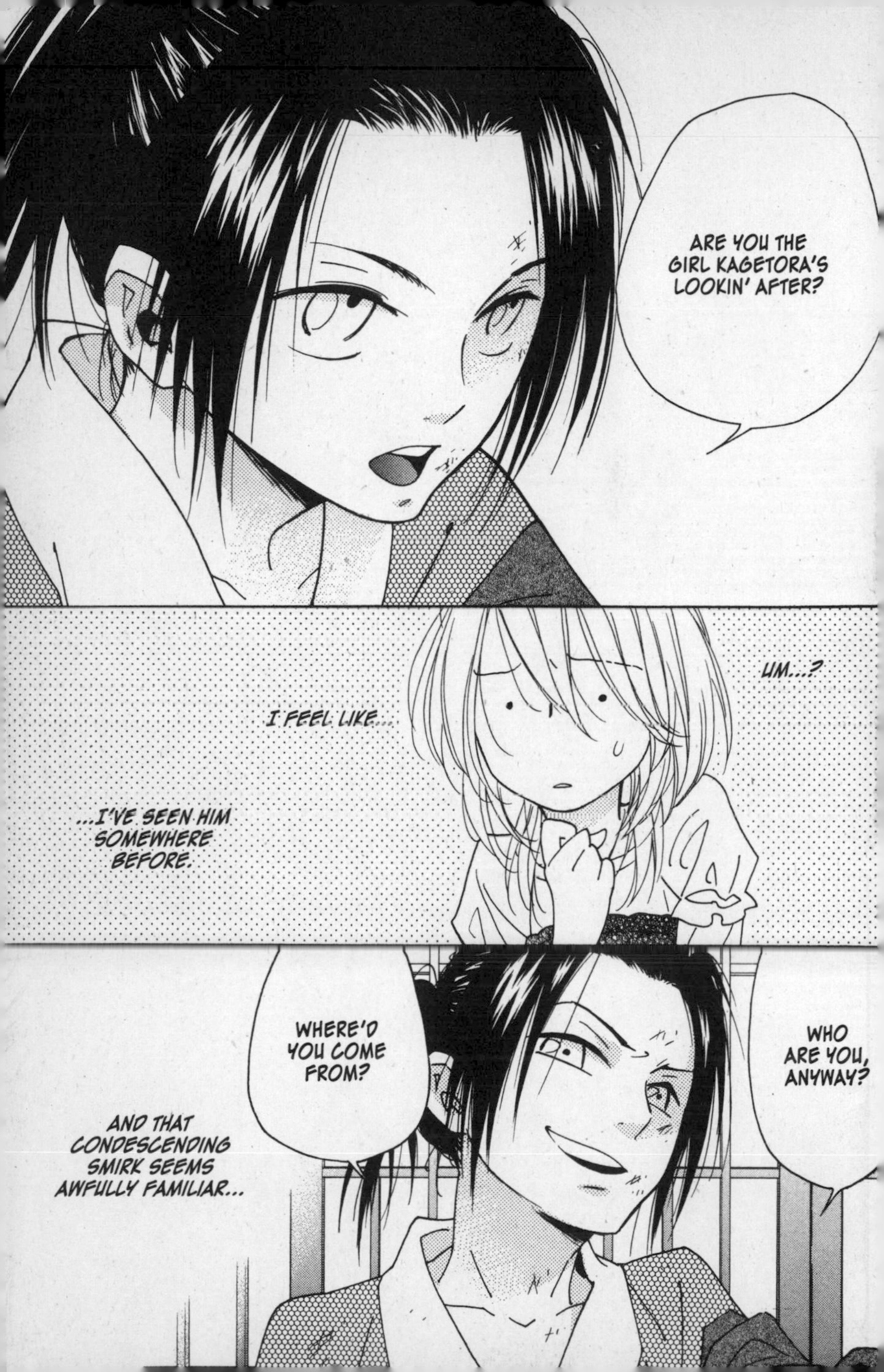
ARE YOU THE GIRL KAGETORA'S LOOKIN' AFTER?
UM...?
I FEEL LIKE...
...I'VE SEEN HIM SOMEWHERE BEFORE.
WHO ARE YOU, ANYWAY?
WHERE'D YOU COME FROM?
AND THAT CONDESCENDING SMIRK SEEMS AWFULLY FAMILIAR...

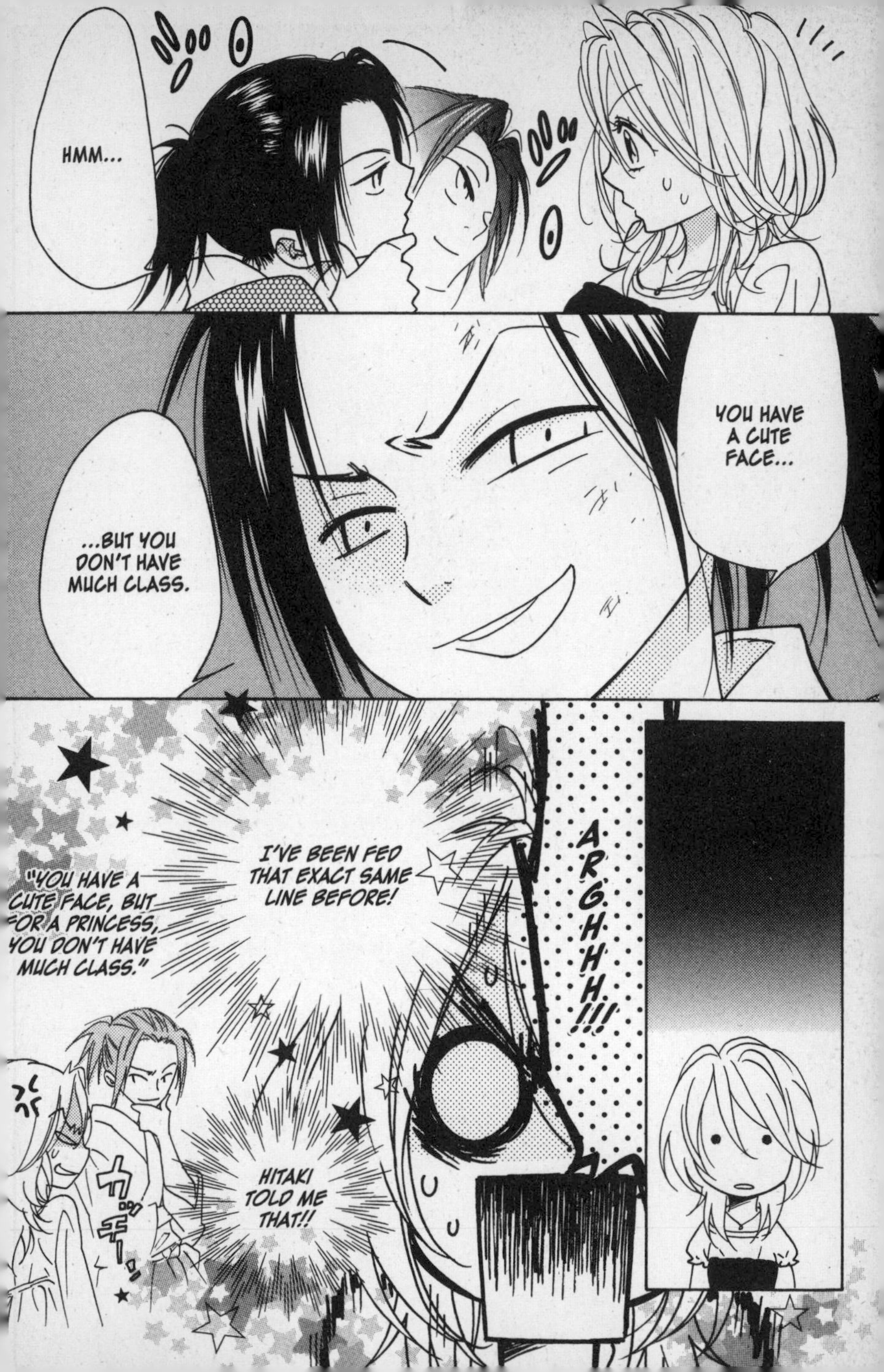
HMM...
YOU HAVE A CUTE FACE...
...BUT YOU DON'T HAVE MUCH CLASS.
ARGHHH!!!
I'VE BEEN FED THAT EXACT SAME LINE BEFORE!
"YOU HAVE A CUTE FACE, BUT FOR A PRINCESS, YOU DON'T HAVE MUCH CLASS."
HITAKI TOLD ME THAT!!

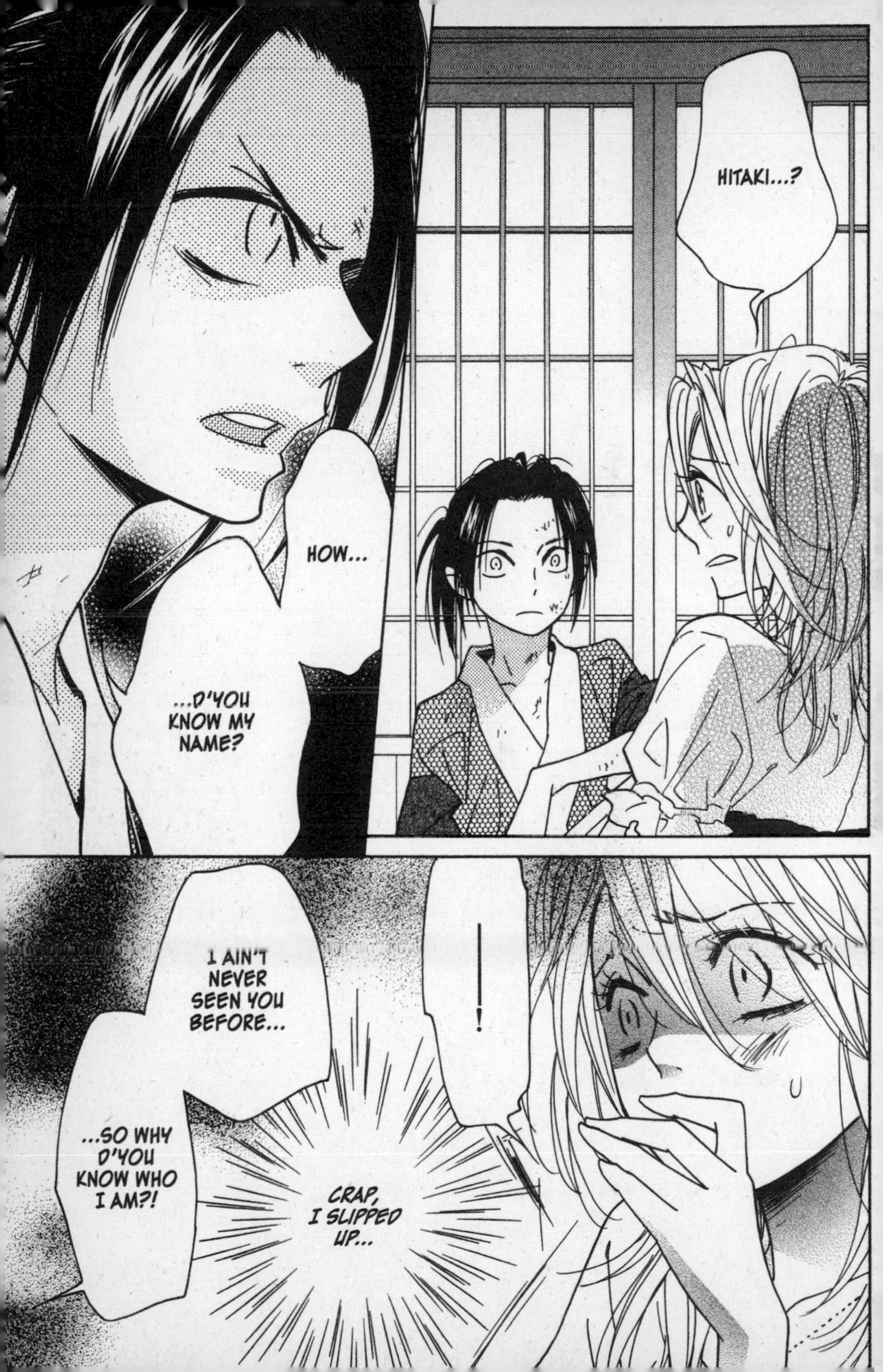
HITAKI...?
HOW...
...D'YOU KNOW MY NAME?
!
I AIN'T NEVER SEEN YOU BEFORE...
...SO WHY D'YOU KNOW WHO I AM?!
CRAP, I SLIPPED UP...

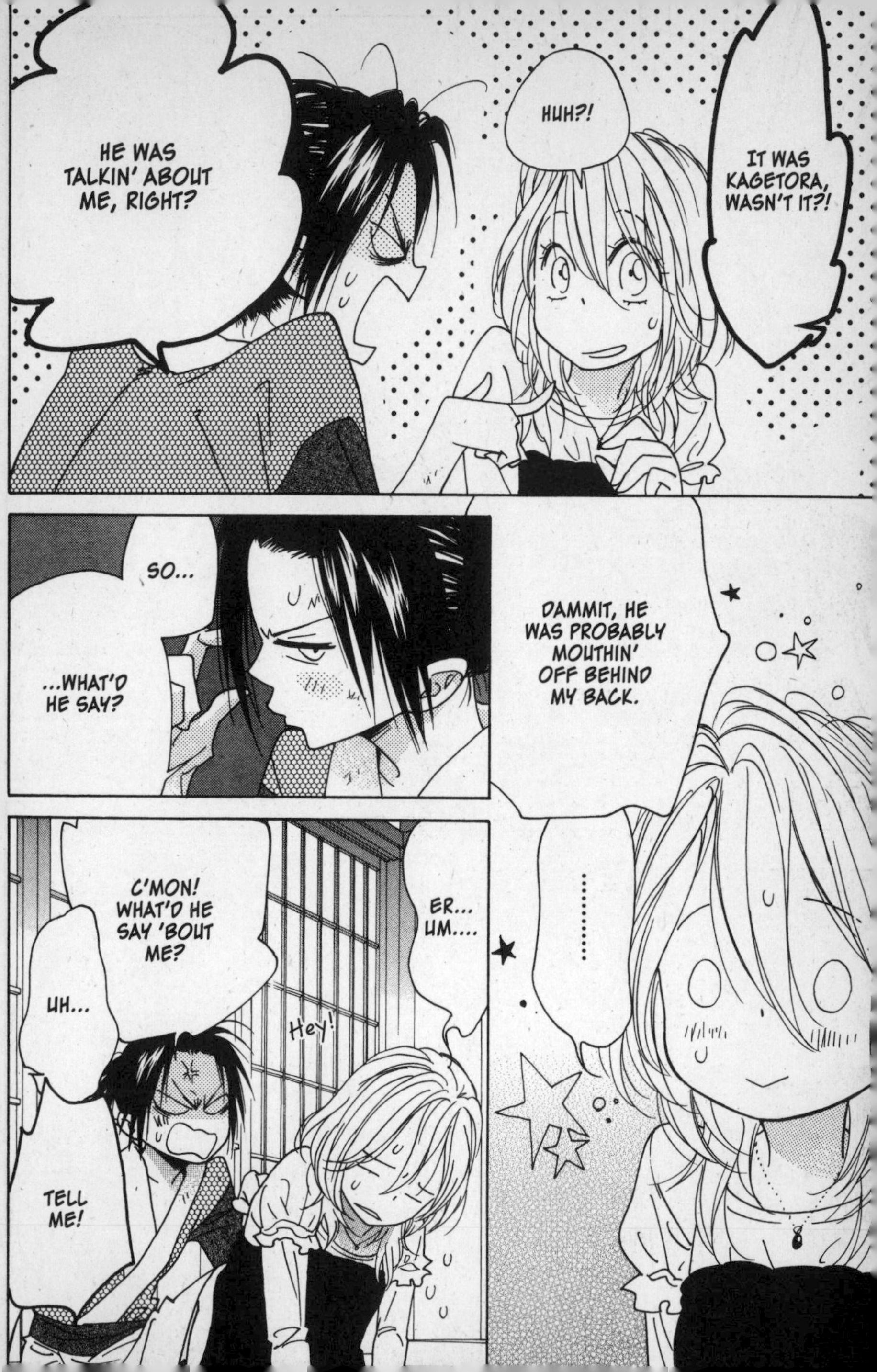
IT WAS KAGETORA, WASN'T IT?!
HUH?!
HE WAS TALKIN' ABOUT ME, RIGHT?
DAMMIT, HE WAS PROBABLY MOUTHIN' OFF BEHIND MY BACK.
SO...
...WHAT'D HE SAY?
......
ER... UM....
C'MON! WHAT'D HE SAY 'BOUT ME?
Hey!
UH...
TELL ME!

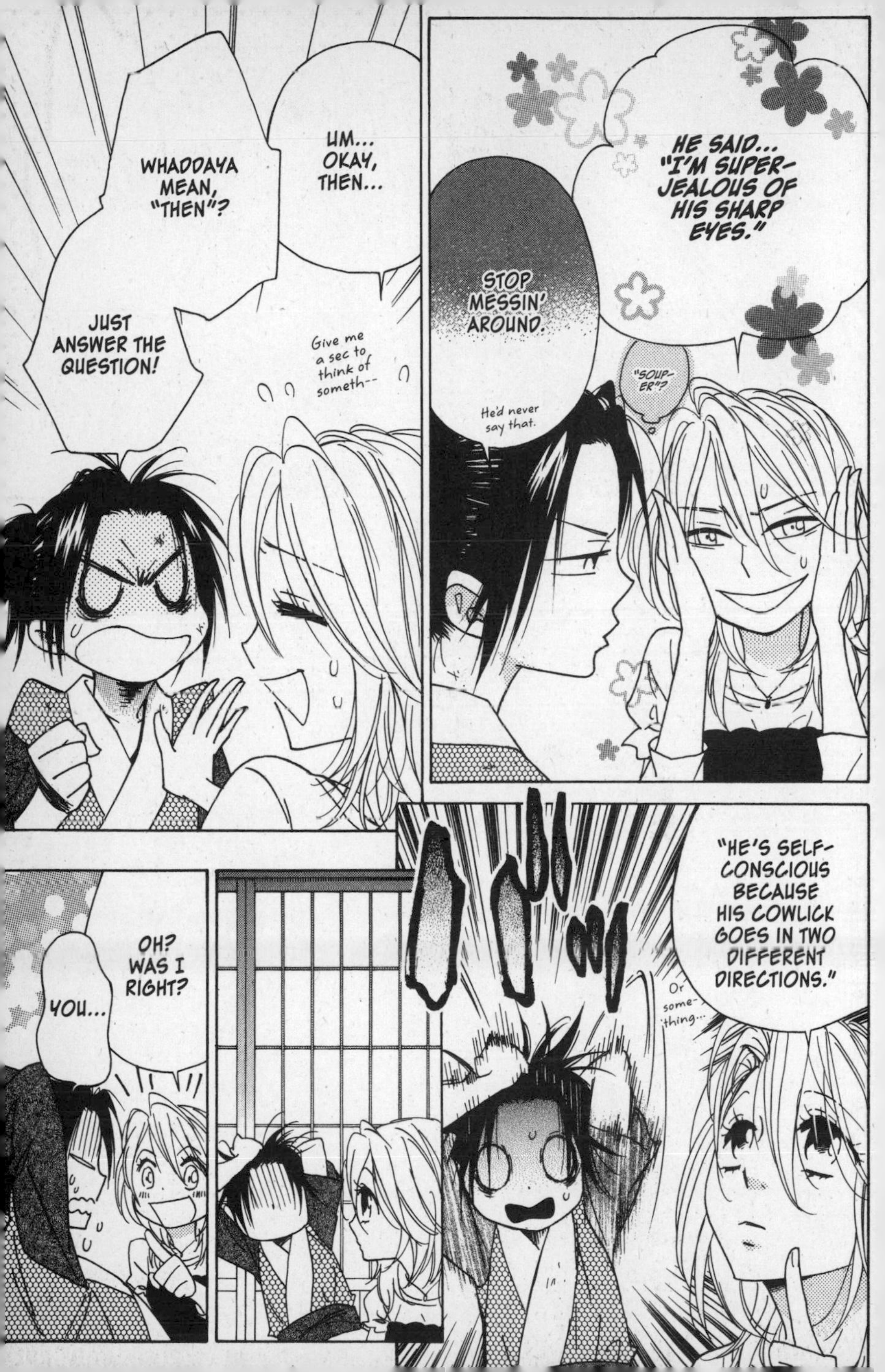
HE SAID... "I'M SUPER-JEALOUS OF HIS SHARP EYES."
STOP MESSIN' AROUND.
He'd never say that.
"SOUP-ER"?
UM... OKAY, THEN...
Give me a sec to think of someth--
WHADDAYA MEAN, "THEN"?
JUST ANSWER THE QUESTION!
"HE'S SELF-CONSCIOUS BECAUSE HIS COWLICK GOES IN TWO DIFFERENT DIRECTIONS."
Or some-thing...
OH? WAS I RIGHT?
YOU...

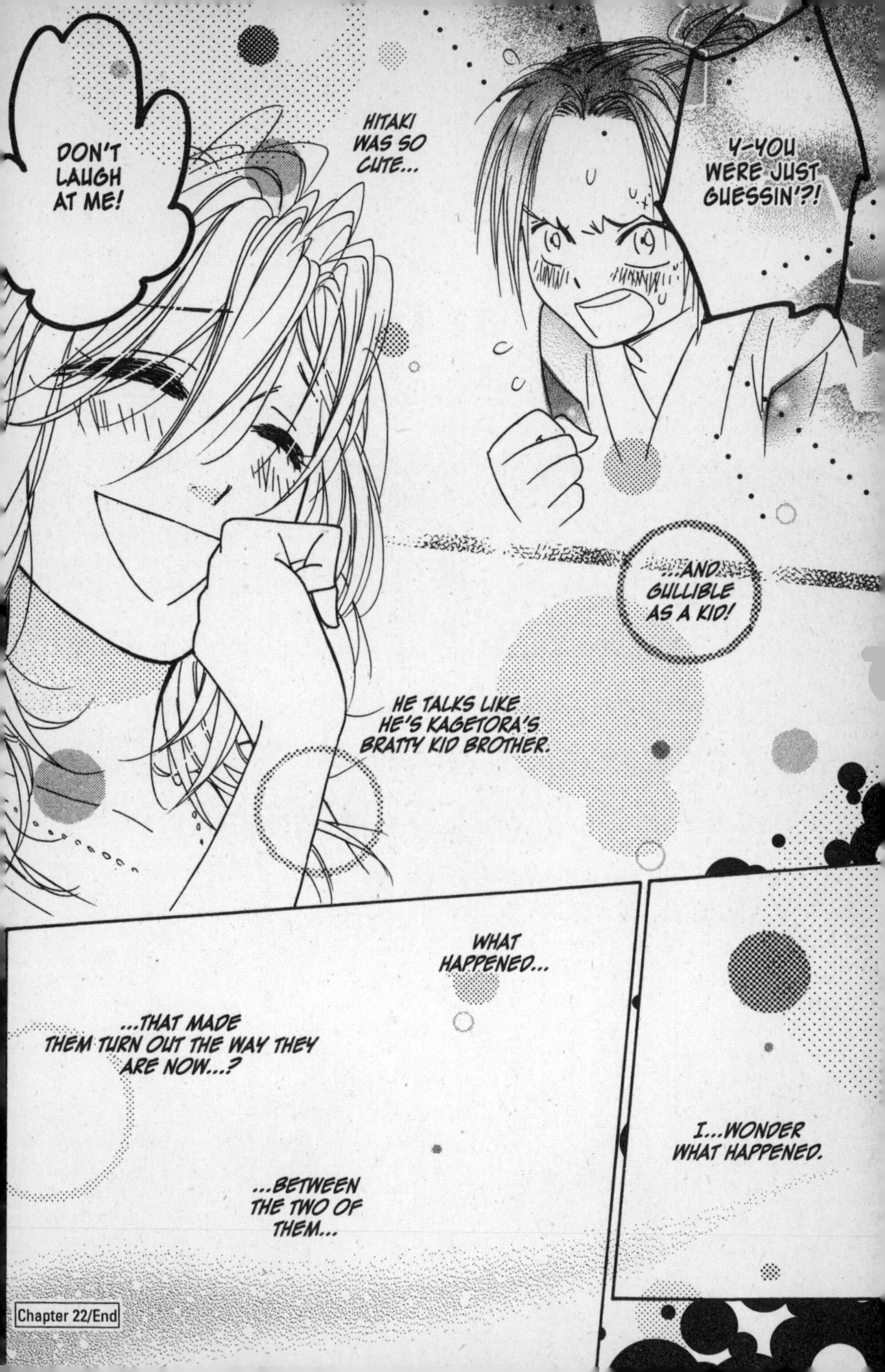

Y-YOU WERE JUST GUESSIN'?!
HITAKI WAS SO CUTE...
DON'T LAUGH AT ME!
...AND GULLIBLE AS A KID!
HE TALKS LIKE HE'S KAGETORA'S BRATTY KID BROTHER.
I...WONDER WHAT HAPPENED.
WHAT HAPPENED...
...THAT MADE THEM TURN OUT THE WAY THEY ARE NOW...?
...BETWEEN THE TWO OF THEM...
Chapter 22/End

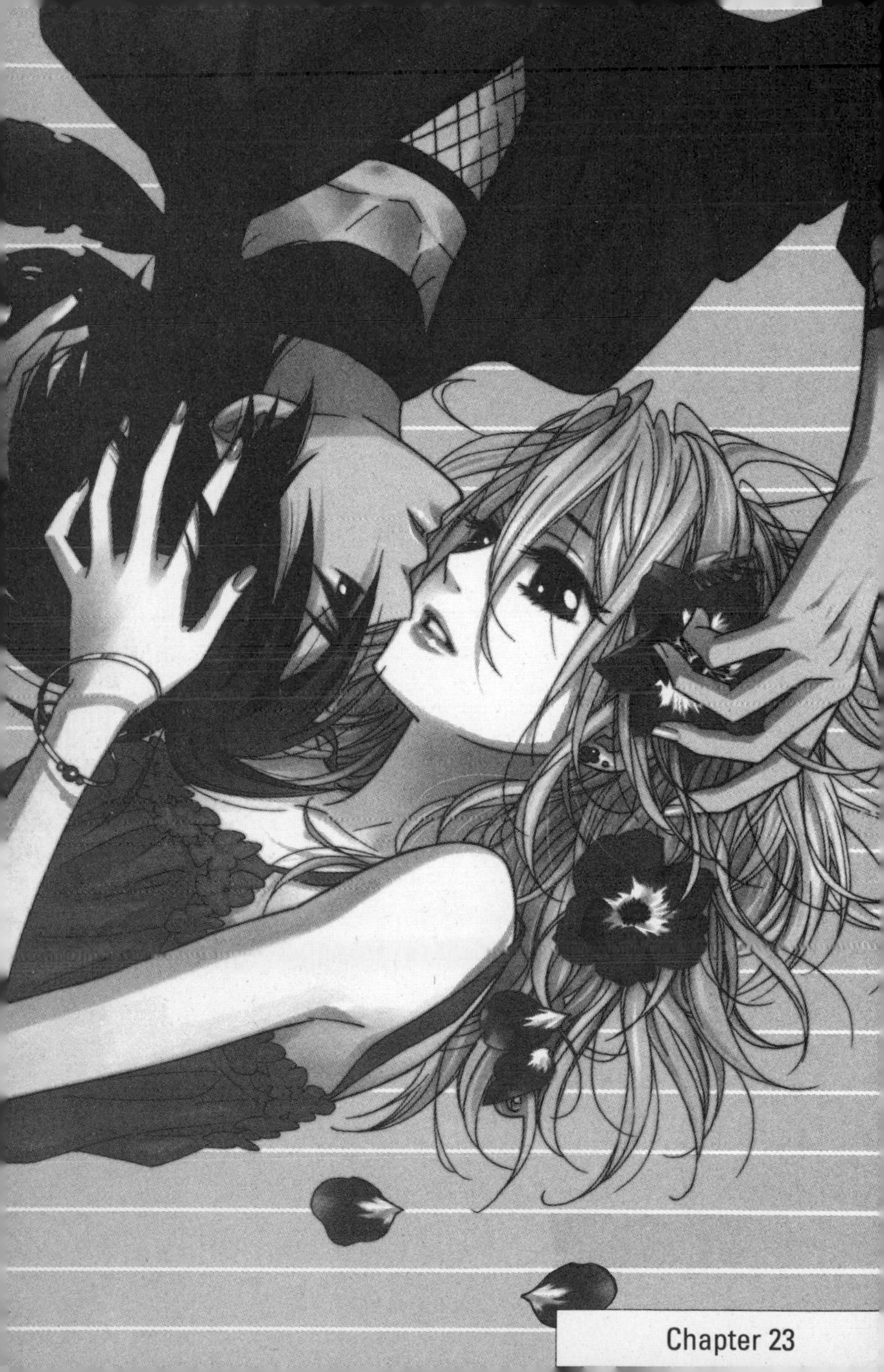

Chapter 23

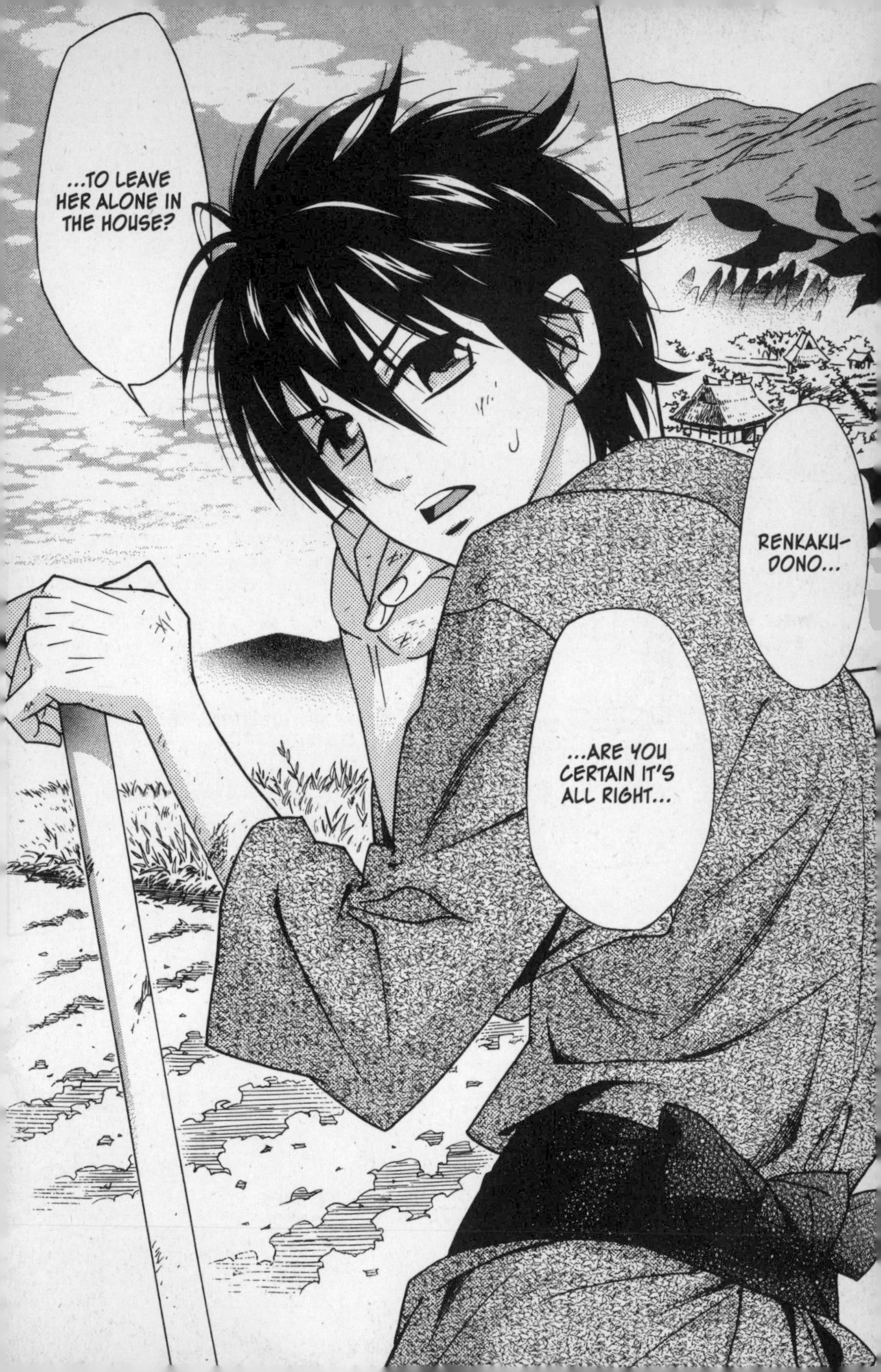
RENKAKU-DONO...
...ARE YOU CERTAIN IT'S ALL RIGHT...
...TO LEAVE HER ALONE IN THE HOUSE?

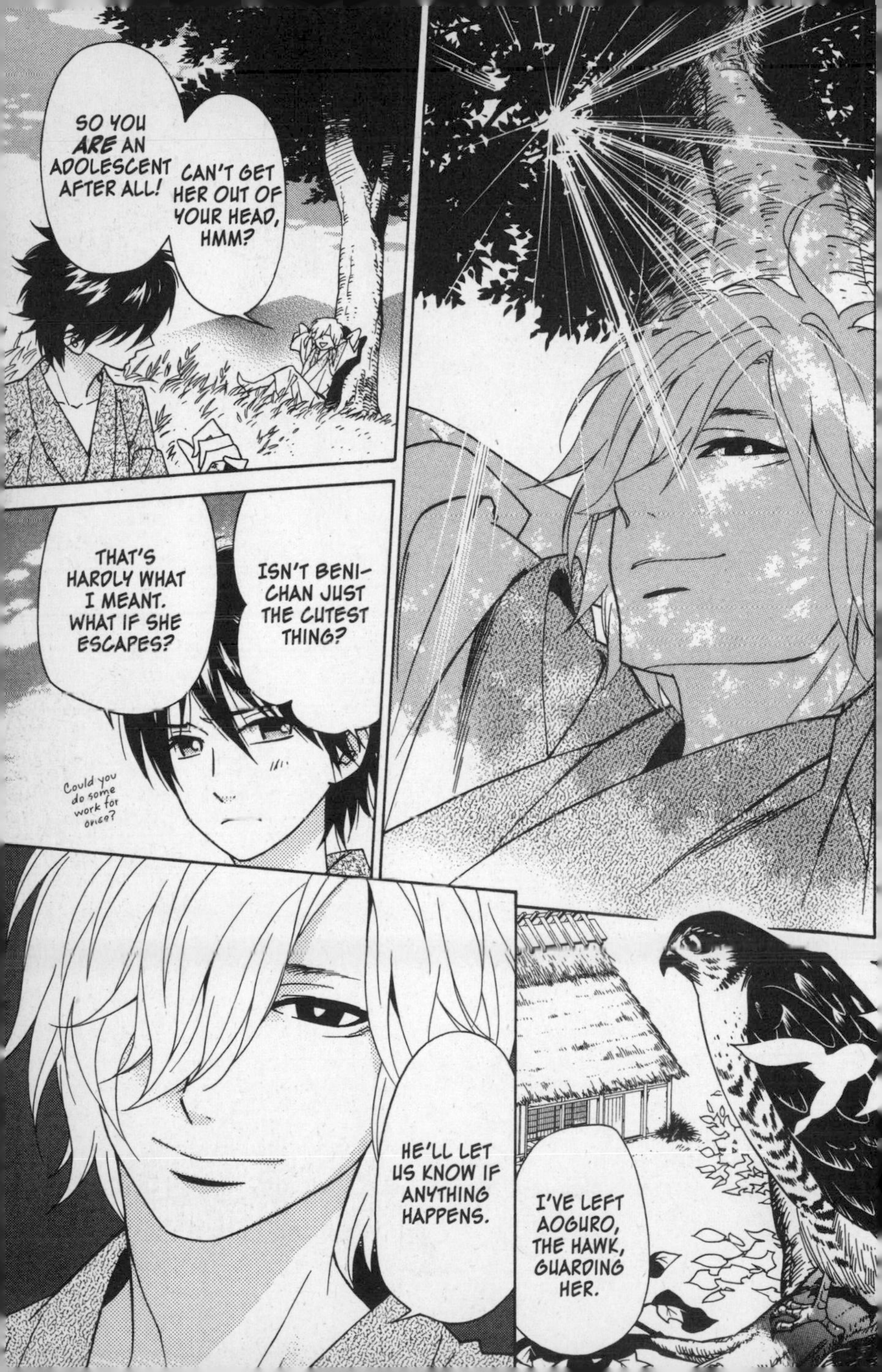
CAN'T GET HER OUT OF YOUR HEAD, HMM?
SO YOU ARE AN ADOLESCENT AFTER ALL!
ISN'T BENI-CHAN JUST THE CUTEST THING?
THAT'S HARDLY WHAT I MEANT. WHAT IF SHE ESCAPES?
Could you do some work for once?
I'VE LEFT AOGURO, THE HAWK, GUARDING HER.
HE'LL LET US KNOW IF ANYTHING HAPPENS.

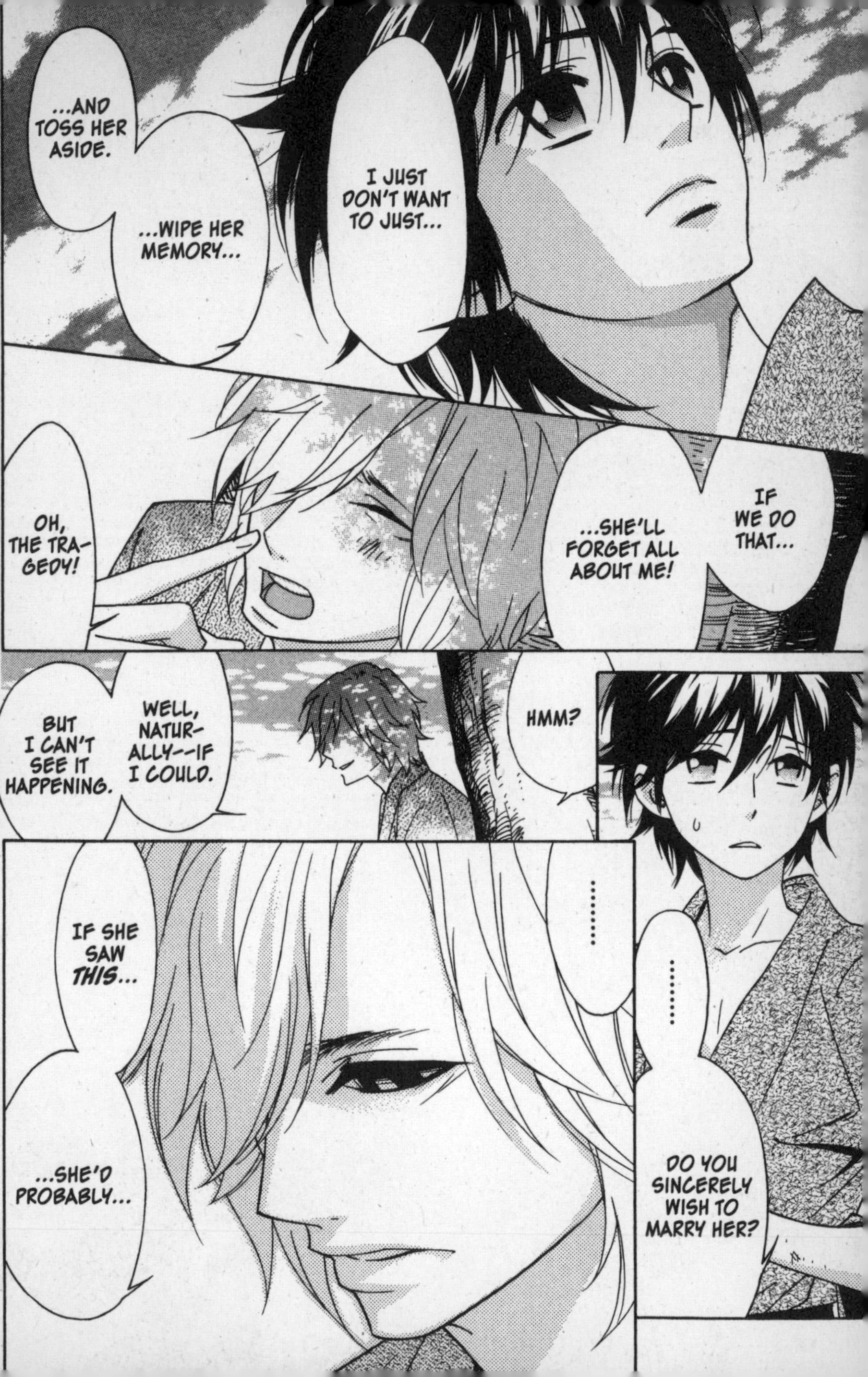
I JUST DON'T WANT TO JUST...
...WIPE HER MEMORY...
...AND TOSS HER ASIDE.
IF WE DO THAT...
...SHE'LL FORGET ALL ABOUT ME!
OH, THE TRA-GEDY!
HMM?
DO YOU SINCERELY WISH TO MARRY HER?
WELL, NATUR-ALLY--IF I COULD.
BUT I CAN'T SEE IT HAPPENING.
......
......
IF SHE SAW *THIS*...
...SHE'D PROBABLY...

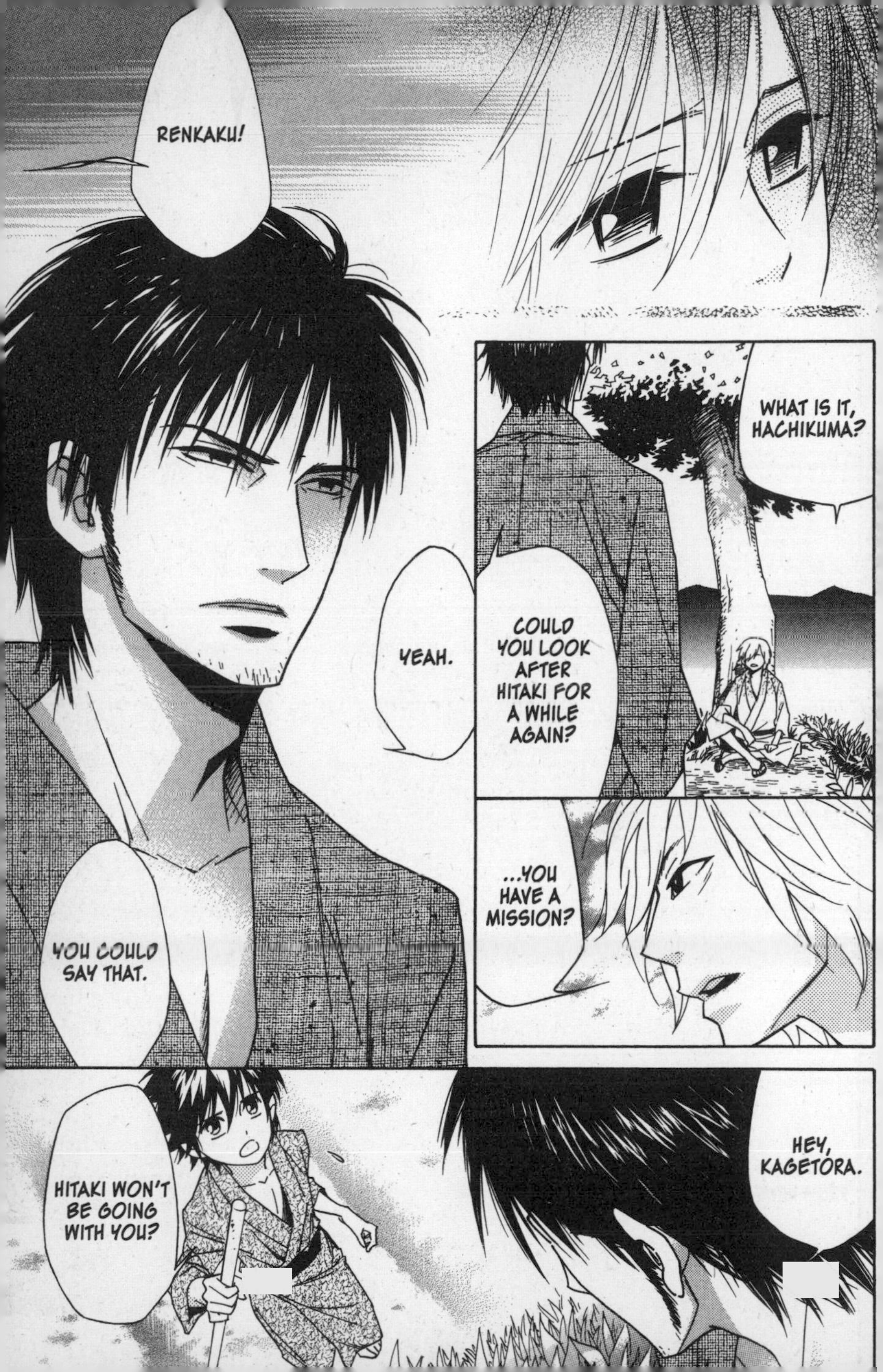
RENKAKU!
WHAT IS IT, HACHIKUMA?
COULD YOU LOOK AFTER HITAKI FOR A WHILE AGAIN?
YEAH.
...YOU HAVE A MISSION?
YOU COULD SAY THAT.
HEY, KAGETORA.
HITAKI WON'T BE GOING WITH YOU?

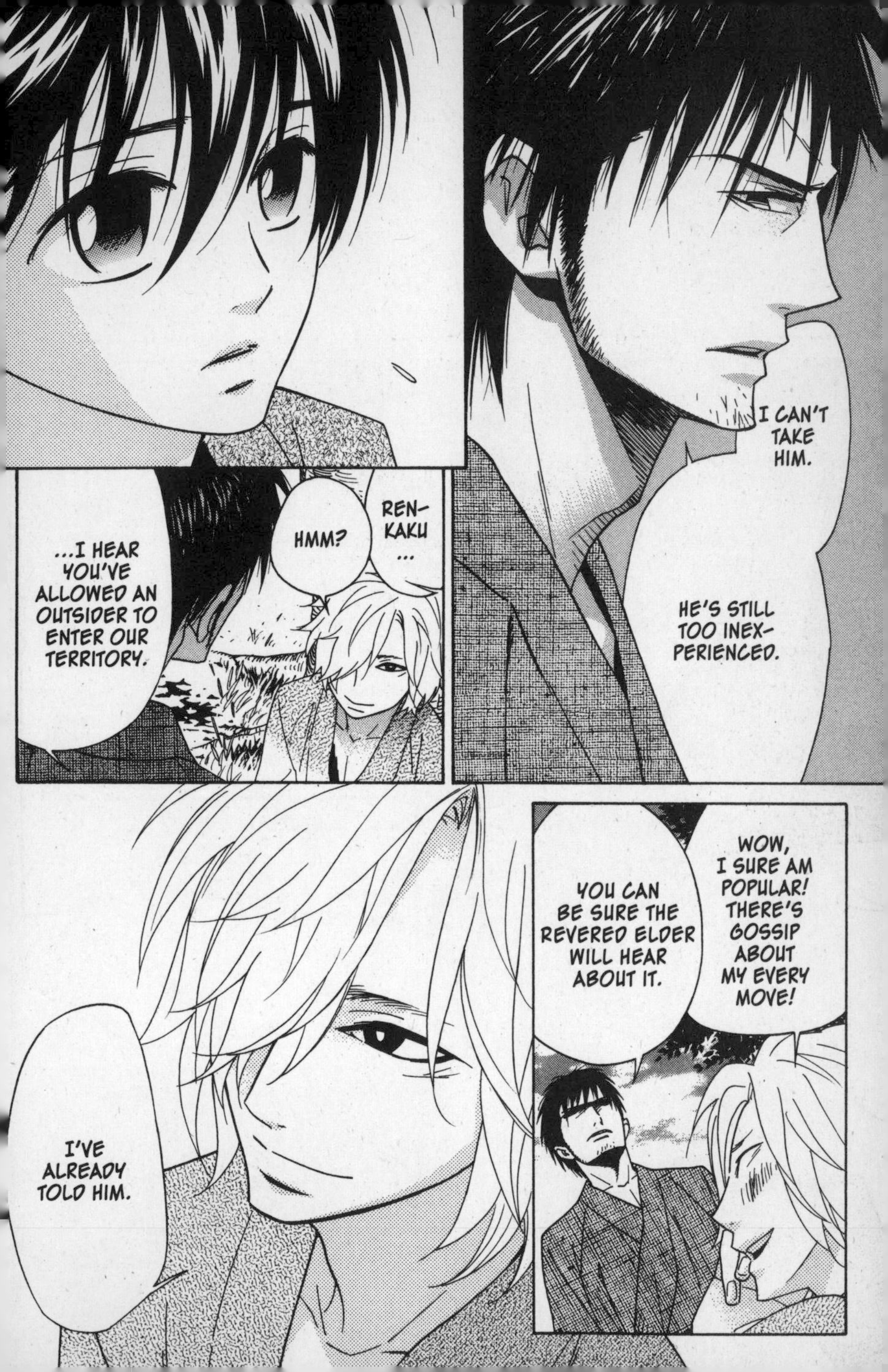
I CAN'T TAKE HIM.
HE'S STILL TOO INEXPERIENCED.
REN-KAKU...
HMM?
...I HEAR YOU'VE ALLOWED AN OUTSIDER TO ENTER OUR TERRITORY.
WOW, I SURE AM POPULAR! THERE'S GOSSIP ABOUT MY EVERY MOVE!
YOU CAN BE SURE THE REVERED ELDER WILL HEAR ABOUT IT.
I'VE ALREADY TOLD HIM.

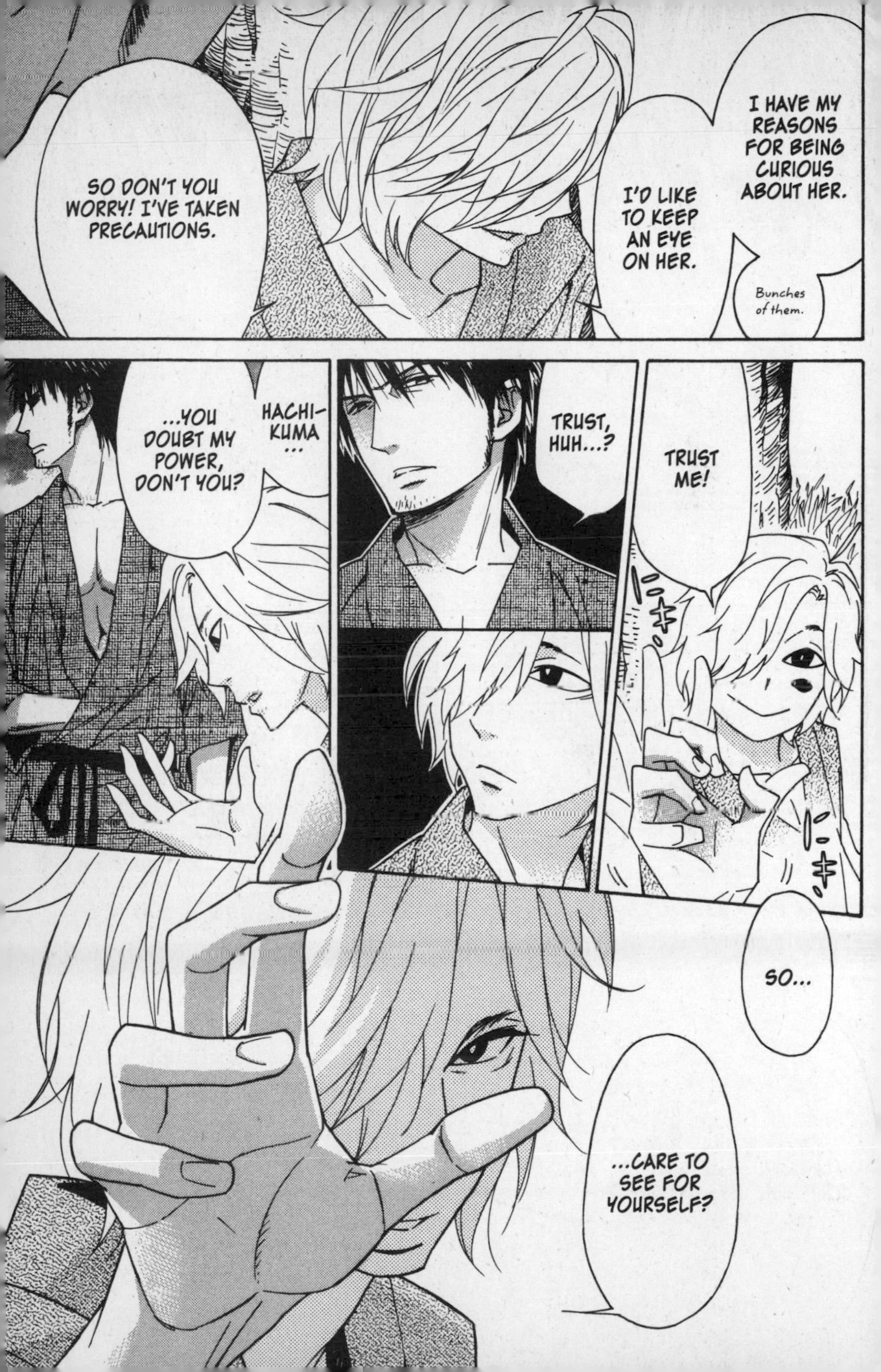
I HAVE MY REASONS FOR BEING CURIOUS ABOUT HER.
Bunches of them.
I'D LIKE TO KEEP AN EYE ON HER.
SO DON'T YOU WORRY! I'VE TAKEN PRECAUTIONS.
TRUST ME!
TRUST, HUH...?
HACHI-KUMA ...
...YOU DOUBT MY POWER, DON'T YOU?
SO...
...CARE TO SEE FOR YOURSELF?

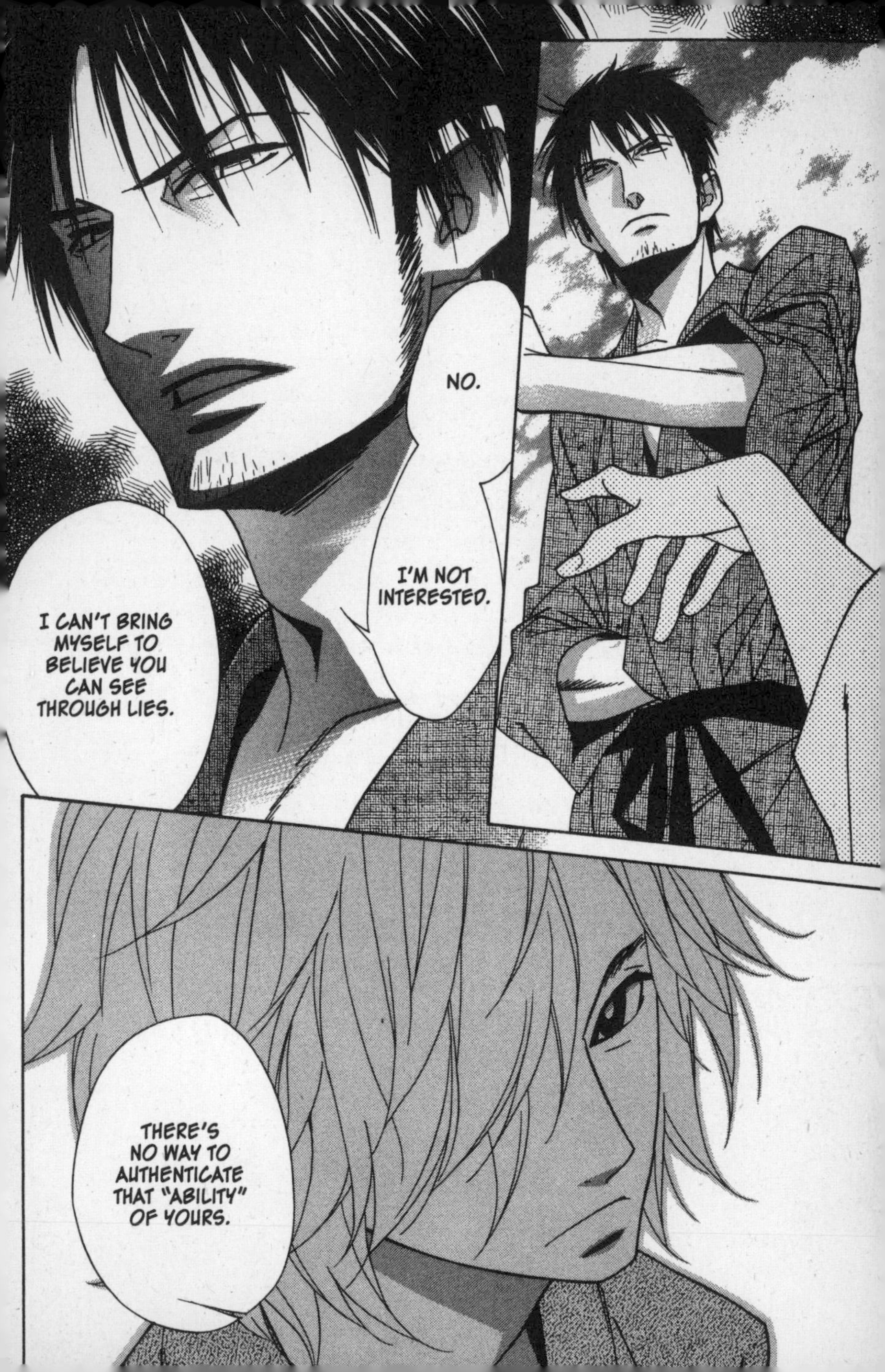
NO.
I'M NOT INTERESTED.
I CAN'T BRING MYSELF TO BELIEVE YOU CAN SEE THROUGH LIES.
THERE'S NO WAY TO AUTHENTICATE THAT "ABILITY" OF YOURS.

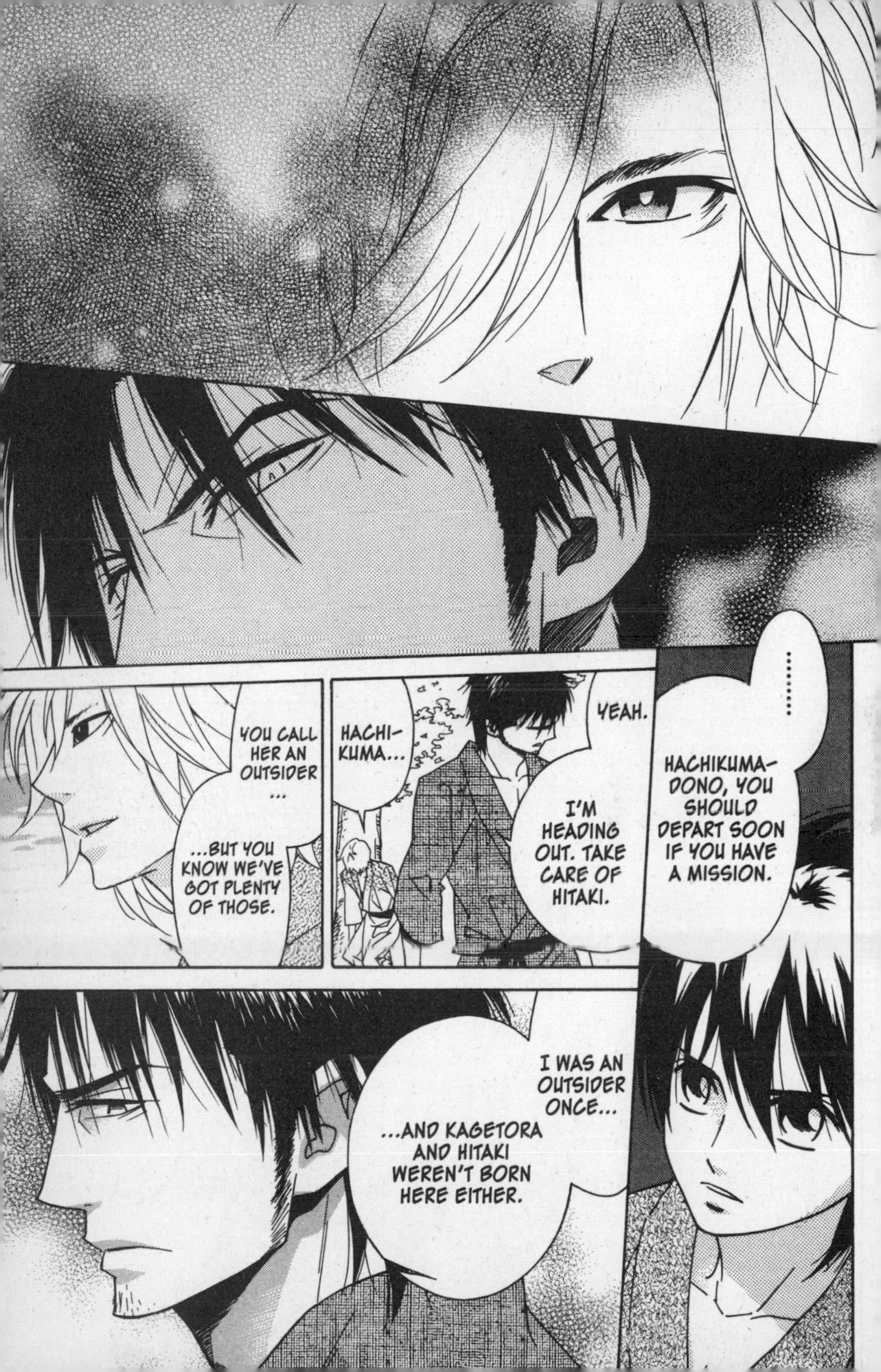
......
HACHIKUMA-DONO, YOU SHOULD DEPART SOON IF YOU HAVE A MISSION.
YEAH.
I'M HEADING OUT. TAKE CARE OF HITAKI.
HACHI-KUMA...
YOU CALL HER AN OUTSIDER ...
...BUT YOU KNOW WE'VE GOT PLENTY OF THOSE.
I WAS AN OUTSIDER ONCE...
...AND KAGETORA AND HITAKI WEREN'T BORN HERE EITHER.

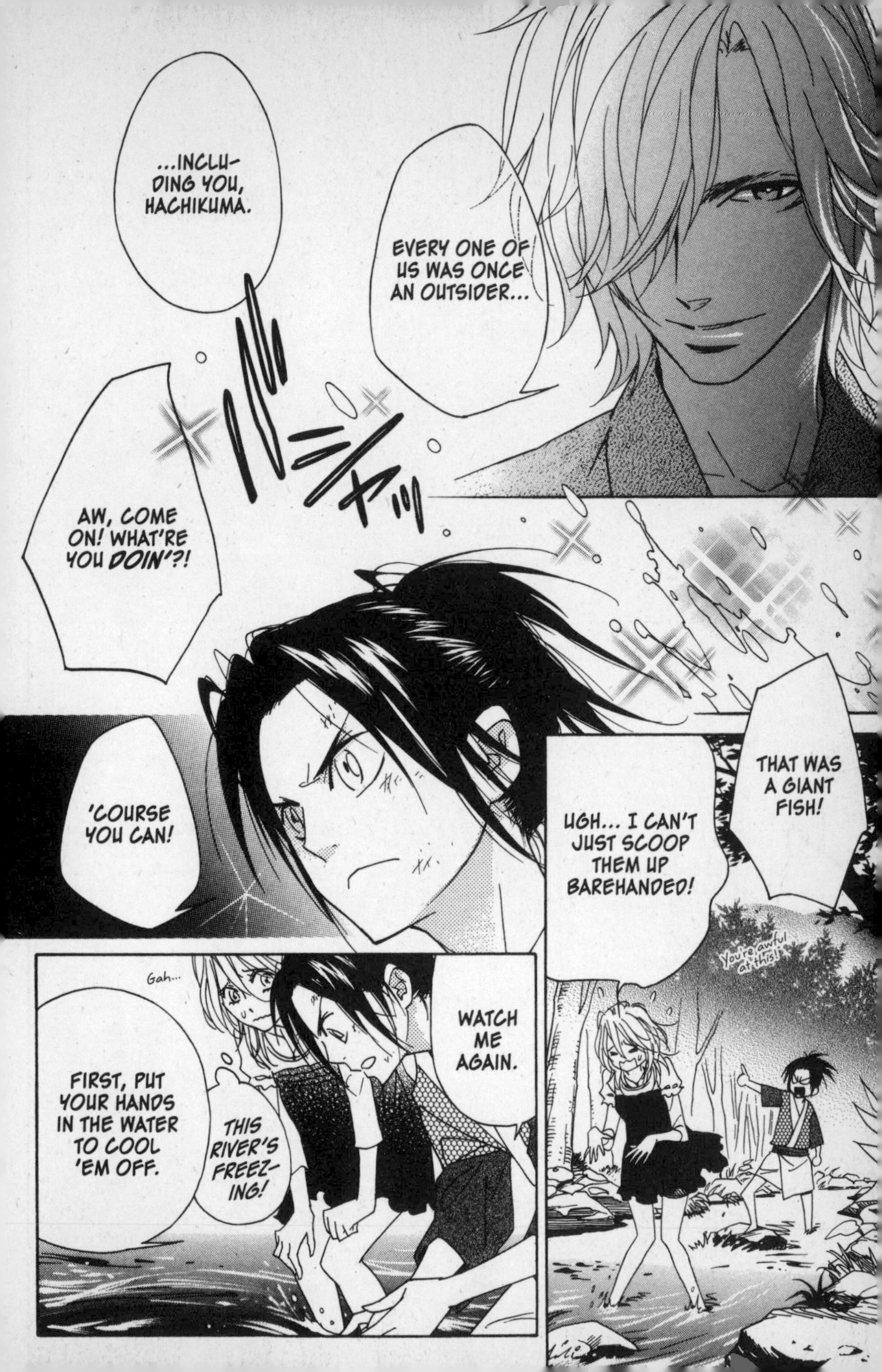
EVERY ONE OF US WAS ONCE AN OUTSIDER...
...INCLU-DING YOU, HACHIKUMA.
THAT WAS A GIANT FISH!
UGH... I CAN'T JUST SCOOP THEM UP BAREHANDED!
You're awful at this!
AW, COME ON! WHAT'RE YOU *DOIN'*?!
'COURSE YOU CAN!
WATCH ME AGAIN.
Gah...
THIS RIVER'S FREEZ-ING!
FIRST, PUT YOUR HANDS IN THE WATER TO COOL 'EM OFF.

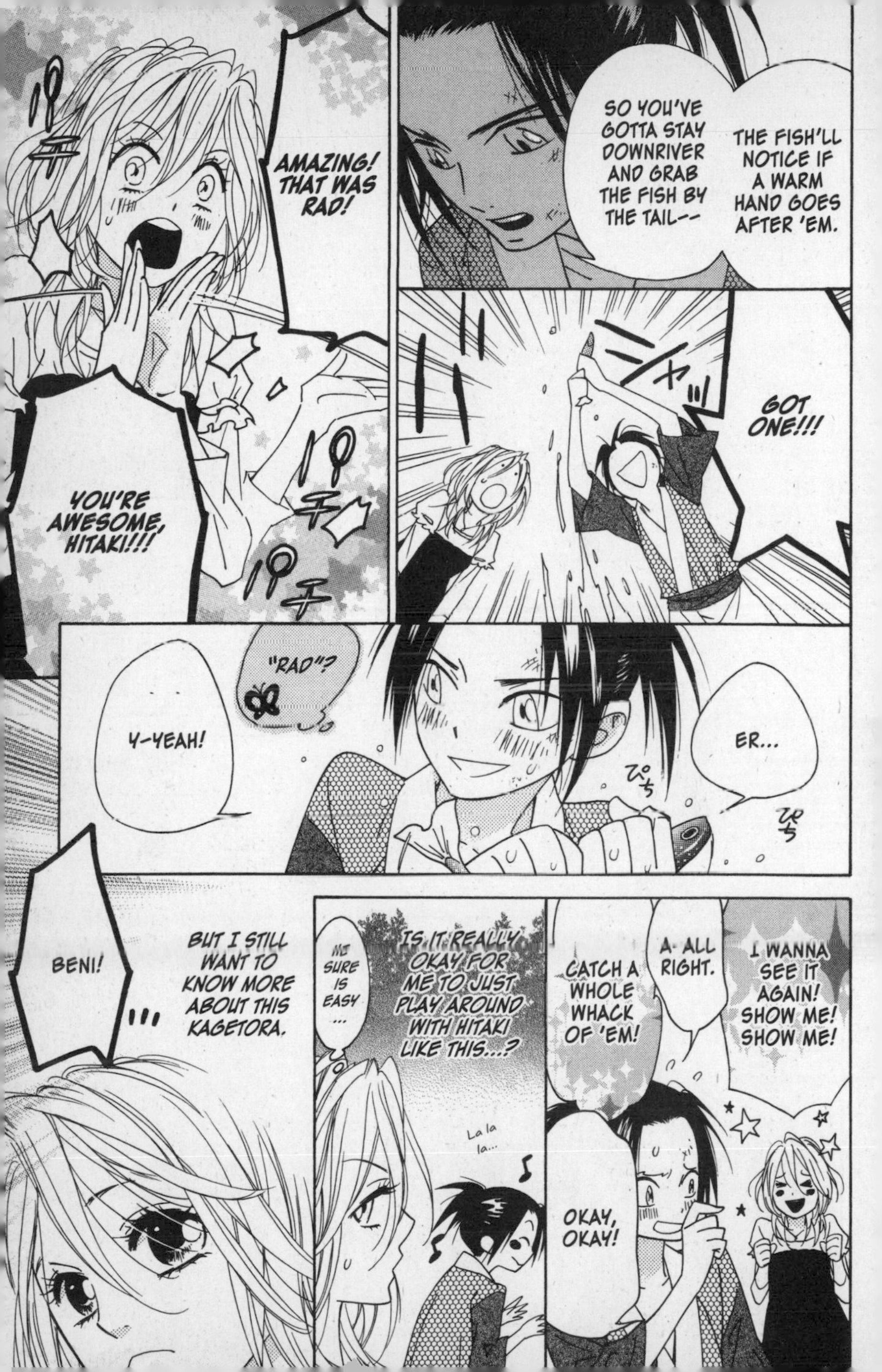
THE FISH'LL NOTICE IF A WARM HAND GOES AFTER 'EM.
SO YOU'VE GOTTA STAY DOWNRIVER AND GRAB THE FISH BY THE TAIL--
GOT ONE!!!
AMAZING! THAT WAS RAD!
YOU'RE AWESOME, HITAKI!!!
ER...
"RAD"?
Y-YEAH!
I WANNA SEE IT AGAIN! SHOW ME! SHOW ME!
A-ALL RIGHT.
CATCH A WHOLE WHACK OF 'EM!
OKAY, OKAY!
IS IT REALLY OKAY FOR ME TO JUST PLAY AROUND WITH HITAKI LIKE THIS...?
HE SURE IS EASY...
La la la...
BUT I STILL WANT TO KNOW MORE ABOUT THIS KAGETORA.
BENI!
...

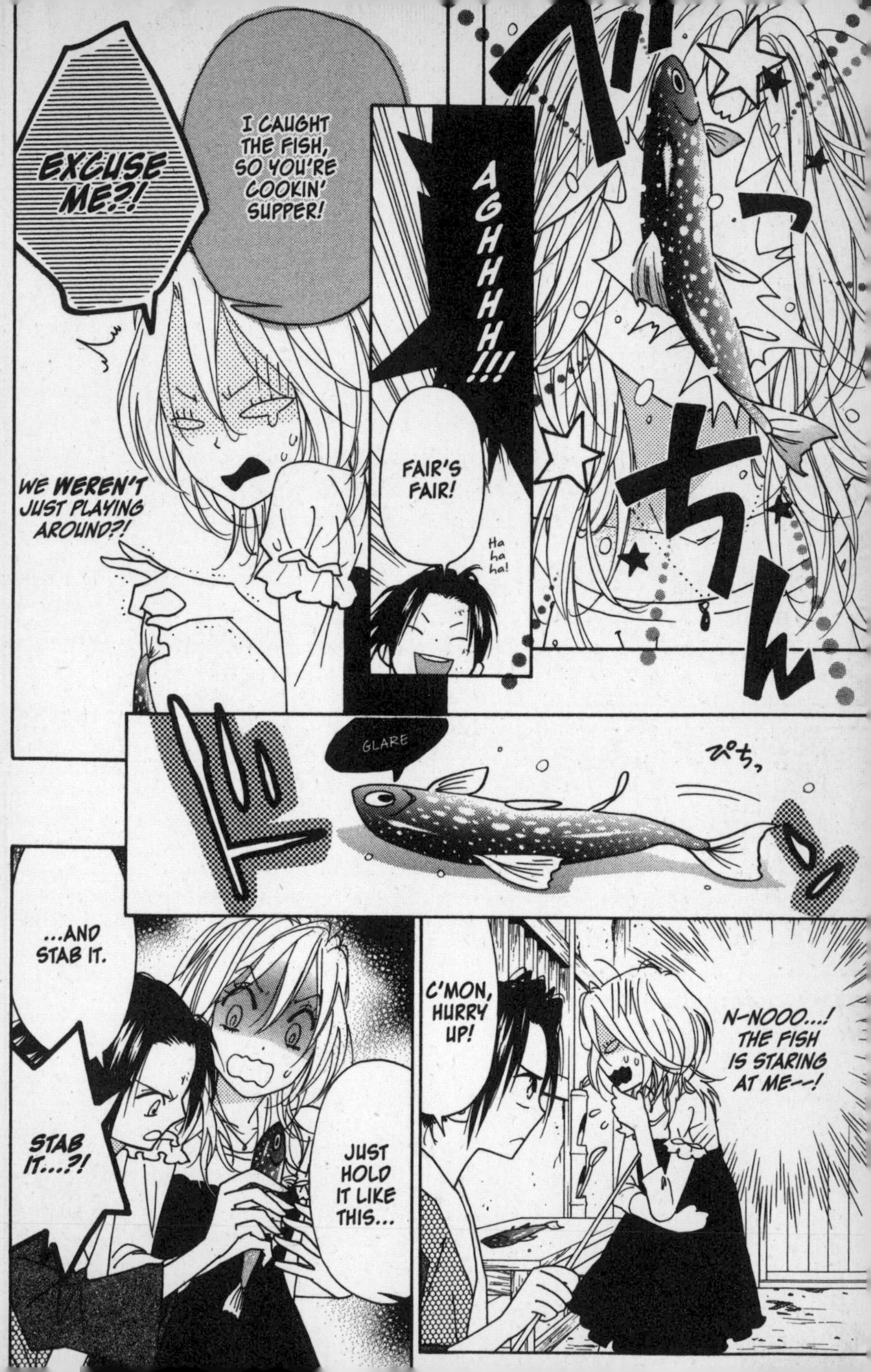

AGHHHHHH!!!
FAIR'S FAIR!
Ha ha ha!
I CAUGHT THE FISH, SO YOU'RE COOKIN' SUPPER!
EXCUSE ME?!
WE WEREN'T JUST PLAYING AROUND?!
GLARE
ぴちっ
N-NOOO...! THE FISH IS STARING AT ME--!
C'MON, HURRY UP!
JUST HOLD IT LIKE THIS...
...AND STAB IT.
STAB IT...?!

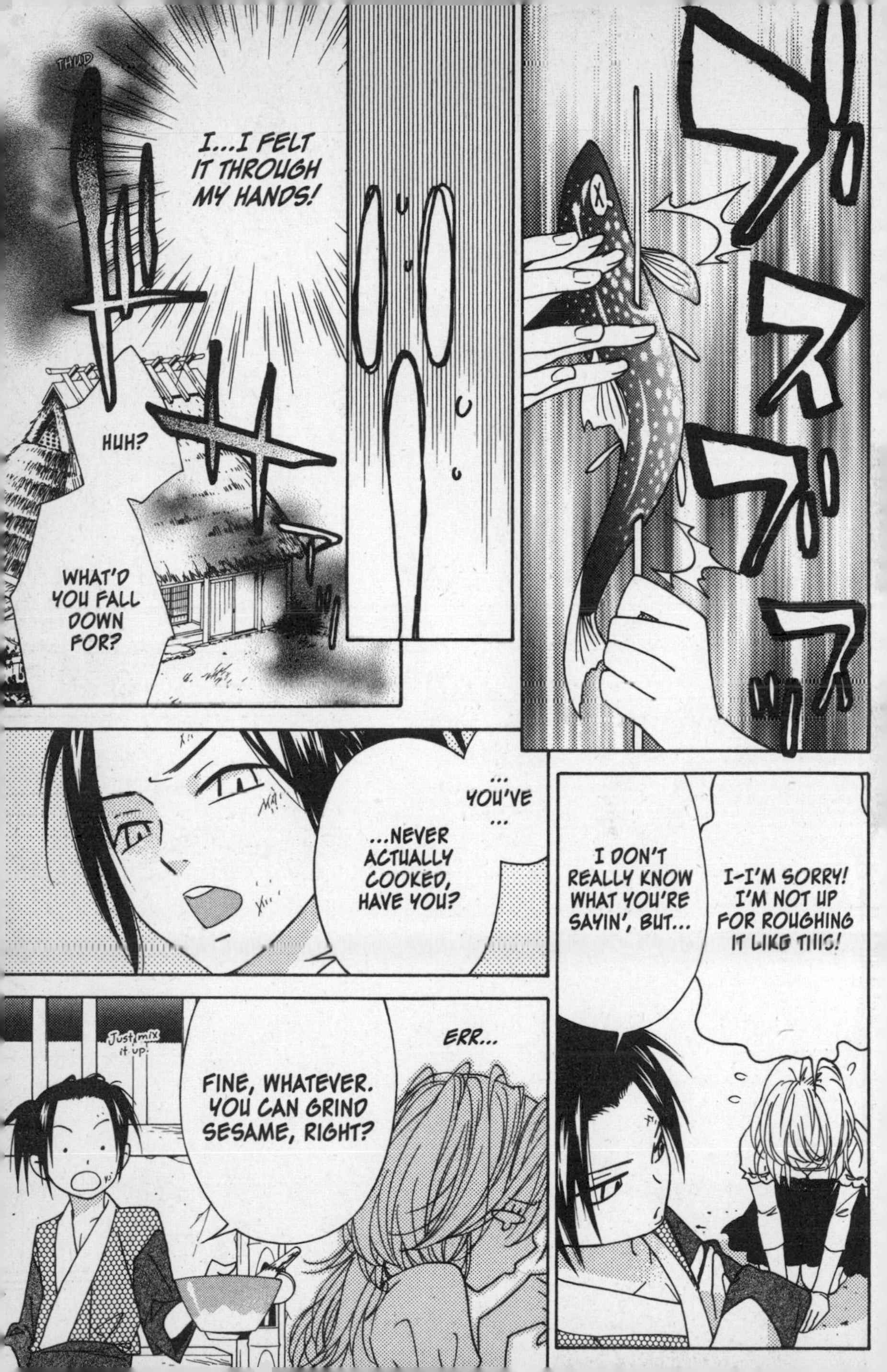
THUD
I...I FELT IT THROUGH MY HANDS!
HUH?
WHAT'D YOU FALL DOWN FOR?
I-I'M SORRY! I'M NOT UP FOR ROUGHING IT LIKE THIS!
I DON'T REALLY KNOW WHAT YOU'RE SAYIN', BUT...
... YOU'VE ...
...NEVER ACTUALLY COOKED, HAVE YOU?
ERR...
FINE, WHATEVER. YOU CAN GRIND SESAME, RIGHT?
Just mix it up.

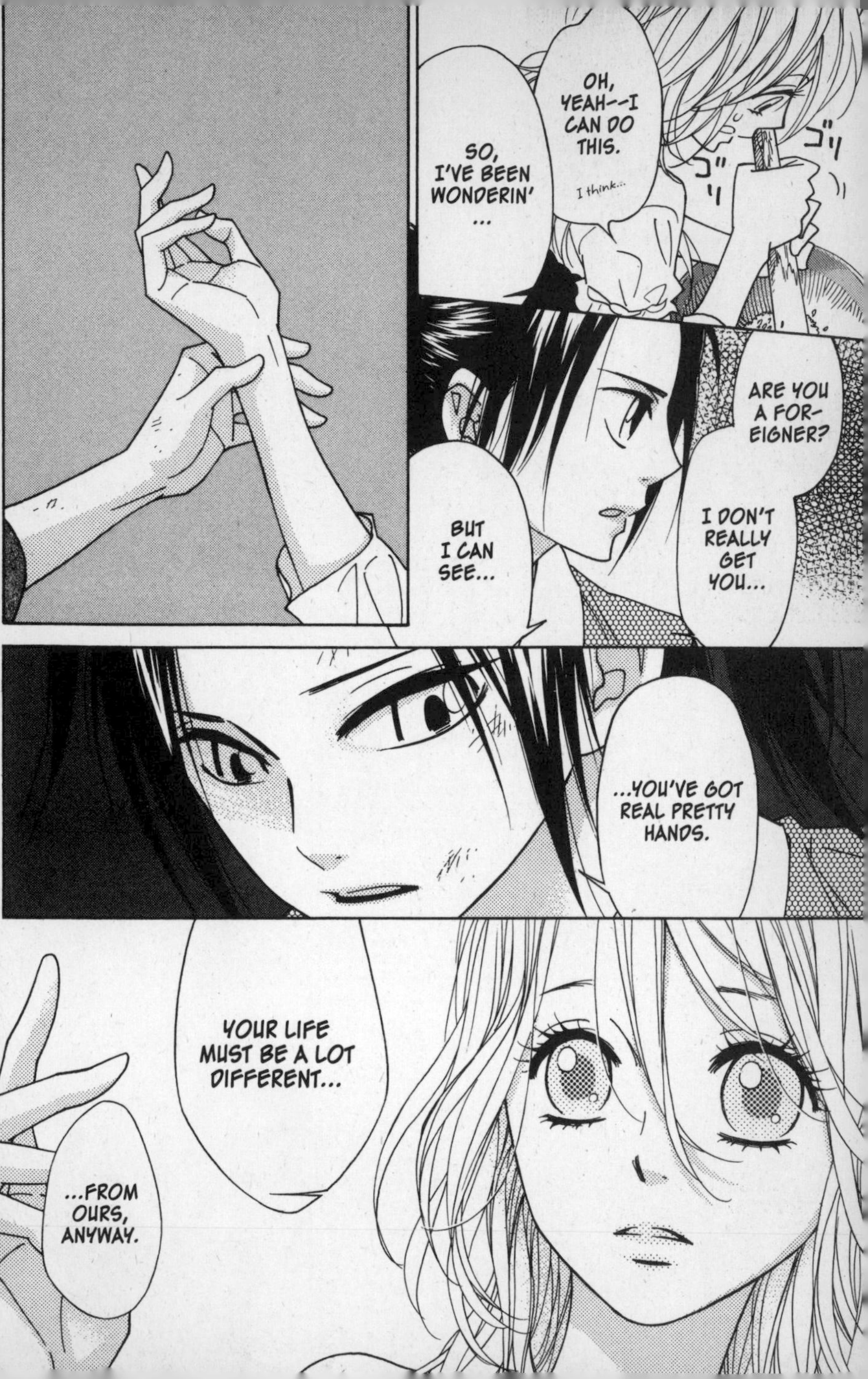
OH, YEAH--I CAN DO THIS.
I think...
ゴリ
ゴリ
SO, I'VE BEEN WONDERIN' ...
ARE YOU A FOR-EIGNER?
I DON'T REALLY GET YOU...
BUT I CAN SEE...
...YOU'VE GOT REAL PRETTY HANDS.
YOUR LIFE MUST BE A LOT DIFFERENT...
...FROM OURS, ANYWAY.

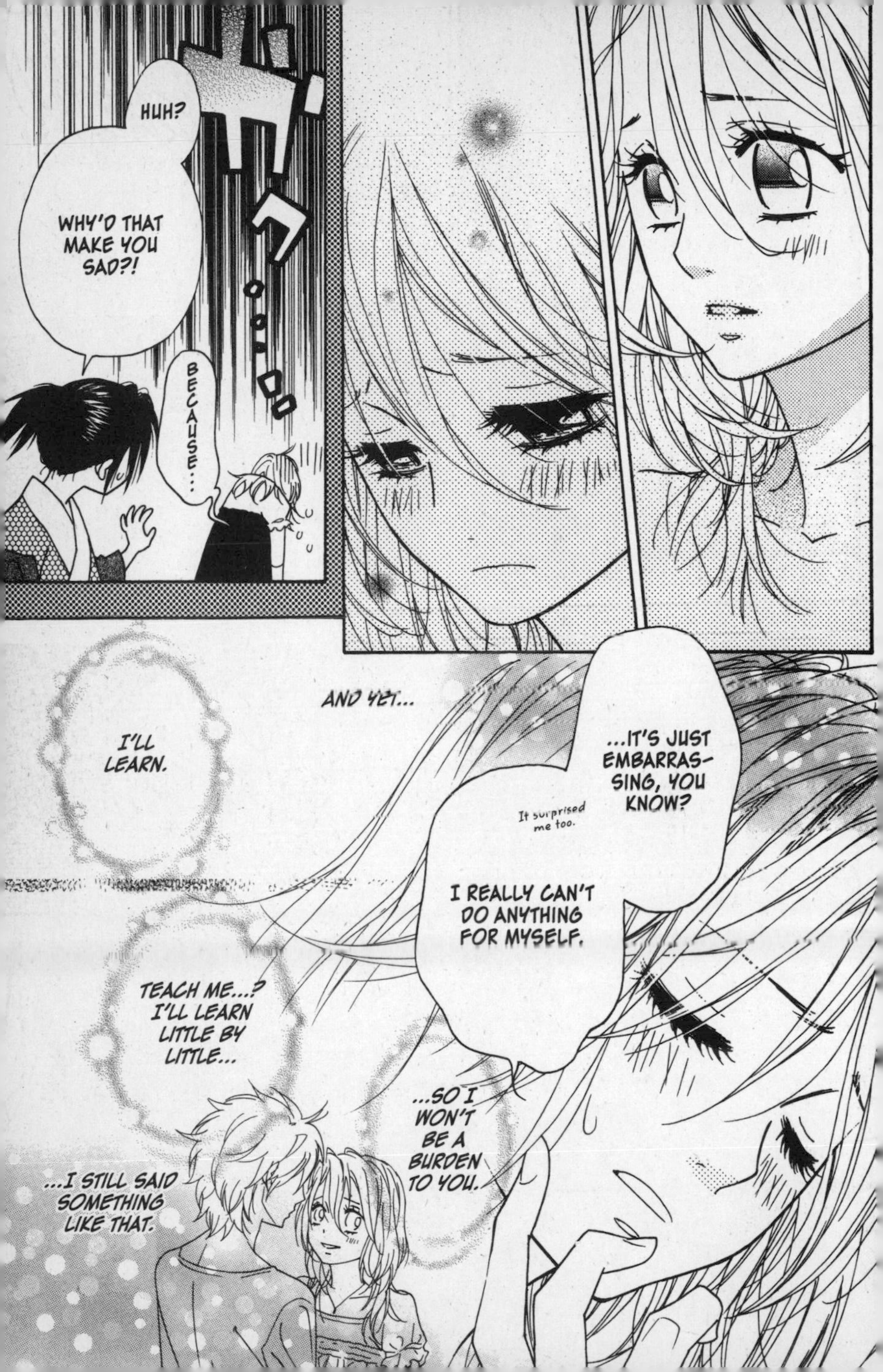
HUH?
WHY'D THAT MAKE YOU SAD?!
BECAUSE...
...IT'S JUST EMBARRAS-SING, YOU KNOW?
It surprised me too.
I REALLY CAN'T DO ANYTHING FOR MYSELF.
AND YET...
I'LL LEARN.
TEACH ME...? I'LL LEARN LITTLE BY LITTLE...
...SO I WON'T BE A BURDEN TO YOU.
...I STILL SAID SOMETHING LIKE THAT.

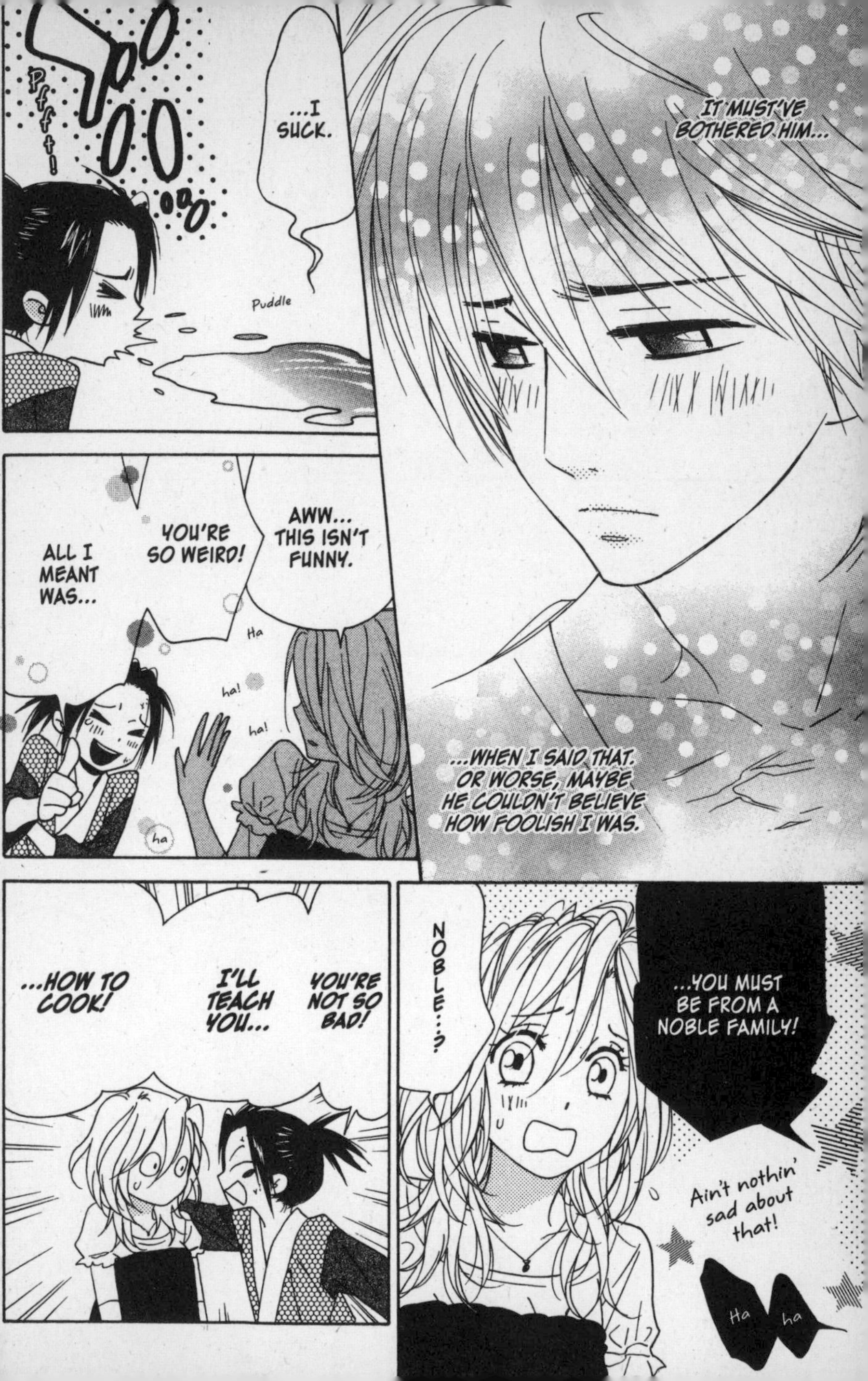
IT MUST'VE BOTHERED HIM...
...WHEN I SAID THAT. OR WORSE, MAYBE HE COULDN'T BELIEVE HOW FOOLISH I WAS.
...I SUCK.
Pffft!
Puddle
AWW... THIS ISN'T FUNNY.
YOU'RE SO WEIRD!
ALL I MEANT WAS...
Ha
ha!
ha!
ha
...YOU MUST BE FROM A NOBLE FAMILY!
NOBLE...?
Ain't nothin' sad about that!
Ha
ha
YOU'RE NOT SO BAD!
I'LL TEACH YOU...
...HOW TO COOK!

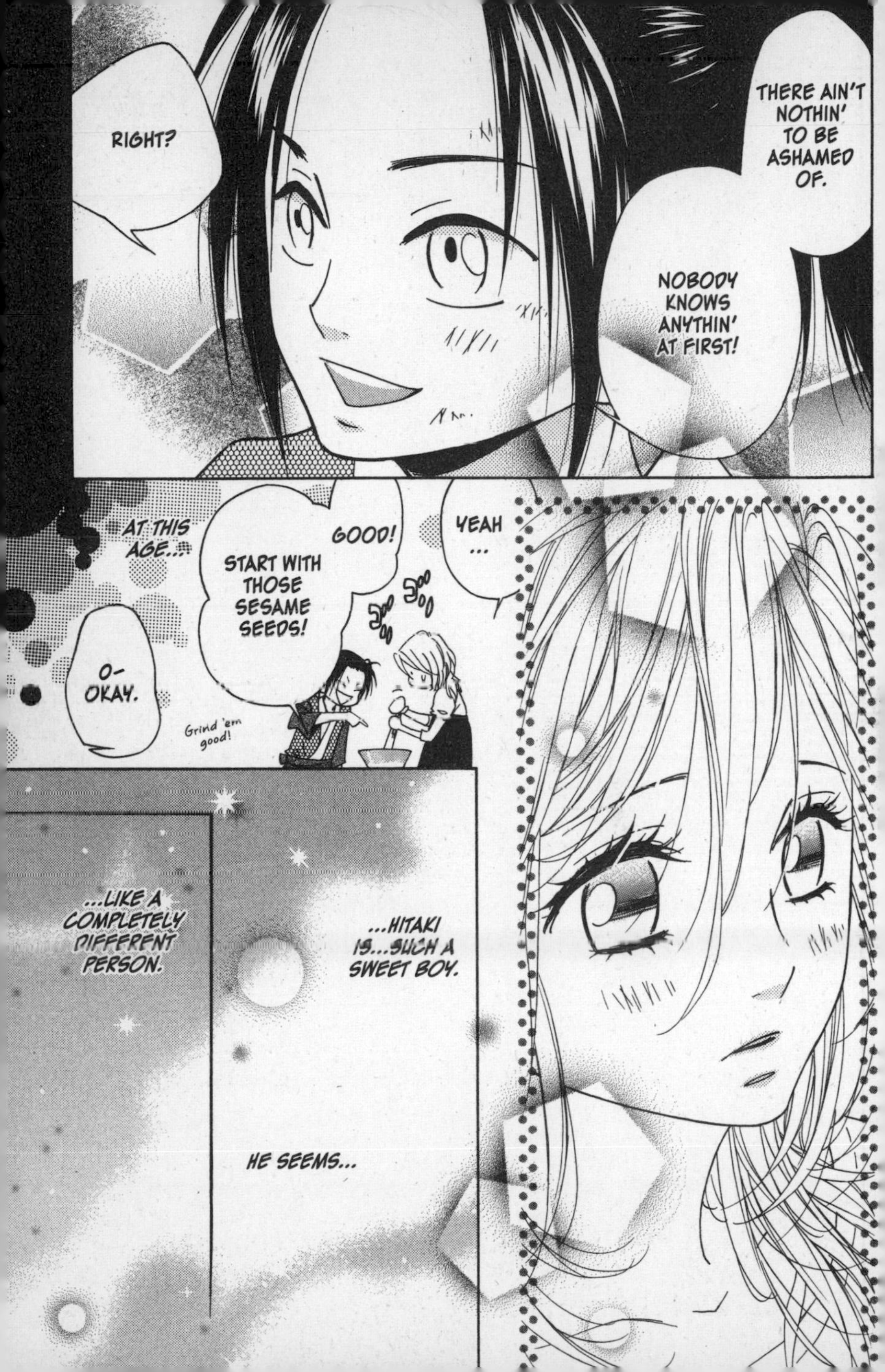
THERE AIN'T NOTHIN' TO BE ASHAMED OF.
NOBODY KNOWS ANYTHIN' AT FIRST!
RIGHT?
YEAH ...
GOOD!
START WITH THOSE SESAME SEEDS!
AT THIS AGE...
O-OKAY.
Grind 'em good!
...HITAKI IS...SUCH A SWEET BOY.
...LIKE A COMPLETELY DIFFERENT PERSON.
HE SEEMS...

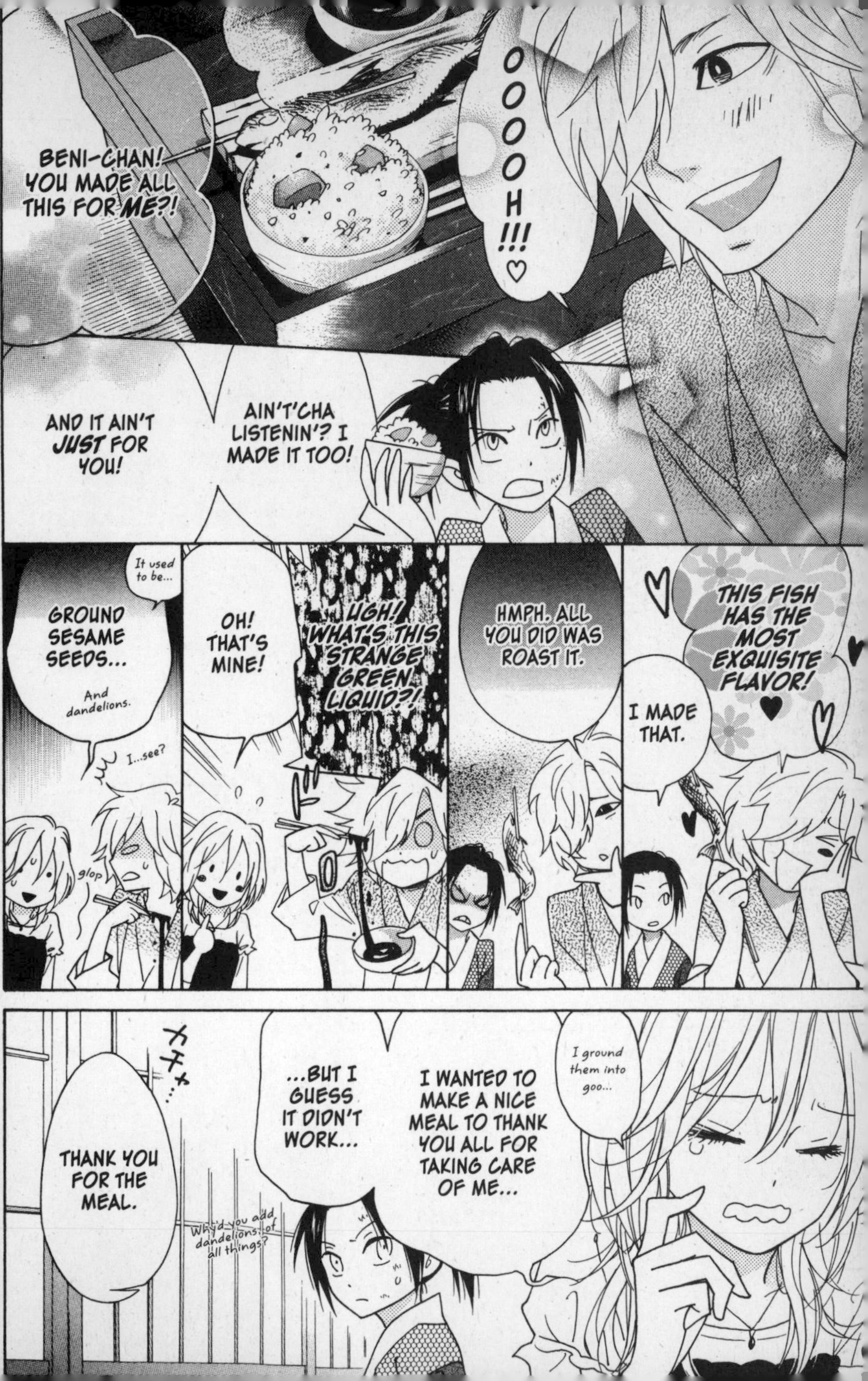
OOOOOH!!! ♡
BENI-CHAN! YOU MADE ALL THIS FOR ME?!
AIN'T'CHA LISTENIN'? I MADE IT TOO!
AND IT AIN'T JUST FOR YOU!
THIS FISH HAS THE MOST EXQUISITE FLAVOR!
I MADE THAT.
HMPH. ALL YOU DID WAS ROAST IT.
UGH! WHAT'S THIS STRANGE GREEN LIQUID?!
OH! THAT'S MINE!
It used to be...
GROUND SESAME SEEDS...
And dandelions.
I...see?
glop
I ground them into goo...
I WANTED TO MAKE A NICE MEAL TO THANK YOU ALL FOR TAKING CARE OF ME...
...BUT I GUESS IT DIDN'T WORK...
Why'd you add dandelions, of all things?
THANK YOU FOR THE MEAL.

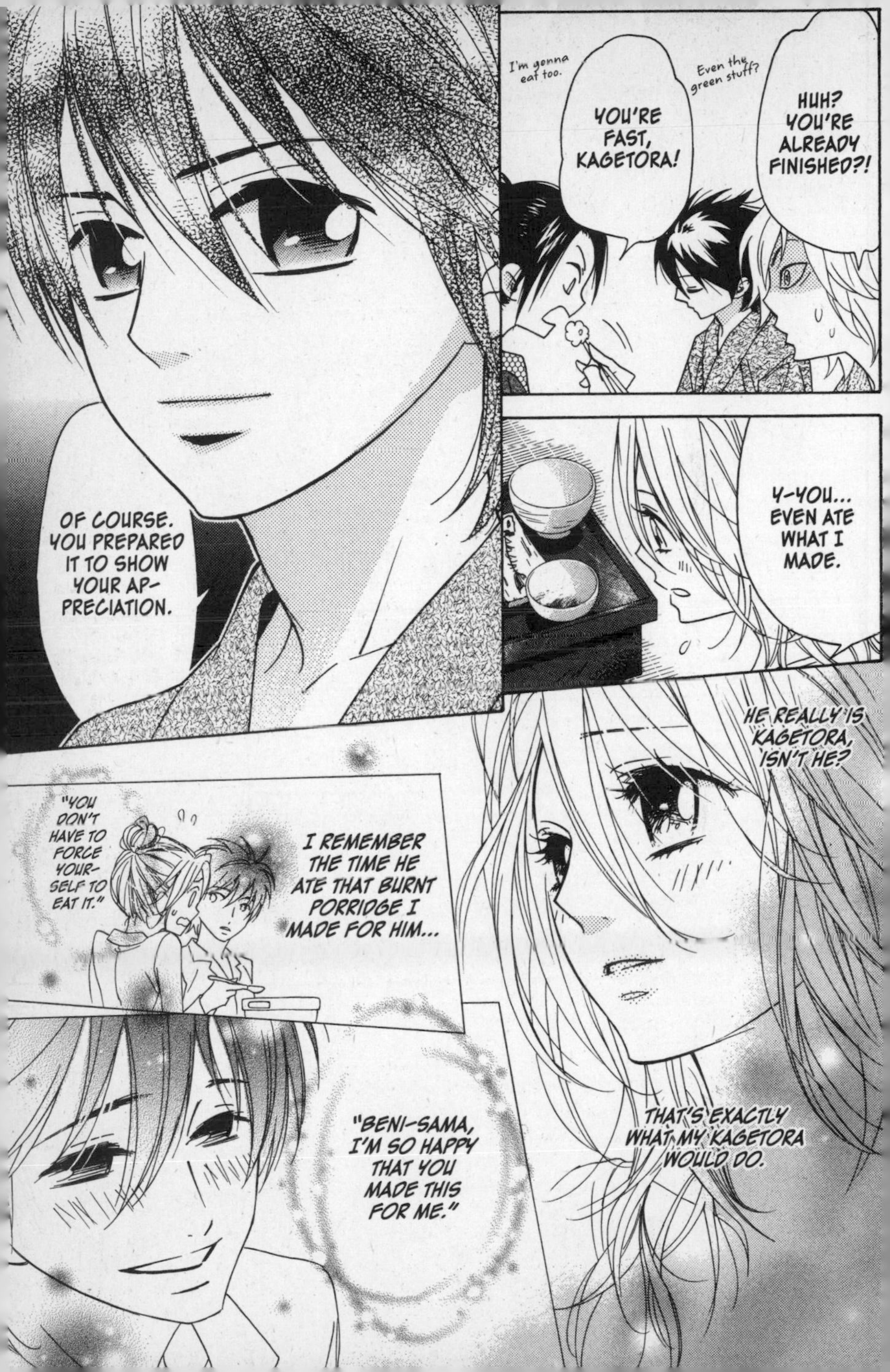
HUH? YOU'RE ALREADY FINISHED?!
Even the green stuff?
YOU'RE FAST, KAGETORA!
I'm gonna eat too.
Y-YOU... EVEN ATE WHAT I MADE.
OF COURSE. YOU PREPARED IT TO SHOW YOUR AP-PRECIATION.
HE REALLY IS KAGETORA, ISN'T HE?
I REMEMBER THE TIME HE ATE THAT BURNT PORRIDGE I MADE FOR HIM...
"YOU DON'T HAVE TO FORCE YOUR-SELF TO EAT IT."
"BENI-SAMA, I'M SO HAPPY THAT YOU MADE THIS FOR ME."
THAT'S EXACTLY WHAT MY KAGETORA WOULD DO.

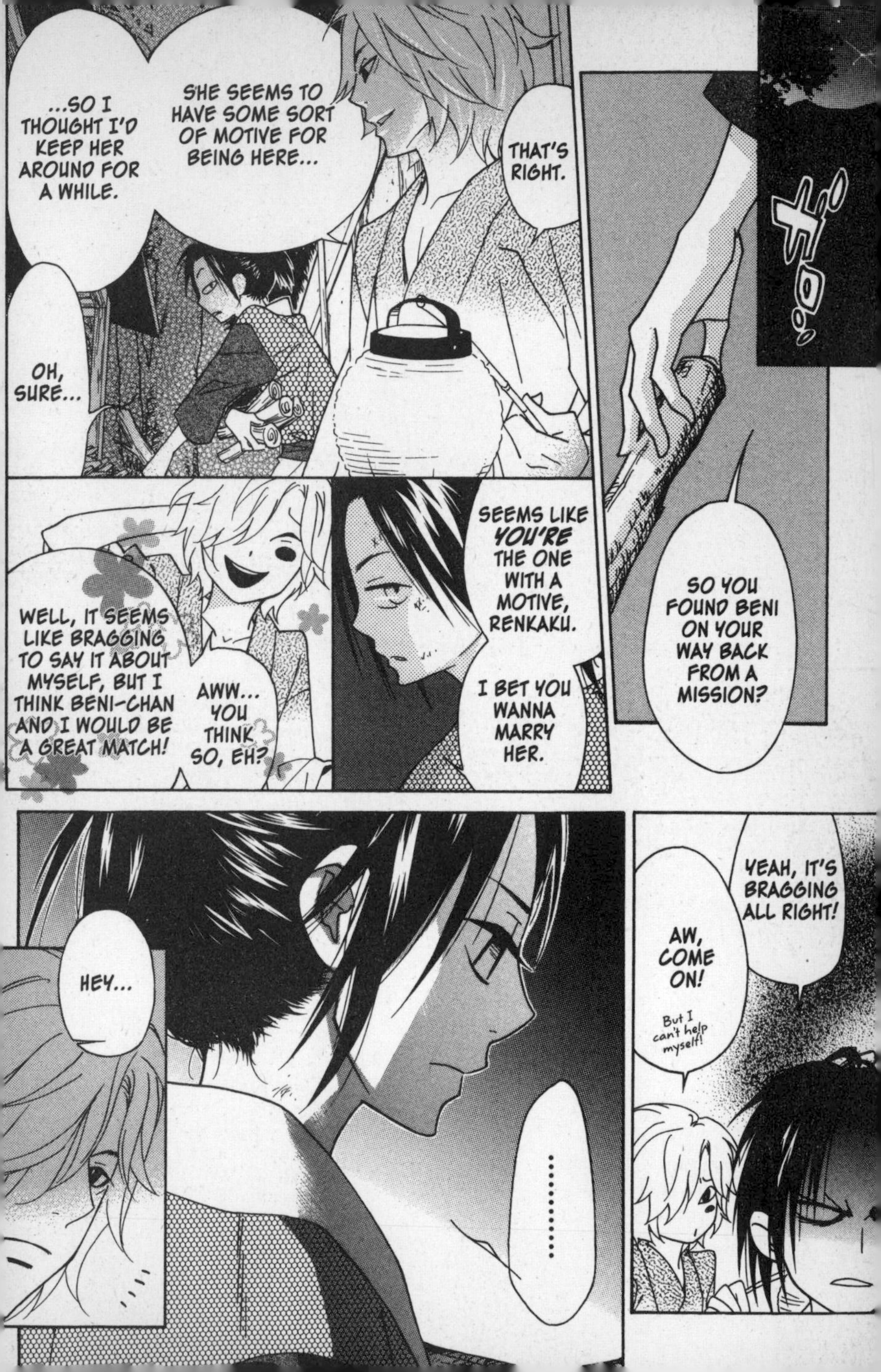
SO YOU FOUND BENI ON YOUR WAY BACK FROM A MISSION?
THAT'S RIGHT.
SHE SEEMS TO HAVE SOME SORT OF MOTIVE FOR BEING HERE...
...SO I THOUGHT I'D KEEP HER AROUND FOR A WHILE.
OH, SURE...
SEEMS LIKE *YOU'RE* THE ONE WITH A MOTIVE, RENKAKU.
I BET YOU WANNA MARRY HER.
AWW... YOU THINK SO, EH?
WELL, IT SEEMS LIKE BRAGGING TO SAY IT ABOUT MYSELF, BUT I THINK BENI-CHAN AND I WOULD BE A GREAT MATCH!
YEAH, IT'S BRAGGING ALL RIGHT!
AW, COME ON!
But I can't help myself!
HEY...
......

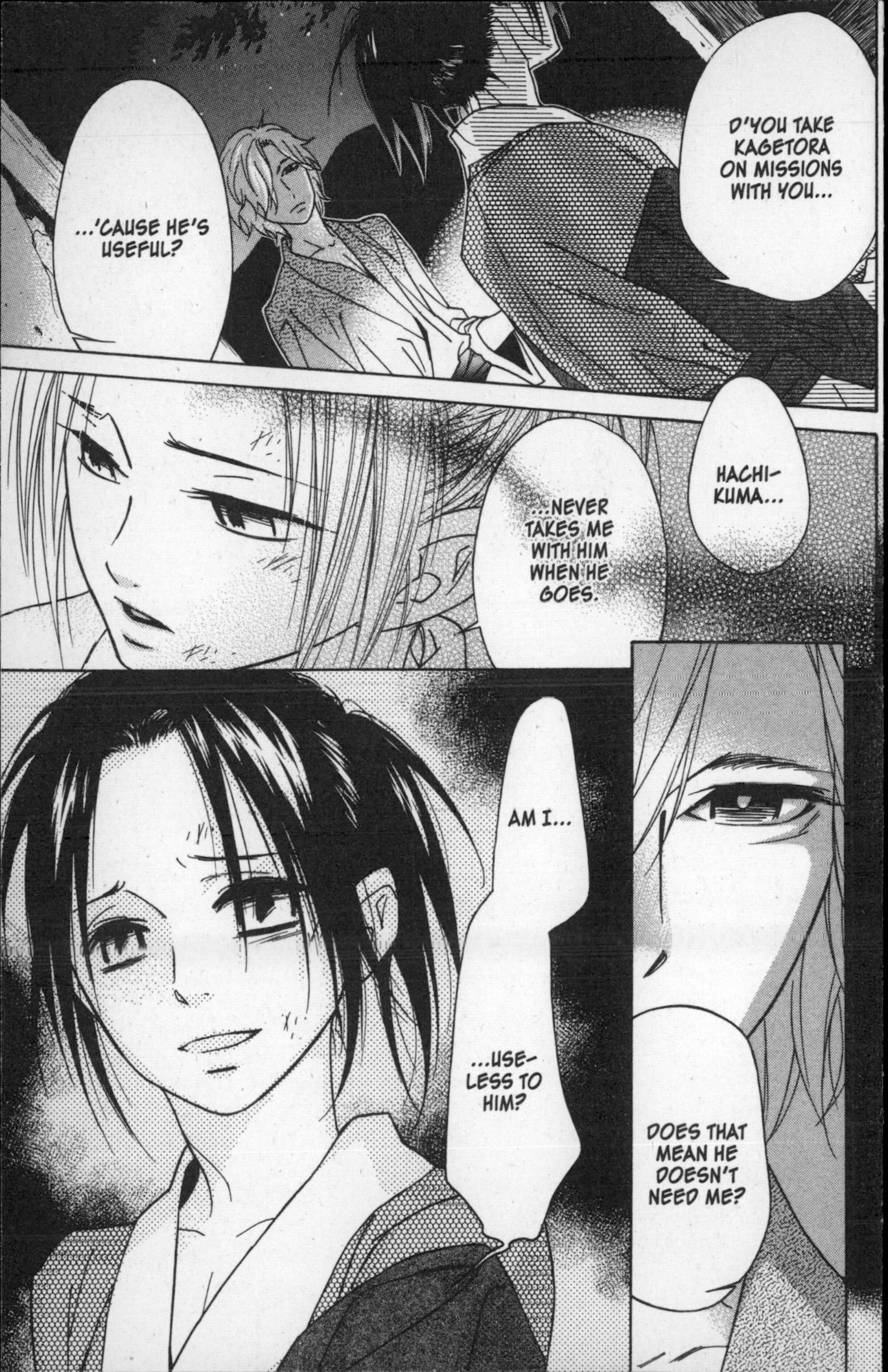
D'YOU TAKE KAGETORA ON MISSIONS WITH YOU...
...'CAUSE HE'S USEFUL?
HACHI-KUMA...
...NEVER TAKES ME WITH HIM WHEN HE GOES.
DOES THAT MEAN HE DOESN'T NEED ME?
AM I...
...USE-LESS TO HIM?

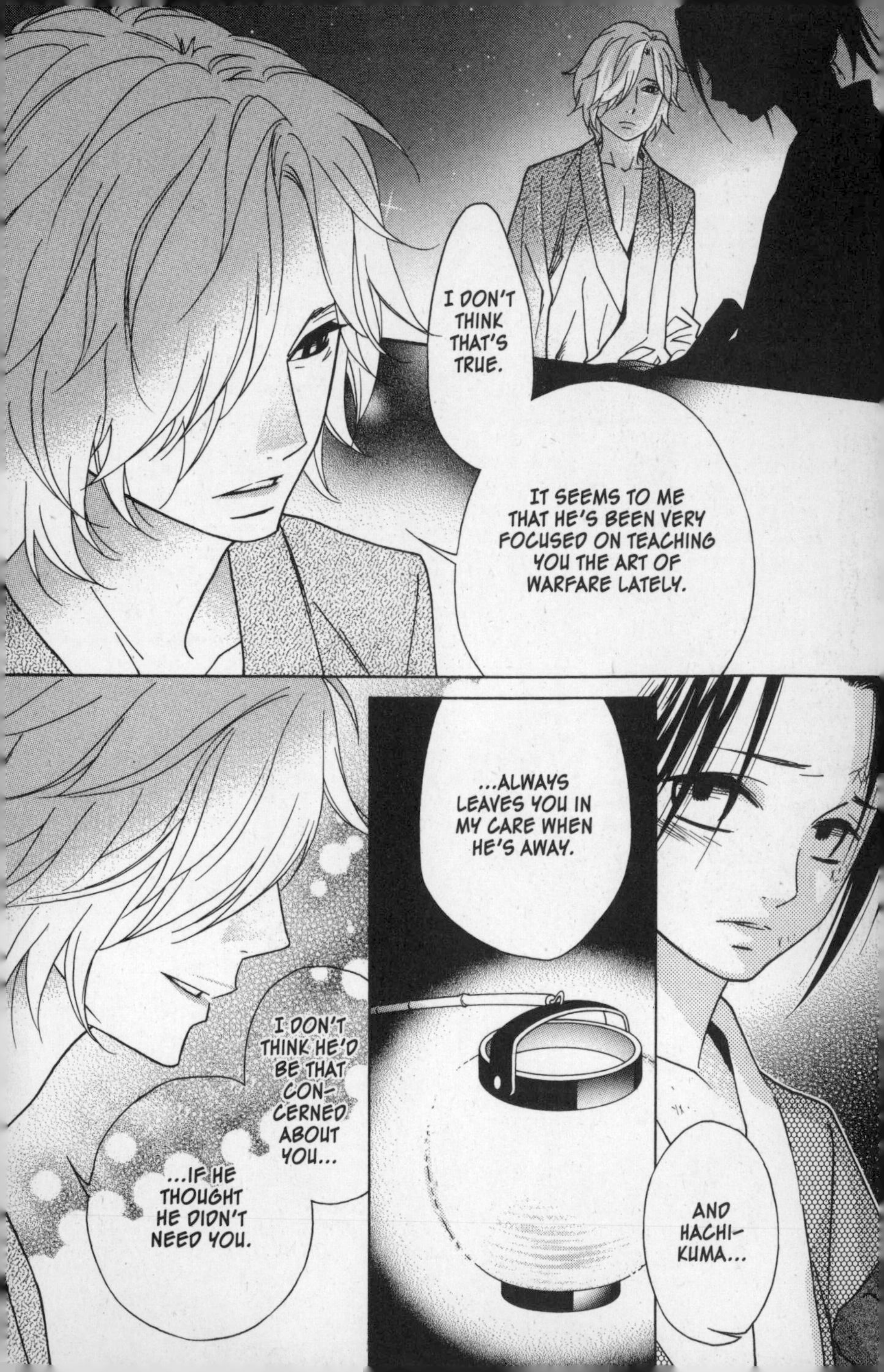
I DON'T THINK THAT'S TRUE.
IT SEEMS TO ME THAT HE'S BEEN VERY FOCUSED ON TEACHING YOU THE ART OF WARFARE LATELY.
AND HACHI-KUMA...
...ALWAYS LEAVES YOU IN MY CARE WHEN HE'S AWAY.
I DON'T THINK HE'D BE THAT CON-CERNED ABOUT YOU...
...IF HE THOUGHT HE DIDN'T NEED YOU.

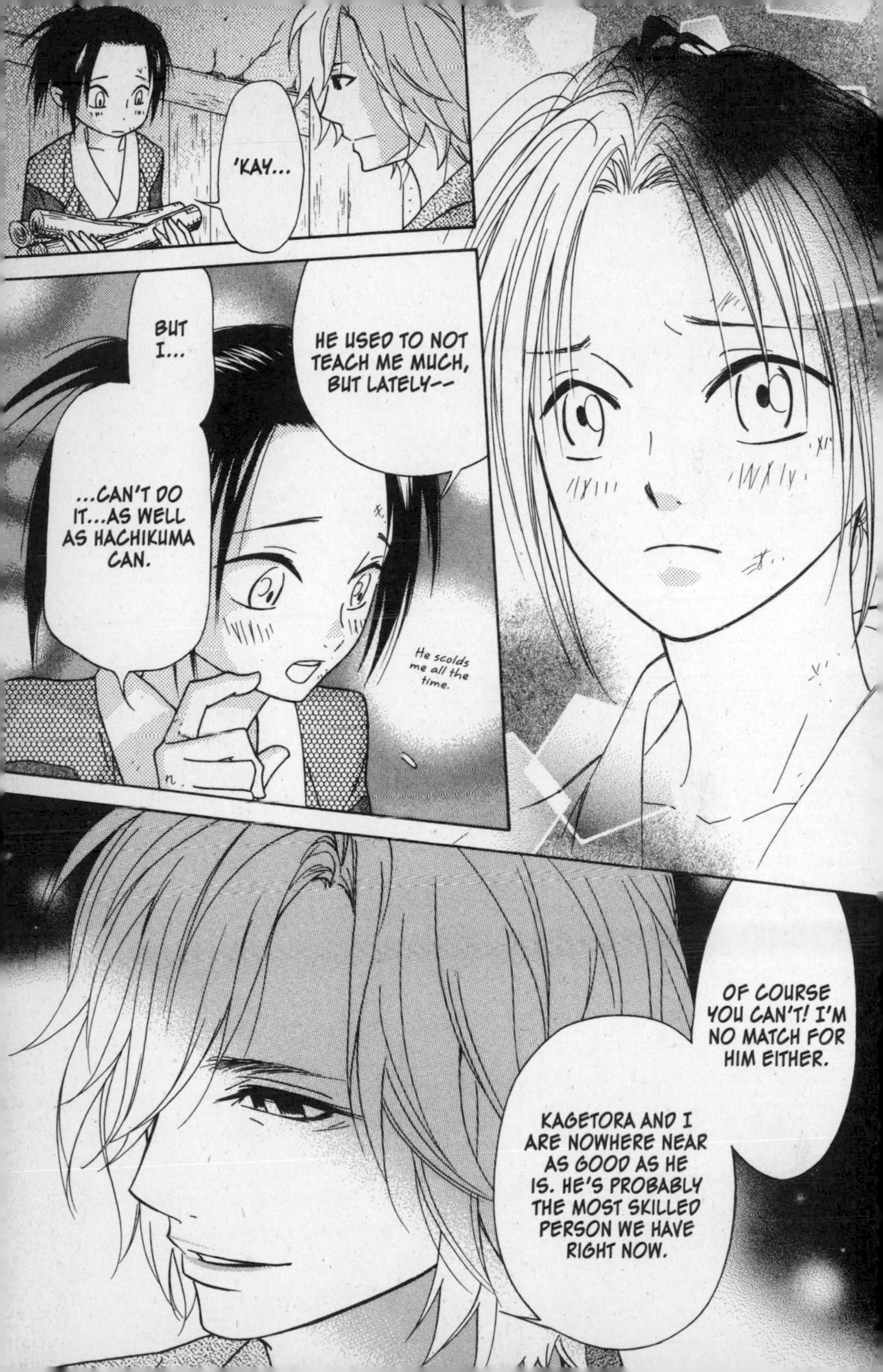
'KAY...
HE USED TO NOT TEACH ME MUCH, BUT LATELY--
BUT I...
...CAN'T DO IT...AS WELL AS HACHIKUMA CAN.
He scolds me all the time.
OF COURSE YOU CAN'T! I'M NO MATCH FOR HIM EITHER.
KAGETORA AND I ARE NOWHERE NEAR AS GOOD AS HE IS. HE'S PROBABLY THE MOST SKILLED PERSON WE HAVE RIGHT NOW.

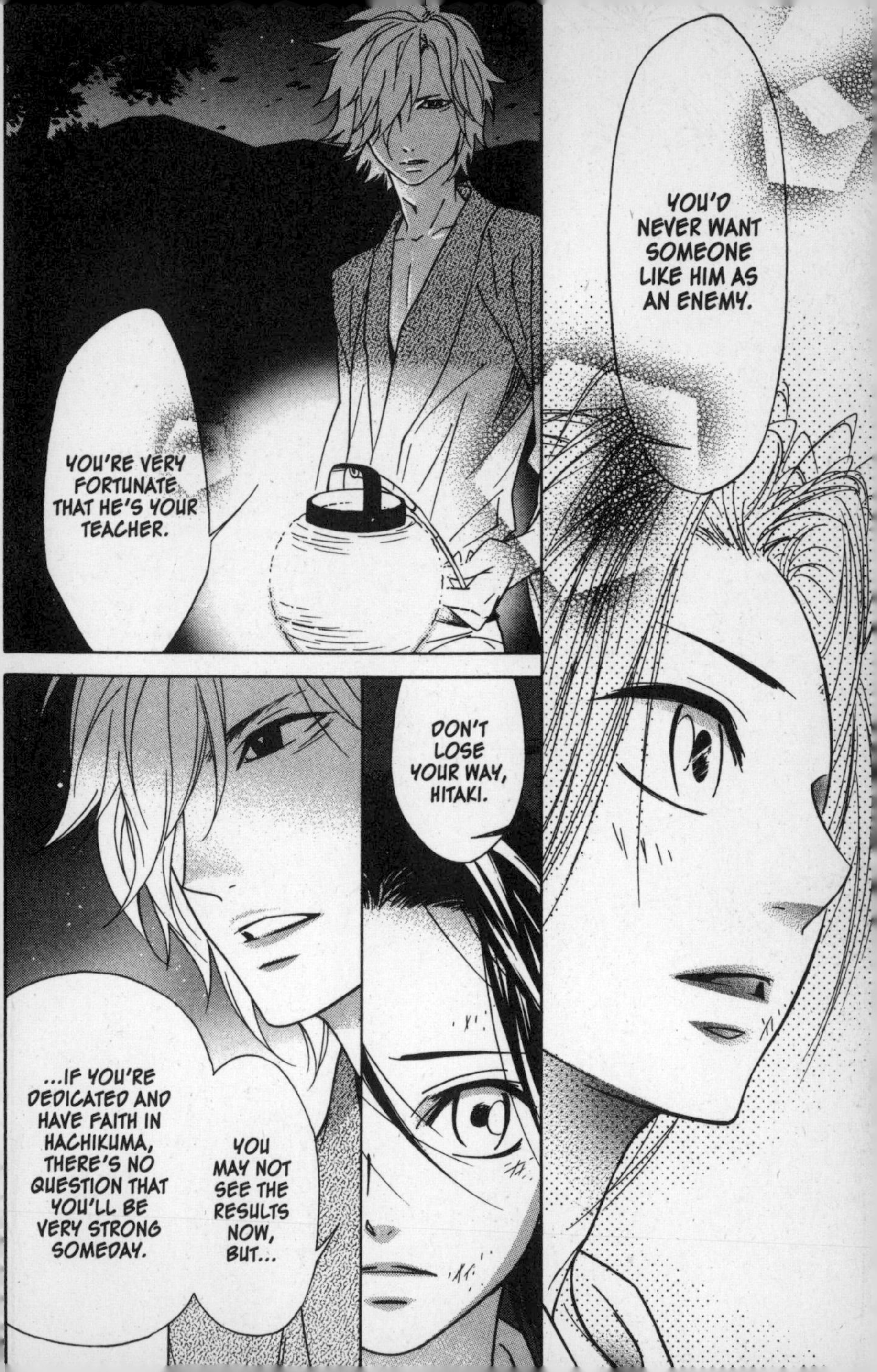
YOU'RE VERY FORTUNATE THAT HE'S YOUR TEACHER.
YOU'D NEVER WANT SOMEONE LIKE HIM AS AN ENEMY.
YOU MAY NOT SEE THE RESULTS NOW, BUT...
...IF YOU'RE DEDICATED AND HAVE FAITH IN HACHIKUMA, THERE'S NO QUESTION THAT YOU'LL BE VERY STRONG SOMEDAY.
DON'T LOSE YOUR WAY, HITAKI.

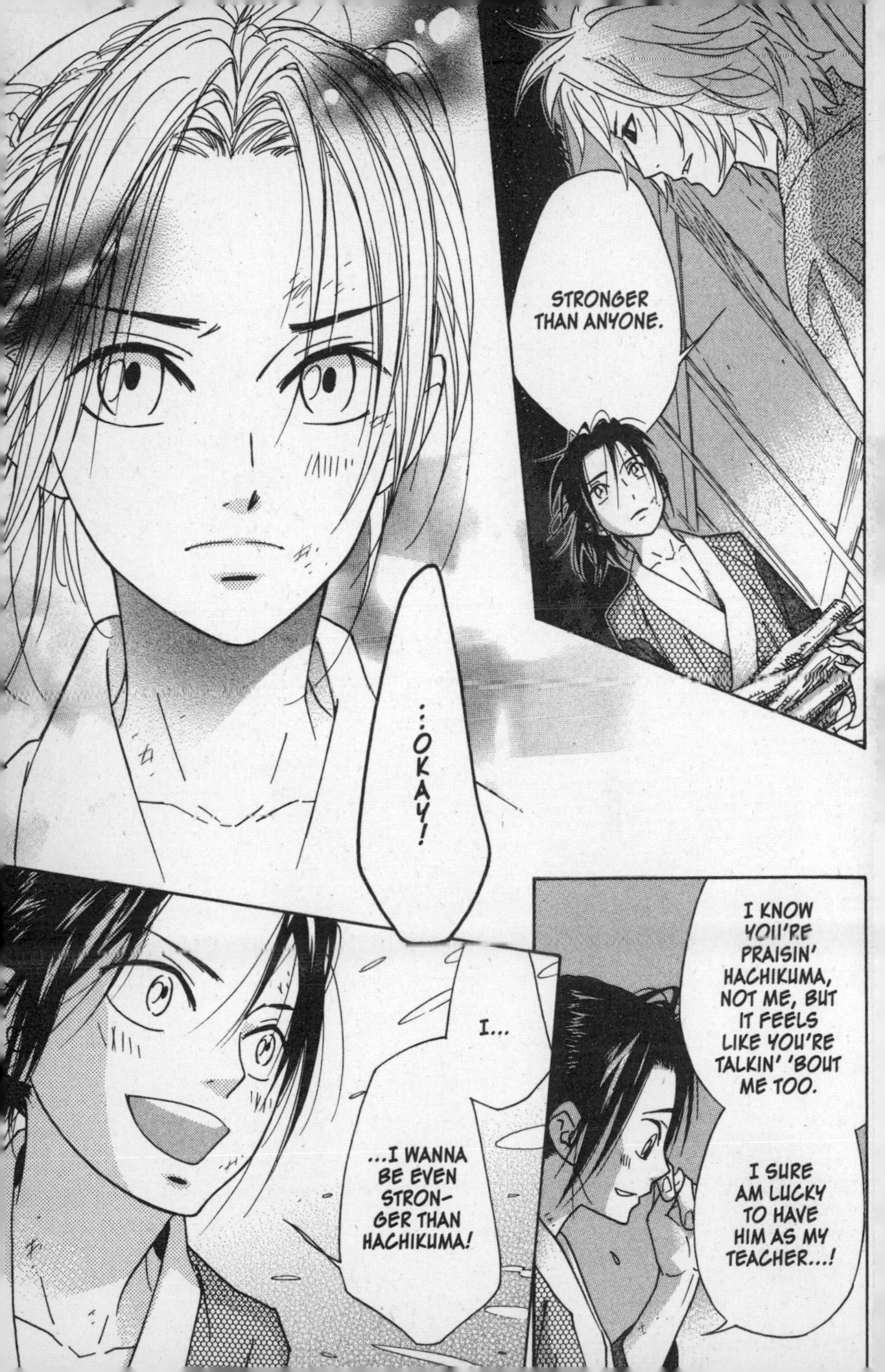
STRONGER THAN ANYONE.
...OKAY!
I KNOW YOU'RE PRAISIN' HACHIKUMA, NOT ME, BUT IT FEELS LIKE YOU'RE TALKIN' 'BOUT ME TOO.
I SURE AM LUCKY TO HAVE HIM AS MY TEACHER...!
I...
...I WANNA BE EVEN STRON-GER THAN HACHIKUMA!

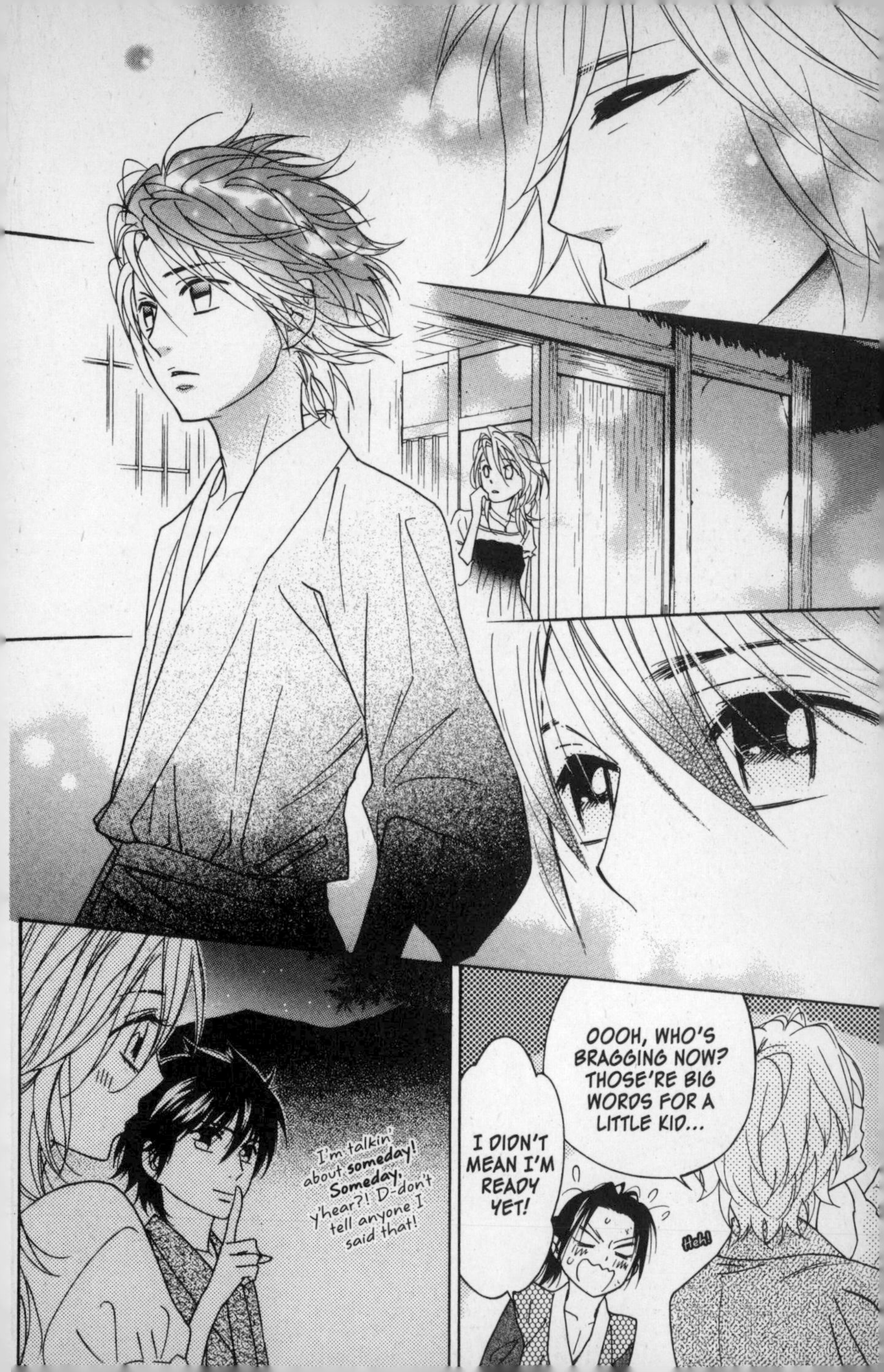
OOOH, WHO'S BRAGGING NOW? THOSE'RE BIG WORDS FOR A LITTLE KID...
Heh!
I DIDN'T MEAN I'M READY YET!
I'm talkin' about someday! Someday, y'hear?! D-don't tell anyone I said that!

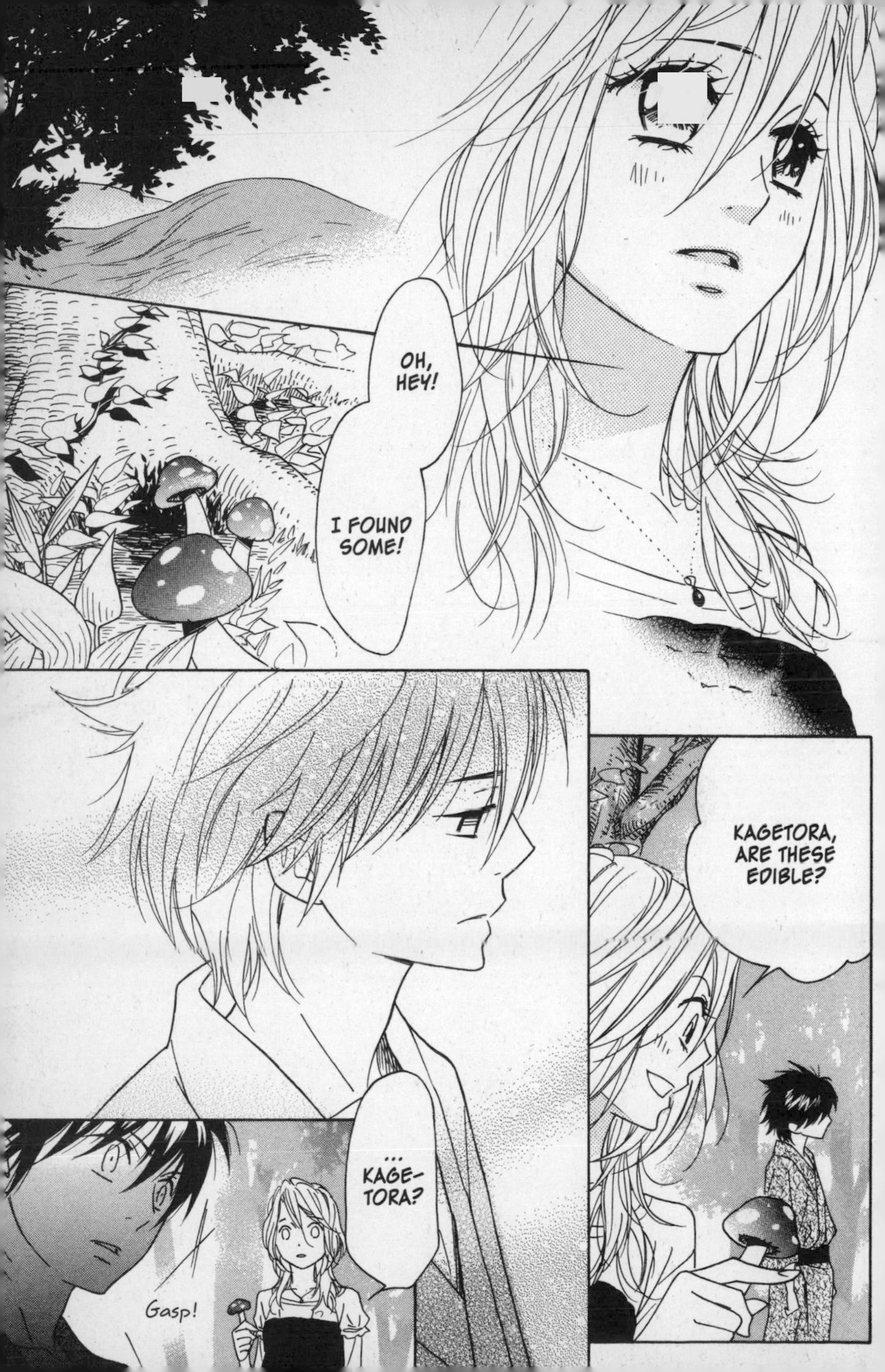
OH, HEY!
I FOUND SOME!
KAGETORA, ARE THESE EDIBLE?
... KAGE-TORA?
Gasp!

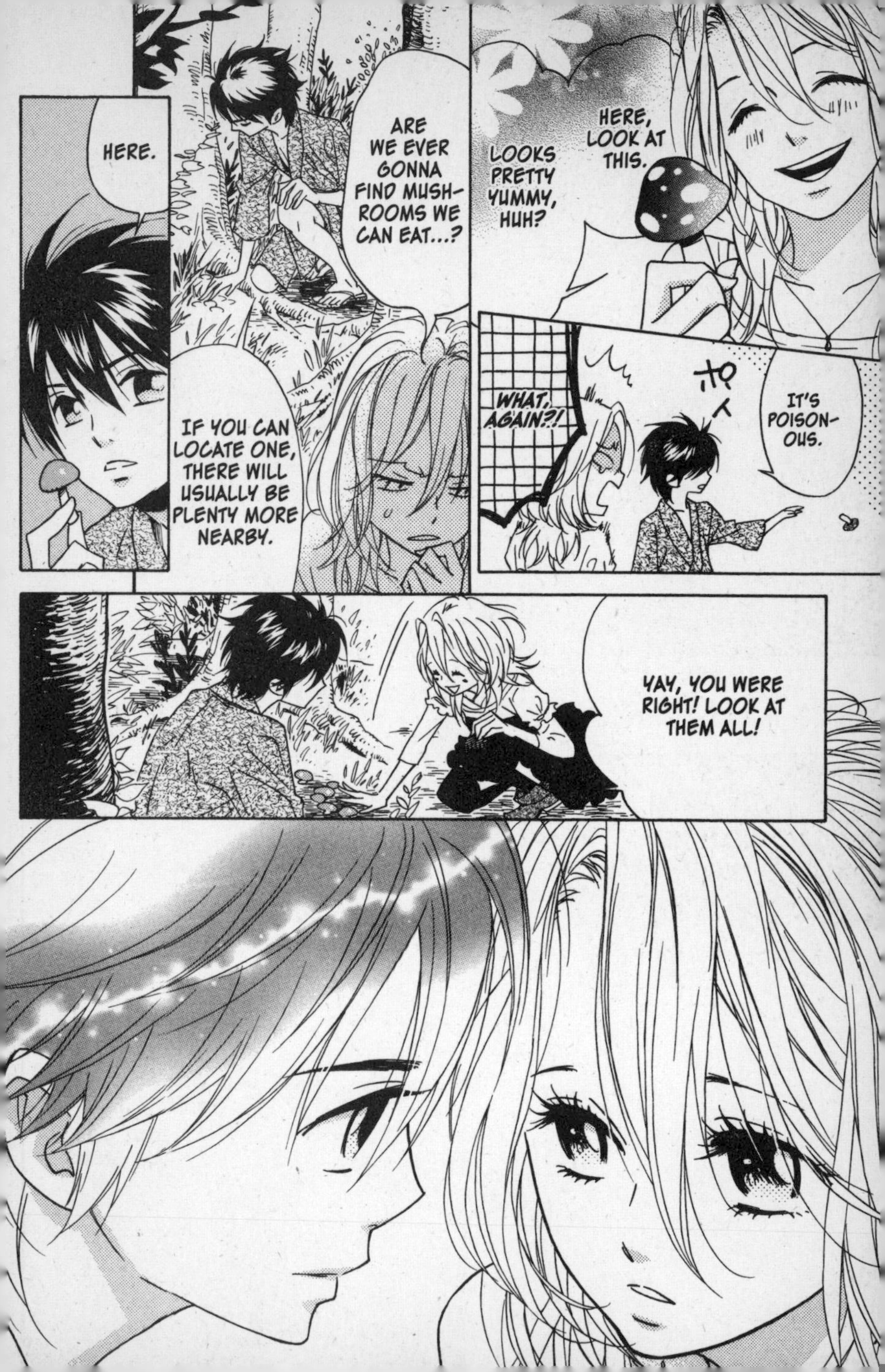
HERE, LOOK AT THIS.
LOOKS PRETTY YUMMY, HUH?
IT'S POISON-OUS.
ポイ
WHAT, AGAIN?!
ARE WE EVER GONNA FIND MUSH-ROOMS WE CAN EAT...?
HERE.
IF YOU CAN LOCATE ONE, THERE WILL USUALLY BE PLENTY MORE NEARBY.
YAY, YOU WERE RIGHT! LOOK AT THEM ALL!

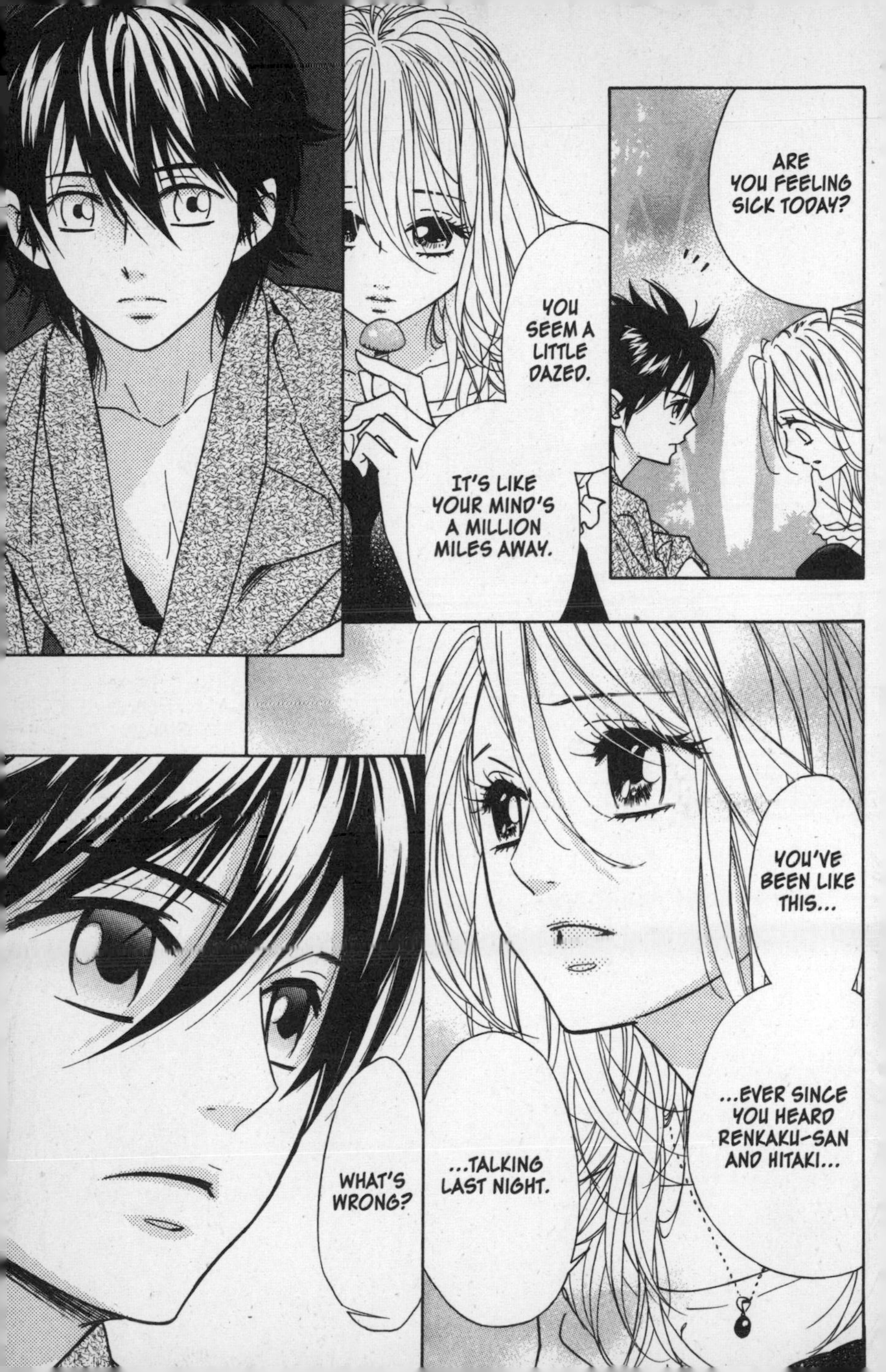
ARE YOU FEELING SICK TODAY?
YOU SEEM A LITTLE DAZED.
IT'S LIKE YOUR MIND'S A MILLION MILES AWAY.
YOU'VE BEEN LIKE THIS...
...EVER SINCE YOU HEARD RENKAKU-SAN AND HITAKI...
...TALKING LAST NIGHT.
WHAT'S WRONG?

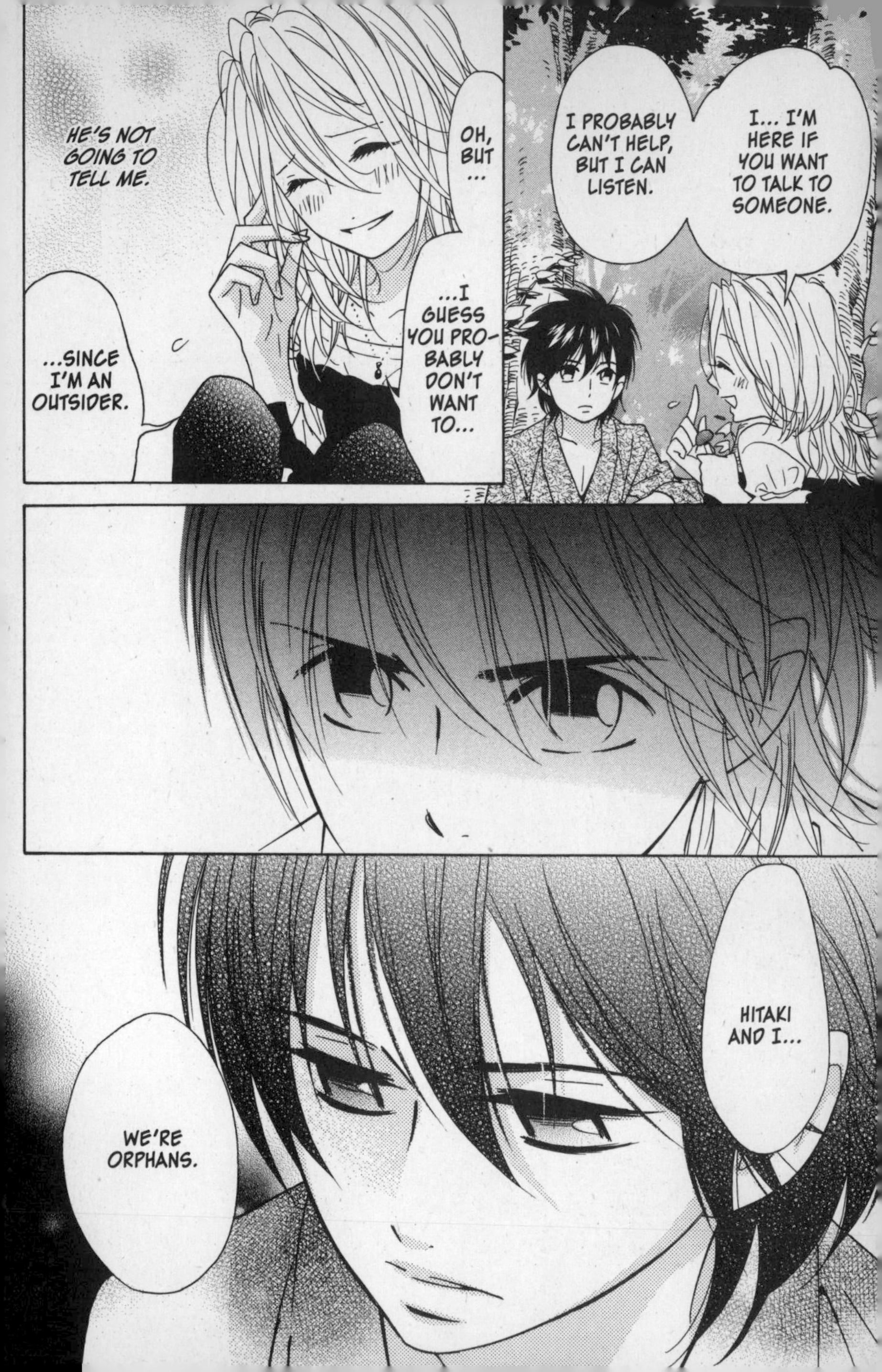
I... I'M HERE IF YOU WANT TO TALK TO SOMEONE.
I PROBABLY CAN'T HELP, BUT I CAN LISTEN.
OH, BUT ...
...I GUESS YOU PROBABLY DON'T WANT TO...
HE'S NOT GOING TO TELL ME.
...SINCE I'M AN OUTSIDER.
HITAKI AND I...
WE'RE ORPHANS.

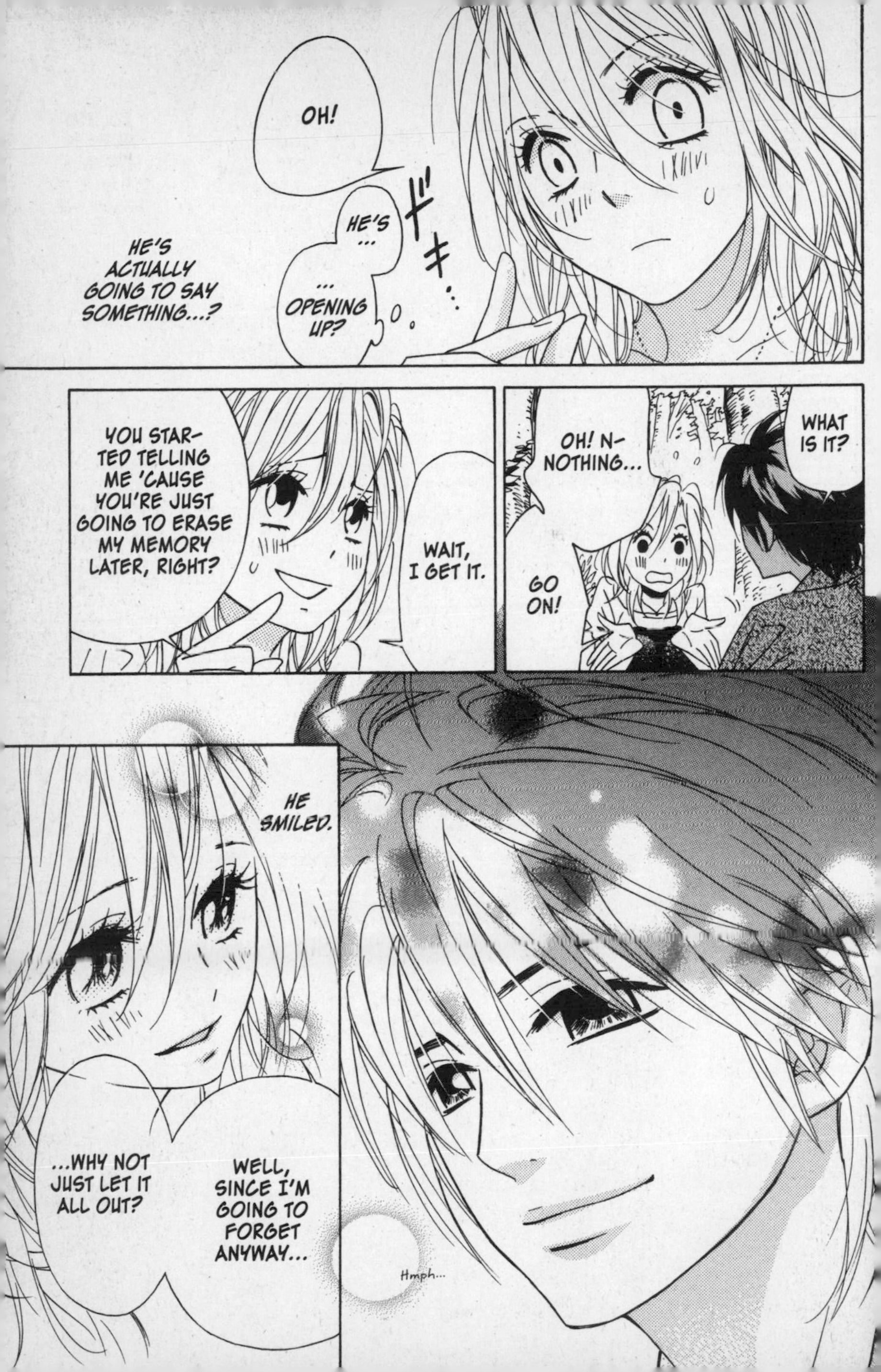
OH!
HE'S ...
... OPENING UP?
ドキ...
HE'S ACTUALLY GOING TO SAY SOMETHING...?
WHAT IS IT?
OH! N-NOTHING...
GO ON!
WAIT, I GET IT.
YOU STAR-TED TELLING ME 'CAUSE YOU'RE JUST GOING TO ERASE MY MEMORY LATER, RIGHT?
HE SMILED.
Hmph...
WELL, SINCE I'M GOING TO FORGET ANYWAY...
...WHY NOT JUST LET IT ALL OUT?

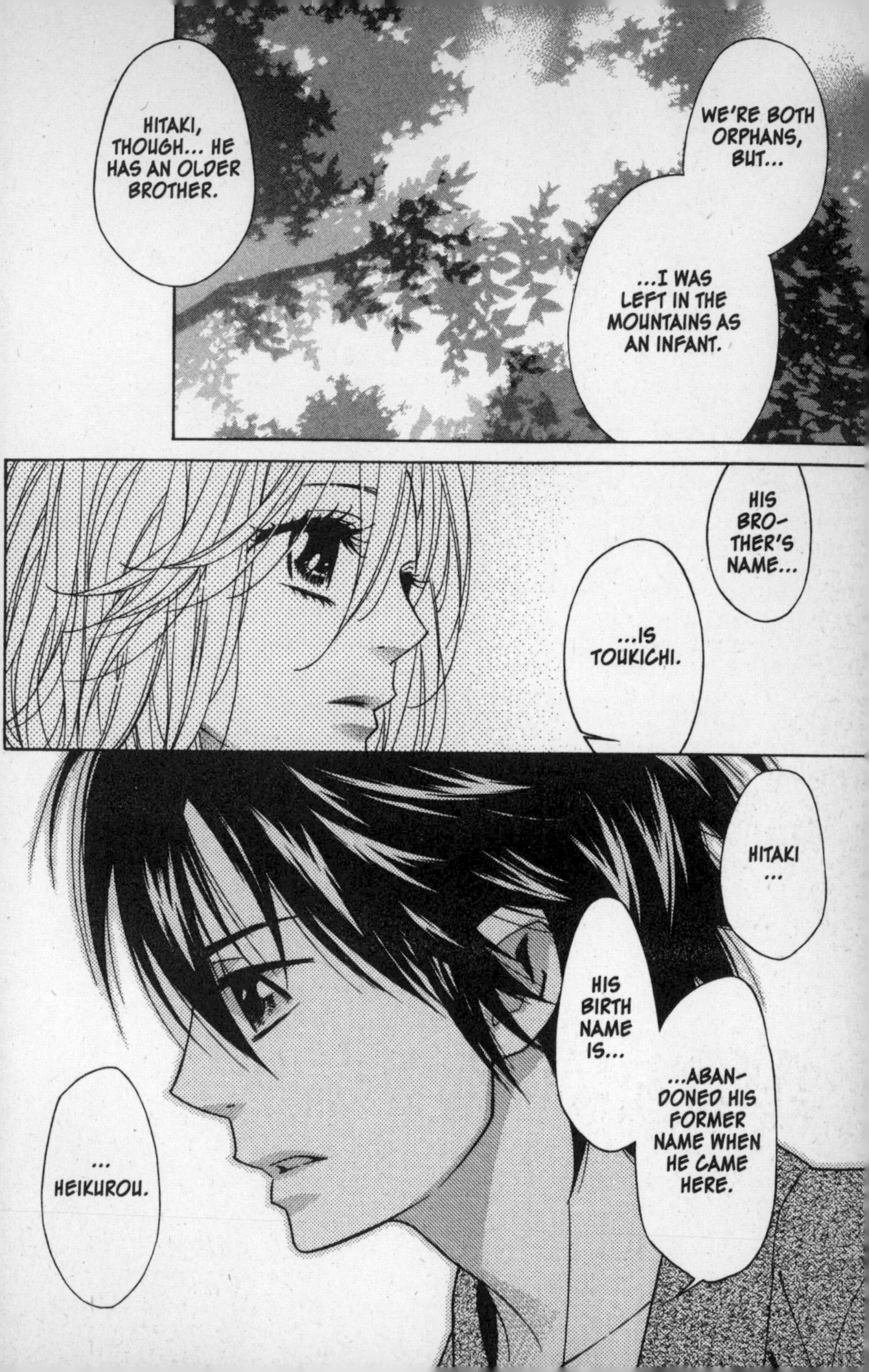
WE'RE BOTH ORPHANS, BUT...
...I WAS LEFT IN THE MOUNTAINS AS AN INFANT.
HITAKI, THOUGH... HE HAS AN OLDER BROTHER.
HIS BRO-THER'S NAME...
...IS TOUKICHI.
HITAKI ...
...ABAN-DONED HIS FORMER NAME WHEN HE CAME HERE.
HIS BIRTH NAME IS...
... HEIKUROU.

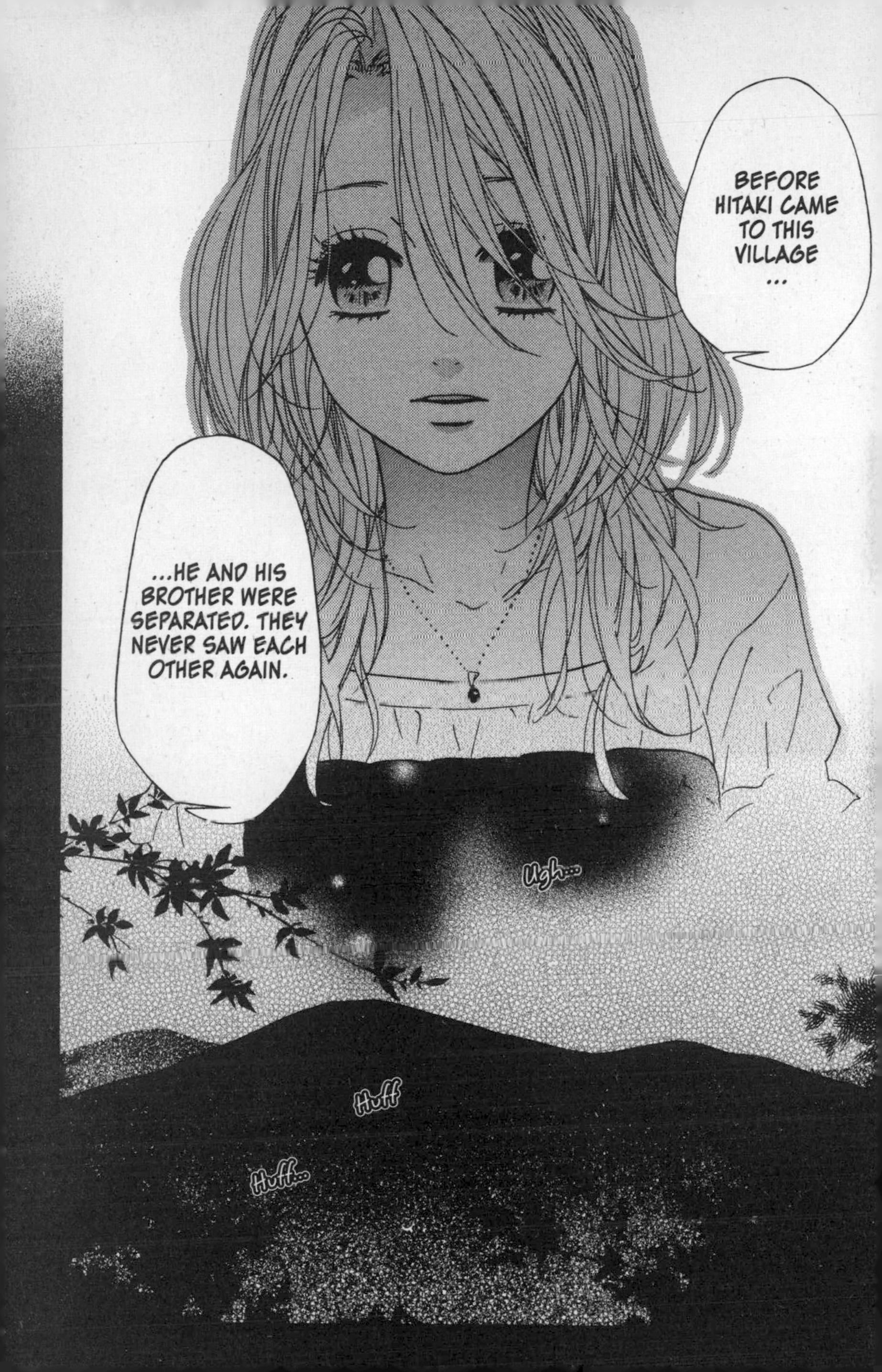
BEFORE HITAKI CAME TO THIS VILLAGE ...
...HE AND HIS BROTHER WERE SEPARATED. THEY NEVER SAW EACH OTHER AGAIN.
Ugh...
Huff
Huff...

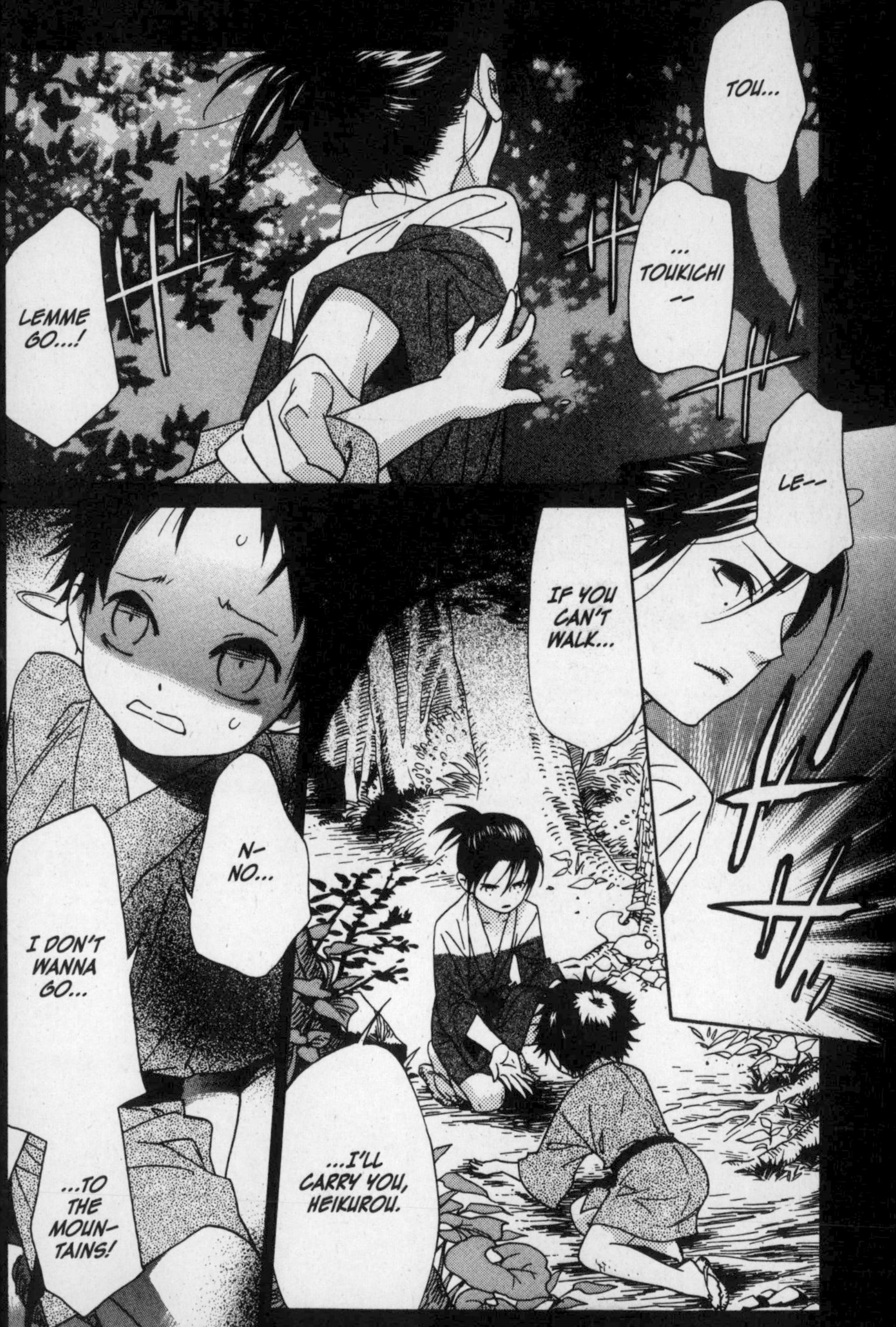
TOU...
... TOUKICHI --
LEMME GO...!
LE--
IF YOU CAN'T WALK...
...I'LL CARRY YOU, HEIKUROU.
N- NO...
I DON'T WANNA GO...!
...TO THE MOUN-TAINS!

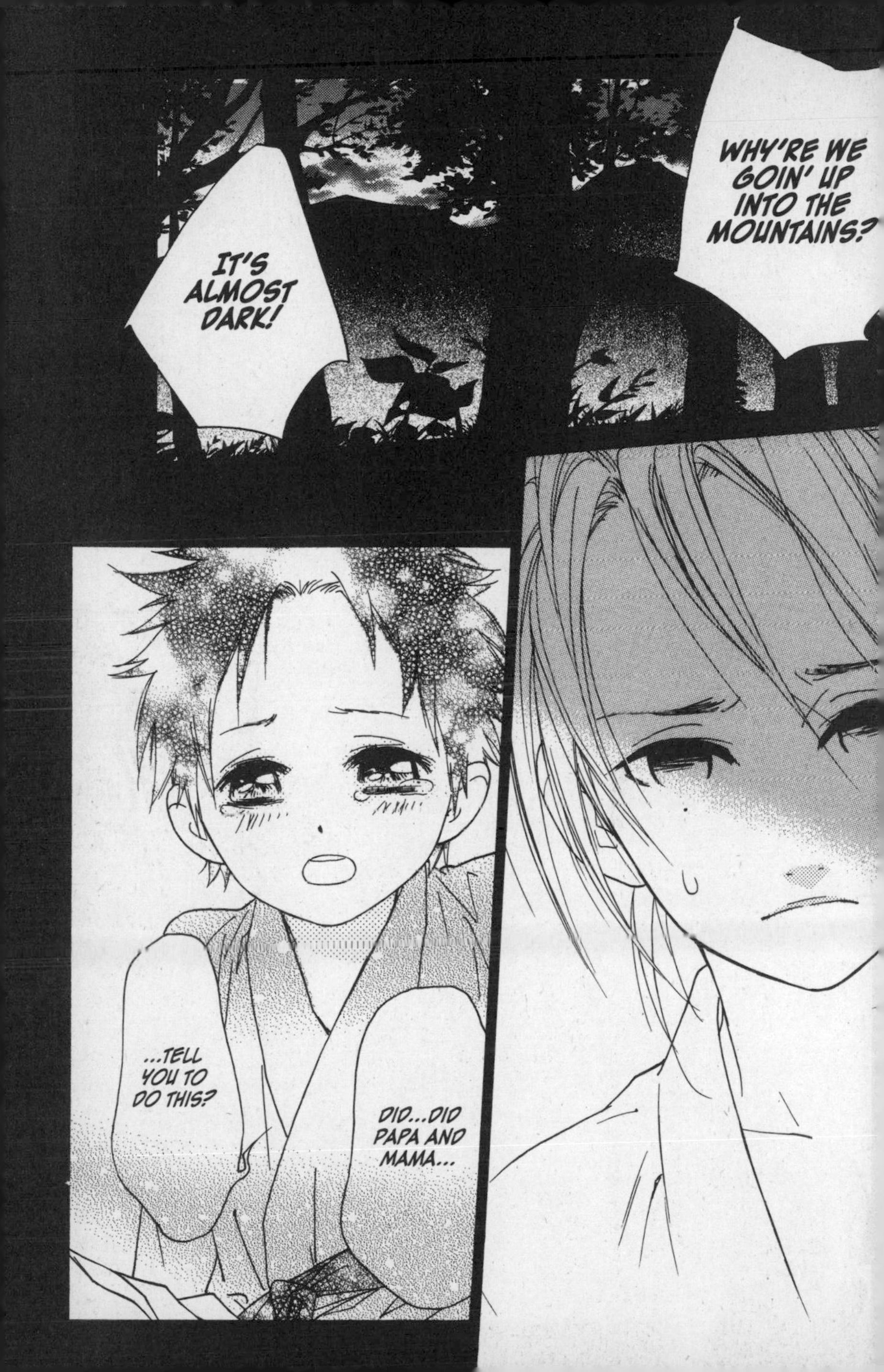
WHY'RE WE GOIN' UP INTO THE MOUNTAINS?
IT'S ALMOST DARK!
DID...DID PAPA AND MAMA...
...TELL YOU TO DO THIS?

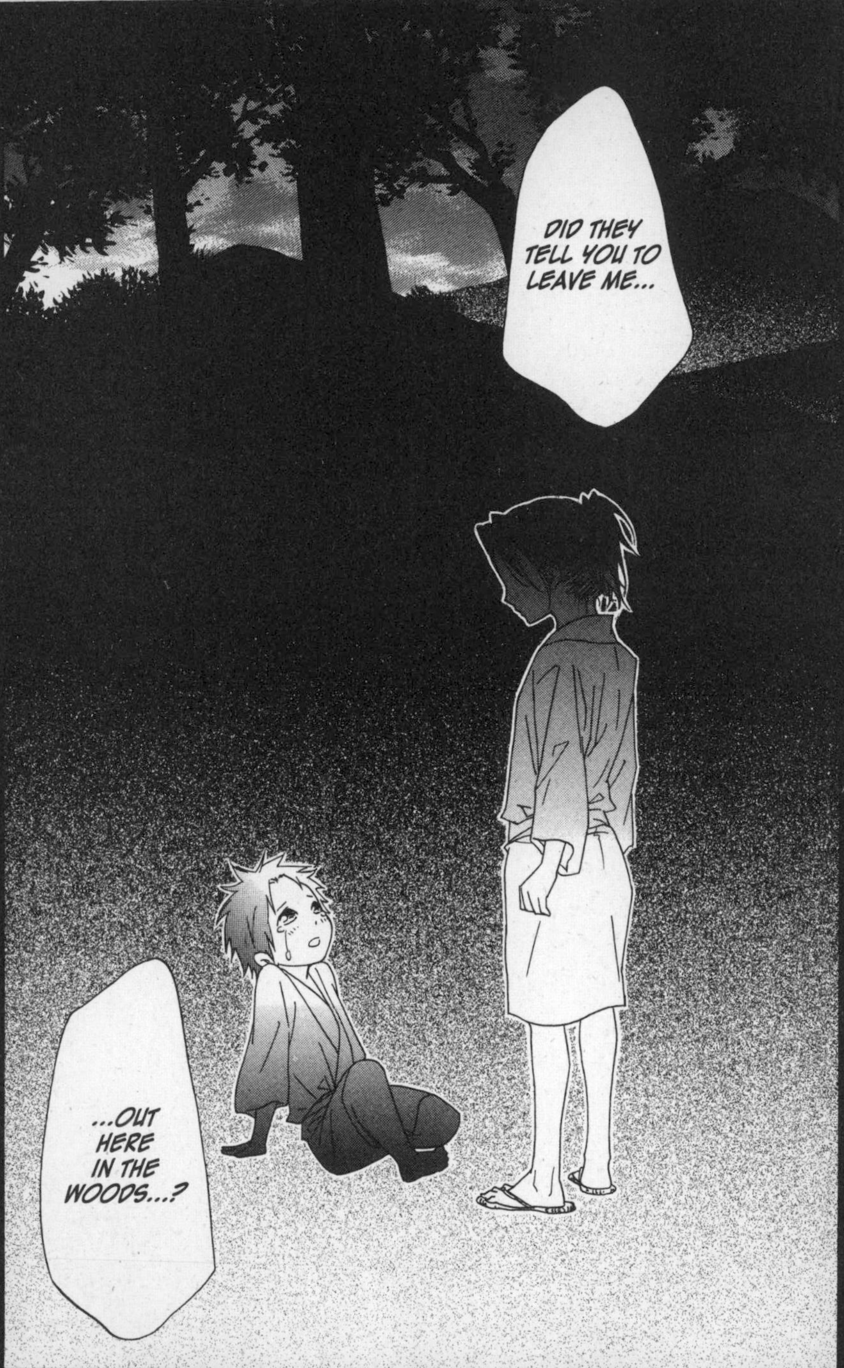
DID THEY TELL YOU TO LEAVE ME...
...OUT HERE IN THE WOODS...?

Chapter 23/End

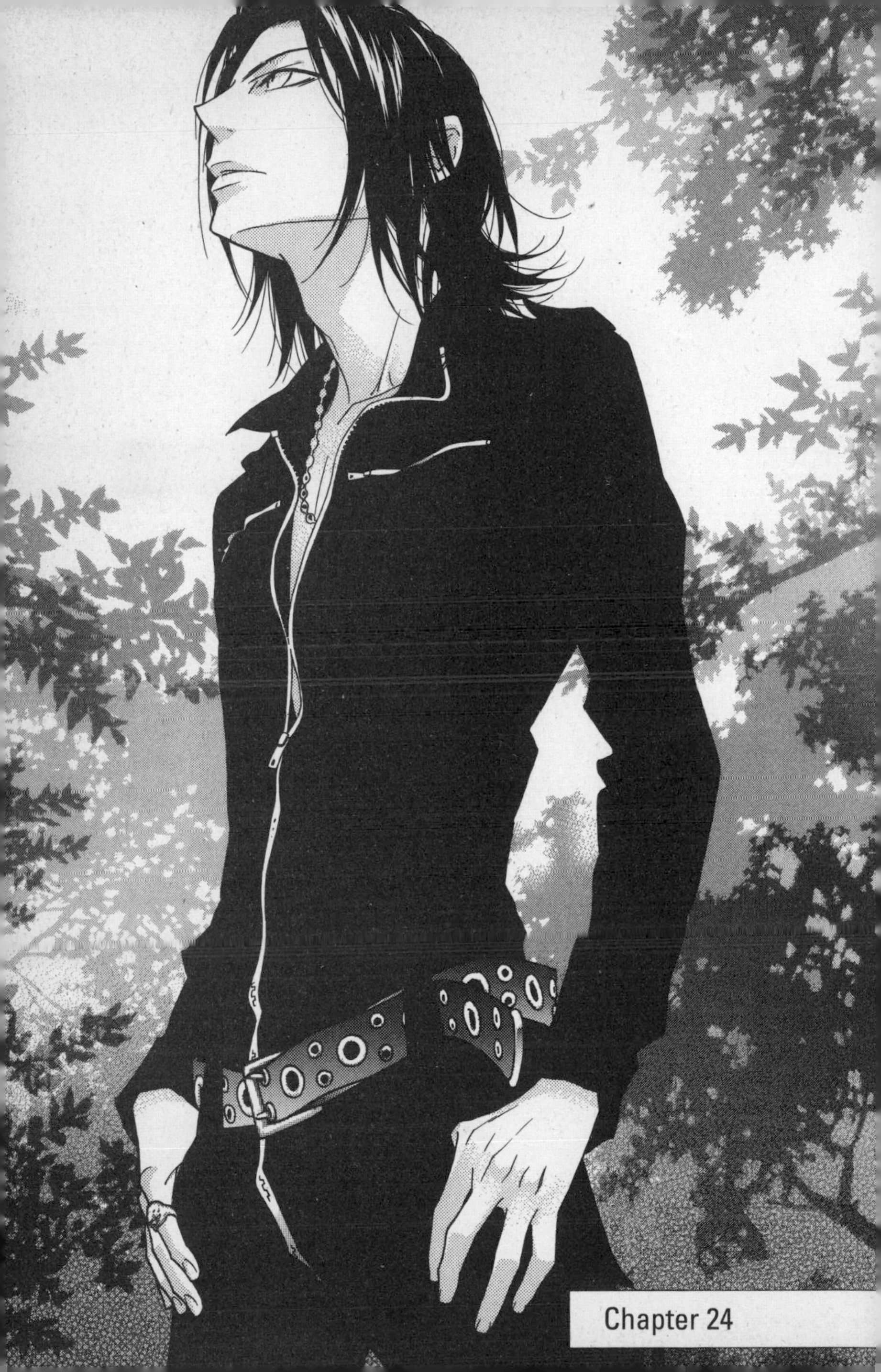

Chapter 24

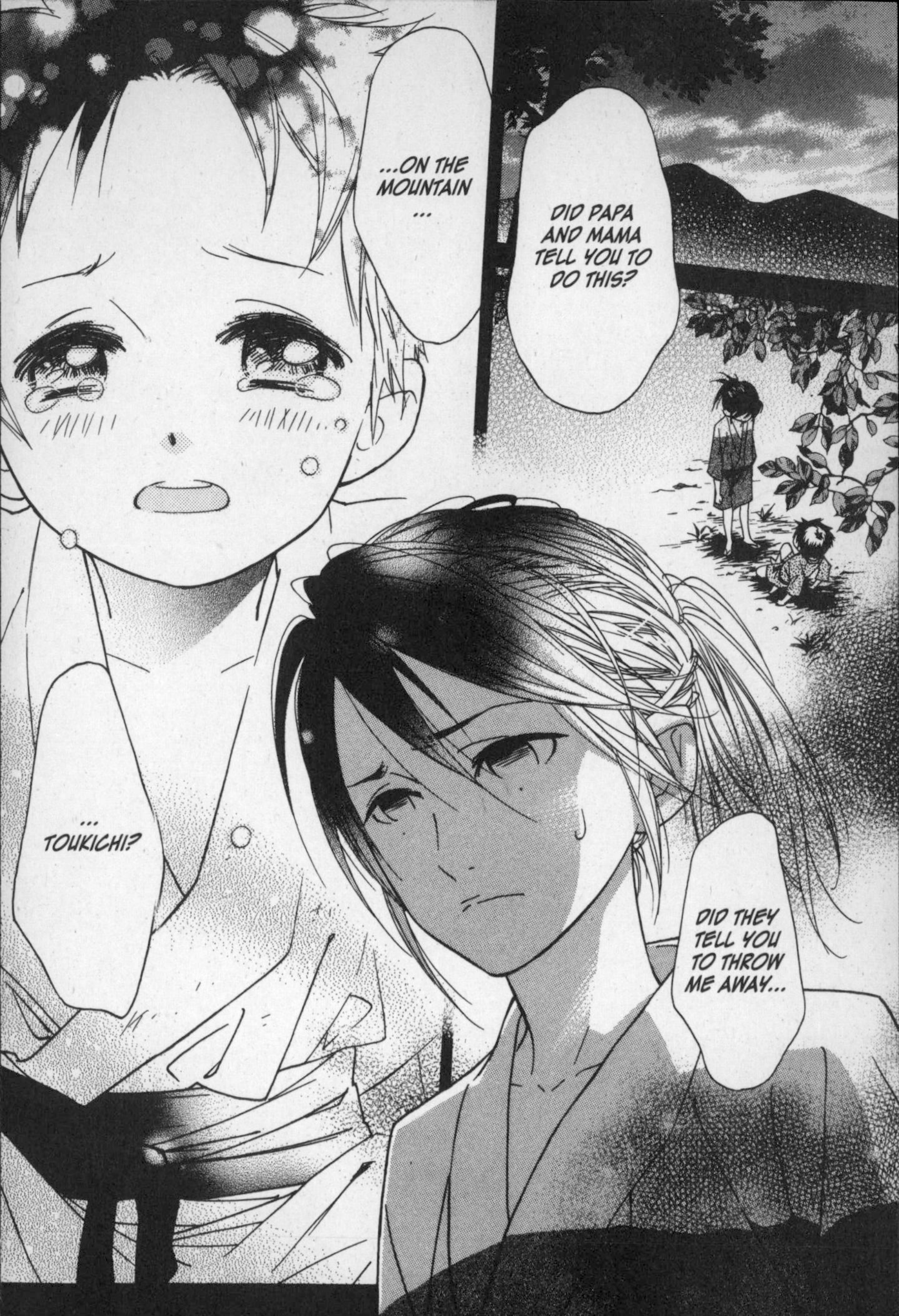
DID PAPA AND MAMA TELL YOU TO DO THIS?
DID THEY TELL YOU TO THROW ME AWAY...
...ON THE MOUNTAIN ...
... TOUKICHI?

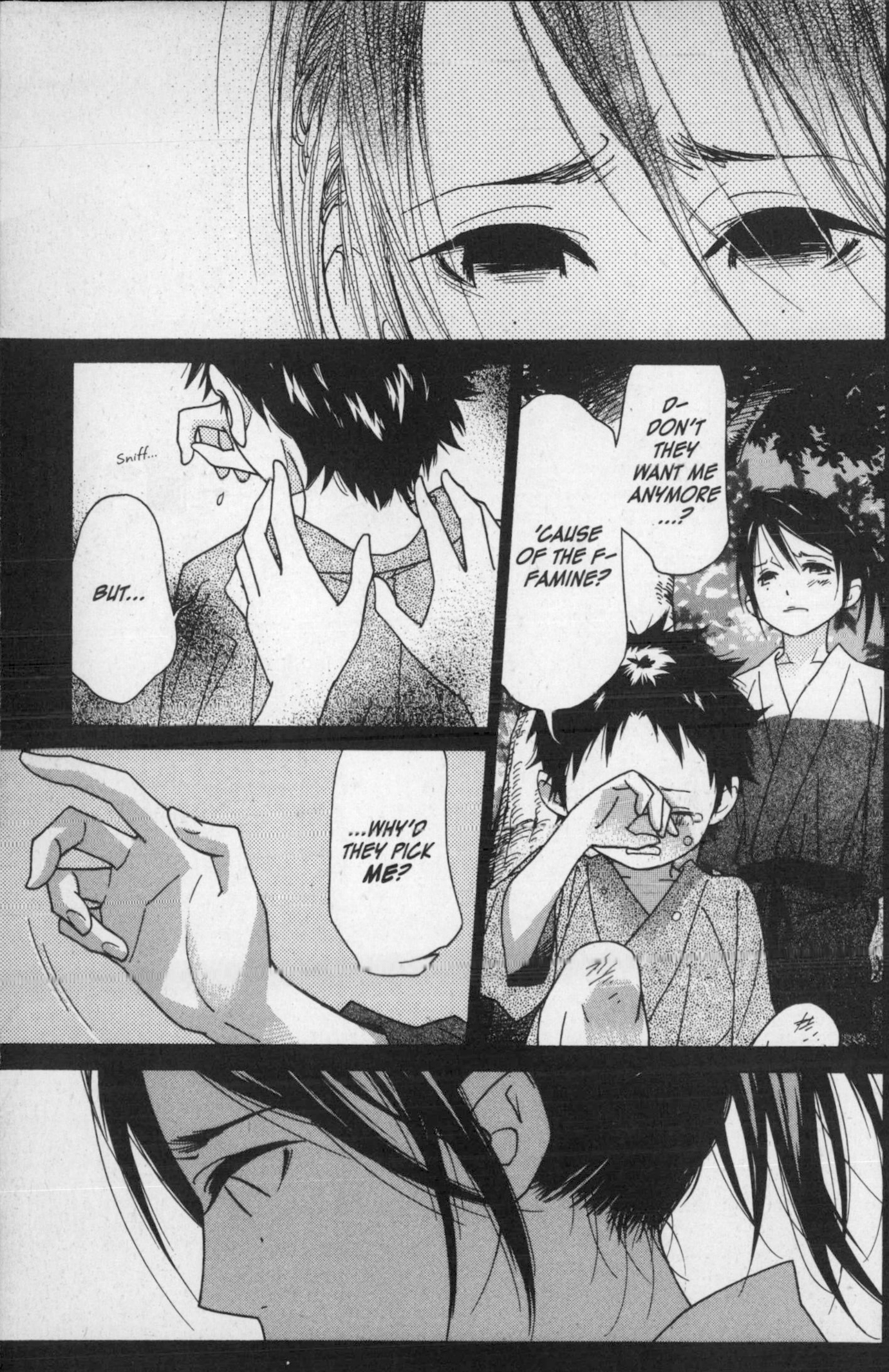
D-DON'T THEY WANT ME ANYMORE ...?
'CAUSE OF THE F-FAMINE?
Sniff...
BUT...
...WHY'D THEY PICK ME?

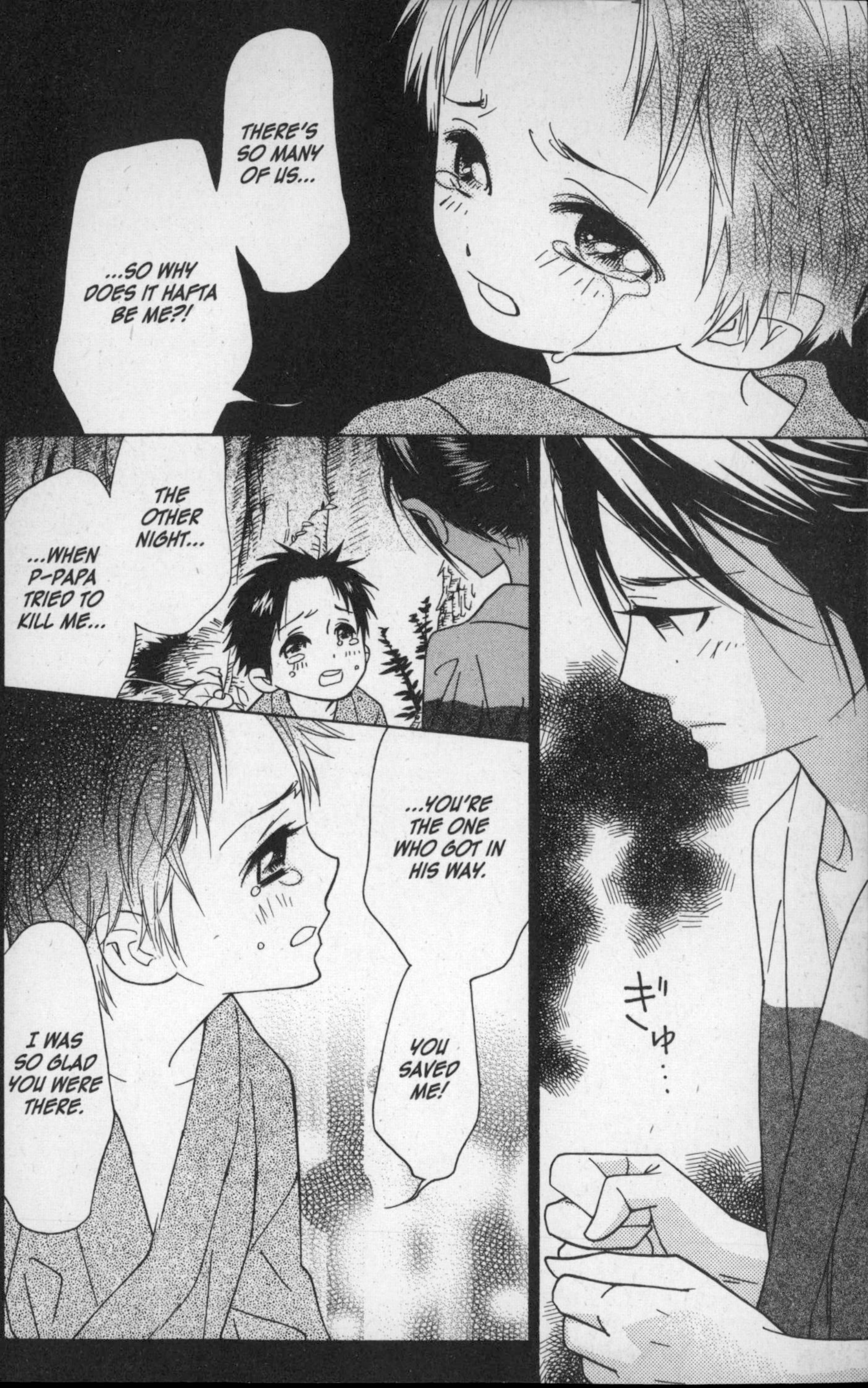
THERE'S SO MANY OF US...
...SO WHY DOES IT HAFTA BE ME?!
THE OTHER NIGHT...
...WHEN P-PAPA TRIED TO KILL ME...
...YOU'RE THE ONE WHO GOT IN HIS WAY.
YOU SAVED ME!
I WAS SO GLAD YOU WERE THERE.
ぎゅ...

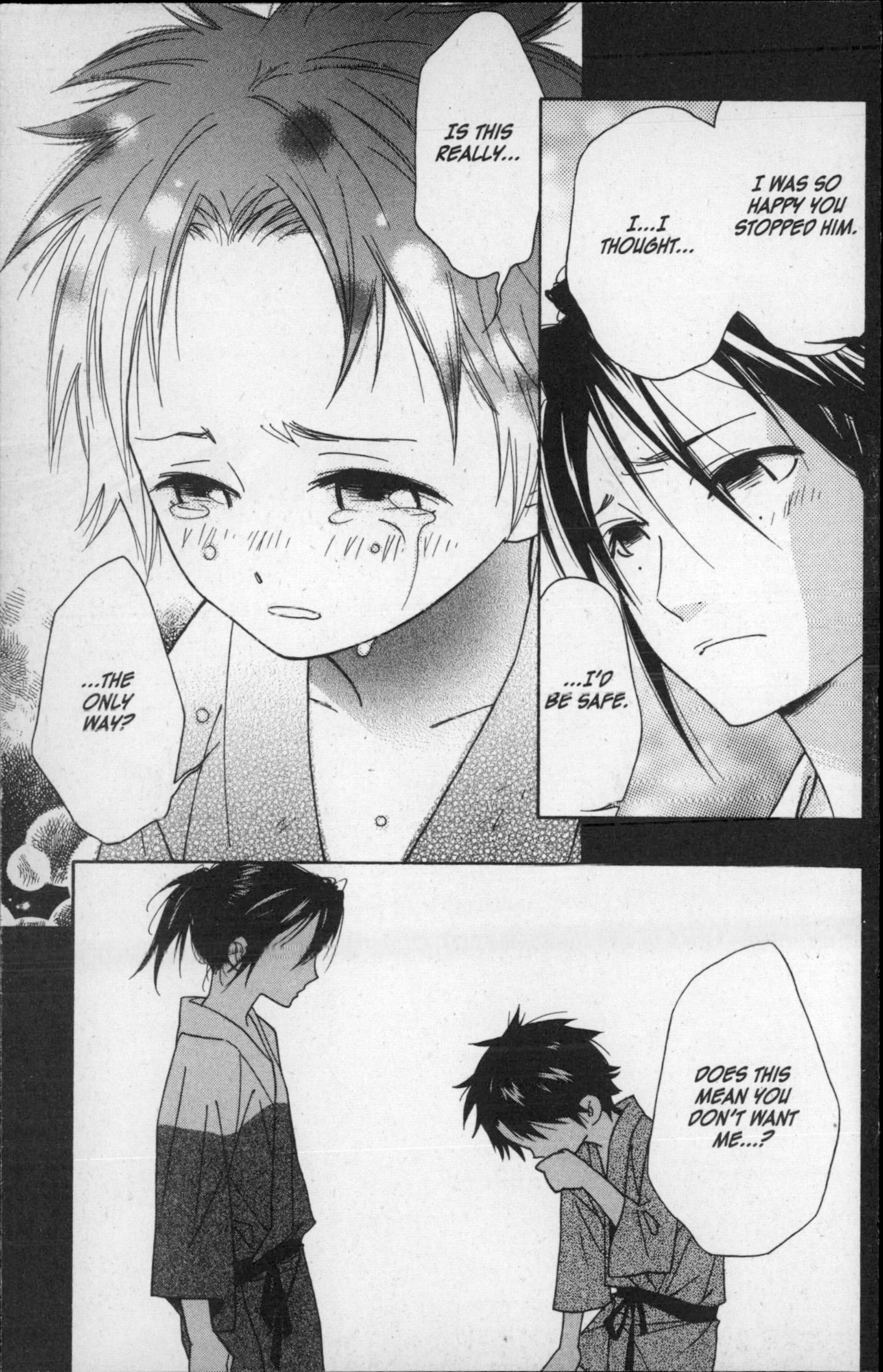
IS THIS REALLY...
...THE ONLY WAY?
I WAS SO HAPPY YOU STOPPED HIM.
I...I THOUGHT...
...I'D BE SAFE.
DOES THIS MEAN YOU DON'T WANT ME...?

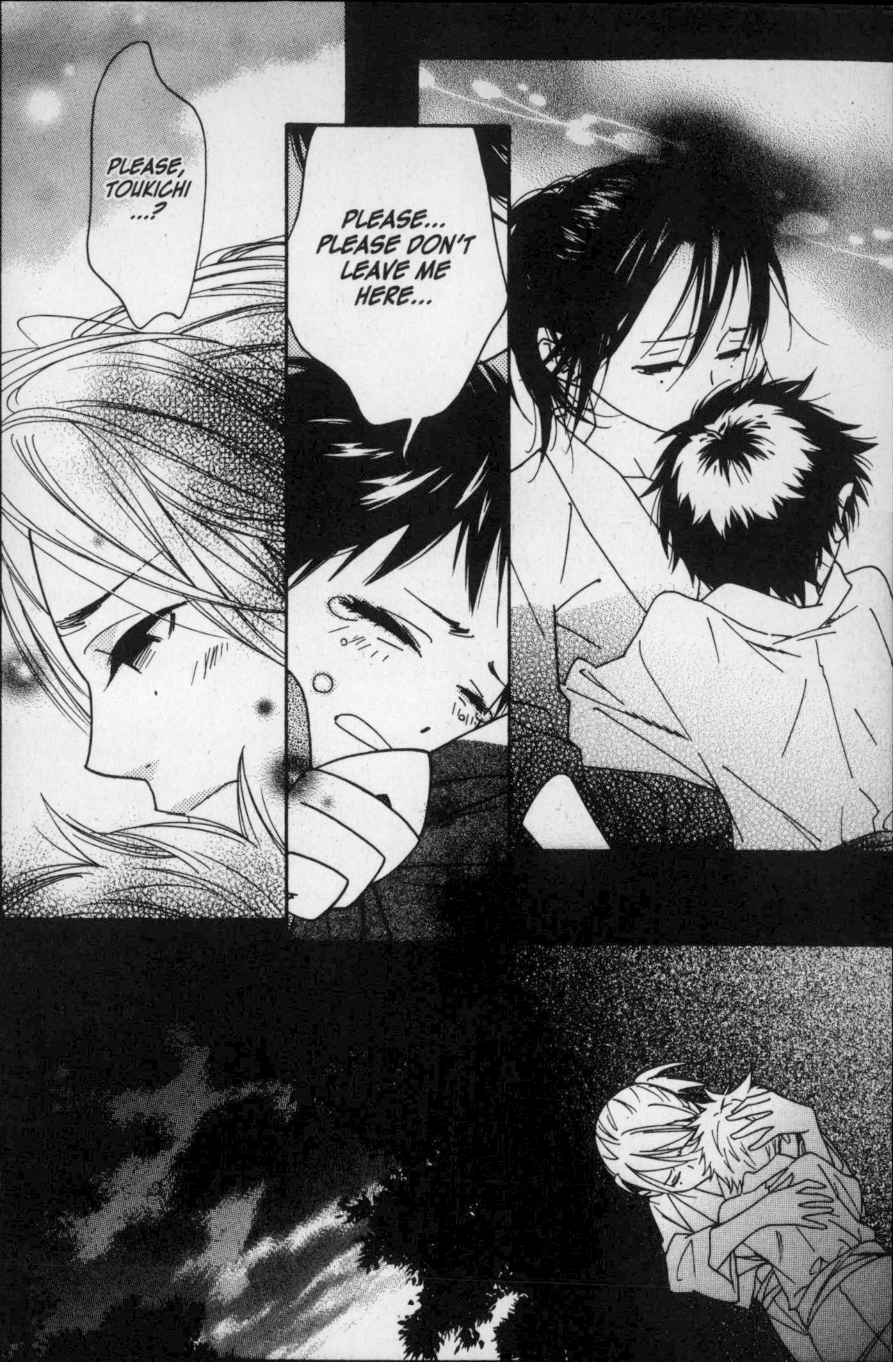
PLEASE...
PLEASE DON'T
LEAVE ME
HERE...
PLEASE,
TOUKICHI
...?

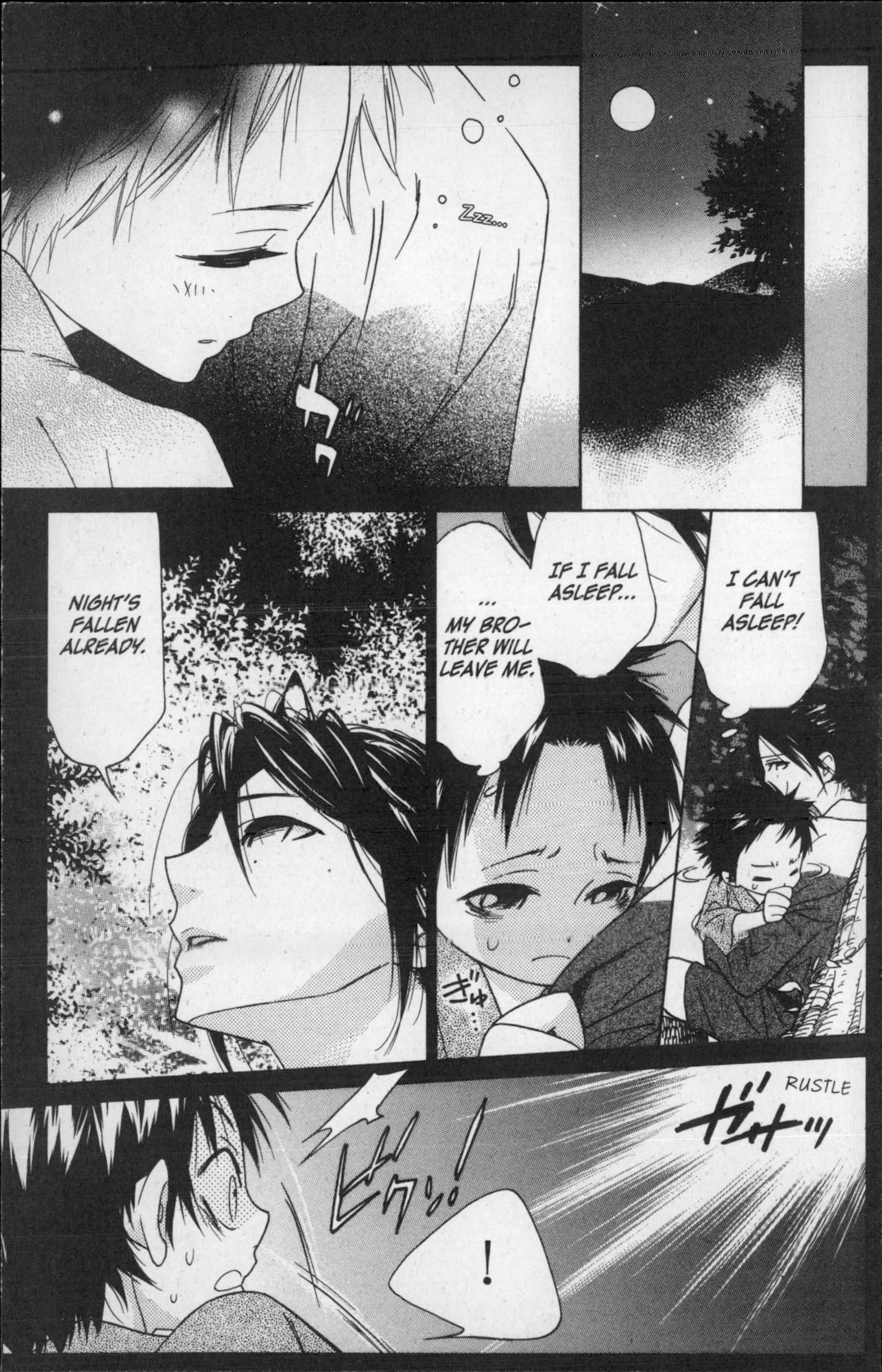
Zzz...
NIGHT'S FALLEN ALREADY.
I CAN'T FALL ASLEEP!
IF I FALL ASLEEP...
... MY BROTHER WILL LEAVE ME.
RUSTLE
!

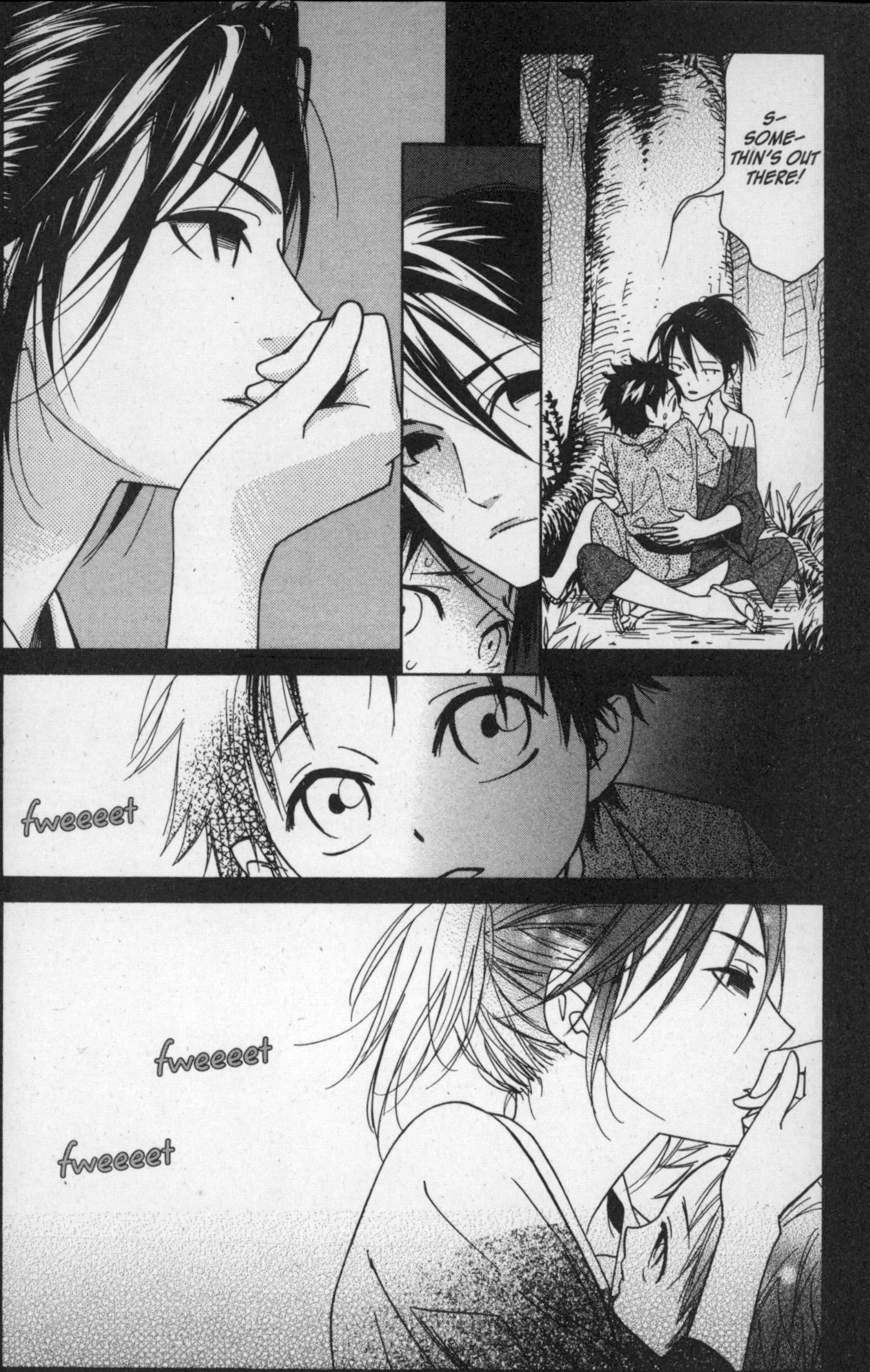
S-SOME-THIN'S OUT THERE!
fweeeet
fweeeet
fweeeet

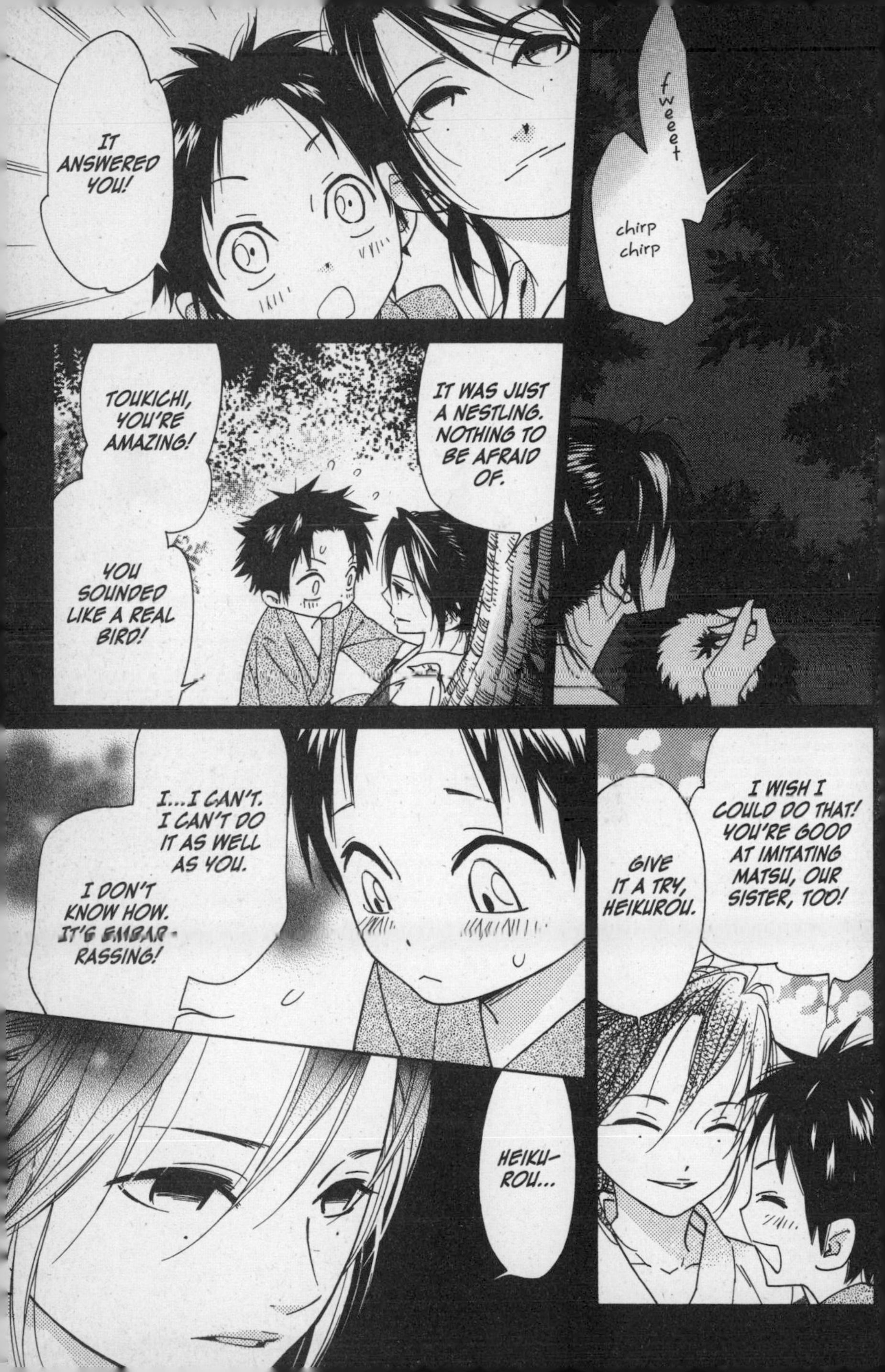
fweeet
chirp chirp
IT ANSWERED YOU!
IT WAS JUST A NESTLING. NOTHING TO BE AFRAID OF.
TOUKICHI, YOU'RE AMAZING!
YOU SOUNDED LIKE A REAL BIRD!
I WISH I COULD DO THAT! YOU'RE GOOD AT IMITATING MATSU, OUR SISTER, TOO!
GIVE IT A TRY, HEIKUROU.
I...I CAN'T. I CAN'T DO IT AS WELL AS YOU.
I DON'T KNOW HOW. IT'S EMBAR-RASSING!
HEIKU-ROU...

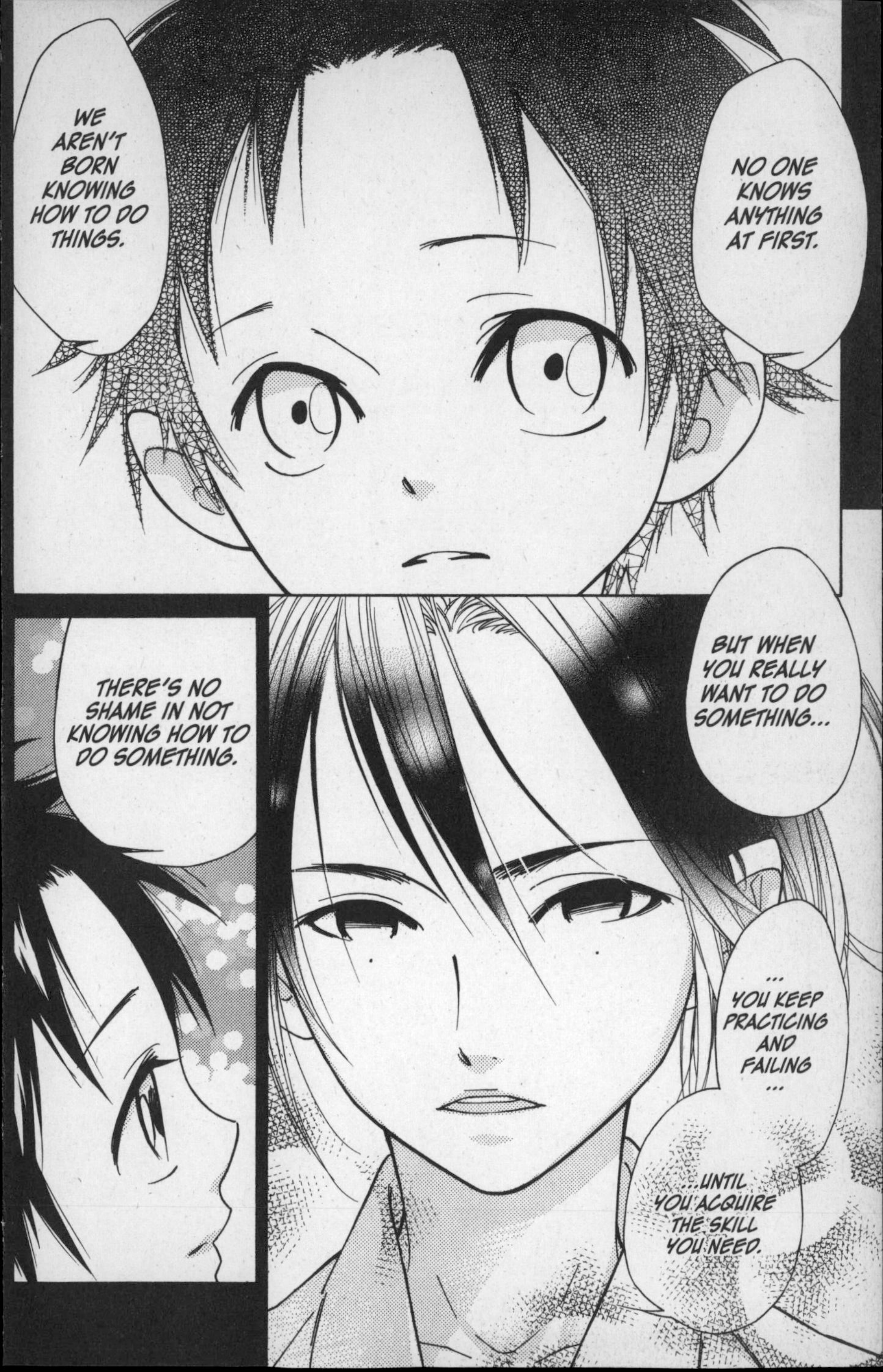
NO ONE KNOWS ANYTHING AT FIRST.
WE AREN'T BORN KNOWING HOW TO DO THINGS.
BUT WHEN YOU REALLY WANT TO DO SOMETHING...
... YOU KEEP PRACTICING AND FAILING ...
...UNTIL YOU ACQUIRE THE SKILL YOU NEED.
THERE'S NO SHAME IN NOT KNOWING HOW TO DO SOMETHING.

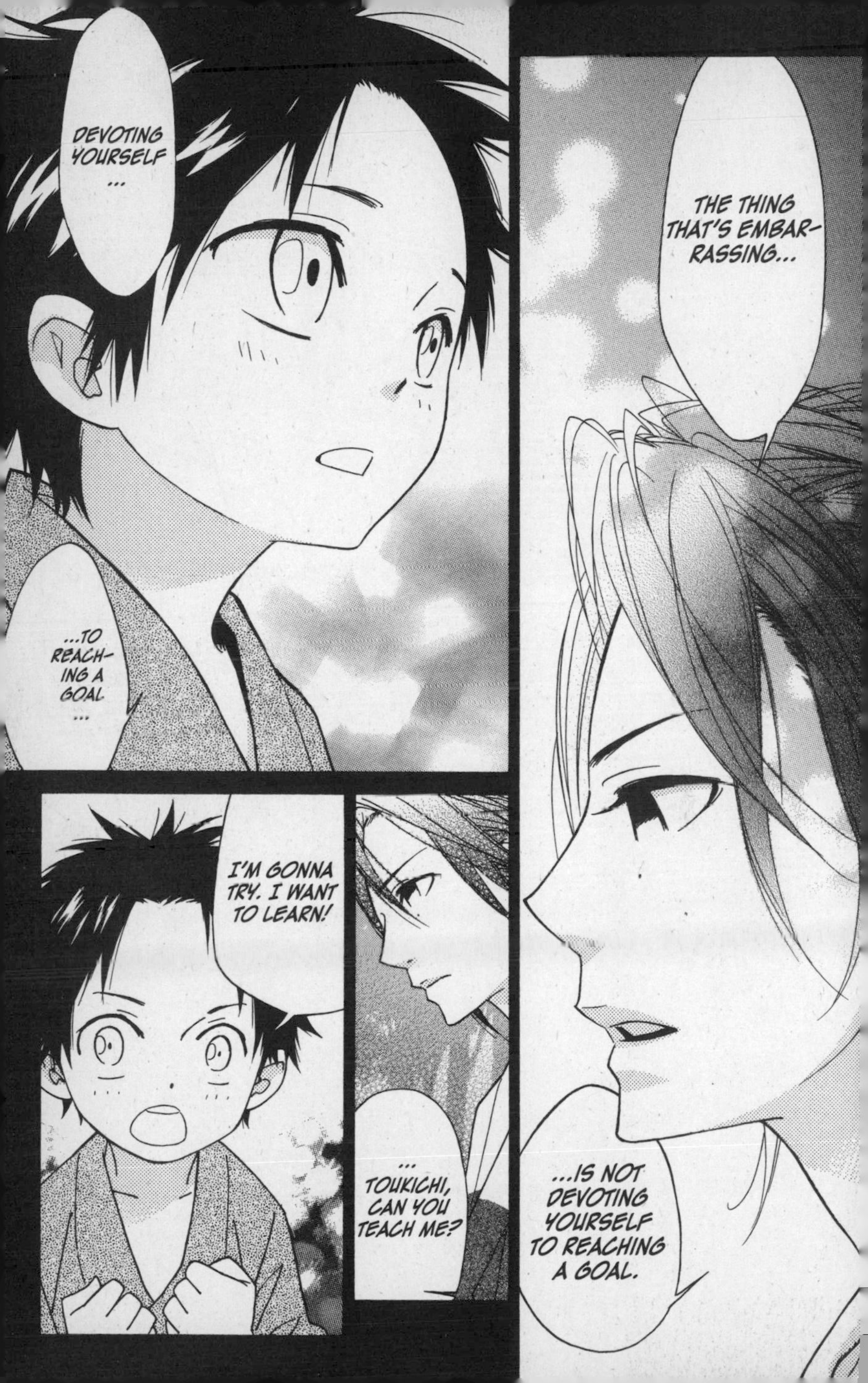
THE THING THAT'S EMBARRASSING...
...IS NOT DEVOTING YOURSELF TO REACHING A GOAL.
DEVOTING YOURSELF ...
...TO REACHING A GOAL ...
... TOUKICHI, CAN YOU TEACH ME?
I'M GONNA TRY. I WANT TO LEARN!

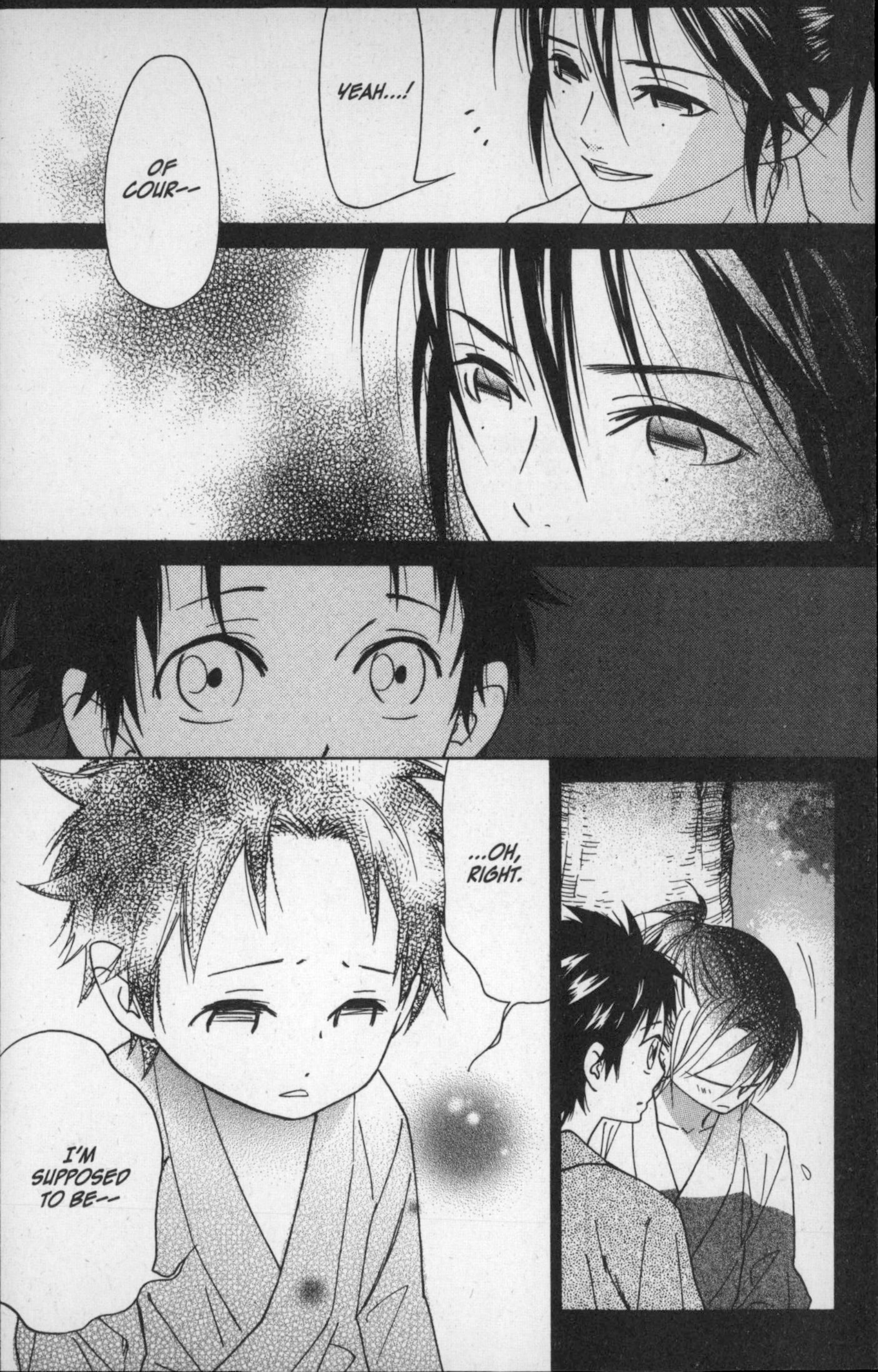
YEAH...!
OF COUR--
...OH, RIGHT.
I'M SUPPOSED TO BE--

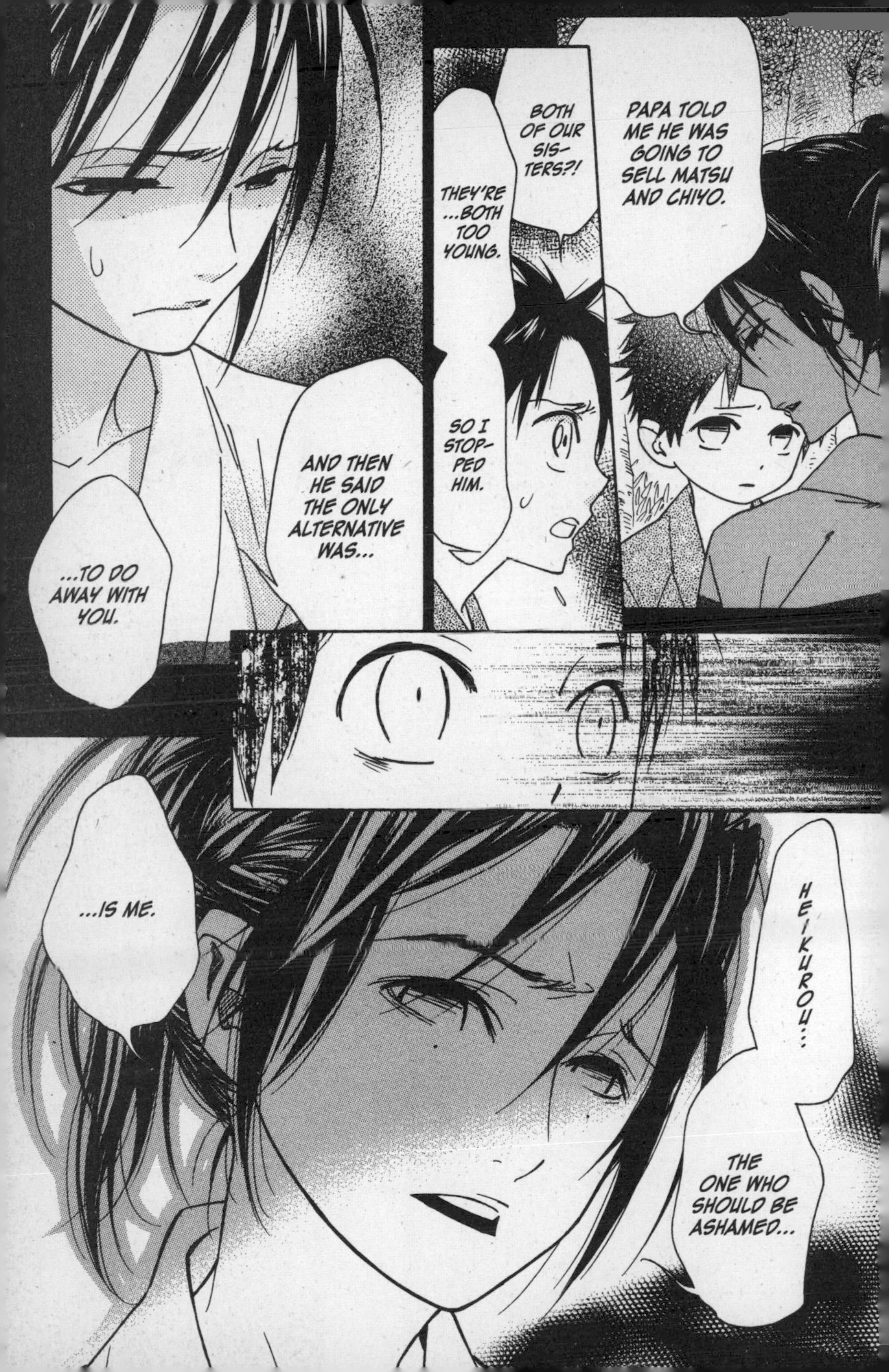
PAPA TOLD ME HE WAS GOING TO SELL MATSU AND CHIYO.
BOTH OF OUR SIS-TERS?!
THEY'RE ...BOTH TOO YOUNG.
SO I STOP-PED HIM.
AND THEN HE SAID THE ONLY ALTERNATIVE WAS...
...TO DO AWAY WITH YOU.
HEIKUROU...
THE ONE WHO SHOULD BE ASHAMED...
...IS ME.

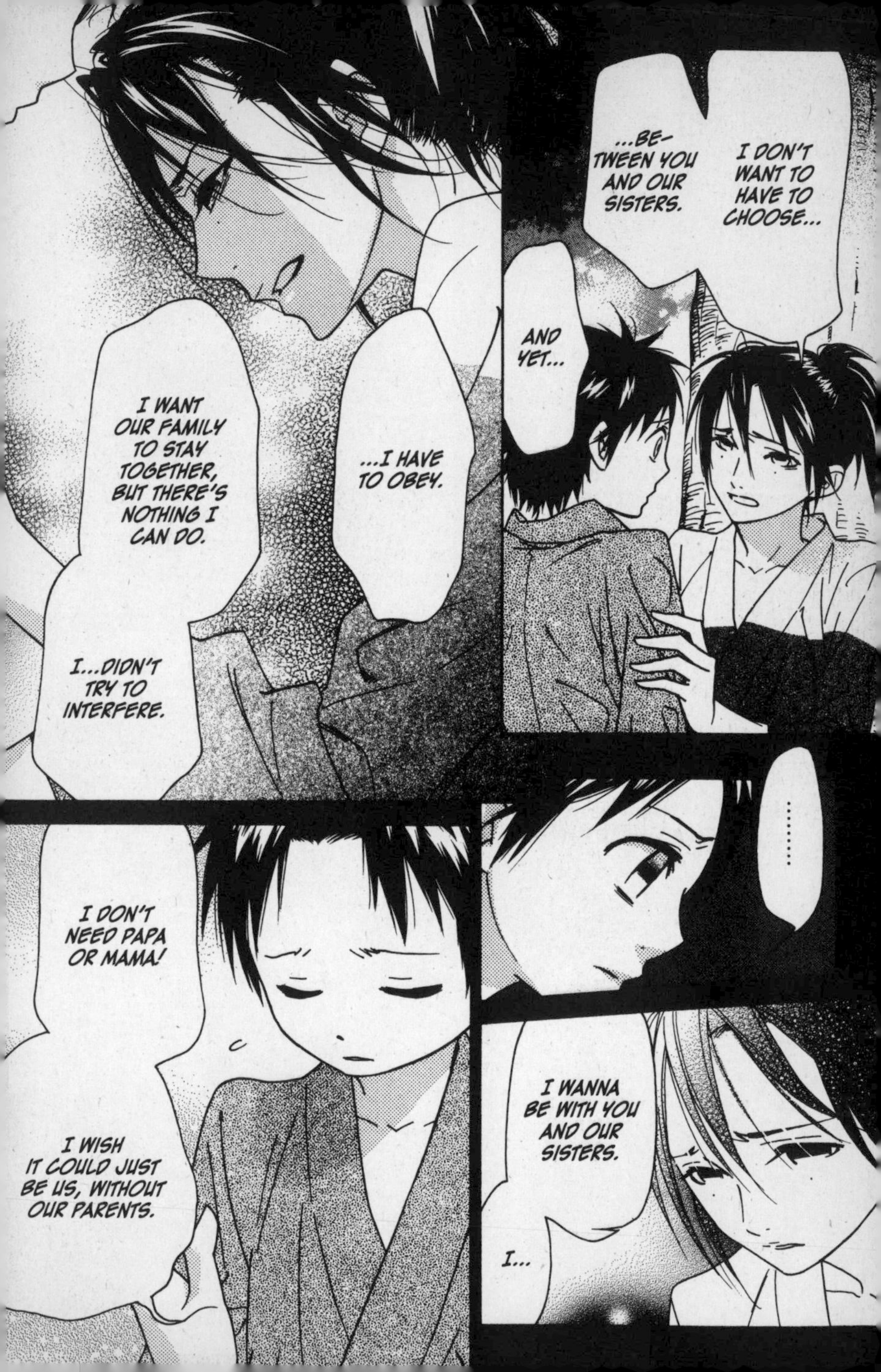
I DON'T WANT TO HAVE TO CHOOSE...
...BE-TWEEN YOU AND OUR SISTERS.
AND YET...
...I HAVE TO OBEY.
I WANT OUR FAMILY TO STAY TOGETHER, BUT THERE'S NOTHING I CAN DO.
I...DIDN'T TRY TO INTERFERE.
......
I WANNA BE WITH YOU AND OUR SISTERS.
I...
I DON'T NEED PAPA OR MAMA!
I WISH IT COULD JUST BE US, WITHOUT OUR PARENTS.

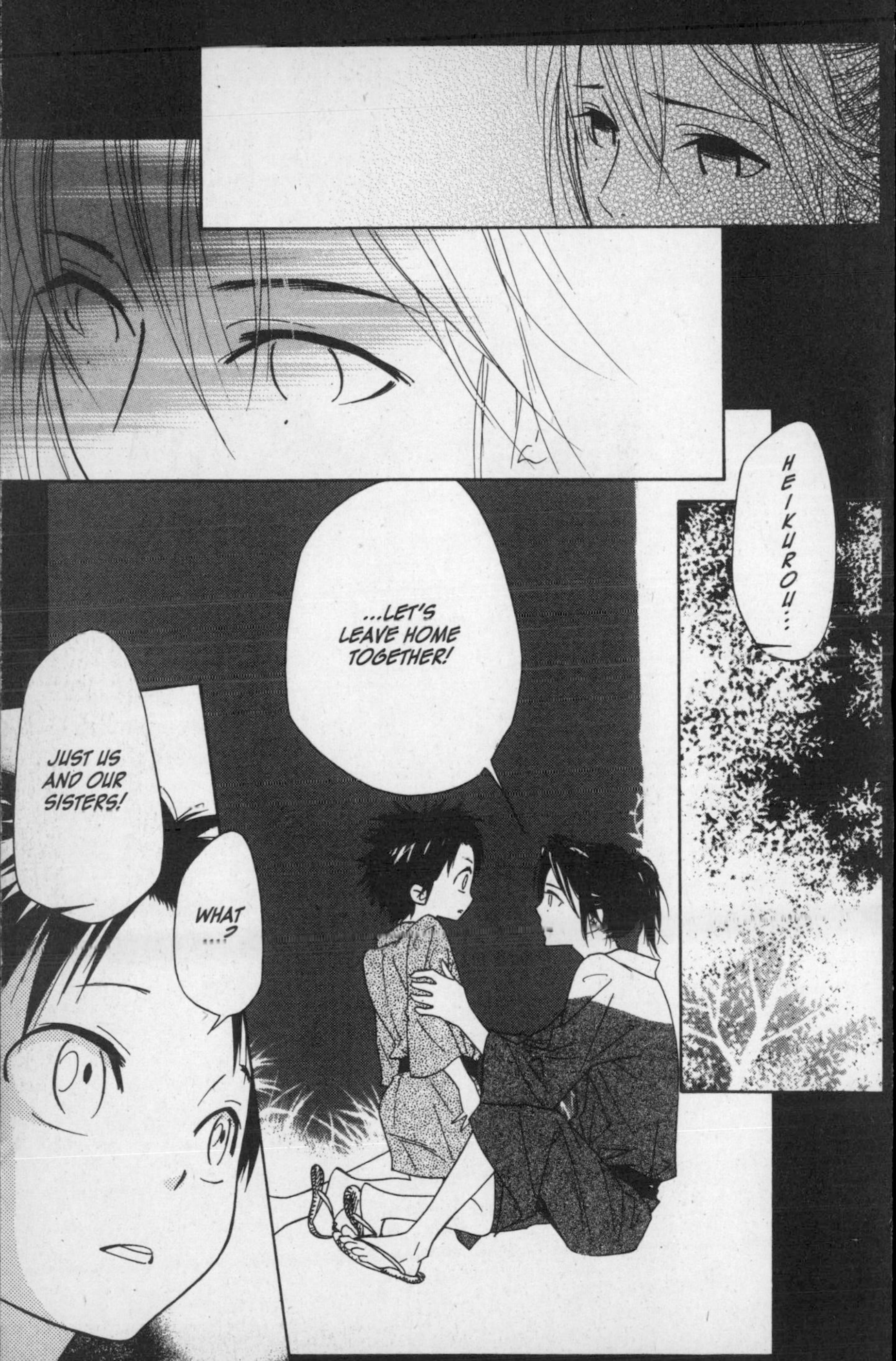
HEIKUROU...
...LET'S LEAVE HOME TOGETHER!
JUST US AND OUR SISTERS!
WHAT...?

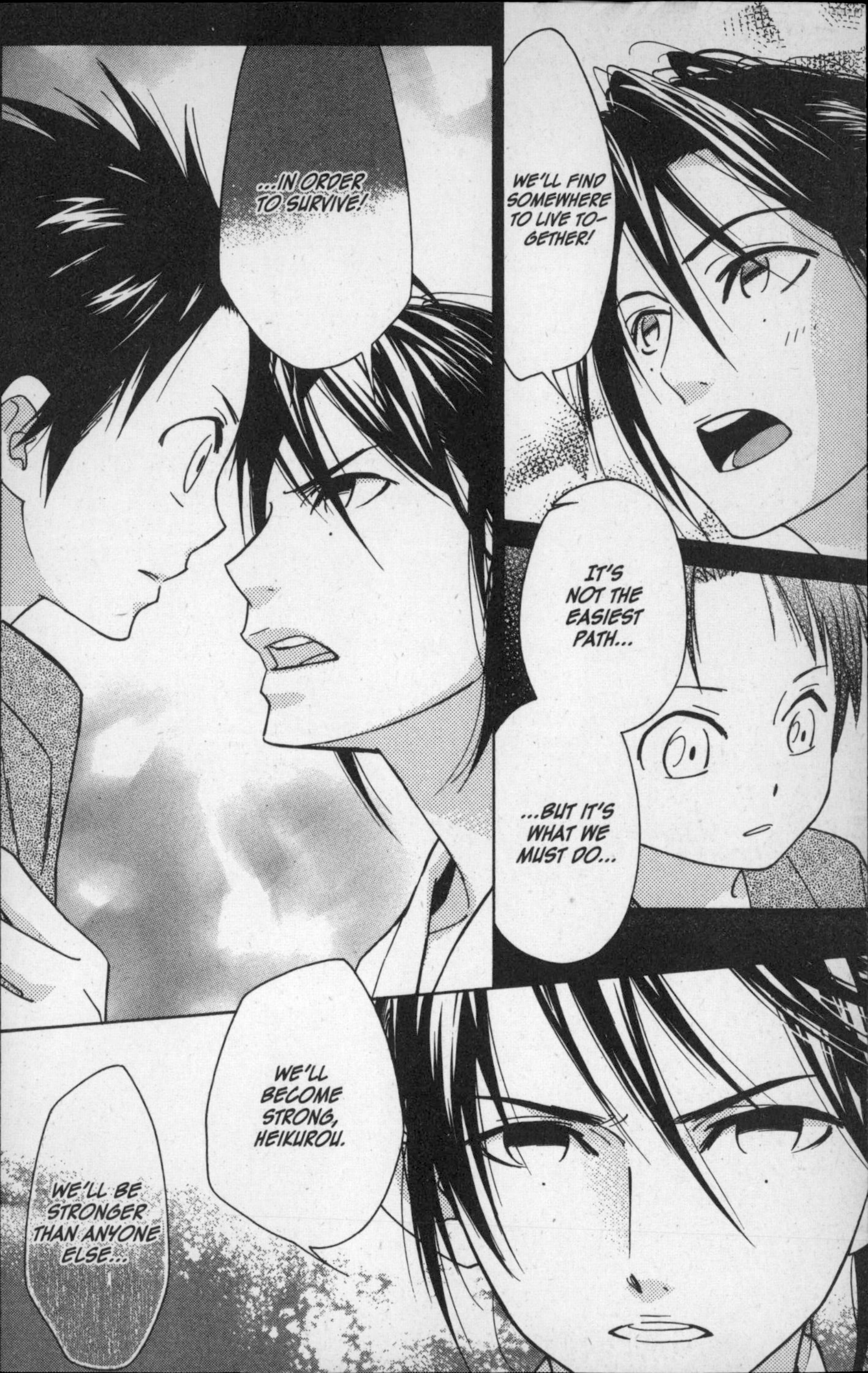
WE'LL FIND SOMEWHERE TO LIVE TO-GETHER!
...IN ORDER TO SURVIVE!
IT'S NOT THE EASIEST PATH...
...BUT IT'S WHAT WE MUST DO...
WE'LL BECOME STRONG, HEIKUROU.
WE'LL BE STRONGER THAN ANYONE ELSE...

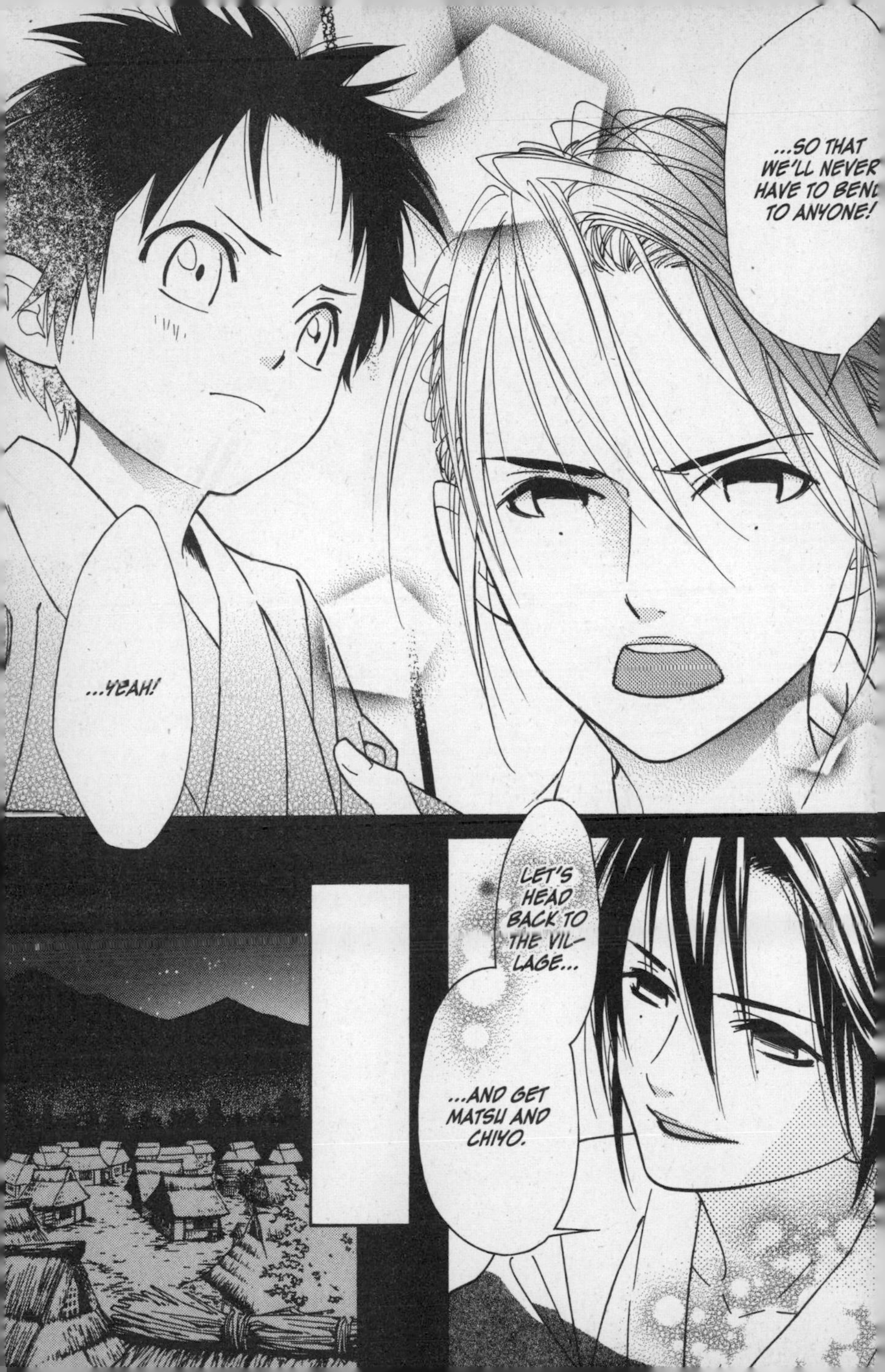
...SO THAT WE'LL NEVER HAVE TO BEND TO ANYONE!
...YEAH!
LET'S HEAD BACK TO THE VIL-LAGE...
...AND GET MATSU AND CHIYO.

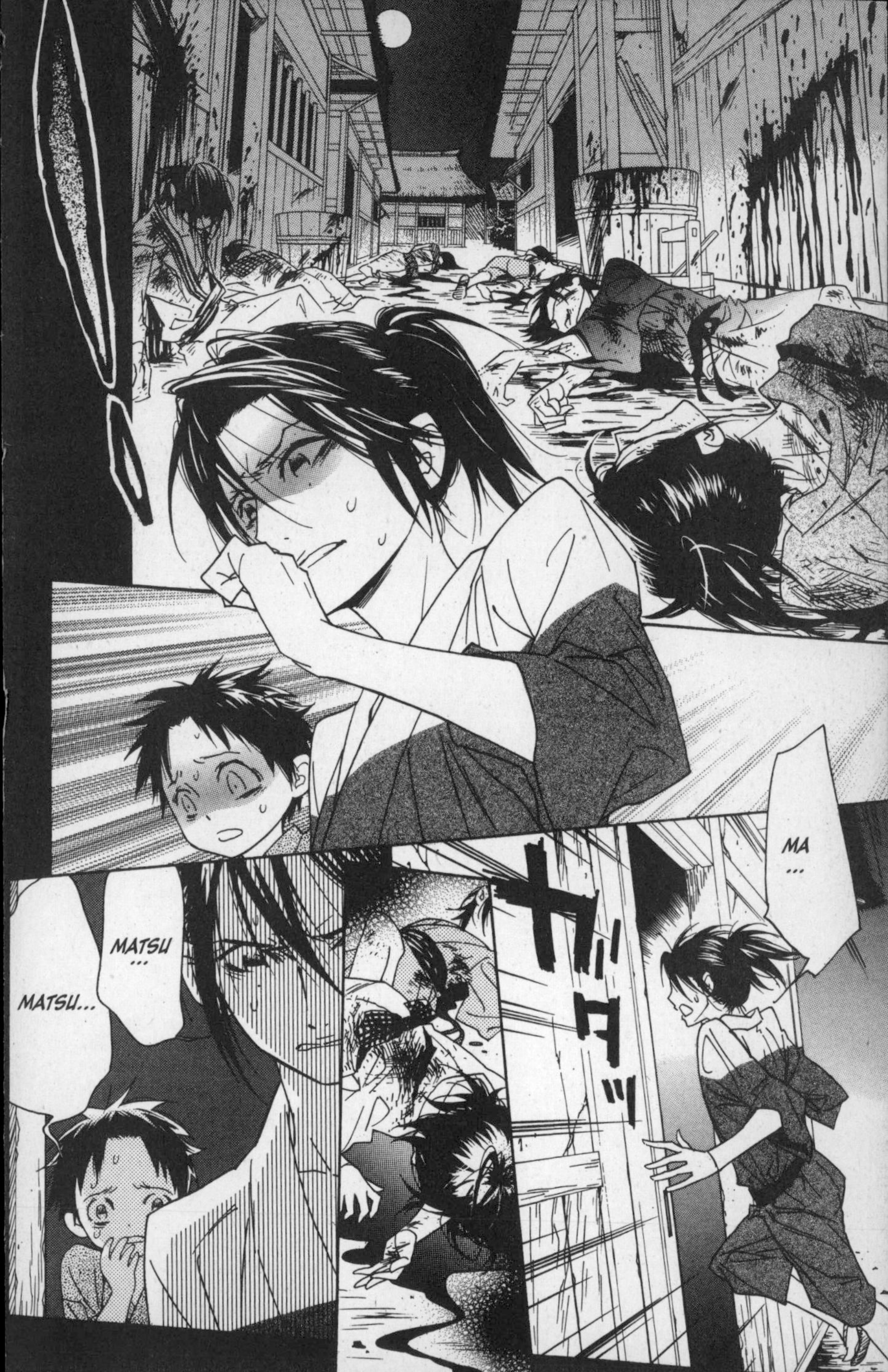
MA
...
ガタッ
MATSU
...
MATSU...

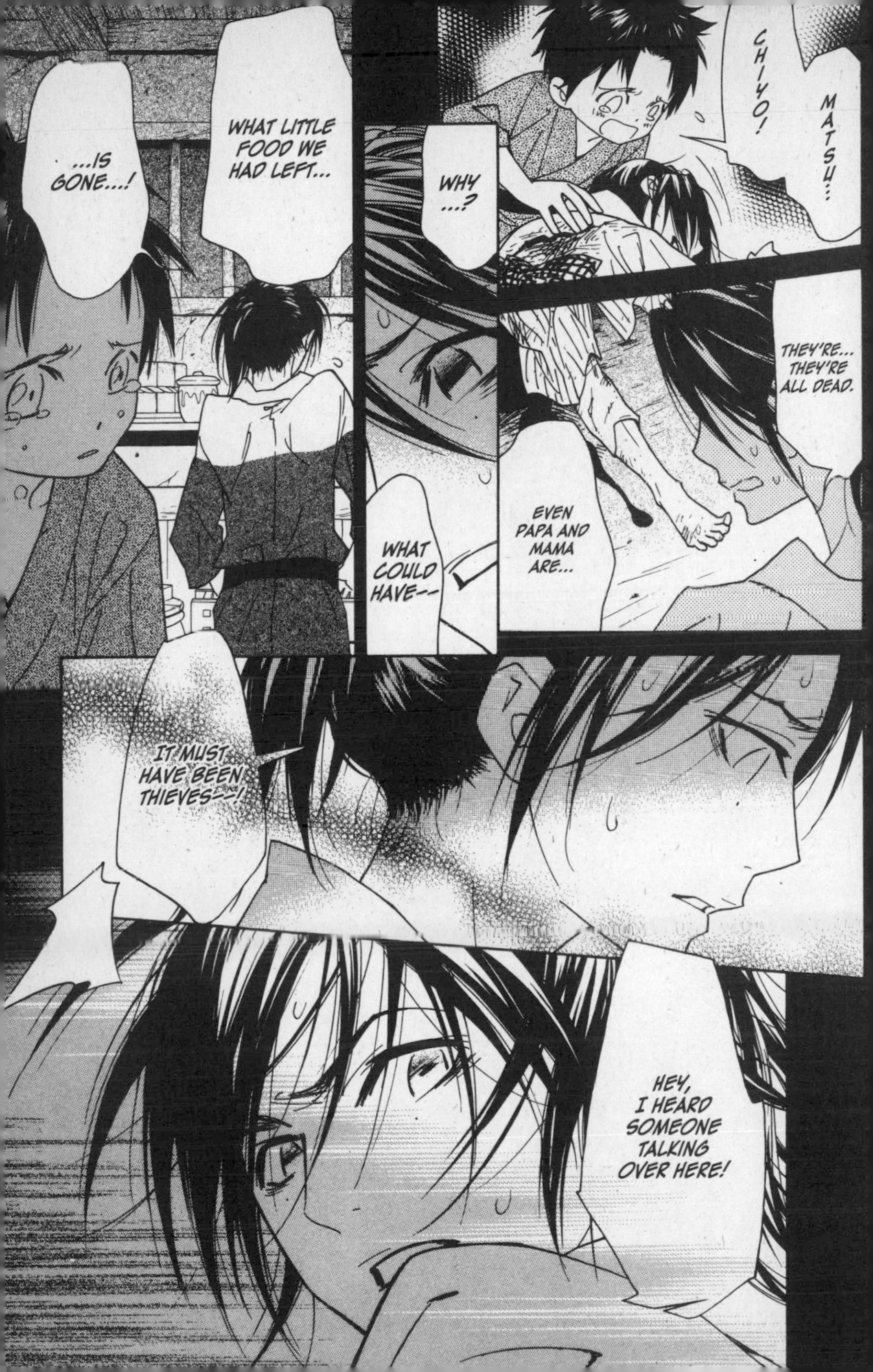
MATSU...
CHIYO!
THEY'RE... THEY'RE ALL DEAD.
EVEN PAPA AND MAMA ARE...
WHY ...?
WHAT COULD HAVE--
WHAT LITTLE FOOD WE HAD LEFT...
...IS GONE...!
IT MUST HAVE BEEN THIEVES---!
HEY, I HEARD SOMEONE TALKING OVER HERE!

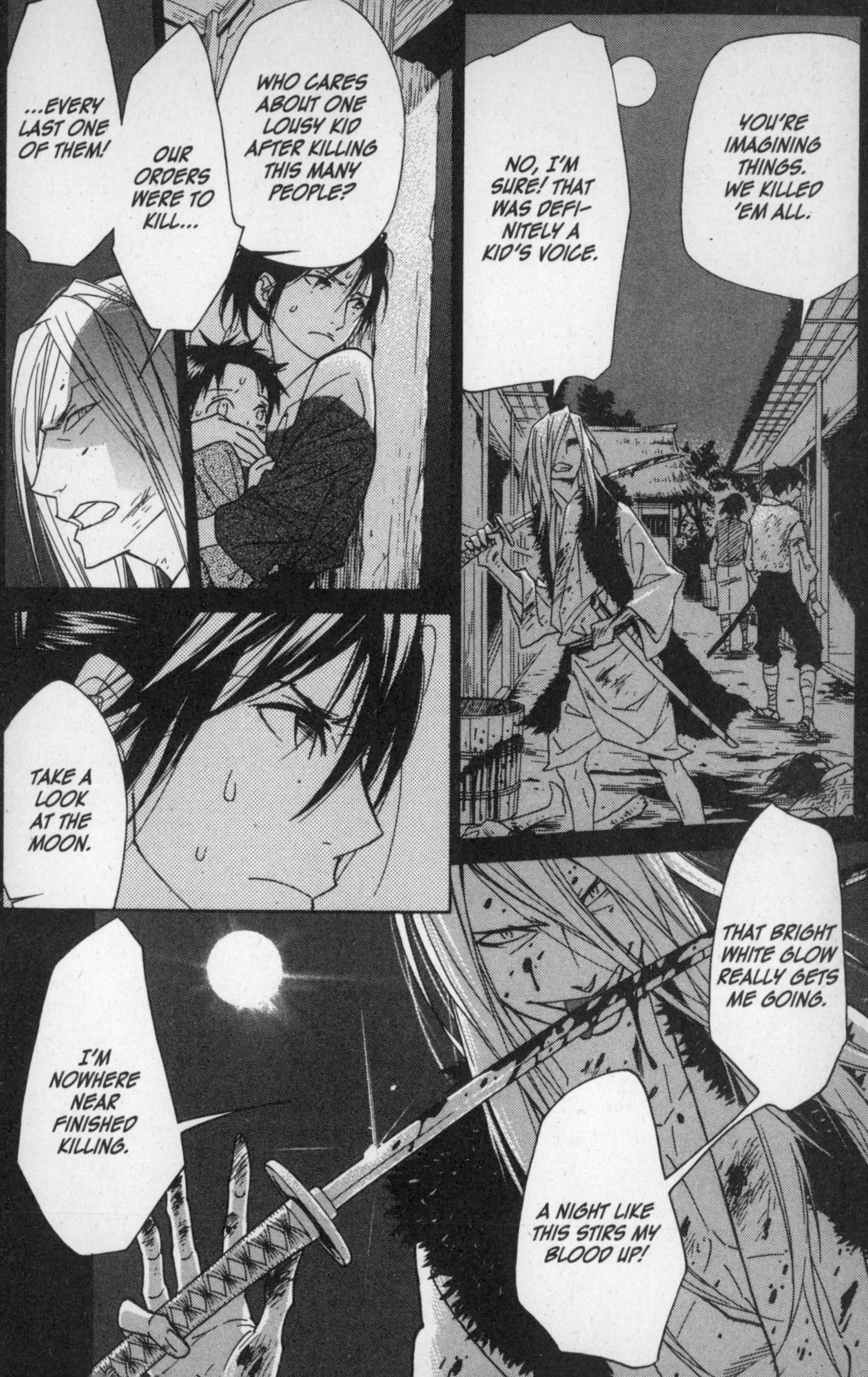
YOU'RE IMAGINING THINGS. WE KILLED 'EM ALL.
NO, I'M SURE! THAT WAS DEFI-NITELY A KID'S VOICE.
WHO CARES ABOUT ONE LOUSY KID AFTER KILLING THIS MANY PEOPLE?
OUR ORDERS WERE TO KILL...
...EVERY LAST ONE OF THEM!
TAKE A LOOK AT THE MOON.
THAT BRIGHT WHITE GLOW REALLY GETS ME GOING.
A NIGHT LIKE THIS STIRS MY BLOOD UP!
I'M NOWHERE NEAR FINISHED KILLING.

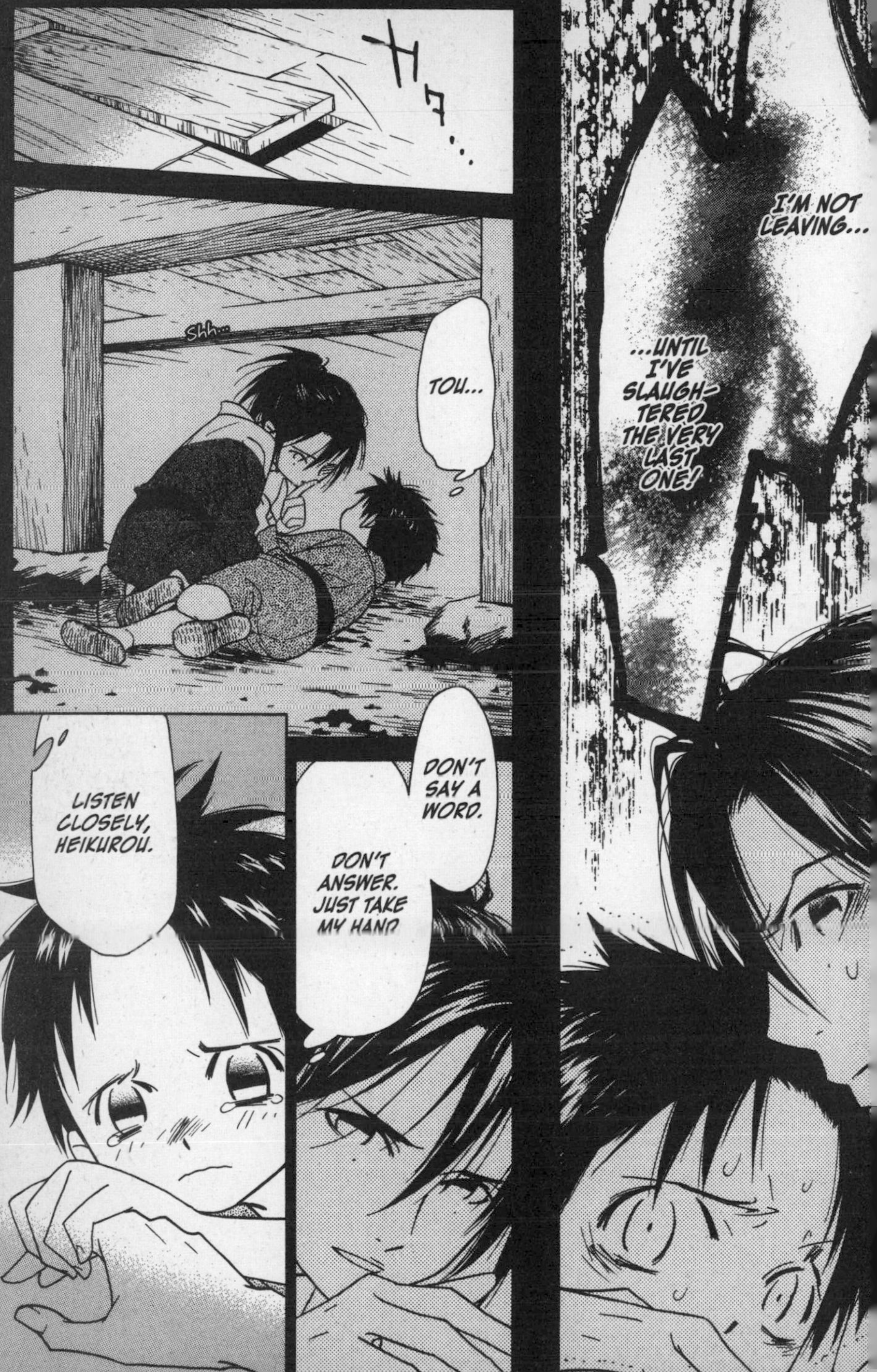
I'M NOT LEAVING...
...UNTIL I'VE SLAUGHTERED THE VERY LAST ONE!
TOU...
Shh...
DON'T SAY A WORD.
DON'T ANSWER. JUST TAKE MY HAND
LISTEN CLOSELY, HEIKUROU.

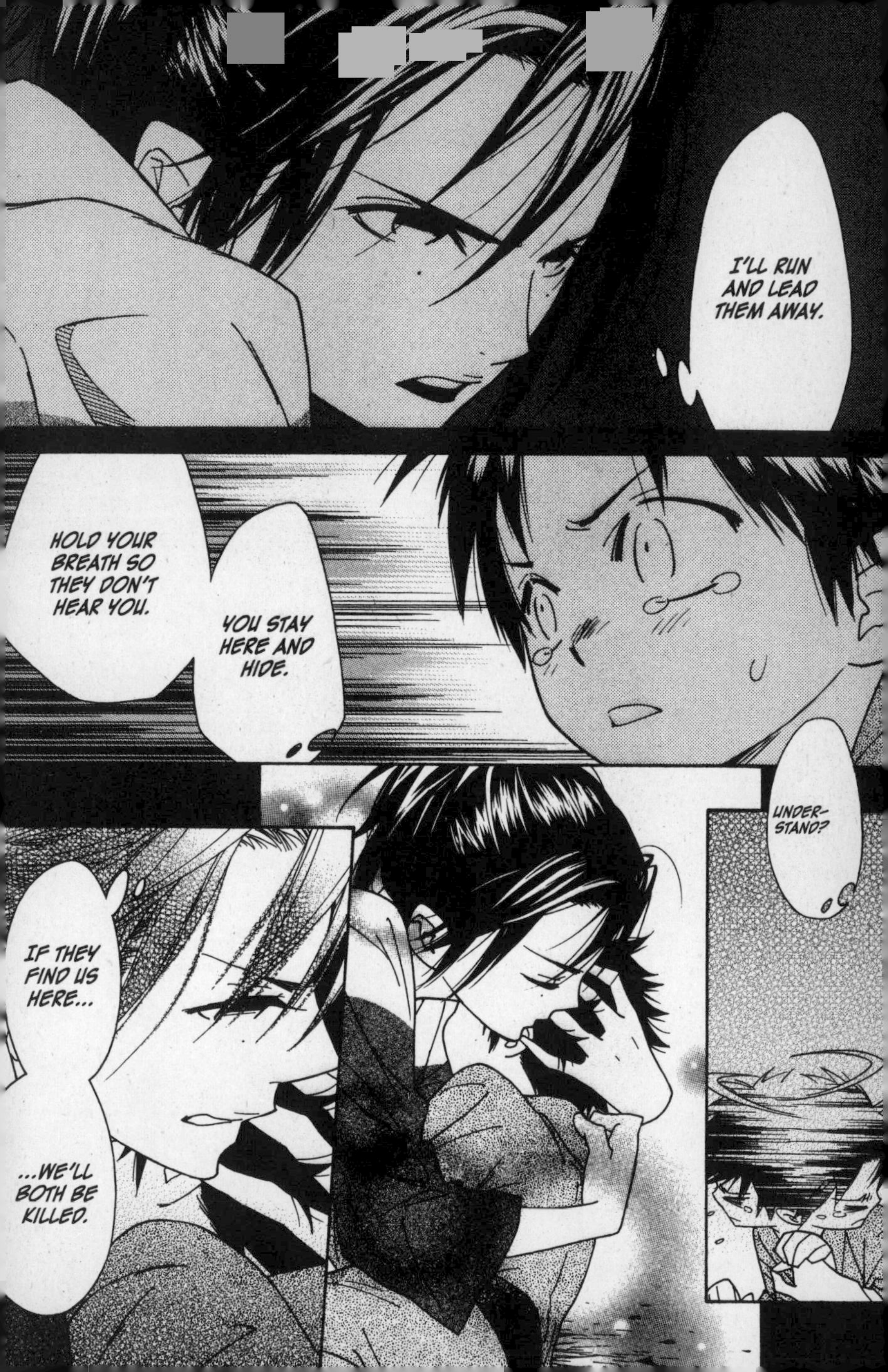
I'LL RUN AND LEAD THEM AWAY.
YOU STAY HERE AND HIDE.
HOLD YOUR BREATH SO THEY DON'T HEAR YOU.
UNDER-STAND?
IF THEY FIND US HERE...
...WE'LL BOTH BE KILLED.

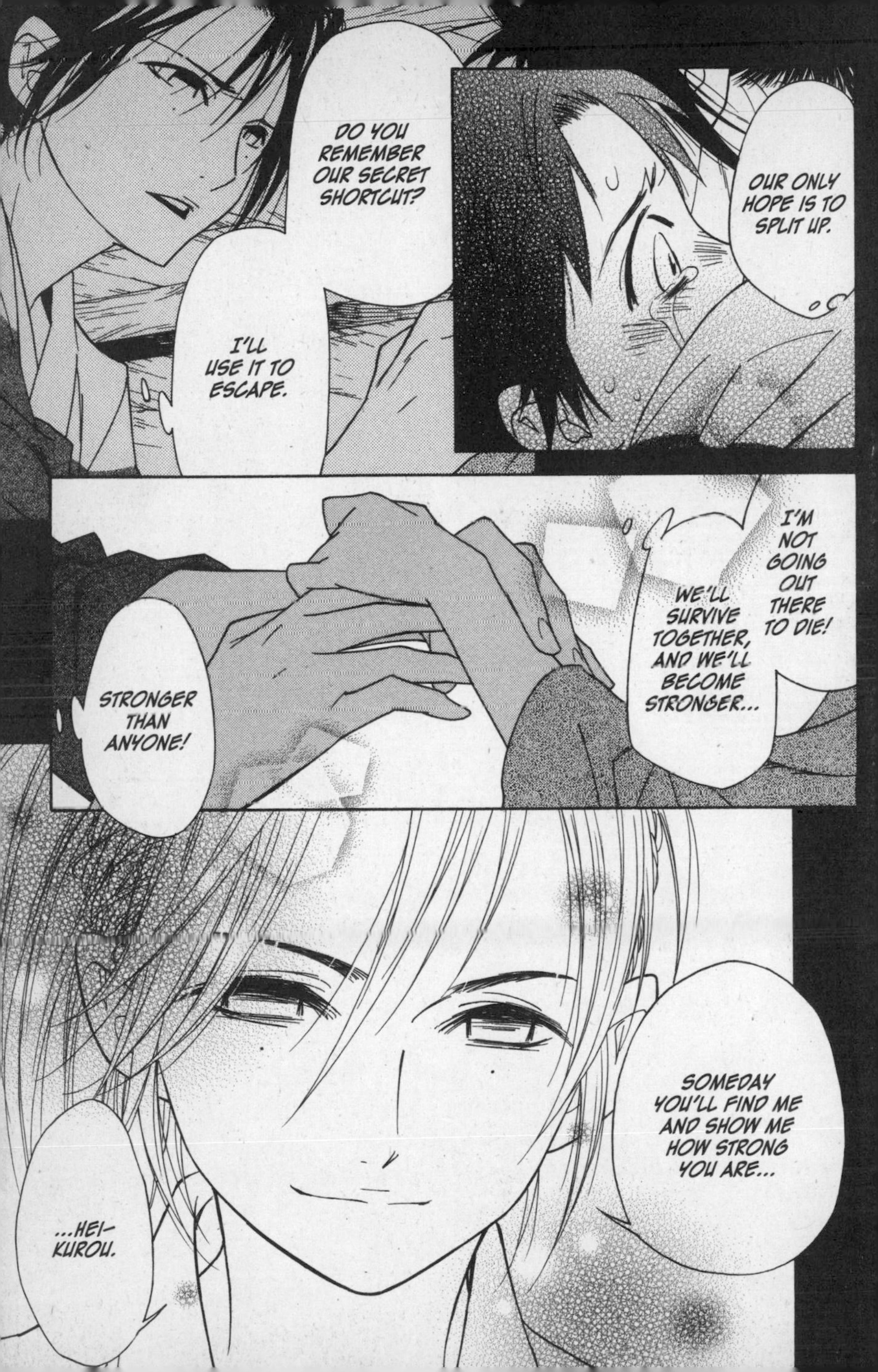
OUR ONLY HOPE IS TO SPLIT UP.
DO YOU REMEMBER OUR SECRET SHORTCUT?
I'LL USE IT TO ESCAPE.
I'M NOT GOING OUT THERE TO DIE!
WE'LL SURVIVE TOGETHER, AND WE'LL BECOME STRONGER...
STRONGER THAN ANYONE!
SOMEDAY YOU'LL FIND ME AND SHOW ME HOW STRONG YOU ARE...
...HEI-KUROU.

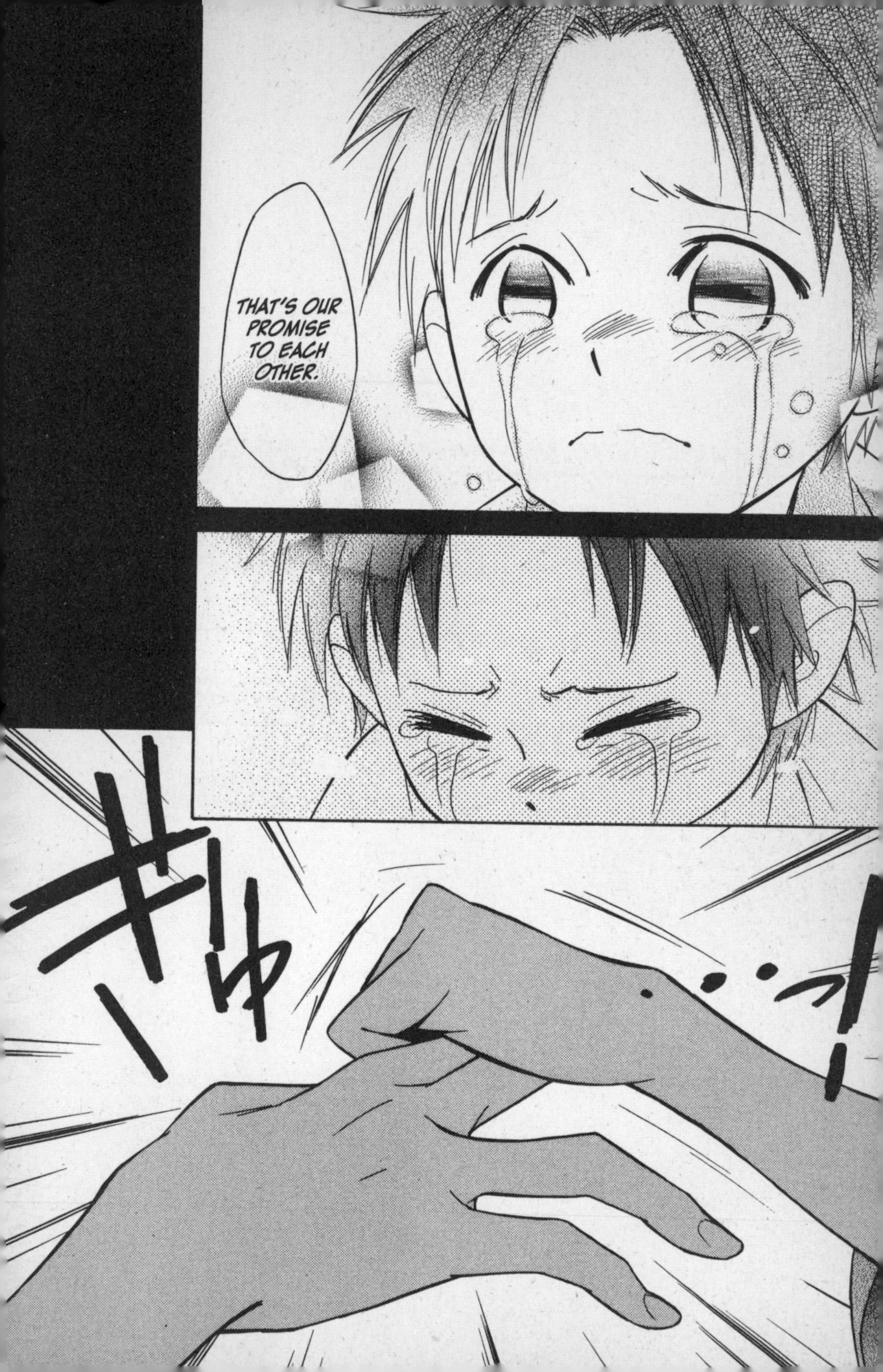
THAT'S OUR PROMISE TO EACH OTHER.
ぎゅ
…っ!

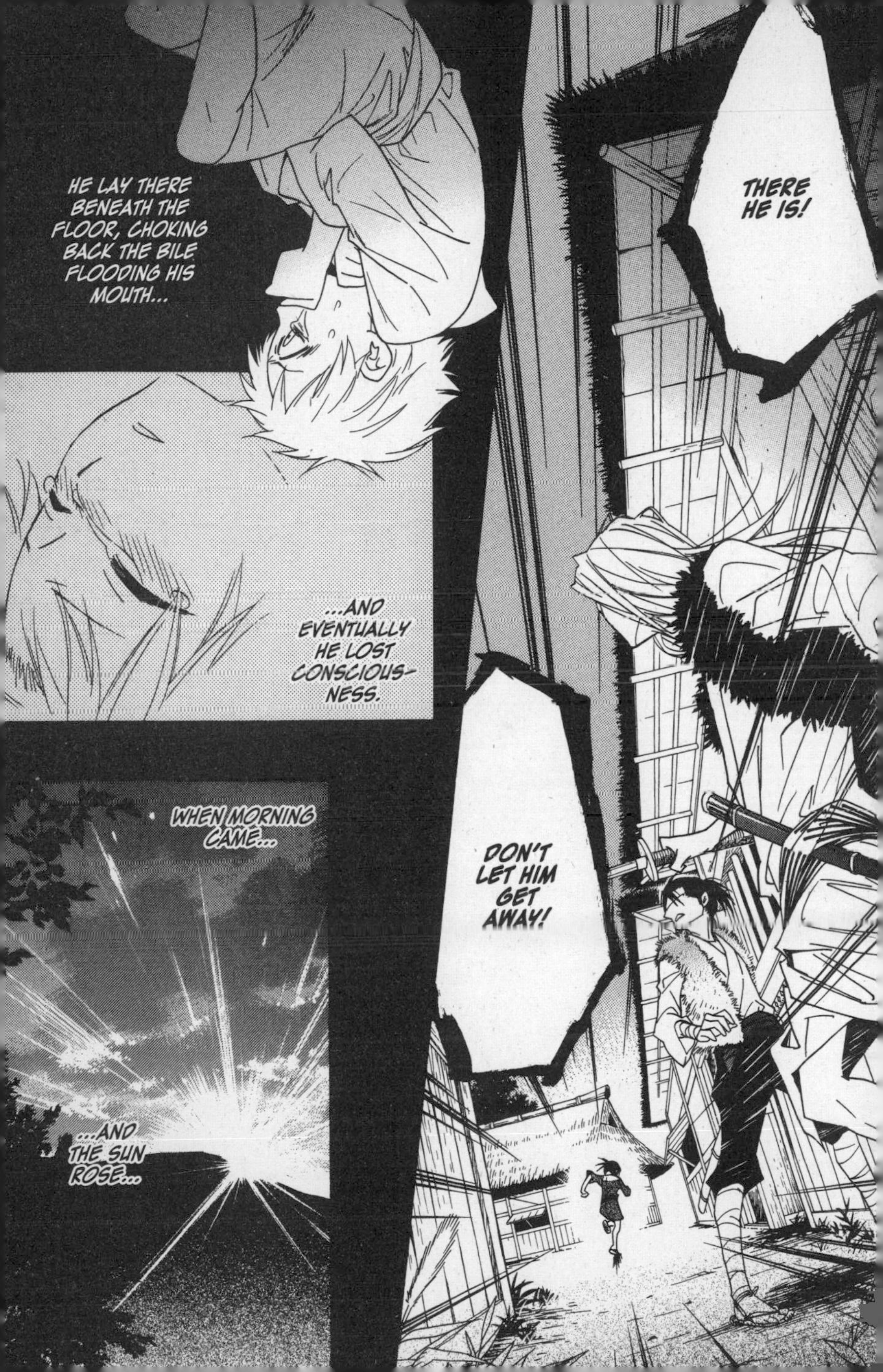
HE LAY THERE BENEATH THE FLOOR, CHOKING BACK THE BILE FLOODING HIS MOUTH...
...AND EVENTUALLY HE LOST CONSCIOUS-NESS.
WHEN MORNING CAME...
...AND THE SUN ROSE...
THERE HE IS!
DON'T LET HIM GET AWAY!

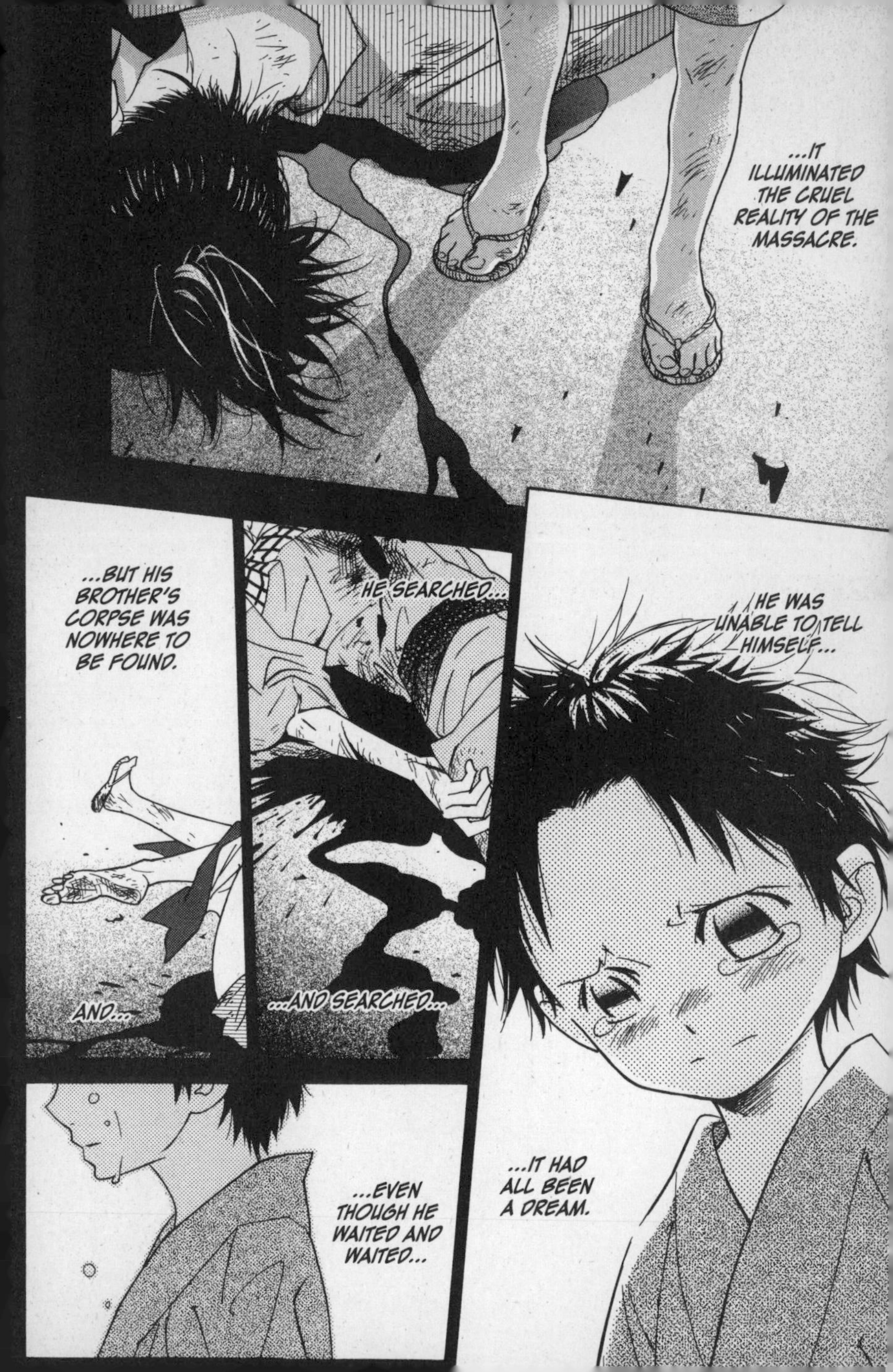
...IT ILLUMINATED THE CRUEL REALITY OF THE MASSACRE.
HE SEARCHED...
...AND SEARCHED...
...BUT HIS BROTHER'S CORPSE WAS NOWHERE TO BE FOUND.
AND...
...EVEN THOUGH HE WAITED AND WAITED...
HE WAS UNABLE TO TELL HIMSELF...
...IT HAD ALL BEEN A DREAM.

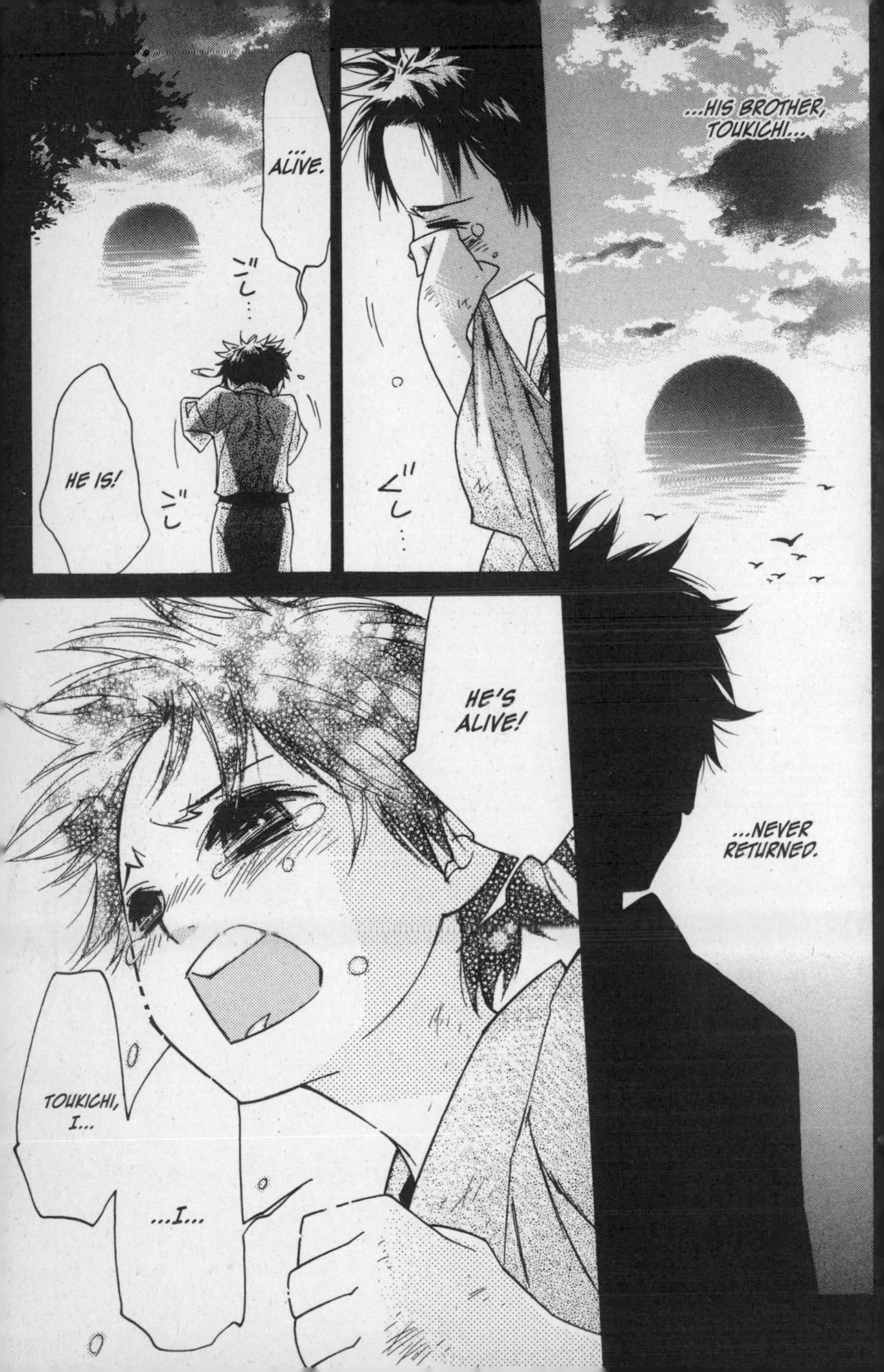
...HIS BROTHER, TOUKICHI...
...ALIVE.
ごし…
HE IS!
ごし
ごし…
HE'S ALIVE!
...NEVER RETURNED.
TOUKICHI, I...
...I...

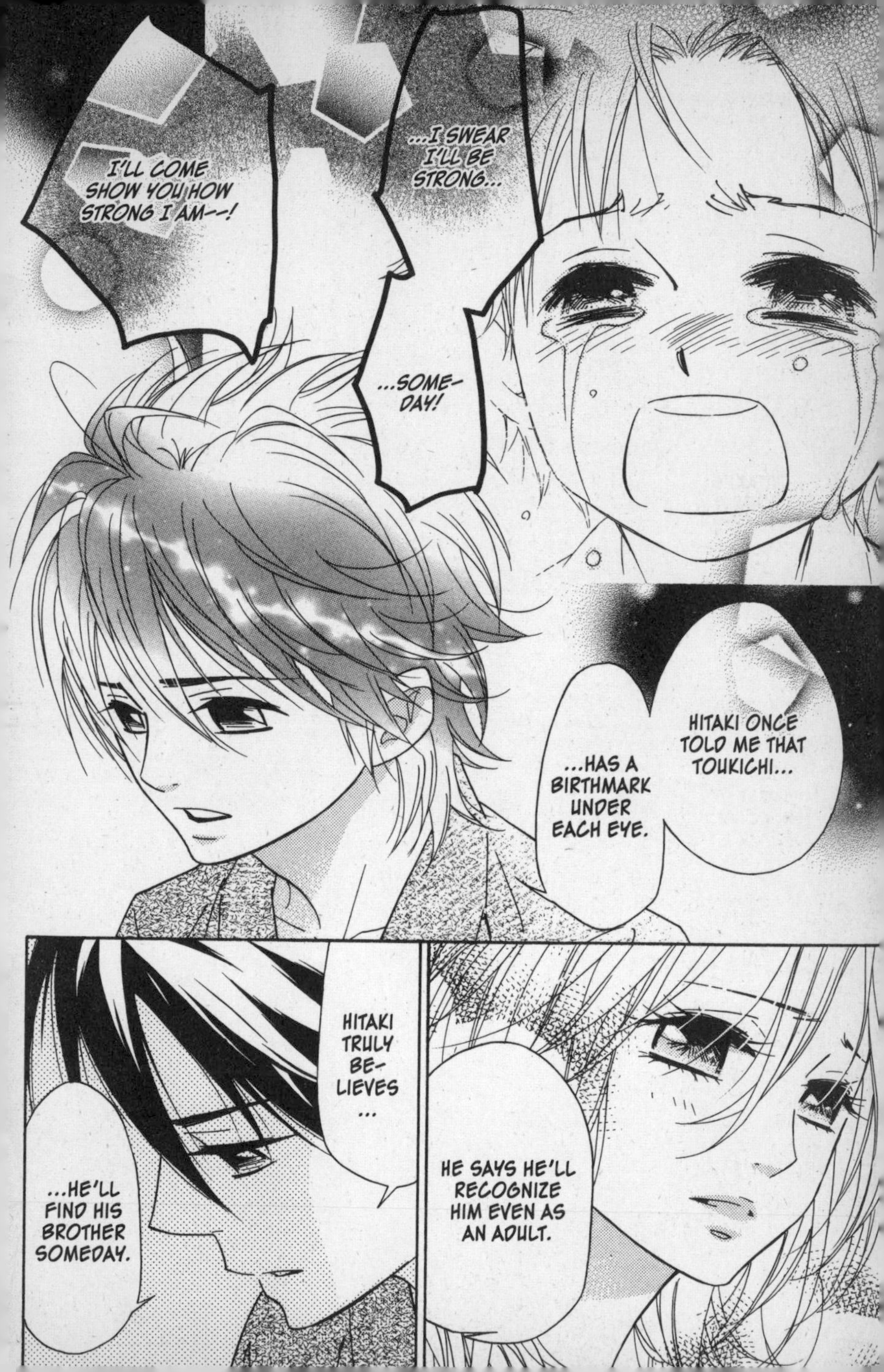
...I SWEAR I'LL BE STRONG...
...SOMEDAY!
I'LL COME SHOW YOU HOW STRONG I AM--!
HITAKI ONCE TOLD ME THAT TOUKICHI...
...HAS A BIRTHMARK UNDER EACH EYE.
HE SAYS HE'LL RECOGNIZE HIM EVEN AS AN ADULT.
HITAKI TRULY BE-LIEVES...
...HE'LL FIND HIS BROTHER SOMEDAY.

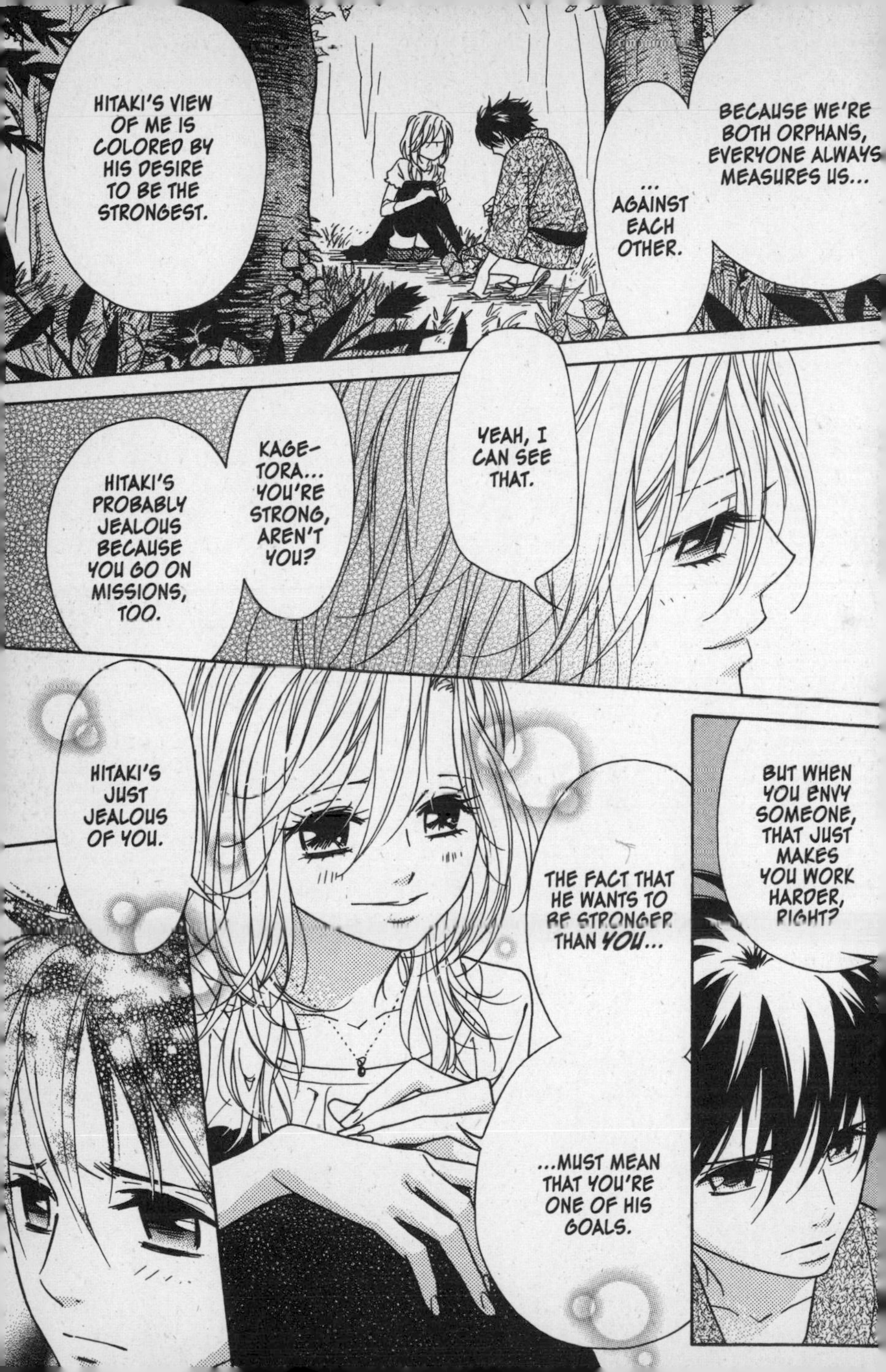
BECAUSE WE'RE BOTH ORPHANS, EVERYONE ALWAYS MEASURES US...
...AGAINST EACH OTHER.
HITAKI'S VIEW OF ME IS COLORED BY HIS DESIRE TO BE THE STRONGEST.
YEAH, I CAN SEE THAT.
KAGE-TORA... YOU'RE STRONG, AREN'T YOU?
HITAKI'S PROBABLY JEALOUS BECAUSE YOU GO ON MISSIONS, TOO.
BUT WHEN YOU ENVY SOMEONE, THAT JUST MAKES YOU WORK HARDER, RIGHT?
THE FACT THAT HE WANTS TO BE STRONGER THAN *YOU*...
...MUST MEAN THAT YOU'RE ONE OF HIS GOALS.
HITAKI'S JUST JEALOUS OF YOU.

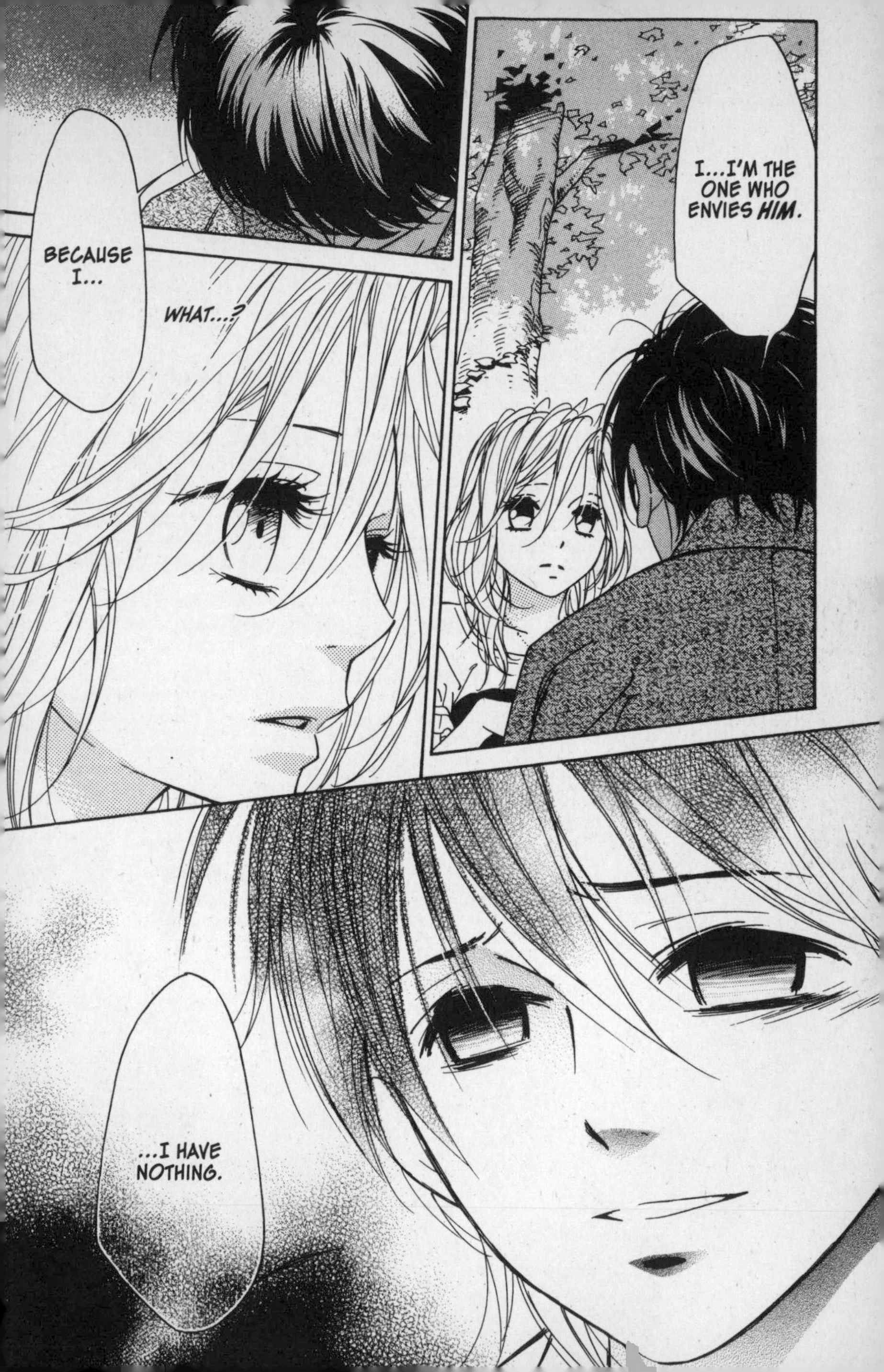
I...I'M THE ONE WHO ENVIES HIM.
BECAUSE I...
WHAT...?
...I HAVE NOTHING.

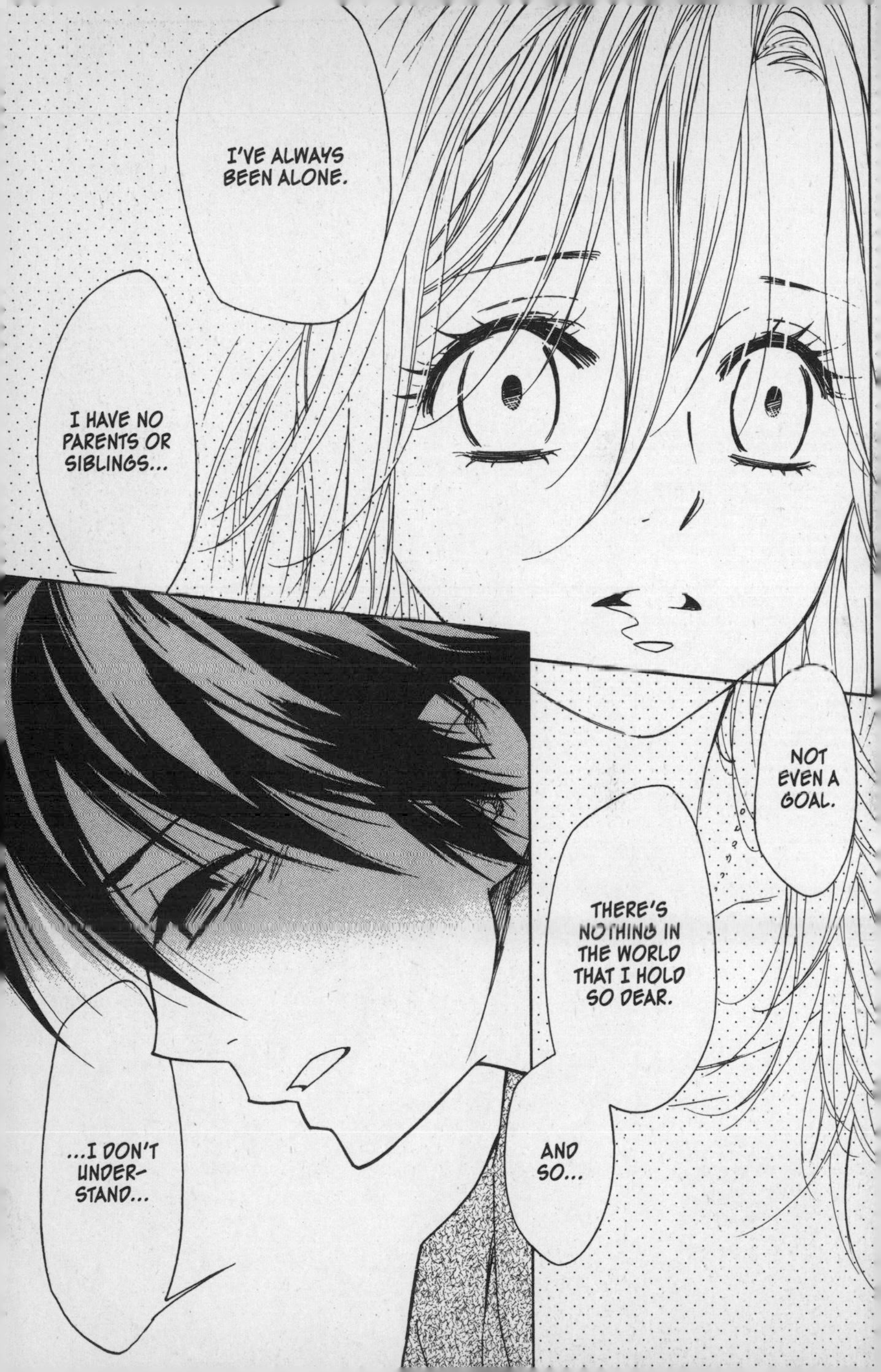
I'VE ALWAYS BEEN ALONE.
I HAVE NO PARENTS OR SIBLINGS...
NOT EVEN A GOAL.
THERE'S NOTHING IN THE WORLD THAT I HOLD SO DEAR.
AND SO...
...I DON'T UNDER-STAND...

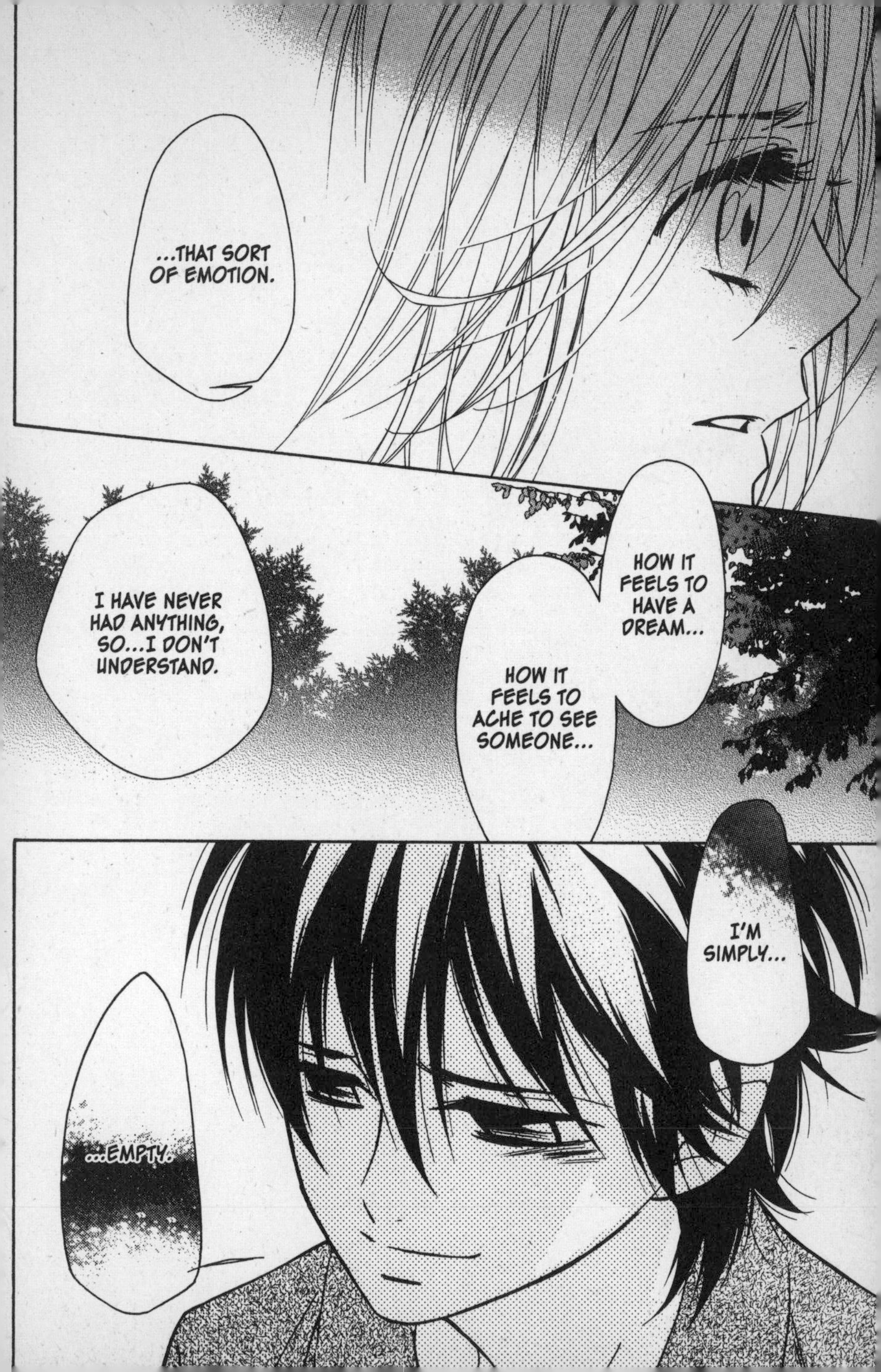
...THAT SORT OF EMOTION.
HOW IT FEELS TO HAVE A DREAM...
HOW IT FEELS TO ACHE TO SEE SOMEONE...
I HAVE NEVER HAD ANYTHING, SO...I DON'T UNDERSTAND.
I'M SIMPLY...
...EMPTY.

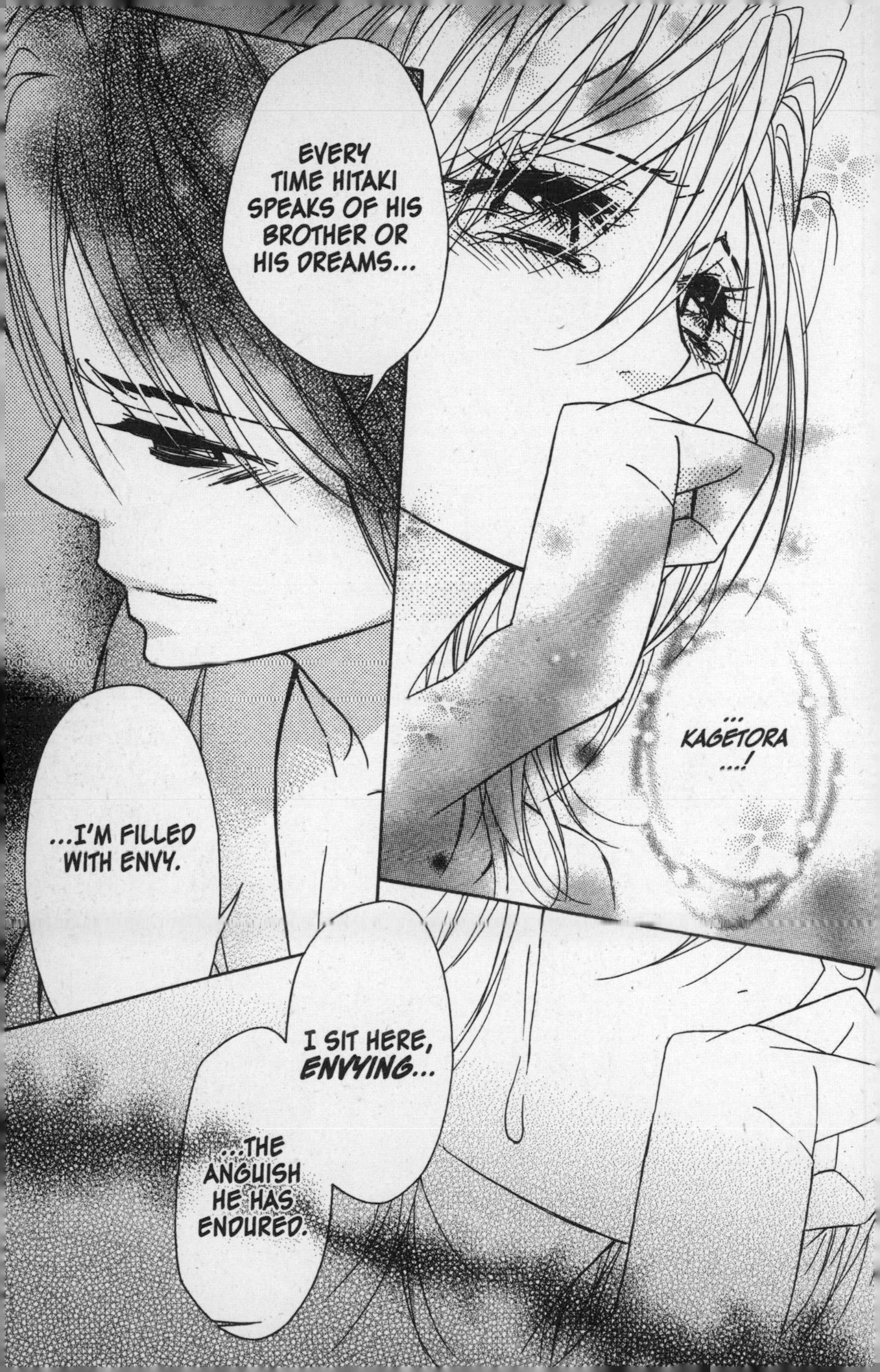
EVERY TIME HITAKI SPEAKS OF HIS BROTHER OR HIS DREAMS...
...KAGETORA ...!
...I'M FILLED WITH ENVY.
I SIT HERE, ENVYING...
...THE ANGUISH HE HAS ENDURED.

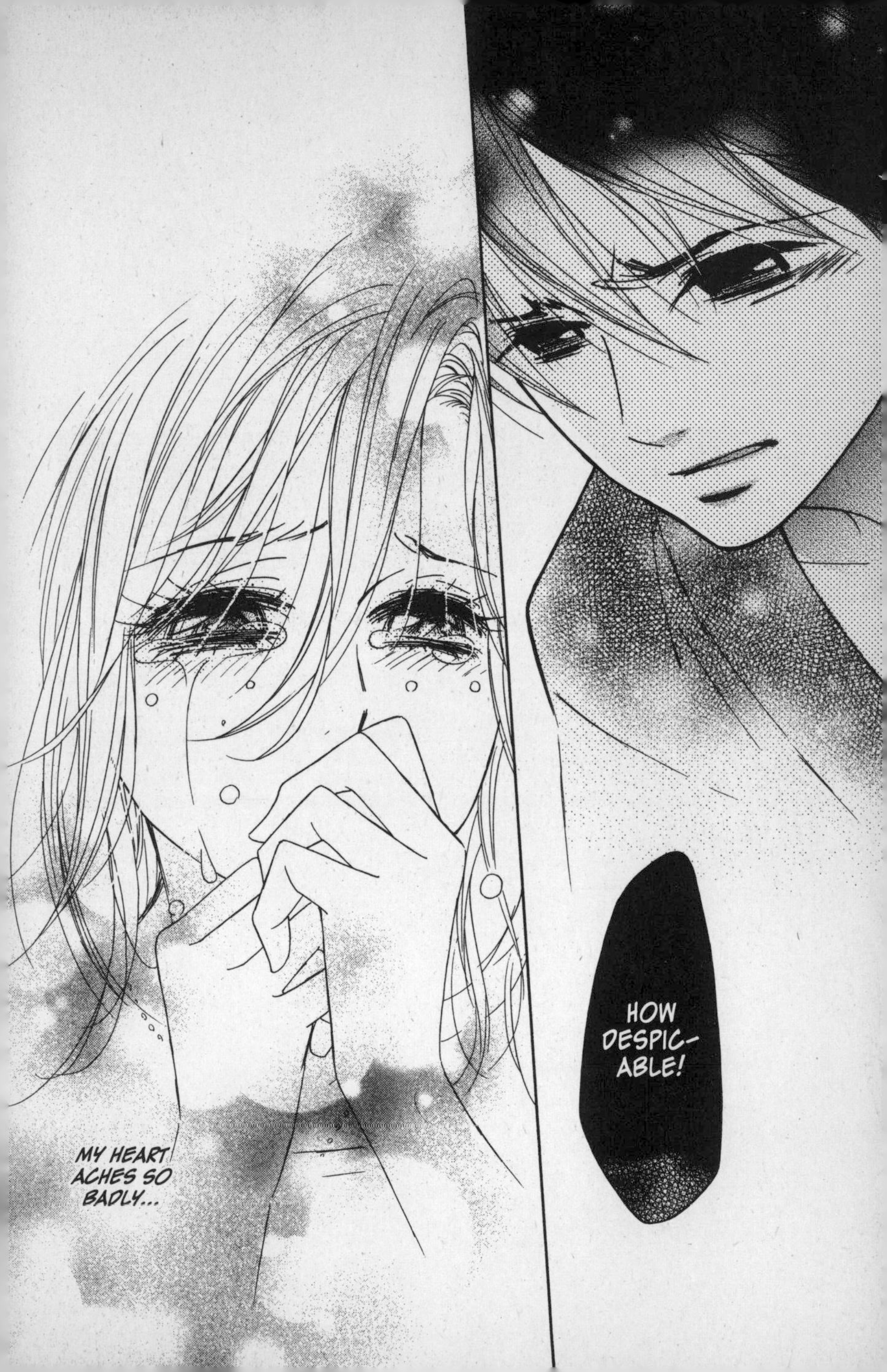
HOW DESPIC-ABLE!
MY HEART ACHES SO BADLY...

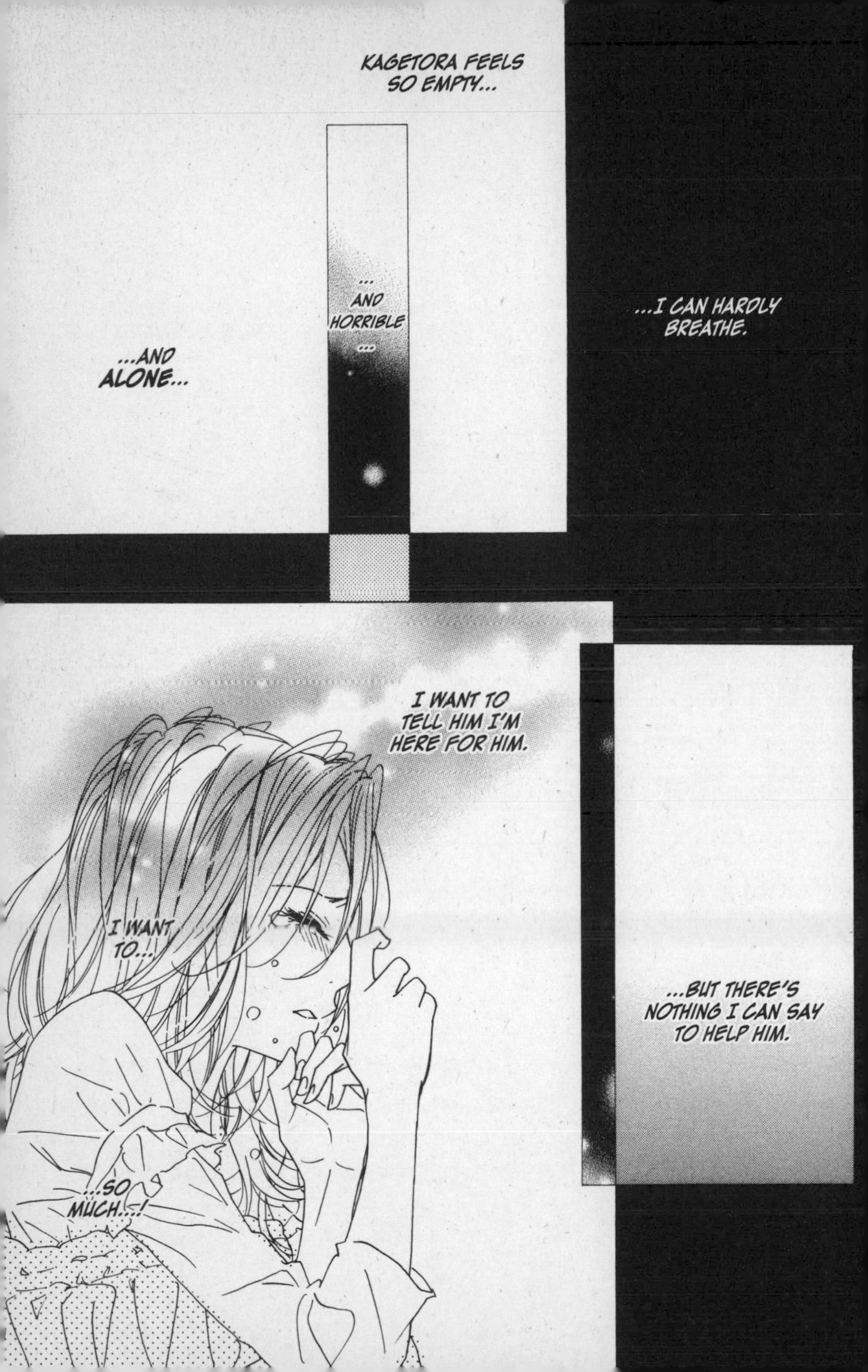
KAGETORA FEELS SO EMPTY...
... AND HORRIBLE ...
...AND ALONE...
...I CAN HARDLY BREATHE.
I WANT TO TELL HIM I'M HERE FOR HIM.
...BUT THERE'S NOTHING I CAN SAY TO HELP HIM.
I WANT TO...
...SO MUCH...!

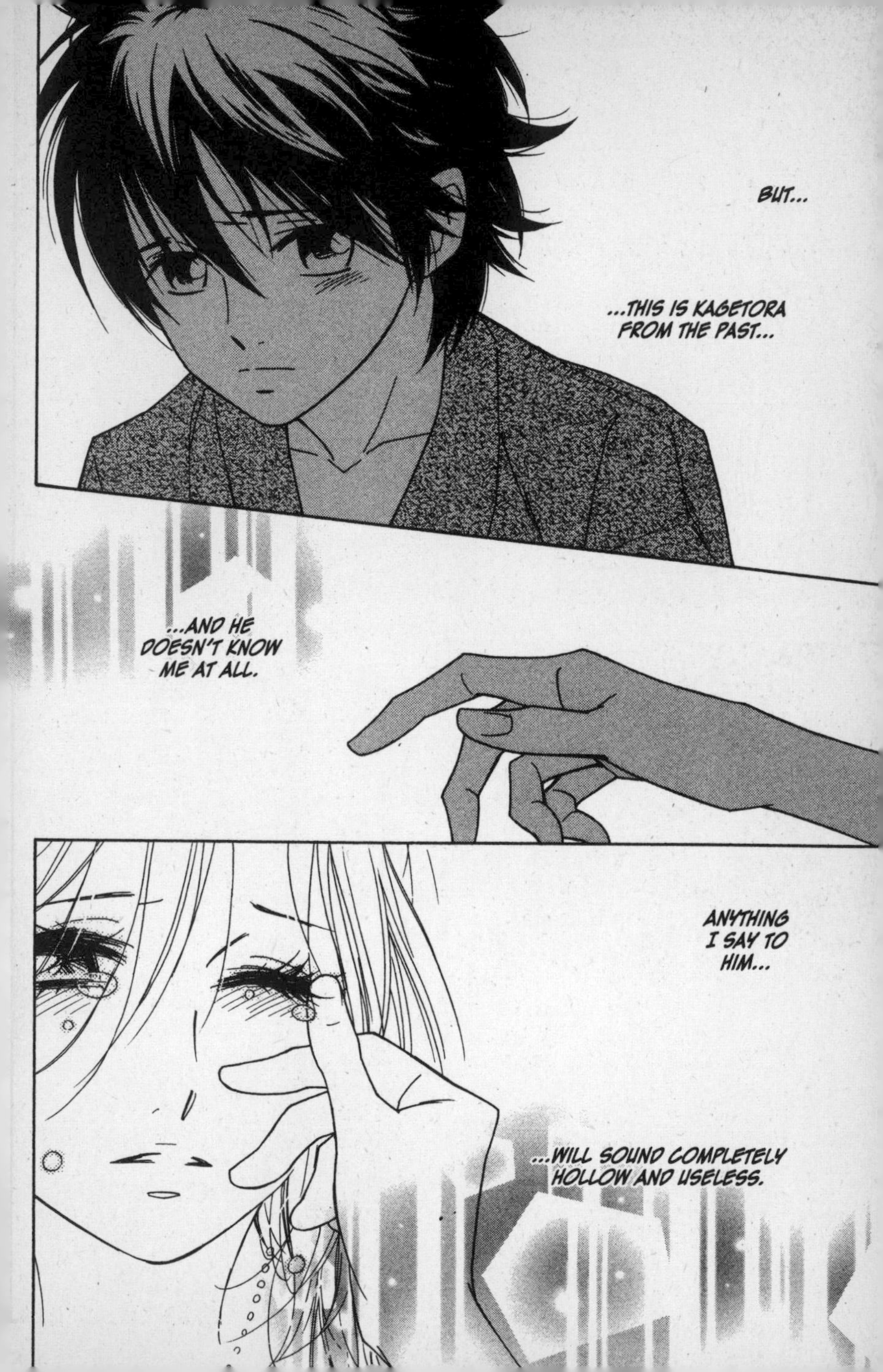
BUT...
...THIS IS KAGETORA FROM THE PAST...
...AND HE DOESN'T KNOW ME AT ALL.
ANYTHING I SAY TO HIM...
...WILL SOUND COMPLETELY HOLLOW AND USELESS.

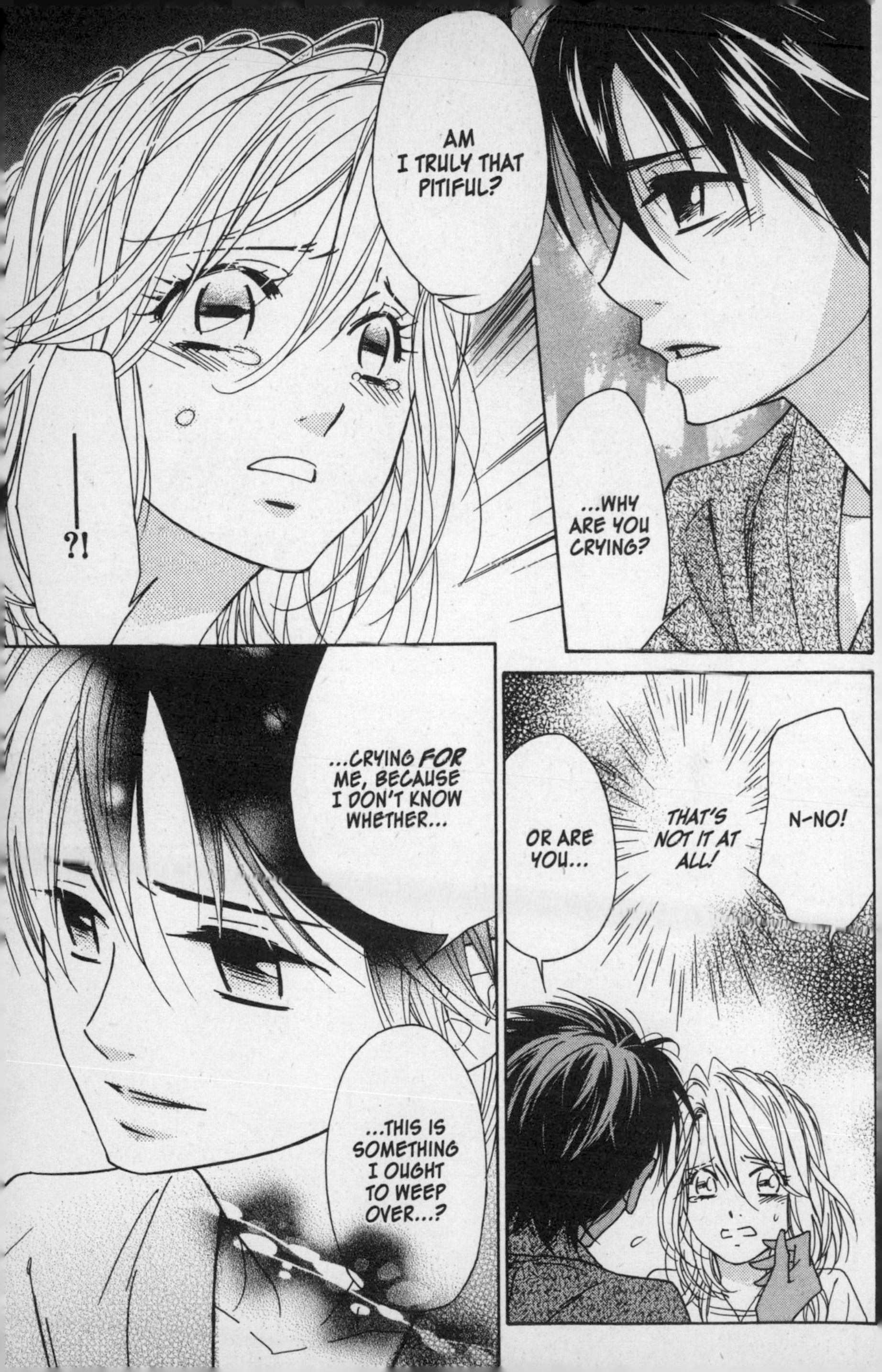
AM I TRULY THAT PITIFUL?
...WHY ARE YOU CRYING?
?!
N-NO!
THAT'S NOT IT AT ALL!
OR ARE YOU...
...CRYING FOR ME, BECAUSE I DON'T KNOW WHETHER...
...THIS IS SOMETHING I OUGHT TO WEEP OVER...?

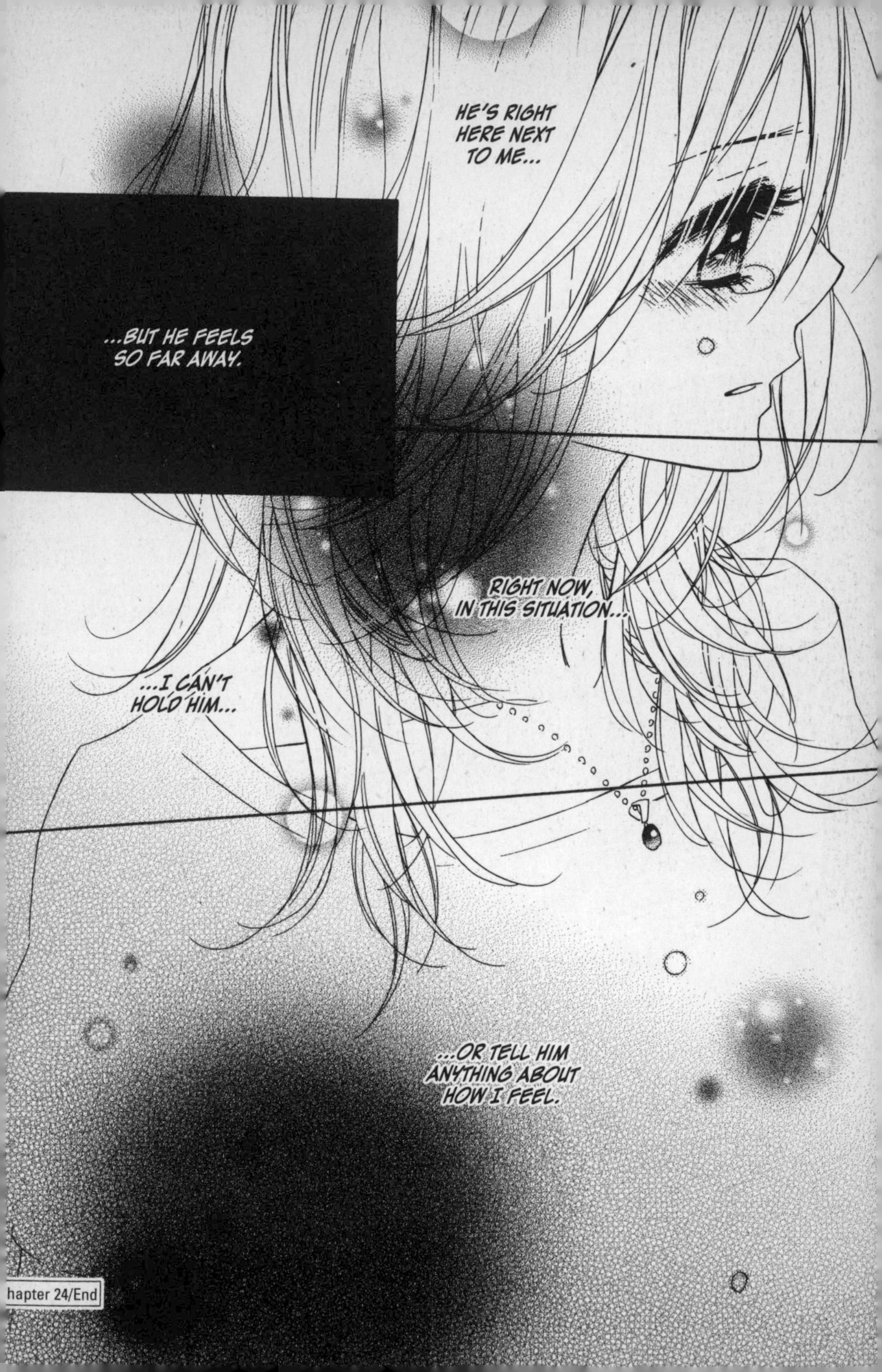
HE'S RIGHT HERE NEXT TO ME...
...BUT HE FEELS SO FAR AWAY.
RIGHT NOW, IN THIS SITUATION...
...I CAN'T HOLD HIM...
...OR TELL HIM ANYTHING ABOUT HOW I FEEL.
hapter 24/End

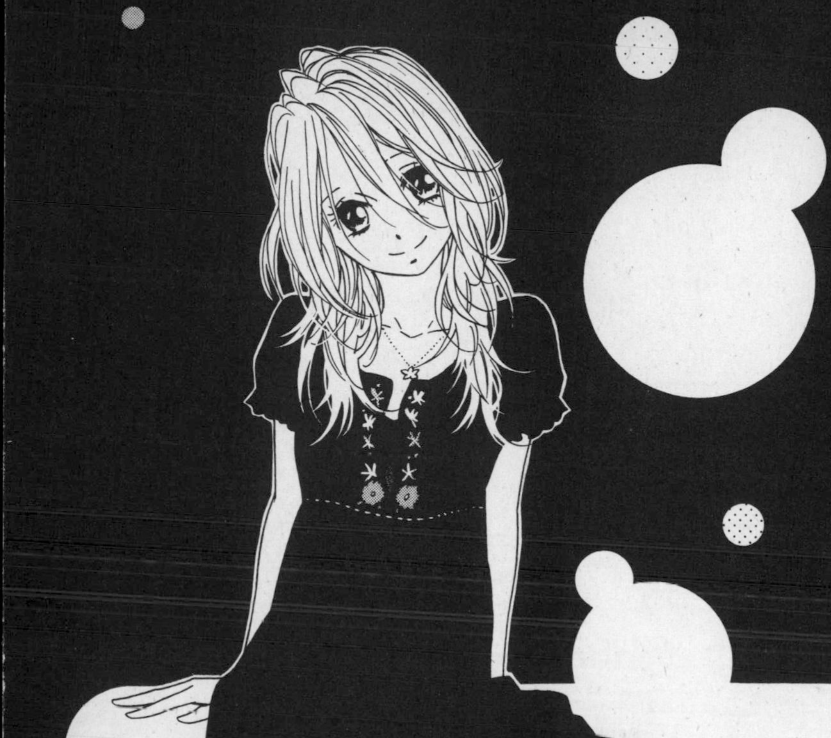

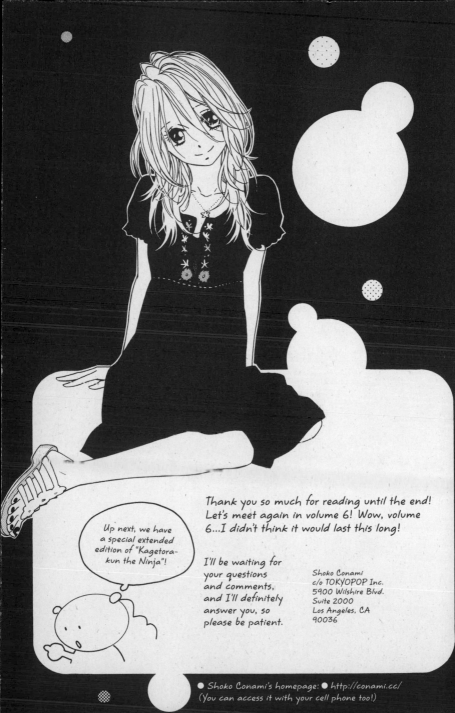

Thank you so much for reading until the end! Let's meet again in volume 6! Wow, volume 6...I didn't think it would last this long!

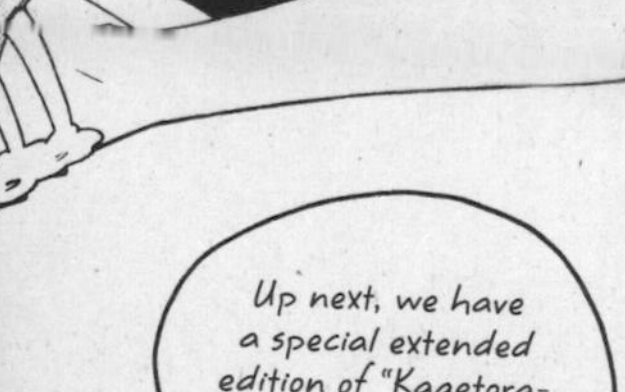
Up next, we have a special extended edition of "Kagetora-kun the Ninja"!

I'll be waiting for your questions and comments, and I'll definitely answer you, so please be patient.

Shoko Conami
c/o TOKYOPOP Inc.
5900 Wilshire Blvd.
Suite 2000
Los Angeles, CA
90036

● Shoko Conami's homepage: ● http://conami.cc/
(You can access it with your cell phone too!)

Bonus Manga!

● Kagetora-kun the Ninja! ●

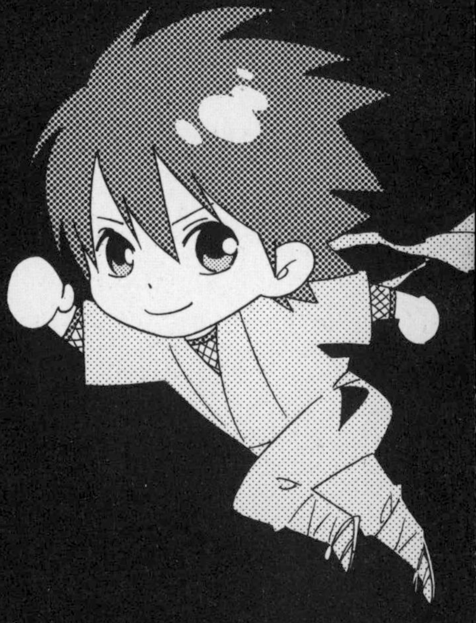

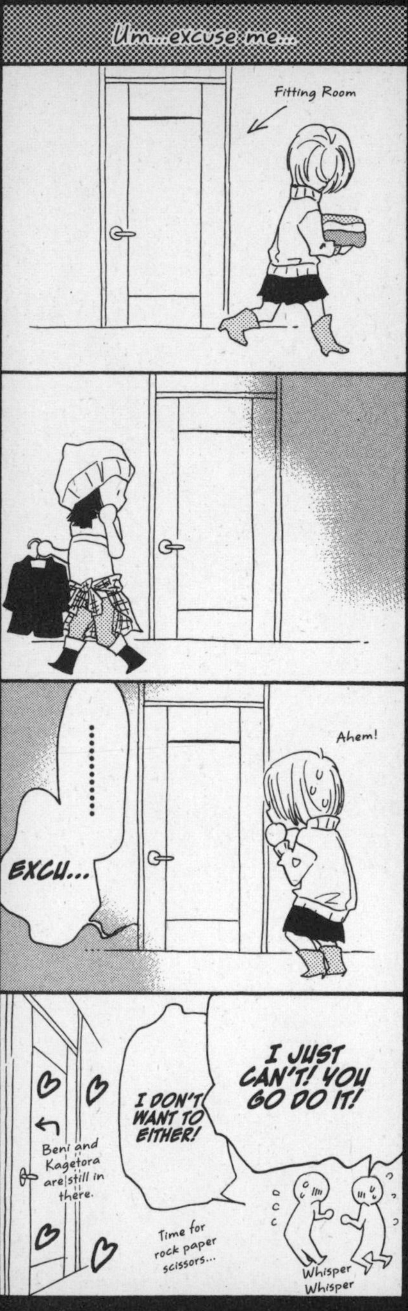
Um...excuse me...
Fitting Room
......
Ahem!
EXCU...
I JUST CAN'T! YOU GO DO IT!
I DON'T WANT TO EITHER!
Beni and Kagetora are still in there.
Time for rock paper scissors...
Whisper Whisper

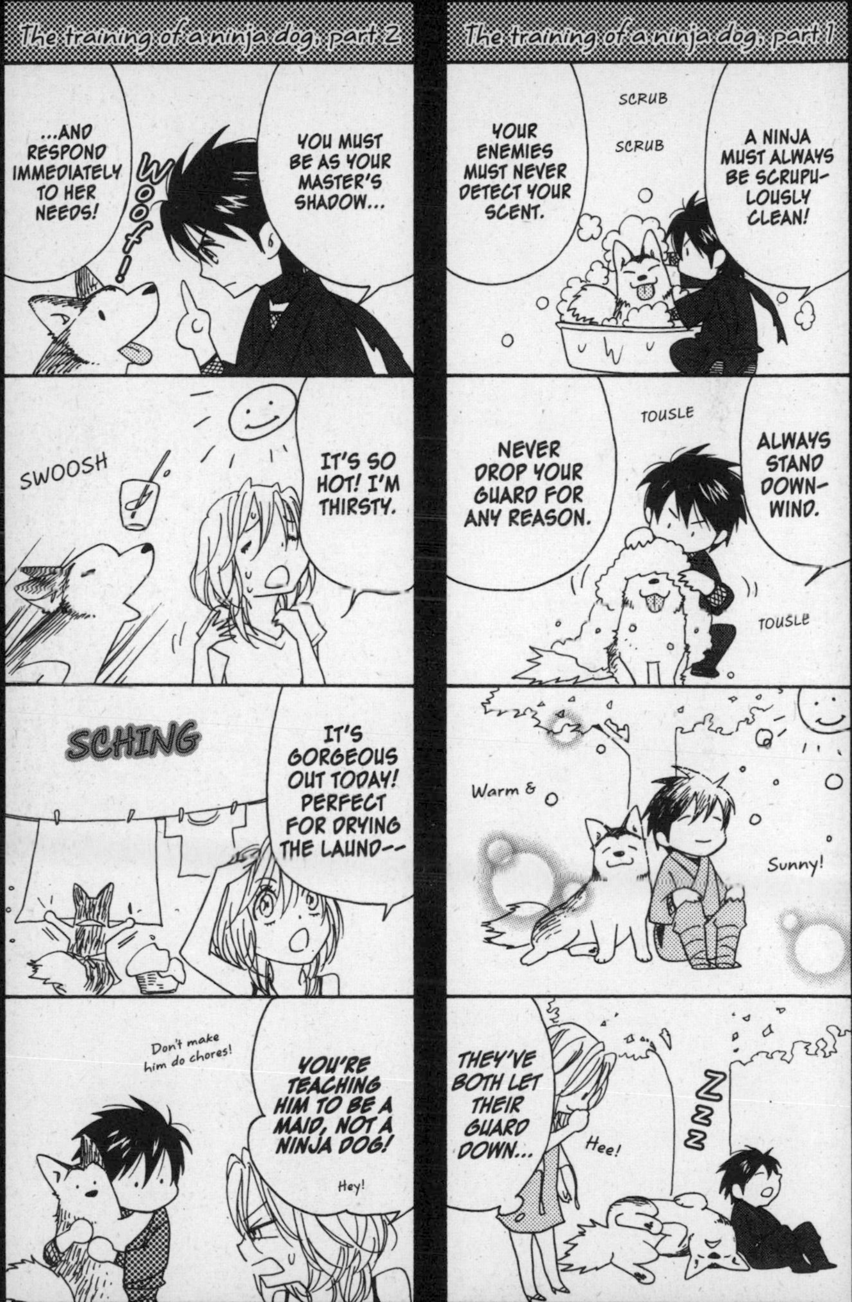
The training of a ninja dog, part 1
A NINJA MUST ALWAYS BE SCRUPULOUSLY CLEAN!
SCRUB
SCRUB
YOUR ENEMIES MUST NEVER DETECT YOUR SCENT.
ALWAYS STAND DOWNWIND.
TOUSLE
NEVER DROP YOUR GUARD FOR ANY REASON.
TOUSLE
Warm &
Sunny!
THEY'VE BOTH LET THEIR GUARD DOWN...
Hee!
The training of a ninja dog, part 2
YOU MUST BE AS YOUR MASTER'S SHADOW...
Woof!
...AND RESPOND IMMEDIATELY TO HER NEEDS!
IT'S SO HOT! I'M THIRSTY.
SWOOSH
IT'S GORGEOUS OUT TODAY! PERFECT FOR DRYING THE LAUND--
SCHING
YOU'RE TEACHING HIM TO BE A MAID, NOT A NINJA DOG!
Hey!
Don't make him do chores!

Big dog, little dog

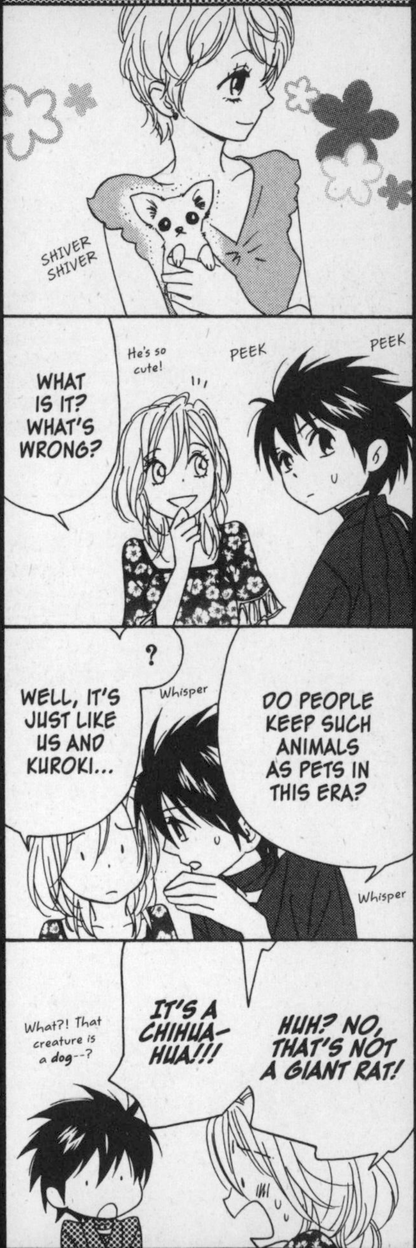
SHIVER SHIVER
PEEK
PEEK
He's so cute!
WHAT IS IT? WHAT'S WRONG?
DO PEOPLE KEEP SUCH ANIMALS AS PETS IN THIS ERA?
Whisper
?
WELL, IT'S JUST LIKE US AND KUROKI...
Whisper
HUH? NO, THAT'S NOT A GIANT RAT!
IT'S A CHIHUA-HUA!!!
What?! That creature is a dog--?

One moment please...

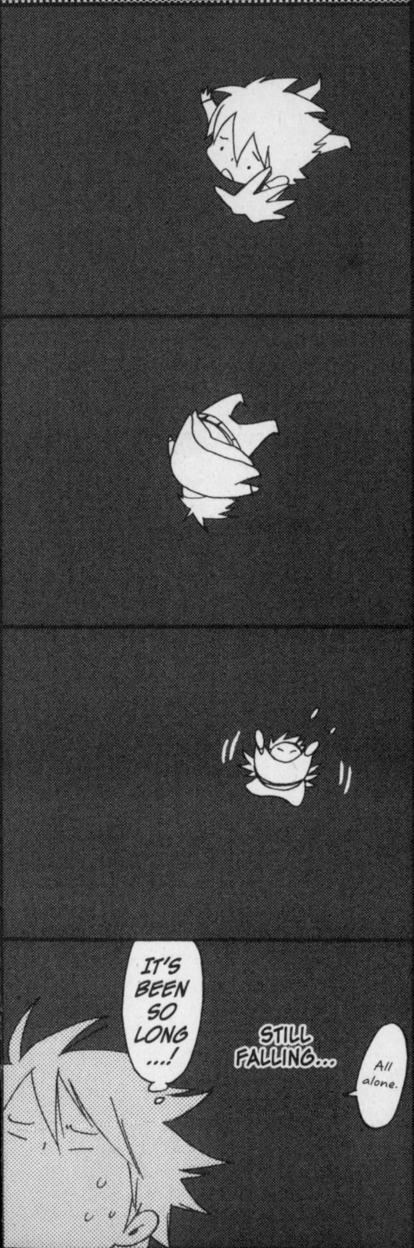
All alone.
STILL FALLING...
IT'S BEEN SO LONG ...!

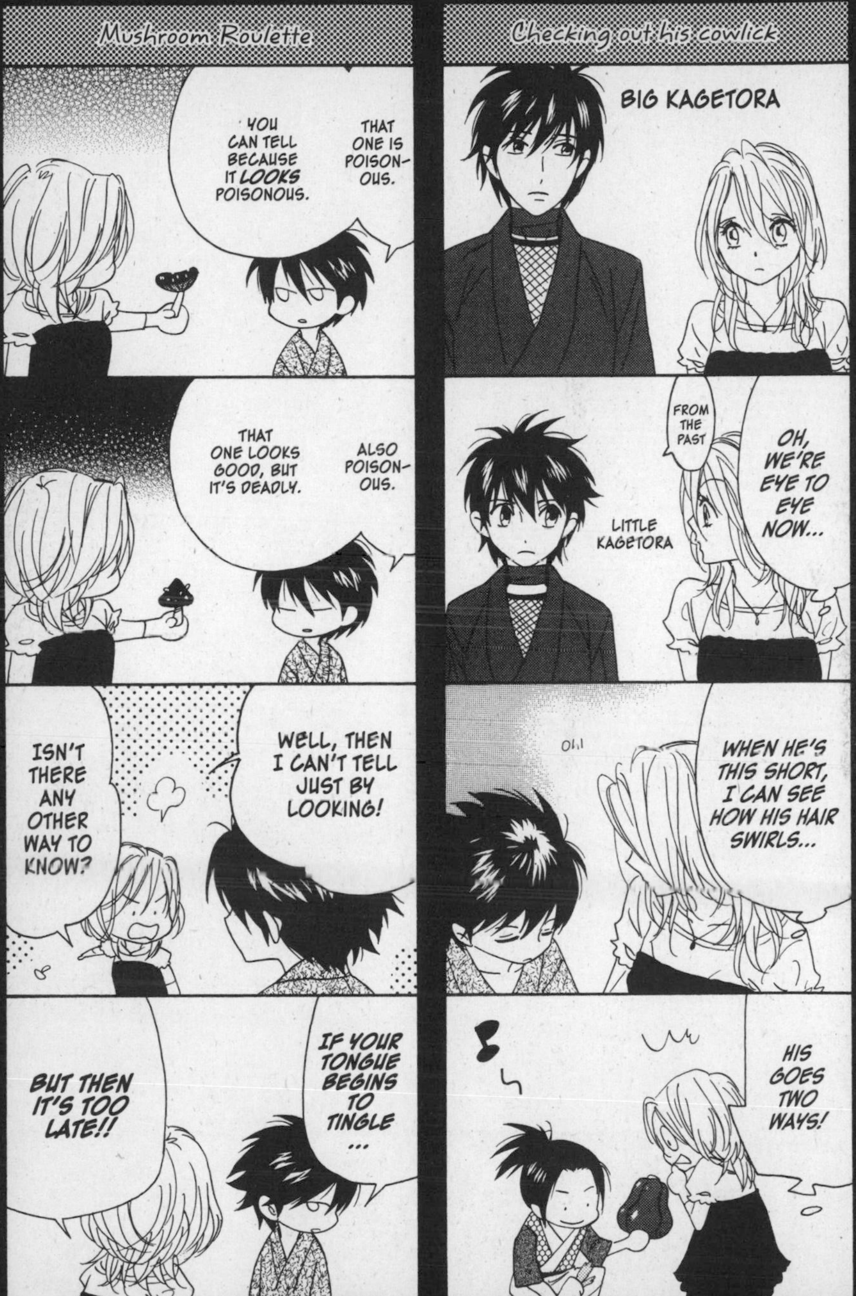
Checking out his cowlick
BIG KAGETORA
OH, WE'RE EYE TO EYE NOW...
FROM THE PAST
LITTLE KAGETORA
WHEN HE'S THIS SHORT, I CAN SEE HOW HIS HAIR SWIRLS...
OH!
HIS GOES TWO WAYS!
Mushroom Roulette
THAT ONE IS POISONOUS.
YOU CAN TELL BECAUSE IT LOOKS POISONOUS.
ALSO POISONOUS.
THAT ONE LOOKS GOOD, BUT IT'S DEADLY.
WELL, THEN I CAN'T TELL JUST BY LOOKING!
ISN'T THERE ANY OTHER WAY TO KNOW?
IF YOUR TONGUE BEGINS TO TINGLE...
BUT THEN IT'S TOO LATE!!

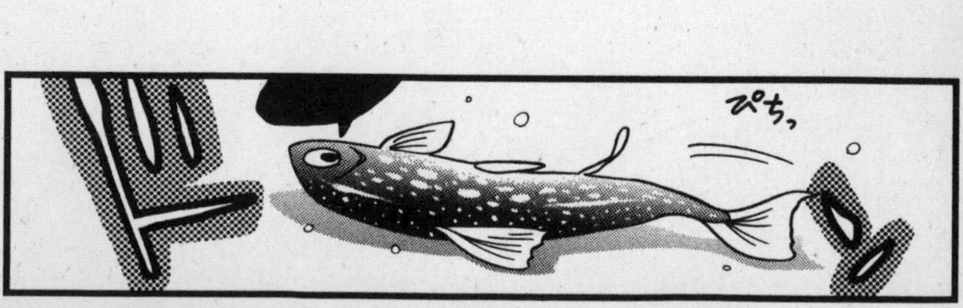
ぴちっ

In the next volume of

BENI'S GOT A NEW KIMONO, BUT SHE'S STILL A LONG WAY FROM FITTING IN TO THE NINJA VILLAGE. AND IT DOESN'T HELP THAT HER NEW FRIENDS HAVE THEIR OWN MYSTERIOUS CIRCUMSTANCES, INCLUDING A SPY IN THEIR MIDST! COULD RENKAKU'S SMILING EXTERIOR HIDE A DARKER MOTIVE? AND WHAT OF HACHIKUMA? NOT TO MENTION THAT WHILE BIG KAGETORA IS SEARCHING FRANTICALLY FOR BENI, LITTLE KAGETORA MAY ACTUALLY BE FALLING FOR HER!

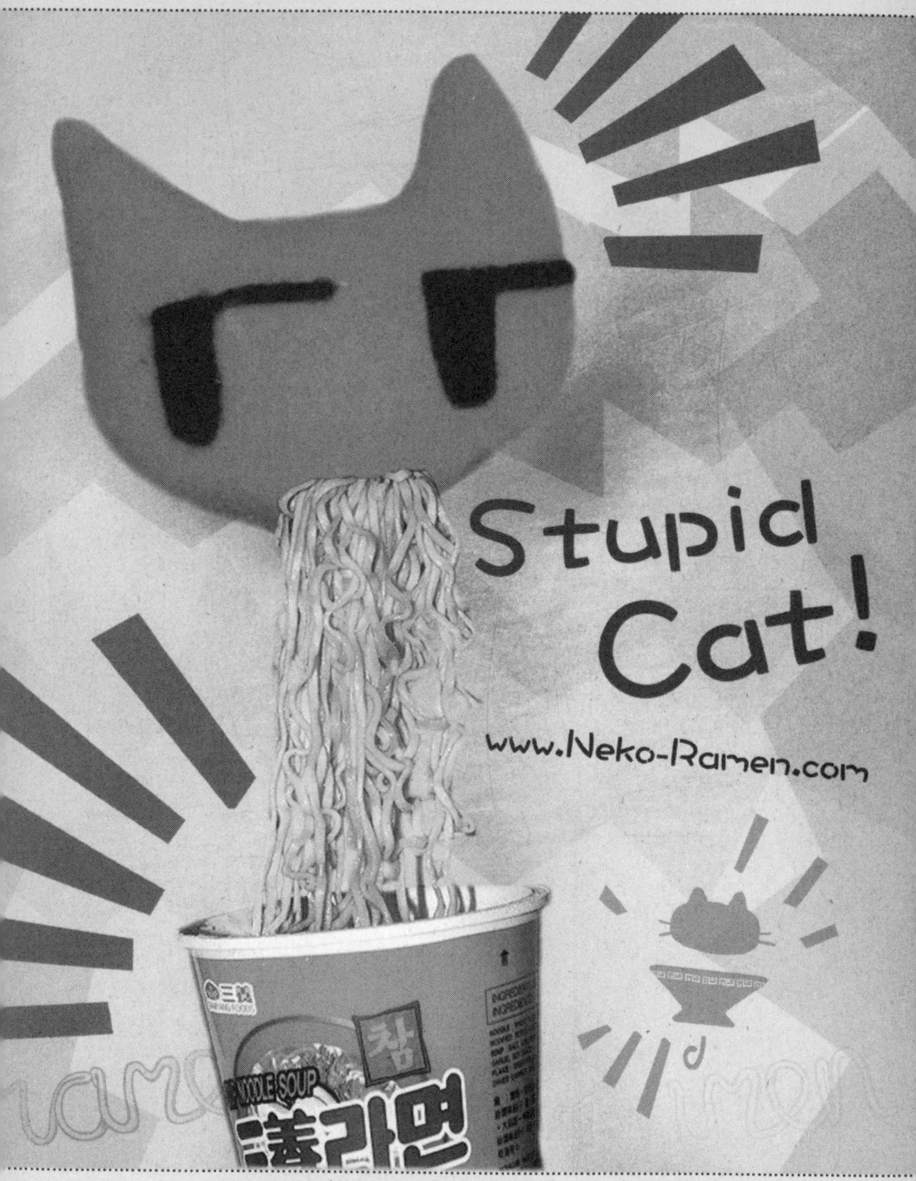
Stupid Cat!
www.Neko-Ramen.com
NOODLE SOUP
라면

THE SMALLEST HERO!?
RATMAN
ラットマン

Shuto Katsuragi is a superhero otaku. Only problem is, he's a shrimp always getting teased for his height...especially when he tries to emulate his favorite superhero! To make matters worse, Shuto suddenly gets abducted by his classmate and tricked into participating in some rather sketchy and super-villainous experiments! Why is it always one step forward and a hundred steps back for this little guy?

ACTION

OT
OLDER TEEN
AGE 16+

WWW.TOKYOPOP.COM/SHOP

The second epic trilogy continues!

Princess Ai: The Prism of Midnight Dawn

Princess Ai
The Prism of Midnight Dawn
Created by Courtney Love & Stuart "D.J. Milky" Levy
Story by Stuart "D.J. Milky" Levy Written by Christine Boylan Art by Misaho Kujiradou
2

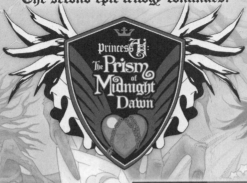

Ai fights to escape the clutches of her mysterious and malevolent captors, not knowing whether Kent, left behind on the Other Side, is even still alive. A frantic rescue mission commences, and in the end, even Ai's magical voice may not be enough to protect her from the trials of the Black Forest.

Dark secrets are revealed, and Ai must use all her strength and courage to face off against the new threat to Ai-Land. But will she ever see Kent again...?

"A very intriguing read that will satisfy old fans and create new fans, too."
– Bookloons

OT OLDER TEEN AGE 16+

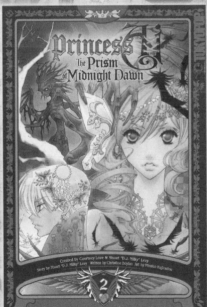

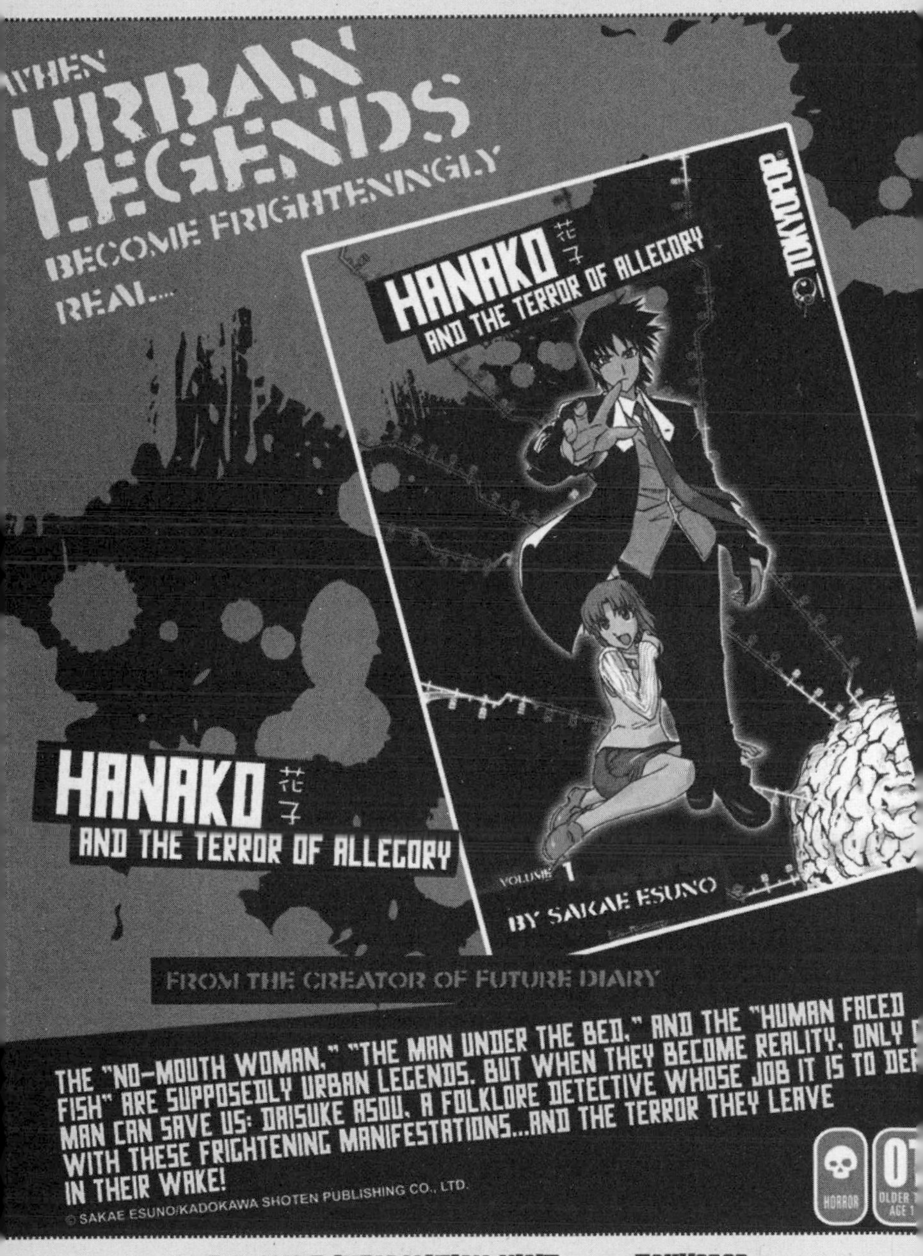
WHEN
URBAN LEGENDS
BECOME FRIGHTENINGLY
REAL...
HANAKO 花子
AND THE TERROR OF ALLEGORY
TOKYOPOP
VOLUME 1
BY SAKAE ESUNO
FROM THE CREATOR OF FUTURE DIARY
THE "NO-MOUTH WOMAN," "THE MAN UNDER THE BED," AND THE "HUMAN FACED FISH" ARE SUPPOSEDLY URBAN LEGENDS. BUT WHEN THEY BECOME REALITY, ONLY ONE MAN CAN SAVE US: DAISUKE ASOU, A FOLKLORE DETECTIVE WHOSE JOB IT IS TO DEAL WITH THESE FRIGHTENING MANIFESTATIONS...AND THE TERROR THEY LEAVE IN THEIR WAKE!
© SAKAE ESUNO/KADOKAWA SHOTEN PUBLISHING CO., LTD.
HORROR
OLDER

Relive the Magic of the World's #1 Shojo Manga!

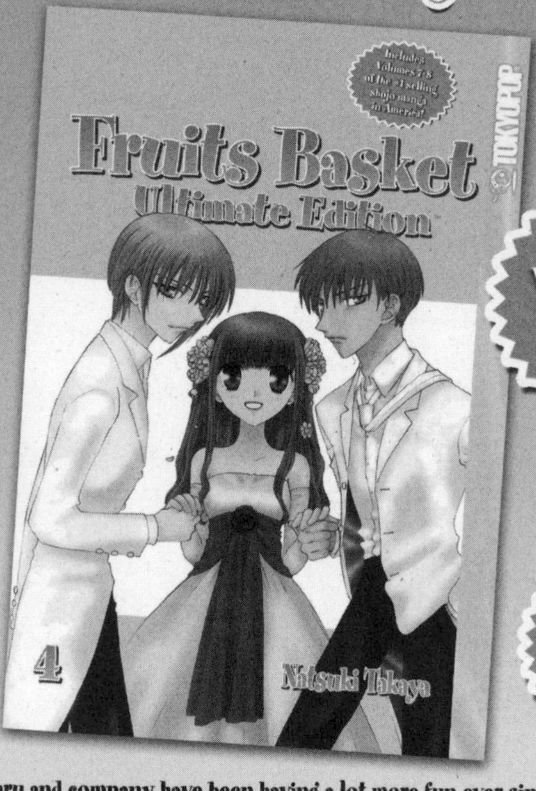
Includes Volumes 7/8 of the #1 selling shojo manga in America!
TOKYOPOP
Fruits Basket
Ultimate Edition
4
Natsuki Takaya

Includes Vols. 7 & 8 of the Original Series!

Hardcover! $14.99

Tohru and company have been having a lot more fun ever since Kisa came to visit. Now it's time for Tohru to meet another member of the Zodiac--the skillfully sarcastic grade-school student, Hiro! Meanwhile, Black Haru is full of more rage than usual, so what will happen when Yuki intervenes? And then there's Ritsu Sohma, whose mom Tohru met at the hot spring...but what's wrong with this kimono-wearing beauty?!

Discover for yourself the Secret of the Zodiac, and find out why *Fruits Basket* has won the hearts of readers the world over!

FOR MORE INFORMATION VISIT: WWW.TOKYOPOP.COM

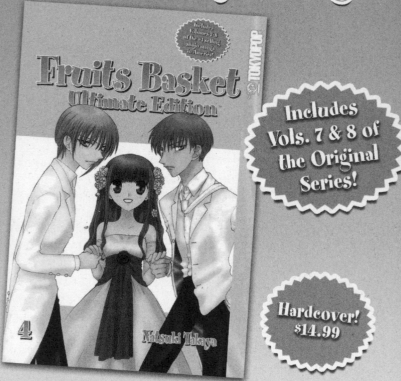

KARAKURI ODETTE

カラクリ オデット

VOL. **2**

KARAKUI ODETTO © 2005 Julietta Suzuki / HAKUSENSHA, Inc.

She's a robot who wants to learn how to be a human... And what she learns will surprise everyone!

Odette is now a sophomore at her high school. She wants to be as close to human as she can, but finds out she still has a long way to go. From wanting to be "cute" by wearing nail polish, to making a "tasty" bento that people would be happy to eat, Odette faces each challenge head-on with the help of her friends Yoko, Chris, the Professor and, of course, Asao!

FROM THE CREATOR OF *AKUMA TO DOLCE*

"A SURPRISINGLY SENSITIVE, FUNNY AND THOUGHT-PROVOKING SCI-FI SHOJO SERIES ... AS GENUINELY CHARMING AND MEMORABLE AS ITS MECHANICAL HEROINE." —ABOUT.COM